CREATING PARADISE

FRONTISPIECE. The third Earl of Carlisle, by William Aikman.
Castle Howard is shown in the background.

Creating Paradise

The Building of the English Country House
1660–1880

RICHARD WILSON *and* ALAN MACKLEY

Hambledon and London

London and New York

Hambledon and London
102 Gloucester Avenue
London NW1 8HX

838 Broadway
New York
NY 10003–4812

First Published 2000

ISBN 1 85285 252 6

A description of this book is available from
the British Library and from the Library of Congress.

Typeset by Carnegie Publishing, Carnegie House
Chatsworth Road, Lancaster, LA1 4SL

Printed on acid-free paper and bound in
Great Britain by Cambridge University Press

Contents

Illustrations

Plates

Figures

Tables

Illustration Acknowledgements

The authors and the publisher wish to thank the following for their kind permission to reproduce figures and plates:

Messrs Agnew's, 4; the Ashmolean Museum, 58; Viscount Astor, 133; Bedfordshire Record Office, 106–107; the Bodleian Library, 93; Buckinghamshire Record Office, 22; the British Architectural Library, Royal Institute of British Architects, 23, 47, 51, 86, 90, 95; the British Library, 37, 87; the Castle Howard Collection, frontispiece, 20; the Trustees of the Chatsworth Settlement, 50; Cheshire Record Office, 71; The Marquess of Cholmondeley, 14; *Country Life*, 74, 80, 82, 98, 108, 113, 119; the Courtauld Institute of Art, 6, 19, 30, 43, 45, 75–76, 114, 120–121; Doncaster Archives, 103–104; Mrs Freda English, 5; English Heritage, 116–118, 125–127; English Heritage, National Monuments Record, 17, 24, 48, 83, 134; Mrs Jane Fenner-Fust, 132; The Earl of Harewood, 112, 122; Julia Ionides, 109; Mr Philip Judge, 27–28; Mr Anthony Kersting, 41, 62, 97, 102, 123; Mr Nicholas Kingsley, 70, 132; the Laing Art Gallery, Newcastle upon Tyne, 61; the Earl of Leicester, 31–33, 81; Leicestershire Record Office, 111; The Paul Mellon Centre for Studies in British art, 21; Mr Hugh Myers, 64; the National Portrait Gallery, 11, 39, 63, 66; the National Trust, 10, 34–36, 59, 85, 114, 133; Norfolk Air Photography Library, Derek A. Edwards, 26; Norfolk Museums Service (Norwich Castle Museum), 15; Norfolk Record Office, 91; Norfolk Studies Library, 16, 110; Northamptonshire Record Office, 60, 73; Nottinghamshire Record Office, 130–131; Sir William Pennington-Ramsden Bt, 8; Messrs Phillips, 105; Mr P. J. N. Prideaux-Brune, 13; Random House, 38; the Royal Academy of Arts, 55; Mr Eddie Ryle-Hughes, 12, ; Viscount Scarsdale, 43; Mrs Olive Smith, 9; the Trustees of Sir John Soane's Museum, 57; Somerset Record Office, 72, 78, 124; the Earl of Stradbroke, 67, 77; Sir Tatton Sykes, Bt, 120–121; The Marquess Townshend of Raynham, 40; the University of East Anglia, (Mr Michael Brandon-Jones), 1, 7, 25, 42, 44, 46, 49, 54, 65, 68–69, 79, 84, 88–89, 92, 94, 96, 101, 115; Lord Walpole, 75–76; the West Yorkshire Archives Service, Leeds, 52–53; the Duke of Westminster, 2–3; Mr S. C. Whitbread, 19, 90; Dr Tom Williamson, 18; Dr Giles Worsley, 21, 129; Yale Center for British Art, 29.

Abbreviations

BL	British Library
BPP	British Parliamentary Papers
DNB	Dictionary of National Biography
HMC	Royal Commission on Historical Manuscripts
Mason	R. H. Mason, *Norfolk Photographically Illustrated* (Norwich, 1865)
Morris	F. O. Morris, *A Series of Picturesque Views of Seats of the Noblemen and Gentlemen of Great Britain and Ireland*, 6 vols (London, 1880)
Neale	J. P. Neale, *Views of the Seats of Noblemen and Gentlemen in England*, 6 vols (London, 1818–23)
Pyne	W. H. Pyne, *The Microcosm of Arts, Manufactures and Commerce* (London, 1803)
RCHME	Royal Commission on The Historical Monuments of England
Repton	Humphry and John Adey Repton, *Fragments on the Theory and Practice of Landscape Gardening* (London, 1816)
Rutter	John Rutter, *Delineations of Fonthill Abbey*, (1823)
Soane	Sir John Soane, *Plans, Elevations and Sections of Buildings Executed in the Counties of Norfolk, Suffolk, Yorkshire, Staffordshire, Warwickshire, Hertfordshire, et caetera* (London, 1788).
Watts	William Watts, *The Seats of the Nobility and Gentry* (London, 1779)
Williamson	G. C. Williamson, *Life and Works of Ozias Humphrey R.A.* (London, 1918)

Preface

The country house was the creation of large landowners. In the period we discuss, 1660–1880, they prospered, dominating local and national government alike. They were the chief beneficiaries of the prolonged expansion of the British economy in these years, a growth based upon agricultural as well as industrial progress. Their outlook in general therefore was one of unbroken confidence. This optimism and the power that they shared were above all expressed in the country house.

Our book, however, is not restricted to the great territorial magnates and their palaces which have hitherto dominated country house literature. English land-owners were a varied group. We look at the building activities of the whole gamut, from the fabulously rich and grand to the small country squire whose estate and income barely sustained his standing at county level. The paradise they sought to create was not only achieved through the endeavours of themselves and their architects, but also of the various craftsmen and labourers who turned their visions into reality. These visions of course included gardens and parks as well as houses. But it is the country house – the centre-piece of a formidable statement being made about wealth, authority and status – with which we are principally concerned. It is the whole process of their construction which we therefore attempt to encompass, from the young Grand Tourist's thrill at first viewing Palladio's sunlit villas in the Veneto to the time, often decades later, when he moved his family into a big, new, somewhat chilly home in the English countryside.

Studies of the country house are numerous. They embrace wares of many descriptions: beautifully illustrated surveys of houses, their architecture and archi-tects; serious monographs; erudite National Trust booklets to its properties, and guide books to every house open to the public; the century-long series of *Country Life* articles and publications devoted to the British country house. Life in them across the centuries is captured in accounts of owners and servants alike.

We bring a different approach. This is a book not about architects and archi-tecture of country houses but about their builders and building. It attempts to provide the economic and social context of a remarkable creative phenomenon. At its heart is a study of building accounts, at least those surviving in reasonable completeness. From them it introduces practical and financial dimensions to the field of country house studies, one hitherto dominated by the stylistic and aesthetic concerns of architectural historians.

Some of the research for the book was undertaken with an Economic and Social Research Council grant (R000221311), and we are indebted to the assessors of our final report to the Council for their perceptive appraisals. A version of chapter seven appeared in the *Economic History Review* (1999). We are grateful to the editors and those of the *Georgian Group Journal* and *Norfolk Archaeology* for their permission to reproduce material which was published in their journals, and now appears here rewritten and pruned. We have profited enormously from the comments of Dr Malcolm Airs, Dr Bill Mathew and Professor Michael Thompson who kindly read our manuscript.

Our colleagues in the School of History at the University of East Anglia, especially Dr Tom Williamson as always bursting with ideas about houses and landscapes, have given us advice and encouragement, as have those scholars in other universities where we have presented papers about our research. Many people have helped us during the past half dozen years and we would particularly like to express our gratitude to Dr John Barney, Dr Ian Gordon Brown, Brett Harrison, Michael Brandon-Jones, Philip Judge, Nicholas Kingsley, the Earl of Leicester, Anthony Mitchell, Norman Scarfe, Sir Tatton Sykes, Jenni Tanimoto, the Marquess Townshend of Raynham, Lord and Lady Walpole, Mavis Wesley, Sam Whitbread, Edmund Wilson and Dr Giles Worsley. We would also like to thank the staffs of the Berkshire, Cheshire, Dorset, Gloucestershire, Leicestershire, Norfolk, Northamptonshire, Nottinghamshire, Somerset and Suffolk Record Offices, the West Yorkshire Archives Service and the Yorkshire Archaeological Society, for their expertise and assistance. In the task of collecting illustrations Dr Jane Cunningham and Melanie Blake in the Photographic Survey Department of the Courtauld Institute were especially helpful. Martin Sheppard, our publisher, guided the book through all the stages of production, calmly and efficiently.

Our wives, Marian and Ursula, enjoying many excursions to country houses, remained amazingly uncomplaining about our neglect of them and their gardens during the other, more protracted stages of research, writing and revision.

*'When one lives in Paradise, how hard it must be
to ascend in heart and mind to Heaven.'*

Lady Frederick Cavendish, writing of Cliveden,
Buckinghamshire, in 1863.

1

The English Country House

Vita Sackville-West began her little book *English Country Houses* in the *Britain in Pictures* series, 'There is nothing quite like the English Country House anywhere else in the world ... it may be large, it may be small; it may be manorial; it may be the seat of aristocracy or the home of the gentry'. And, writing in 1944, she unsurprisingly and gloomily concluded with the question, 'One wonders for how long?'[1] But the point about their variety is a valid one, evident even now when a significant proportion of the houses which flourished in her youth have been demolished, reduced in size or put to other uses.[2] She opined with a mounting, unfettered run of generalities (Vanbrugh's *oeuvre* especially got short shrift), that 'the English are a rural-minded people on the whole'. Whereas 'our cities generally speaking are deplorable', English villages and country houses were the inheritors of a different tradition and spirit. Again, the contrast she invoked has been an important one in English history. Certainly, no part of this vision, so wilfully failing to encompass Britain's industrial and urban heart land, has been a more potent reminder of our past than the country house. Physically, powerfully, they continue to expound to us the key role played by their owners in politics, in taste and culture, and in the development of the landscape across the past four centuries.

As a consequence, historians and writers of every hue continue to produce a varied and ever-burgeoning literature about them. Its more academic segment consists of two main sectors, one provided by historians of architecture, the other by those writing about landownership more generally. The architectural historians, who traditionally have supplied the better end of the market, are naturally preoccupied with styles, architects and craftsmen, and the relationship between architecture and other arts, literature, painting and landscape gardening. With a few notable exceptions, they have not been very interested in linking the evolution of the country house to the economic and social history of landownership.[3] Often houses are treated in isolation, like the vast, century-old series of *Country Life* articles, a house in Cumbria one week, another in Essex the next; or presented,

as in Pevsner's immensely influential *Buildings of England* series, as entries providing
erudite guides for the educated sightseer but which contain hardly a word about
their builders or costs. In this literature the builders of country houses are
represented as an implausibly uniform class. Their finances and economic
prospects especially are almost totally ignored, the pace and scale of building
activity is passed over. At worst, the same examples of architectural distinction
are paraded time after time. We begin to see the world of the country house in
the two centuries after the Restoration through the lenses of Blenheim and Castle
Howard, Holkham and Houghton. It is a *Brideshead Revisited* view of the English
county house in which the sheer variety of their size and the scale of their
numbers is ignored.

The agenda of the historians of landownership in the period between 1660 and
1880 period is very different.[4] Basically, they are faced with the task of explaining
a paradox of great significance in English history. How, in an economy increasingly
driven by industrial and commercial forces, did the landed class retain their
traditional influence past 1832 into the last quarter of the nineteenth century? Did
their political authority, their embrace of the country's industrial and financial
leaders, mean a faltering of Britain's early economic supremacy? How easily did
the progressive British economy, in contrast to that of the southern states of
America for example, carry the weight of a traditional seigneurial class? The
accounts of historians attempting to answer these big questions have concentrated upon issues such as the growth in the size of the landed estate, especially
between the 1720s and its apogee in the mid Victorian period, and the absorption
(or otherwise) of newcomers into the landowners' ranks. Contrariwise, they have
also elucidated the ways in which some landowners themselves were increasingly
involved in the processes of industrial, urban and transport developments as well
as of agrarian improvement. In this literature analysing the growing wealth and
survival of English landowners, the specific aspects of country house building
have been relatively neglected in the attempt to explain the complex and varied
growth of estates over a long period. Again there has been a tendency amongst
historians of landownership to cite the atypical example, those wonder houses
whose construction was pivotal in the development of architectural styles and
sometimes crucial in the fate of individual family fortunes.

There is a need therefore to examine the full compass of country house building
in its golden age between 1660 and 1880 in terms of numbers, activity, distribution
and costs. Sir John Summerson, forty years ago, stated the position succinctly:

'Nobody, I believe, has attempted to estimate the number of country houses built, the amount of money spent on them, or their distribution throughout the Kingdom – elementary desiderata, surely, if country house building is to be considered historically.' The difficulties of providing an acceptable estimate of costs and numbers, however, even in the second half of the nineteenth century when the evidence becomes fuller, are forbidding, and the literature provides little guide even as a starting point. Sir John himself performed some rather vague calculations about 150 great houses built between 1710 and 1740. He found one-third were built in the five years between 1720 and 1724. But he felt unable to pin-point the causes of this concentration. He offered two explanations, 'The latent stylistic factors' of the new Palladianism and 'remote causes ... embedded in economic and social history [which] cannot be dealt with here'.[5] Subsequently, attention has been drawn to the importance of the subject in relation to capital formation in the eighteenth century. Although acknowledging the pole position of land-owners, profiting handsomely from agrarian improvement, historians have not found the task easy either in establishing a chronology of country house building or the scale of spending on them: 'No attempt has so far been made to establish a chronology of stately home investment, and the task may turn out to be virtually impossible, bearing in mind the difficulty of dating the many hundred, if not thousands of houses involved, as well as of establishing at this distance of time the total expenditure on each building.'[6] Back-of-the-envelope calculations from Pevsner's *Buildings of England* series, and a more intensive sampling, have suggested that in the two centuries after the Restoration peak activity seems to be concentrated in two periods, the 1690s to the 1730s, and the 1790s to the 1830s.[7] The territory of expenditure remains uncharted.

Our agenda of calculating numbers and costs, of defining periods of activity across two centuries, of examining the economic history of the English country house as a whole is then, as others have outlined, a tough one.[8] This book attempts to provide some answers by looking at the phenomenon across England, the core of the work being a detailed study of six counties, Cheshire, Gloucestershire, Norfolk, Northamptonshire, Suffolk, and Yorkshire.[9] The choice is neither random nor watertight. Different factors weighed in our attempt to provide a reasonable cross-section of England: convenience (Norfolk and Suffolk); our existing know-ledge (Yorkshire); a good secondary literature (Cheshire, Gloucestershire and Northamptonshire). Mainly we have looked at surviving building accounts (full sets are rare) within the context of the number of houses built between 1660 and

1880. It has also entailed assimilating a wide range of material: estate and family records; the views of numerous contemporaries who visited and wrote about country houses; and some of the vast literature on architecture and landownership.

It is necessary to say something about the use of the word 'builder' and attempt to define what we mean by 'country house'. Neither task is as straightforward as it seems. Who was the builder? Indeed, who was the architect? One dictionary defines 'builder' as follows: 'builder now equals master artisan, who is instructed by the architect, and employs the manual labourers'.[10] The term was not used in the seventeenth and eighteenth centuries in this way. At the start of our period, the various forms of organising the building of the country house preclude the application of a strict definition to the terms builder or architect. With the increasing specialisation of roles this changed. In the eighteenth century the professional architect emerged from the ranks of gentlemen-designers, craftsmen-builders and the trained officials of the Office of Works. By 1830 the codification of the architect's relationship with his clients created the professional we would recognise today. As the scope of the architect's role increased, hitherto autonomous craftsmen became subservient to a single controlling designer. During the nineteenth century the responsibilities of master craftsmen for the employment and management of men within their own crafts shifted to general building contractors, as building by contract replaced individual craft agreements and directly recruited workforces. Consequently the meaning of the terms architect and builder changed and depend upon context. For example, Thomas Coke (1697–1759), first Earl of Leicester, was the architect, client and builder of Holkham Hall, one of the greatest houses of its age. Yet he cannot possibly be confused with an artisan 'builder', whether an individual or the manager of the construction process. Nor did he perform the same role as a professional architect a century later, boasting a portfolio of clients, responsible for the design of a building, the preparation of specifications and bills of quantities, the recommendation of a contractor, and the overall supervision of construction. A lack of precision in the use of the labels architect and builder simply reflects the problem that they describe activities which changed over time. We, however, use the term 'builder of the country house' to mean the client or patron. What we now think of as builders we refer to as 'master craftsmen' – masons, joiners, plasterers etc. – in the seventeenth and eighteenth centuries and, increasingly, as building contractors in the Victorian period.

The second question, 'What do we mean by a country house?', similarly defies precise definition. Saturated in our heritage and armed with National Trust membership, we all know in our mind's eye: a large, old house with numerous outbuildings, surrounded by gardens and park, the main residence, at least historically, of a sizeable landed estate – a statement of exclusiveness and authority, of expense and status. Yet these are imprecise considerations when divorced from definitions of estate size or income. Whereas, for example, Bateman identified 183 estates of over one thousand acres in size in Norfolk in the 1870s, Burke's and Savills *Guide to Country Houses* of 1981 – even after the demolition of at least twenty-seven large houses and the wholesale breakup of estates in the intervening century – lists no fewer than 450 country houses.[11] It is clear that its compilation was imperceptibly influenced by forty years of escalating house prices and estate agents' hype, by the fact that the old gentry, where they survive, often live in smaller houses in the later twentieth century, and many pre-1700 manor houses which abound in Norfolk have only recently come back into the country house repertoire with their refurbishment. Nowhere is the amount of land attached to them disclosed. Entries therefore do not necessarily constitute a list of country houses which would have been recognised as such in the eighteenth and nineteenth centuries. The *Guide* goes well down the scale into those domains beloved by estate agents – the old rectory.

When we turn to Victorian directories (Plate 1), or the numerous editions of Walford's *County Families of the United Kingdom*, for their listing of 'the Seats of the Nobility, Gentry and Clergy', we find these are not necessarily more helpful: both compilations tend to record houses of the magistracy which, even in the 1840s, when county membership of the bench was almost entirely confined to the gentry and clergy, was not the same thing as a list of country houses.[12] Essentially, the directories and Walford are recording membership of the county community (including many 'superior' clergy and some urban plutocrats), not providing an accurate catalogue of either country houses or estates in any given year.

For the construction of an objective database of country houses the options are limited. To confine ownership of them to the titled aristocracy is much too exclusive. And status as defined by Gregory King in the 1690s and by subsequent political economists, in an attempt to calculate the size and incomes of the titled and gentry classes, founders on estimates of the number of 'gentlemen' and, at least for our purposes, fails to take account of the crucial relationship between

LIST OF THE

PRINCIPAL SEATS IN CHESHIRE,

With Reference to the Places under which they will be found in this Volume.

PAGE

Abbots Moss, Hon. Mrs. Cholmondeley, see Marton ... 353
Acresbank, Ralph Bates esq. J.P. see Stalybridge......... 435
Adlington hall, Mrs. Legh, see Adlington 18
Agden hall, Charles Lister esq. J.P. see Agden 159
Alderley park, Lord Stanley of Alderley, see Alderley... 19
Aldersey hall, Thomas Aldersey esq. see Aldersey......... 234
Appleton hall, Thomas Hy. Lyon esq. J.P. see Appleton 31
Apsley cottage, Lieut.-Col. Samuel Wright Wilkinson J.P. see Stockport.. 452
Arderne hall, Earl of Haddington, see Tarporley 482
Arley hall, Piers Egerton-Warburton esq. J.P. see Aston-by-Budworth... 35
Arrowe hall, Fredk. Jas. Harrison esq. J.P. see Arrowe 512
Ashbrook hall, Mrs. Brooke, see Church Minshull 233
Ashfield, Thomas Collier esq. J.P. see Chester 229
Ashfield, Joshua O. Nicholson esq. J.P. see Upton......... 400
Ashfield hall, Uvedale Corbett esq. M.A., J.P. see Great Neston 372
Ashford, Wm. Wycliffe Barlow esq. J.P. see Fulshaw ... 508
Ashton Hayes, William Hayes esq. see Ashton 34
Astle hall, Lieut.-Col. George Dixon J.P. see Chelford... 180
Aston hall, Hervey Talbot esq. see Dutton.................. 315
Aston lodge, James Geo. Best esq. see Aston-by-Sutton 36
Bache hall, Mrs. Hudson, see Bache.......................... 38
Backford hall, Birkenhead Glegg esq. see Backford 38
Bank house, Robt. Oliver Orton esq. J.P. see Tattenhall 486
Beach cottage, Saml. Outram Hermon esq. see Hartford 283
Beaconhurst, Henry Reynolds esq. J.P. see Netherton ... 276
Beeches (The), Wm. Dickson Houghton esq. see Moore 250
Beechfield, George C. Greenwell esq. J.P. see Poynton... 397
Beechfield, George Gordon McRae esq. J.P. see Hartford 283
Beechwood, Geo. Charnley Dewhurst esq. J.P. see Lymm 322
Birtles hall, John Brooks Close Brooks esq. see Over Alderley 20
Birtles Old hall, Mrs. Frank Hibbert, see Birtles 398
Bolesworth Castle, George Barbour esq. M.A., D.L., J.P. see Broxton 46
Bolling (The), Lord Dudley, see Malpas 346
Bonis hall, James Thomas Dorrington esq. see Butley... 398
Boothfield house, Edward Lewis Ashworth esq. J.P. see Over Knutsworth 311
Bostock hall, Col. Charles Hosken France-Hayhurst D.L., J.P. see Bostock... 251
Bothams hall, James Kirk esq. J.P. see Yeardsley-cum-Whaley 519
Boughton hall, Col. William Vesey Brownlow C.B. see Great Boughton 162
Boxes (The), Lieut.-Col. John Sprot Tait D.L., J.P. see Hartford 284
Bramhall hall, Chas. Hy. Nevill esq. J.P. see Bramhall 165
Bredbury hall, James Edward Mills esq. see Bredbury 166
Brereton hall, John Moir esq. see Brereton.................. 167
Brinnington Manor house, James Leigh esq. J.P. see Brinnington 468
Brockhurst (The), Joseph Verdin esq. D.L., J.P. see Danebridge 385
Bromborough hall, Robert Norris Dale esq. see Bromborough.. 168
Brook house, Wm. Philip Brabazon esq. M.D., J.P. see Lymm 322
Brookbank, Edward Hibbert esq. J.P. see Godley......... 302
Brookdale, James Jardine esq. D.L., J.P. see Chester ... 229
Brookfield, Edmund Howard Sykes J.P. see Cheadle Bulkeley.. 177
Brookside, Major John Kennedy J.P. see Arclid 421

PAGE

Broxton Old hall, William Graham Crum esq. J.P. see Broxton 46
Buglawton hall, Samuel Pearson esq. see Buglawton ... 171
Burland hall, Miss Dutton, see Burland 17
Burton hall, Wm. Congreve esq. D.L., J.P. see Burton 174
Butley hall, William Coare Brocklehurst esq. J.P. see Butley.. 398
Caldy manor, Alfred Barton esq. J.P. see Caldy 306
Calveley hall, Mrs. H. R. Peel, see Calveley 172
Capenhurst hall, Richard Taswell Richardson esq. J.P. see Capenhurst.. 175
Capesthorne hall, William Bromley-Davenport esq. M.P., J.P. see Capesthorne... 176
Carden park, John Hurleston Leche esq. D.L., J.P. see Carden 489
Carlett park, Rev. Wm. Edward Torr M.A see Eastham 264
Cassia lodge, Oswald Moseley Leigh esq. J.P. see Marton 353
Castle park, Misses Wright, see Netherton................. 275
Cedar Lawn, Major John Rd. Pickmere J.P. see Thelwall 487
Cedars (The), James Maddock J.P. see Alsager 21
Cherry hill, Sl. Hy. Sandbach esq. J.P. see Cuddington 347
Cholmondeley Castle, John Henry Gartside esq. see Cholmondeley 346
Chorlton hall, Frederick Dresser esq. see Chorlton 38
Christleton hall, Mrs. Ince, see Christleton 231
Church Lawton hall, William Laurence Chew esq. J.P. see Church Lawton... 232
Cliffe (The), Sir Henry Fox Q.C., F.R.G.S. see Hough ... 517
Cogshall hall, John Highfield esq. see Cogshall............ 169
Combermere Abbey, Viscount Combermere J.P. see Burley Dam 174
Copley, Stephen Williamson esq. M.P. see Thornton-Hough 487
Corbrook house, Thomas Latham Boote esq. J.P. see Audlem 36
Crag hall, Francis Wm. Ashton esq. see Wildboarclough 504
Cranage hall, Robert Miller esq. see Cranage 240
Cresswellshawe, Francis Henry Randle Wilbraham esq. J.P. see Alsager 21
Crewe hall, Lord Crewe, see Crewe.......................... 242
Crewe hill, Mrs. Barnston, see Crewe........................ 273
Cringle house, Thomas Hardcastle Sykes J.P. see Cheadle Bulkeley 177
Crofton lodge, Samuel Beckett Chadwick esq. J.P. see Runcorn 408
Crowton house, Rev. Charles William Spencer-Stanhope M.A. see Crowton... 249
Cuddington hall, Thomas Brassey esq. see Cuddington 346
Daisy Bank, Dennis Bradwell esq. J.P. see Hulme Walfield.. 293
Dale (The), Miss Massey, see Moston 362
Daresbury hall, Robert Iorwerth Wynne-Jones esq. see Daresbury.. 249
Darnhall hall, William Henry Verdin esq. J.P. see Darnhall 392
Davenham hall, Christopher Kay esq. D.L., J.P. see Davenham... 251
Davenport hall, Miss Tippinge, see Davenport 480
Davenshaw house, Capel Wilson Hogg esq. J.P. see Buglawton 171
Delamere house, Roger William Wilbraham esq. J.P. see Cuddington 499
Doddington hall, Louis Delves Broughton esq. see Doddington 255
Dorfold hall, Henry James Tollemache esq. M.P., J.P. see Acton 17

PLATE 1. The definition of principal country seat used in nineteenth-century directories, as in this list from Kelly's 1892 edition for Cheshire, embraced many that were not associated with significant landed estates.

land and country house ownership. Two other choices remain: the size of house and size of estate. It is the latter we have chosen to define the country house.[13]

It was an approach first delineated by Michael Thompson.[14] He subjected the Return of Owners of Land (the celebrated New Domesday of 1873 which tells us more about the structure of land ownership than at any other point in our history), and the subsequent verification of the holdings of 'Great Landowners' by John Bateman, to careful analysis.[15] He found there were 363 great estates of more than 10,000 acres, around 1000 'greater gentry' owning between 3000 and 10,000 acres, and some 2000 'squires' with between 1000 and 3000 acres. Together this tiny population of landowners owned an incredible 53.5 per cent of England. They all enjoyed annual incomes in excess of £1000 which was thought to be the minimum necessary to support the lifestyle of a landed gentleman. A figure therefore of around 5000 country houses – some of the largest landowners owning more than one and some aristocrats several – is probably not far from the total of English country houses if we firmly link the country house to defined amounts of land and income.

There are, of course, obvious drawbacks with this estimation. There are problems at the margin. First, there were some few landholdings of more than 1000 acres which supported no country house. Secondly, there were many estates of less than 1000 acres which nevertheless did include a sizeable country house, because their owners derived, especially by the nineteenth century, the major part of their incomes from non-landed sources. A key group here were the new rich, principally those who continuously from the 1690s derived their fortunes from industry, trade and finance. Did they buy big estates and houses or were they content with, at most, a few hundred acres, happy to live a country life in miniature? Before the great depression in agriculture (1873–96), most of the richest new men did buy landed estates; but there were also increasing numbers of plutocrats who often lived more comfortably than the old gentry in houses that were not the centre of a fully-fledged landed estate.[16] Certainly, the major part of the new men's incomes was not derived from land rentals. They nevertheless enjoyed almost all of a landed estate's amenities, sizeable and stylish homes, with immaculate gardens, extensive hot-houses and stables, all surrounded by neat small parks. Benjamin Gott (1761–1840), one-time cloth merchant and the first large-scale factory owner in the Leeds woollen industry, typifies this kind of owner and house.[17] In 1803 he bought a modest Georgian house with 200 acres

of land from another merchant at Armley on the edge of Leeds. He engaged
Sir Robert Smirke to build him a stylish villa in the latest Grecian style, and
Humphry Repton to set out a landscape park on an unpromising site with a
distant view of the smoke-laden town. He filled his house with fine paintings
and the sculptures of a distant cousin in Rome, Joseph Gott. Half a century later
the family owned 770 acres around Leeds. Their holding was never a country
estate, but Armley was a fine house where the family resided until the late 1920s,
as large as, and certainly better furnished and maintained, than the majority of
those owned by the Yorkshire squirearchy. By the mid nineteenth century there
were hundreds of men like Gott, eager to display their wealth and taste, occupying
houses similar to, if less stylish than, Armley.

Most larger towns were surrounded by their villas. As J. A. Houseman observed
in 1800: 'merchants frequently accumulated very large fortunes, if we may judge
from their many and elegant seats with which the neighbourhood of Leeds is
studded'.[18] A map of Norfolk parks of about 1880 shows a marked concentration
around Norwich (a lesser engine of wealth creation than Leeds by the early
nineteenth century), largely accounted for by the establishments of the city's
richest families.[19] Yet there was nothing novel about them. Well-kept villas were
a feature of the English landscape when Celia Fiennes and Daniel Defoe made
their tours in the 1690s and 1720s. Of course these suburban villas especially
proliferated close to London. Defoe wrote of them: 'I find 2000 houses which in
other places would pass for Palaces ... in a word, nothing can be more Beautiful
[than] these Villages fill'd with these Houses, and the Houses surrounded with
Gardens, Walks, Vistas, Avenues, representing all the Beauties of Building, and
all the Pleasures of Planting.'[20]

Yet contemporaries made a clear distinction between the true country house
and the house in the country. They recognised that a *country house* required a
sufficient landed estate to pay for its upkeep, and that it must possess tenanted
land indicating an intention to use the house as a source of influence in the local
community. Only from the mid nineteenth century did these definitions break
down as new money flowed into the countryside. The sizeable houses they built
were used primarily for recreation and for the entertainment of family and business
associates. Clearly these establishments, the home of a rich and often transient
gentry, are a problem in discussing the composition of landed society and in the
definition of the country house. But so long as the association of the house with
a precisely determinable size of landed estate is maintained, a figure of around

5000 such houses is a reasonable estimate. The chief strength of the method is that it identifies the country house with its surrounding tenanted farms, cottages and all the other appurtenances of a large landed estate. Thus it is defined by its role and purpose as family seat, 'power house' and community focus.

For our purposes, examining the numbers and wealth of landowners as potential country house builders under three heads, the peerage, the landed gentry, and newcomers to the latter, is instructive, allowing for the above strictures (and many more in the voluminous literature on landowners) about rigid categorisation.[21] We consider the development and meaning of the country house, and those influences which motivated their builders – the pressures of a highly emulative and consumer-driven society, the impact of the Grand Tour, the constant peer group appraisal of houses in England, and the increasing tendency for them to spend long periods in London. The roles of the builders of country houses changed as the architectural profession gradually emerged. At the Restoration the former's position in design and construction was pivotal; by the third quarter of the nineteenth century they simply went to an architect and building contractor with their requirements. We examine the process of building a country house, looking at the key function of the clerk of the works, of workforces more generally, and at the procurement of materials and their transport. A more difficult topic – inevitably statistical in its dimensions – is the pattern of country house building activity across two centuries and the extent of regional variations. Lastly we attempt to answer questions about the cost of country houses and the means to finance building activity. What was the range within most landowners operated? Did costs escalate as incomes rose? How did builders provide for these expenditures? What were their sources of income and did building overstretch their resources and lead them into debt? Is it possible to provide an estimate of total investment in country houses from building accounts, insurance records and taxation data? To what extent did the creation of private paradises contribute to the wider economy?

PLATE 2.   The first Duke of Westminster by Sir John Millais.

2

The Builders of the English Country House

'But what do you think of young Sir James Lowther, who, not of age, becomes
master of one or two and forty thousand pounds a year. England will become
a Heptarchy, the property of six or seven people! The Duke of Bedford is fallen
to be not above the fourth rich man in the island.'

Horace Walpole to George Montagu, 20 April 1756.[1]

The first Duke of Westminster (1825–1899) was the beau ideal of a Victorian
nobleman (Plate 2). Descended from a companion of William the Conqueror, he
fathered a large family of fifteen children from two marriages. A man of great
good works, he was at home equally on the racecourse (he won the Derby five
times but never bet), the grouse moor or at a missionary meeting. His income
more than matched his activities. In the 1870s his country estates, principally in
Cheshire, and not large by ducal standards, produced a gross annual rental of
£39,000, but his metropolitan properties, 'the most valuable London estate held
by any of Her Majesty's subjects', yielded in excess of £250,000 a year by his
death. In the 1870s he spent a truly colossal £600,000 on rebuilding the Grosvenors'
Cheshire seat, Eaton Hall, to the designs of Alfred Waterhouse (Plate 3).[2]

In contrast, about a century earlier, a first-generation Norfolk squire, Edmund
Rolfe of Heacham (1738–1817) (Plate 4), worried when making his will whether
he had sufficient resources to leave his widow an income of £1200 a year and
his only son a clear one of £3000 – 'I hope in God sufficient for all your wants'.
In 1814 these were not marginal incomes for the landed gentry. But they had
been hard garnered by the Rolfes. In the course of the eighteenth century they
had put together an estate bordering the Wash of over 2000 acres and had greatly
extended the family home in the late 1770s at a cost of £4128 (Plate 5). It was an
enterprise which thoroughly stretched Edmund Rolfe's resources in the 1780s.[3]

The Grosvenors and the Rolfes fix the polarities between English country house
builders. The Duke of Westminster remains the country's richest landowner;

PLATE 3.   Eaton Hall, Cheshire (Alfred Waterhouse, 1870–82). The entrance front.

Waterhouse's vast pile has been demolished and twice rebuilt. The Heacham estate was sold by the Rolfes in the 1900s, the house pulled down forty years later. The fate of these two families underlines the diversity amongst the land-owning class in terms of their wealth as much as of their origins. The relative difference between the income of the Westminsters and the Rolfes by the late nineteenth century was far greater than that between the duke's most prosperous tenant farmer and his most indigent agricultural labourer. And this, of course, in large measure explains the remarkable variety of country houses which Vita Sackville-West commented upon during the Second World War. But it was also a phenomenon not peculiar to the late Victorian period. Two centuries earlier, the famous calculations of England's wealth and social structure in 1688 made by the herald and statistician Gregory King established essentially the same point about the heterogeneity of the landowning class. He identified a roughly tripartite division: 160 peers (with average incomes of £2800) and 26 bishops (£1300); 800 baronets (£800), 600 knights (£650) and 3000 esquires (£450); and lastly 12,000 gentlemen (£280).[4]

Twentieth-century economic historians have tended to dispute the fine print of King's figures. Since there was much variation between incomes within each of his ranks, some maintain it makes more sense to regroup the landowning class into two divisions, greater and lesser, cutting across distinctions of title.[5] Most accept that his estimate of the number of gentlemen is especially problematic, since contemporaries found it impossible to agree about the size, wealth or status of the group.[6] But the incomes and ranking of his other 4586 landowners, ranging from great duke to parish squire, and roughly equating with a population of

PLATE 4.
Edmund Rolfe by
Pompeo Battoni
(Rome, 1762).

PLATE 5.   Heacham Hall, Norfolk (demolished). A photograph *c*. 1890 showing the large
additions of the late 1770s.

around 5000 country houses, are more plausible, except in that the incomes of
the peerage are much understated (all the evidence suggesting wide variations
and an *average* of twice King's figure) and in that there were a number of
landowners without peerages whose wealth at least equalled that of the average
member of the House of Lords.[7]

The beauty of isolating the English peerage, to review its size and wealth as a
background to financing its building proclivities, is that at least there is near-
precision about its numbers. King was accurate enough with his estimate of 160
in 1688. A century later (the first two Georges especially balking at its extension),
there were still only 220 in 1780. Thereafter numbers rose quite sharply, to 267
in 1800 and 400 in the 1860s. By the end of the nineteenth century the House of
Lords would have required, had attendance been regular, double the seating of
a century earlier.[8] Creations were more prolific than these figures suggest, for
peerages (as even the most superficial perusal of the thirteen volumes of the
Complete Peerage reveals) frequently became extinct, especially between 1670 and

1770, years of demographic crisis that spared neither those of high birth nor full stomach.[9] Taking into account that the population of England and Wales increased six times between 1700 and 1900, creations proportionately were not excessive. The English peerage, unlike its continental counterparts, remained small, exclusive and powerful until the late Victorian period.

What set this tiny group apart? The English peerage had few legal privileges beyond summons (not automatic for Scottish and Irish peers) to the House of Lords. It was not heavily taxed, but this was true of all landowners after 1720, when the exactions of the Land Tax eased, as the government resorted increasingly to loans serviced by revenues raised principally from indirect custom and excise duties spread across the whole population. The small size of the peerage itself guaranteed exclusiveness. There were only 1003 persons who held peerages across the course of the eighteenth century – or as it was put in the 1980s – about the roll of an average comprehensive school, or the crowd at a fourth division football match at Darlington on a wet Saturday afternoon in February. Moreover, recruitment was self-perpetuating, since new members were drawn almost entirely from within the peerage class itself. A few generals, admirals and very successful lawyers were ennobled, but their social connections were usually impeccable. Otherwise, a regular route of advance to the English peerage was laid down: ownership of a large country estate sufficient to sustain a peer's dignity; a prestigious seat in Parliament; a baronetcy; an Irish peerage; and, finally, an English one. But it was often slow progress, requiring frequent application to the King and his ministers. They pondered hard (often longer about peerage claims than over much more pressing issues), their deliberations creating enormous interest amongst the chattering political elite. The peerage also retained political power, although the influence of the Lords vis-à-vis the Commons in the nation's affairs gently waned from the early eighteenth century. But its hold on the Commons, both through the return of Members of Parliament by direct constituency control and more indirectly through family members occupying large numbers of seats, was firm. At its height in the eighteenth century, this embrace was maintained until the reforms of 1884–85. It was, however, in their grip on the country's executive that the peerage's power is most readily illustrated. The 1743 Pelham cabinet of sixteen members included six dukes and the Archbishop of Canterbury. Only as late as 1859, when Britain's industrial leadership was already at its height, was the balance of the cabinet at last tilted in favour of non-peerage members. The English peerage remained significant in executive terms to 1906, and as an influential second chamber to 1911.[10]

The peerage also, of course, had enormous influence at county level. Since its numbers were tiny, those regularly residing in any county could usually be counted on one hand. Demonstrating this pattern as late as 1865, the map illustrating Sandford and Townshend's *Great Governing Families* included 178 peers and only thirty-four other large owners in thirty-nine English counties.[11] In Norfolk, for example, England's foremost agricultural county, never more than half a dozen peers at any one time ruled the roost, although several more held secondary estates there.[12] They provided automatic social leadership in the counties, headed up rival political factions, topped every charitable list. Invariably they filled the office of Lord Lieutenant and, since Lords Lieutenant nominated all justices of the peace, the *de facto* rulers of the countryside in our period, the appointment remained an important one. More generally, enormous deference was paid to peers. Few were as imperious as the proud seventh Duke of Somerset, who insisted that his children remain standing in his presence, but many of the grandest seldom relaxed their dignity, even in the countryside.[13] The first Marquess of Abercorn went shooting kitted out with his Garter sash and star.[14] When Earl and Countess Gower visited Alnwick in 1832, they found the castle 'very imposing ... crowds of footmen await one at the door and lead one to the Duke and Duchess', but they were amused and a little disappointed when they were driven after breakfast around the park in an open carriage, 'not in the glass coach and six which we have been told was likely'. Even so, they were attended by 'a master of the horse, and outriders'.[15] Clearly, the Northumberlands were not going to be outdone by the heir to the Sutherlands. In the late seventeenth and early eighteenth centuries, when they arrived at their country seats from London, members of the peerage received the local gentry and members from the neighbouring corporation, exactly like a minor German prince, to endorse their political and social leadership in the locality. The Irwins of Temple Newsam, placed in considerable financial difficulties in the 1720s and 1730s by the death in quick succession of the third, fourth and fifth Viscounts and the major remodelling of their great old house outside Leeds, borrowed heavily from William Milner (Plate 6). He was the town's wealthiest merchant, its mayor in 1697, and a recent but considerable landowner in his own right, whose son had been created a baronet on his marriage to the Archbishop of York's daughter in 1717. Milner, however, was always careful to wait formally and deferentially upon the Irwins as soon as they returned from town before a more regular exchange of dinners could begin. When the newly created Earl Fitzwalter went down to his Essex estate in the summer of 1730 he 'spent £10 4s. at the Saracen's [Chelmsford] upon my neighbours who came to see me, being the minister and principal inhabitants of the town to the number of 130 and 140 on horseback'.[16]

When he charted the new world of social emulation, leisure and consumption

ANNE HIS WIFE, DAUGHTER
To CHARLES SCARBOROUGH ESQ.

HENRY INGRAM THE SEVENTH
VISCOUNT IRWIN.

PLATE 6. The seventh Viscount Irwin and wife, by Philip Mercier c. 1743. He is holding a design for the saloon of Temple Newsam, remodelled 1738–45 and shown in the background.

in Georgian England, Sir John Plumb concluded that 'money was fundamental to happiness'.[17] If his sybaritic generalisation has meaning, the peerage was in a state of almost continual bliss in the century and a half after 1720. It has been estimated that the average income of the peerage in 1690 was £5000 to £6000; and a century later £10,000.[18] By the 1870s it had at least doubled again. Except during the French wars (1793–1815), these gains were not seriously eroded by inflation; mostly they were real. But averages conceal as much as they reveal. Disparities between peerage incomes were always marked, happiness from Sir John's comment always sharply graded. Struggling to keep pace even with his untitled landowning neighbours, the net income of the second Duke of Manchester in the 1740s was no more than £3000.[19] Already some in his rank boasted means at least ten times as large. By the 1790s, 'the really great *grands seigneurs*, like the Dukes of Bedford, Bridgewater, Devonshire and the Egremonts, Shelburnes and Rockinghams [Fitzwilliams], had incomes approaching forty or even fifty thousand pounds, and were richer than many of the small independent rulers of the Continent'.[20] Certainly, the houses they built, Petworth, Chatsworth, Wentworth Woodhouse, Woburn, were palaces. By the time Bateman came to juggle with the plethora of statistics which the 'New Domesday' of landownership threw up in 1873 these disparities were ever greater. There were fifteen owners in Great Britain and Ireland (with one exception all peers) with landed incomes in excess of £100,000. The Duke of Buccleuch's income from his 460,000 acres, his mineral quarries and his harbour at Granton was £231,855. The Duke of Bedford's was £141,739 without 'his large London property'. The Duke of Westminster, likewise submitting no return from his estates in Mayfair and Belgravia which made him Britain's wealthiest landowner, was not even included in Bateman's super-rich league. In addition, there were fifty-one landed incomes (again unsurprisingly all but six of these of peers) of between £50,000 and £100,000. On the other hand, almost fifty peers, and not invariably of the Scottish and Irish variety, derived incomes of less than £7000 a year from land. That of England's premier marquess, Winchester, was only £4635; that of the premier viscount, Hereford, a mere £2241 from 2100 acres – a marginal entry on both counts. Also Bateman relegated to an appendix a motley list of sixty-six peers and peerages, 'none possess[ing] the double qualification of 2000 acres worth a minimum of £2000 per annum'.[21] Already by the 1870s there were peers – especially those whose titles were recently derived from prominence in the law – who had insufficient means to buy large landed estates and build and maintain a sizeable country house. As creations proceeded apace, and wealth could be more conveniently and profitably held in other forms, a titled plutocracy emerged. After the mid nineteenth century, it was often content to enjoy the fruits of its ennoblement from a London base and from a home in the country either rented or, after 1880, without the burden of broad acres and a vast house.

Nevertheless, Bateman's pages, compiled on the eve of prolonged agrarian depression, reveals a peerage generally at the peak of its prosperity. Nor was it ossified. It responded to change. Certainly it became more cohesive. Newcomers were admitted, and the Scottish and Irish peerages – through intermarriage and long sojourns in London – became thoroughly integrated with their English counterparts. Together, they faced up to a crisis of confidence following the War of American Seccession and the French Revolution by winning a great victory over Napoleon.[22] The ebb in their influence after 1832 was very gradual.

How had the big increases in peerage incomes come about across two centuries? Evidence is not in short supply – the literature on the landed estate is voluminous. Each of the 4500 sizeable estates, scattered randomly across the very diverse agricultural regions of England, experienced a different evolution; each revealed a different demographic profile of ownership. The most recent survey of land-ownership, alive with examples, runs close to 800 pages.[23] Yet whilst historians disagree about the impact, timing and weighting of various factors, all are of the opinion that the growth of the large estate and the increasing wealth of their owners was abundantly evident after 1660.[24]

Three principal causes appear to have worked together to produce the right conditions: the use of the strict settlement or entail allowing estates to be passed from one generation to another largely intact (somewhere between a half and two-thirds of land owned by large landowners was settled); the negotiation of advantageous marriage settlements between landed families and sometimes with the richest bourgeoisie; and the increased reliance upon mortgages to fund territorial expansion, family settlements and estate debt generally. Manipulation of these three features was at the core of all dynastic landed ambition. Classically, they led to the evolution of the great ten, twenty, thirty thousand acre estates which were such a marked feature of British life in the eighteenth and nineteenth centuries. Of course there were wider influences, without which these strategies and devices could not have operated. After 1688 the great upheavals of the seventeenth century, which had so thoroughly destabilised the land market and so troubled landowners, subsided. At home political stability and peace, with few major disturbances, returned. Moreover, the post-Revolution political settlement, enshrining the power of property, was immensely favourable to agricultural and industrial development and to colonial expansion alike. Interest rates after the 1690s were low; agricultural prices and incomes rose appreciably after 1750. When population growth began to accelerate after the 1750s, grain prices increased from the low levels which had generally subsisted since the 1660s. The French wars (1793–1815) further fuelled inflationary trends. Wheat prices almost doubled between the late 1780s from around forty-eight shillings per quarter to eighty-four shillings in 1800. Towards the end of the wars (1809–12) they had reached an average 122 shillings, levels not recorded again until the early 1970s. Rents reflected these increases and also the benefits of enclosure to landlords. During the wars they advanced by some 90 per cent on average, although on some estates by as much as 175 per cent. When peace came cereal prices eased considerably; but, although there were pressures on rents and the length of leases in the worst years of the post-1815 depression, rentals in the 1820s remained around twice their pre-1790 levels. Landowners shared fully in the general prosperity of agriculture after the 1750s.

The recording of negotiations and transactions surrounding settlements and borrowing, purchases, rentals, leases and sales of land filled the muniment rooms and estate offices of every country house. But there were landowners, often the largest, whose incomes were made up from other sources besides land. Some, with spectacular examples such as the first Duke of Chandos, Sir Robert Walpole and the Fox family, did well from political place and office, especially during the many periods when Britain was at war. Cannons and Houghton were monuments to government place. But many a peerage family's finances were reinforced, if less spectacularly, from the profits of office, as the *Extraordinary Red Book* (1816) and John Wade's *Black Book: or Corruption Unmasked* (1819) disclosed. They revealed scores of sinecures, realising thousands of pounds annually for those influential members of the peerage who struggled most successfully to acquire them. When they were gradually abolished after 1832 holders were generously compensated. The Dukes of Grafton received no less than £420,761 between 1809 and 1857 when their sinecure places and perpetual pensions, largely conferred on the first Duke by his father, Charles II, were redeemed. These were sums which allowed them to keep two large houses open and out of debt even when landed incomes dipped sharply after 1880. More often the most notable landed fortunes were increasingly supplemented by urban rentals and mineral rights and way-leaves. Certainly, the

PLATE 7. Sir John Ramsden's landed income disclosed in John Bateman's *Great Landowners of Great Britain* (1883 edn). The Ramsdens owned five country houses in this period.

Great Landowners of Great Britain.			375

** RAMSDEN, Sɪʀ Jᴏʜɴ Wɪʟʟɪᴀᴍ, Bᴀʀᴛ., of Byram, Ferry-Bridge, &c.

		acres.	g. an. val.
Coll. Eton, Trin. Cam.	Lincoln . . .	800	. 1,400
Club. Brooks's, Athenæum,	York, W.R. .	11,248	. 168,420
Travellers'.	Inverness . .	138,000	. 11,474

b. 1831, s. 1839, m. 1865.

Served as Under Secretary for War.   150,048 . 181,294

Sat for Taunton, Hythe, the W.R., and Monmouth. Sits for E. Div. of W.R.

Inclusive of a rental of 1,819*l*. belonging to Hᴏɴ. Mʀs. Rᴀᴍsᴅᴇɴ, his mother. This is one of the cases specially noted in the return, where (in Yorkshire) the gross estimated rental forms no criterion of the income received by the landlord.

RANELAGH, Vɪsᴄᴏᴜɴᴛ, K.C.B., Mulgrave Ho., Fulham, S.W.

Club. Carlton.	Norfolk . . .	3,043	. 5,691

b. 1812, m. 1820. Served in 1st Life Guards.

RANFURLY, Eᴀʀʟ ᴏꜰ, Dungannon Park, Co. Tyrone.

Coll. Harr., Trin. Cam.	Co. Tyrone .	9,647	. 10,958
Club. Carl., White's, Ral.	Fermanagh . .	506	. 279

b. 1856, s. 1875, m. 1880.

		10,153	. 11,237

*** RANKIN, Pᴀᴛʀɪᴄᴋ, of Otter House, Kilfinan, Argyll, N.B.

b. 1844, s. 1873.	Lanark . . .	4,365	. 3,196
Exc. of 2,972*l*. for mines,	Argyll . . .	4,200	. 1,552
the real inc. of which was	Stirling . . .	956	. 719
(1877) much higher.			

		9,521	. 5,467

** RASHLEIGH, Jᴏɴᴀᴛʜᴀɴ, of Menabilly, Par, Cornwall, &c.

Coll. Har., Ball. Ox.	Cornwall . .	30,156	. 9,000
b. 1820, s. 1871, m. 1st 1843,	Devon . . .	242	. 750
2nd 1869.	Co. Mayo . .	5,475	. 883
The Cornish acreage in-	Co. Sligo . .	1,023	. 658
cludes waste, the rental in			
Cornwall is always increas-		36,896	. 11,291
ing as lives drop.			

RANKIN, J., of Bryngwyn.	Heref., Ches.	2,959	. 5,130

PLATE 8. Byram Park, Yorkshire (demolished). The house was remodelled by John Carr and Robert Adam in the 1770s.

majority of those of landowners with incomes in excess of £50,000 in 1873 were derived in part from these sources. Sir John Ramsden of Byram Park, Ferrybridge, found himself in the select band of Bateman's tiny league of super-rich, not because he owned a fair slice of Inverness-shire but because Huddersfield had been developed on his family's property (Plates 7 and 8).[25]

When we turn briefly to expenditure, generalisation is again difficult – in this case because, even with a restricted group like the peerage, members of it were, unlike men in the professions, or merchants, financiers and industrialists, freer to follow their own inclinations. Good, impartial, thoroughly professional advice from agents, attorneys and bankers was nothing like as sound as that provided by accountants and financial advisers in the late twentieth century. Although minorities were far better managed than they had been by the controversial Court of Wards before the Civil War, and the trust had become an established and venerated peculiarly British institution, family members and friends who usually acted as trustees were also no more far-sighted than the general run of landowners. Disputes were settled slowly, almost endlessly, in the Court of Chancery. For all these reasons, landowners still possessed considerable latitude in determining the fate of their estates through their approach to debt and expenditure. Sport, collecting, building and landscaping were compelling pursuits for the class as a whole. Some gambled prodigiously in their London clubs or on the racecourse, keeping strings of racehorses at Newmarket or on nearby downs and wolds and, by the early nineteenth century, stables of hunters in the shires. Lord Lincoln, the twenty-six-year-old heir to the fifth Duke of Newcastle, had racing debts of £230,000 in 1860; in the following year he was fortunate enough to marry (he gallantly said for love) the illegitimate daughter of Henry Thomas Hope, a vastly wealthy London banker, who settled his debts and provided him with an income of £10,000 or £12,000 a year.[26] Others led rackety, debt-ridden lives. The third Earl of Orford, not a little mad but unrestrained, almost wrecked the grand dynastic ambitions of his grandfather, Sir Robert Walpole.

Some peers built beyond their means. The second Earl Verney in 1783 was forced to flee to France to escape his creditors and to sell the contents of the great house he had built. Marrying in 1740 a London mercantile heiress with £40,000, and possessing an income of about £10,000 a year after he succeeded in 1752, he threw himself into building, politics and pleasure with great vigour. Claydon, with the finest suite of rococo rooms in England, is a monument to his folly, gullibility and extravagance (Plate 9). A man of 'magnificent instincts, great artistic taste and

PLATE 9.   Claydon House, Buckinghamshire. Detail of chimney-piece and niches in the north hall.

knowledge', Lord Verney employed a carver of genius, Luke Lightfoot, to carry
out his scheme of constructing a house which would rival nearby Stowe in
magnificence. Lightfoot was dilatory and unbusinesslike. By the time he was
dismissed, in 1769, Verney was over £70,000 in debt. Lightfoot's successor, Sir
Thomas Robinson, brought in to complete the house, was far from a restraining
influence. He too was dismissed two years later, but building, in spite of a
continuing run of unwise speculations by the earl, continued to 1783. The thirty-
year project was then still incomplete on Lord Verney's flight to France. A decade
later his heir wasted no time in pulling down two-thirds of the house (Plate 10).[27]

Lords Lincoln, Orford and Verney exhibited the wilder proclivities of the
nobility. The majority of them were engaged in more profitable pursuits. Increasingly, as the economic benefits of agricultural improvement were brought home
to landowners by a rapidly growing literature on the subject, they invested heavily
in their estates, improving their tenanted farms, providing leadership in agrarian
progress, planting trees for posterity and future gain. Some, like Thomas William
Coke in Norfolk, the Yarboroughs in Lincolnshire, the Sykeses in the East Riding
of Yorkshire, and the Dukes of Northumberland, became model estate owners,

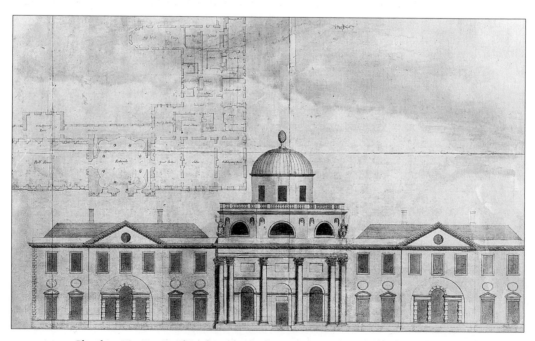

PLATE 10.   Claydon House, Buckinghamshire, showing Sir Thomas Robinson's design of
c. 1770. Only the left-hand portion survives.

their perfection of the landlord-tenant system admired in Britain, on the Continent and in America. There were also landowners, again driven by economic motives, who had the opportunity to exploit either urban expansion or mineral resources on their estates. Many involved themselves, though not necessarily taking the lead, in developing river navigations, turnpike roads and, after 1760, canals. All landowners, even if they made but a small contribution in these productive areas of investment, also condoned the developments in agriculture, industry and transport which slowly transformed Britain, in the two centuries after 1660, into the First Industrial Nation.

To fund dynastic ambitions, control of political institutions, extravagant life-styles, great building schemes or estate improvement, the majority of landowners appear to have resorted to borrowing on the strength of low interest rates and rising incomes. Strict settlements were no bar, indeed they fuelled it. 'Few things are more surprising than the size of the debts which life tenants were able to incur.' Indeed many landowners shared the same culture of debt and insecurity which pervaded the financial, commercial and industrial worlds in this period.[28] The scale of landowners' debts depended of course upon resources and prospects. Lesser landowners, usually more cautious, borrowed a few thousand pounds. But the peerage, again varying in their needs and prudence, could and did borrow profusely. Wealthy they may have been, but this did not necessarily guarantee a high liquidity rating for many of them. Debt was therefore a way of life and one which became a more pronounced feature for all landowners across the eighteenth century.[29] Spending way beyond income across long periods was the usual course. The problems at Houghton after Sir Robert Walpole's death in 1745 were twofold: his grandson was incompetent; but the Prime Minister and his heir, the second Earl of Orford who died in 1751, had already accumulated debts of over £100,000, largely from building, collecting and prodigal lifestyles. Without the fruits of political office and place, these were difficult to sustain on a landed income of only £8000 a year. The fate of Sir Robert's picture collection, the most celebrated of its day, sold at a bargain-basement price of around £40,000 in 1779 to Catherine the Great of Russia, was sealed, in spite of all Horace Walpole's attempts and protestations, from the moment of his father's death.[30] The Duke of Newcastle sustained a long and famous political career, properties in eleven counties, five large houses and seventy servants, with the grandest of ceremonious lifestyles, by servicing an ever-escalating debt. In the early 1720s he enjoyed a net landed income of around £17,500 and earned almost another £5000 from his

Secretaryship of State. At the outset of his career he improved his houses but laid out little on his estates, for spending not investing was the key to the duke's make-up. By 1748 his debts had reached a dizzy £286,000. Inevitably land sales and limited retrenchment followed.[31] Unlike the Duke of Newcastle, the third Duke of Richmond inherited a considerable surplus in 1756. Moreover, he was personally frugal, checking his account books to the penny. But over forty years later he was £95,000 in debt through making land purchases to extend a modest estate and to rebuild a modest house, neither initially matching ducal status.[32] In 1844 it is estimated that the sixth Duke of Devonshire had debts just short of a million pounds.[33] Although many landowners were heavily indebted, they almost all stopped short of the danger point. The Duke of Buckingham's spectacular bankruptcy in 1848 was a rare event, although others tottered on the brink at various times.[34] Conventional practice amongst lenders in the early nineteenth century was based on a formula, based upon net rental income calculations, which allowed lending up to half the value of the property mortgaged.[35]

Massive, increasing wealth, a predilection to borrow, and extravagant, emulative life styles are always powerful forces likely to produce excesses amongst the tiny minority of those who share them. Ample leisure, diverse interests and copious incomes, largely based upon the seeming bedrock and permanence of land, certainly allowed the English peerage between 1660 and 1880 to follow routes and excesses which enlivened the letters and journals of their contemporaries and have fascinated or appalled historians ever since. At the heart of this prodigality was a desire to proclaim to the world their riches, dignity and power. Visually, nothing achieved this better than building, frequently, stylishly, and on the grandest scale.

The 3817 non-peerage landowners, categorised here conveniently as gentry and whom Bateman reckoned owned estates of more than a thousand acres in England and Wales in the 1870s, were indeed a varied bunch, encompassing differences quite equal to those displayed by the peerage. Some 175 possessed estates of ten thousand acres plus, placing them at least on a par with the average peer with whom they almost always had close connections of blood and marriage; just over a thousand gentry owned estates of between three and ten thousand acres; and 2529 lesser gentry occupied between one and three thousand acres.[36] Each county displayed this heterogeneity of gentry population. In Suffolk, for example, the gamut in the 1870s ran from thirty-six greater gentry, owning more than twice the land of the sixty-five lesser gentry. At the top of the tree came Colonel George Tomline MP. No landowner owned a more valuable estate in Suffolk. His vast 18,473 acre estate, centred on Orwell Park near Ipswich, produced £24,005; in addition, he owned 8439 acres in Lincolnshire. Based upon a clerical fortune (his grandfather, George Pretyman, was William Pitt's tutor and secretary; through his patronage he subsequently became Bishop of Lincoln and Winchester), and through a fortuitous inheritance from Marmaduke Tomline 'a stranger in blood', his large landed income allowed Colonel Tomline to dwarf his mid eighteenth-century house with an enormous extension designed by William Burn in 1851–53 and, twenty years later, an observatory tower.[37]

On the other hand, of the sixty-five lesser gentry in Suffolk there were those who struggled on the margins of landed gentility, even when agricultural rents were at their peak in the early 1870s. To keep a household, stable and garden sufficient for the dignity of a justice of the peace and for membership of county society, to marry off daughters and to educate and place sons advantageously at a period when family size was at its most extensive, and to improve farms and cottages, was indeed difficult on the minimum £1000–£1500 a year incomes generated by the smallest estates. Unless there were sizeable earnings from other sources, there was no surplus to build extensively; still less to rent a house in London – the great magnet of landed society by the 1870s – for the season.

Over a century earlier the squirearchy had struggled even harder when rents and agricultural prices plummeted to new depths in the second quarter of the eighteenth century. Davy Durrant of Scottow in Norfolk provides an instructive vignette of their position. Although the Durrants obtained a baronetcy in 1784 and owned 2935 acres a century later, they were average Norfolk squires, even if their incomes were well in excess of King's 1695 guidelines for the gentry. Davy Durrant's day book, revealing his expenses and outgoings from 1738 to 1755, presumably equates with his income since it discloses no repayment of loans. In these eighteen years his expenditure averaged £980. He lived comfortably, enjoying the sufficiency of polite society – regular journeys to Norwich and Yarmouth, a calendar of assemblies and clubs, and the frequent purchase of books and plate. He was a county justice and the bearers at his family's funerals clearly show him as a member of county society; his household included a footman, coachman, gardener, cook and three or four maids. But he could do no more than repair his house and modestly update it, lay a new hall floor, retile the kitchen and barn, install a couple of cheap marble fireplaces, and pay 'the fee for all work and stuff done to ye Pediment of house, £8 10s. *6d.*' A major rebuild, achieved neither stylishly nor extensively, had to wait until the 1780s.[38]

Davy Durrant's spending increased as agricultural prices picked up in the late 1740s; indeed entries for the last year of his day book (1755) record that he spent £1442, almost double that of the lowest point in the series, thirteen years earlier. It seems likely that the gap in income between the average peer and average gentry landowner began to diminish after 1750, as the latter, perhaps managing their resources better, fully enjoyed the fruits of increasing agricultural prosperity.

The mechanism of the gentry's aggrandisement was exactly the same as that we have seen enriching the peerage: the enforcement of strict settlement to assist the descent of estates more or less intact in a period of demographic uncertainty; the negotiation of mortgages to allow the extension and consolidation of estates and to aid bigger family settlements; and the bargaining of marriage settlements to achieve dynastic ambitions and to refuel family resources. Those at the base of the gentry pyramid, although they appear to have operated all these devices, clearly did so less extensively. Those families, like the Ramsdens of Byram Park and the Sykeses of Sledmere, whose estates and enterprises allowed them to benefit from urban land sales and the granting of building leases, from mineral royalties, or from parliamentary enclosure and exceptional agricultural improvement, naturally fared well, especially after the 1780s when the pace of urbanisation, industrialisation and agrarian development quickened. Only in the province of government office and place, which in any case gradually became less lucrative after the 1780s, did the gentry do less well than the peerage, who assumed virtually exclusive rights to shake the tree of state and court patronage.

Lesser titles, baronetcies rather than knighthoods, seem to have constituted distinctions amongst landowners. Jane Austen's Sir Walter Elliot of Kellynch Hall, Somersetshire, plainly believed they did, and the precedence of families of his rank continued to cause many a *placement* headache and slight at the tables of county society. Mrs Lybbe Powys thought Ludlow's assembly in 1771, 'with two lords and six baronets families, might be stil'd tolerable tho' it seem'd a mortyfying thing that Lord Clive's family were at Spaw, and Lady Powis ill in London'.[39] Initially, at least in 1611 when the order of baronets was founded, grants as of right were awarded to those who met the strictly defined criteria of landed wealth and birth. But creations were soon much exceeded by the first three Stuart kings so that the order, originally restricted to 200 members, had swollen to close on a thousand by the early 1680s.[40] The one detailed study of the baronetage, for Yorkshire, reveals an unexpected picture. Of the ninety-three creations between 1611 and 1800 no fewer than seventy-two (77.4 per cent) dated from before 1672. A mere five originated between 1697 and 1775. Nevertheless 'at least in Yorkshire, the order of baronets was characterized by a wide-ranging and growing diversity'. Because creations were chiefly of the early Stuart period, large numbers did not survive the demographic crises which straddled the end of the seventeenth century so menacingly. Sir Walter Elliot derived great satisfaction 'by contemplating the limited remnant of the earliest patents' (his dated from 1660, not a vintage year).[41]

Although the wealth of the Yorkshire baronets varied significantly, the way forward for those who prospered and survived (a dozen were advanced to peerages) was through prestigious marriages, the choice of responsible trustees during minorities, small families, businesslike management, consolidation of the core estate and, above all, the capacity to make realistic wills and settlements. There were casualties, besides those of demographic implosion, who failed to observe these criteria. The most striking was that of Sir Thomas Robinson (c. 1702–77), a notable amateur architect and builder (Plate 11). Enjoying an extended Grand Tour, marrying a daughter of the builder of Castle Howard, the third Earl of Carlisle, being returned an MP for the earl's pocket borough of Morpeth, even possessing a government place in the 1730s as Commissioner of Excise, he acquired notions well beyond that of a recently-created (1731) north Yorkshire baronet of modest estate. Of the neo-Palladian-Burlington school, he completely rebuilt the family seat at Rokeby to his own designs between 1725 and 1731. A highly-individual, compact villa, it was beautifully detailed and expensive (Plate 12). In London he 'gave balls to all the men and women in power and in fashion'. A widower in 1739, he was so in debt that he served as Governor of Barbados between 1742 and 1747, ending up in even worse financial circumstances because his constant itch to build led him to rebuild the official residence, armoury and arsenal without consulting the island's assembly. On his return, he completed Castle Howard for his brother-in-law, was Master of Ceremonies at Ranelagh, and, as we have seen, was involved in one of the most extravagant and ill-fated of Georgian country houses, Claydon. By the early 1770s Sir Thomas, as spendthrift as his last patron, the second Earl Verney at Claydon, was forced to sell Rokeby.[42]

In Norfolk the baronetcy came to occupy estates across the spectrum. In the 1870s, amongst the eleven 10,000 plus acre estates in the county, one was owned by a baronet (Sir Thomas Hare of Stow Bardolph); of the fifty-seven estates of the greater gentry, ten were owned by baronets; and of thirty-one estates of the lesser gentry of 2000 to 3000 acres, three were possessed by baronets.[43] The West Riding of Yorkshire reveals a similar picture, although the dozen baronets were somewhat thinner on the ground. Of the sixteen owners of estates of more than 10,000 acres in the county (there were a further eleven if landholdings outside Yorkshire are taken into account), two were baronets; nine fell into the category of greater gentry. Only one baronet, Sir Joseph Radcliffe of Rudding Park, had fewer than 3000 acres, but he creeps into the greater gentry category when his 457 acres property in Lancashire is taken into account.[44] As might therefore be

PLATE II.
Sir Thomas
Robinson, by
Frans van der
Mijn.

PLATE 12. Rokeby Park, Yorkshire (Sir Thomas Robinson, 1725–31). Painting attributed to George Cuitt.

expected, a baronetcy was usually equated with ownership of a middling-sized landed estate. Although in the nineteenth century baronetcies were granted in increasing numbers, and eventually given to men who adorned the professions, arts and sciences, and the world of business as well as the armed services, the title was granted primarily to men of landed fortune.[45]

It is more difficult to generalise about the conferment of knighthoods because those of the Garter, Thistle and St Patrick were invariably bestowed on the grandest peers, while in the nineteenth century a whole range of orders of knighthood were created to reward talent in different fields. Before 1660 there had been a connection between landowner status and knighthood, one Gregory King still seemed to recognise in 1695. Gradually, however, knighthoods came to reward many eminent statesmen, lawyers, soldiers, seamen, antiquaries, mathematicians, physicians, merchants and learned writers.[46] Again, towards 1900 creations burgeoned. The Prime Minister, the third Marquess of Salisbury, joked, 'you cannot throw a stone at a dog without hitting a knight in London'.[47] Nevertheless, even as late as 1912, numerous as they were, 'the honour more often than not had strong links with the old elite'.[48] It is revealing that amongst the landowners of West Yorkshire and Norfolk in the 1870s there was not a knight bachelor amongst them.

This range of gentry wealth and pretension is, of course, still encapsulated in the country houses surviving at the millennium. There are, however, problems in peeling back the layers of our understanding of them in their original social context. We are conditioned by the immaculate presentations of the National Trust and the piles of capitivatingly illustrated books and magazines devoted to 'our country-house heritage'. We think of them, even the smaller houses, as being formidable undertakings beyond the reach of the largest lottery prize. Perceptions have shifted. When Hilborough Hall in west Norfolk was sold in 1985 it was billed as a major country house, the centre of one of the largest shooting estates in England (created with a nineteenth-century banking fortune). The house had been built in the late 1770s for Ralph Cauldwell, Thomas William Coke's one-time duplicitous agent. He would certainly have counted the thousands he expended upon it on one hand, whereas Holkham, the great eighteenth-century house of his employer, had cost the Cokes £92,000 by the time it was finished two decades earlier. Yet the majority of England's four thousand plus country houses fell into the Hilborough category, buildings which captured in bricks and mortar the means and aspirations of the bulk and bedrock of England's landowners.

A glance at the whole stock of Norfolk's country houses provides a good illustration of this fit between the wealth and heterogeneity of its landowners and the hierarchy of houses they built or remodelled over two centuries. Of course its template does not fit all counties. Whereas Norfolk was a county of great eighteenth-century houses, Jack Simmons believed that Somerset 'cannot claim a single first-class Georgian country house, except Prior Park'.[49] Moreover, chronologies of country house building were far from uniform across England, being much affected by the variable pace of agricultural change across the country, as well as the different stages at which the greater estates were put together and came to predominate in any county; and whether, later, they possessed mining potential or significant industrial and urban dimensions. Norfolk is unusual, being a primarily agrarian county in which the key agricultural changes – rotation and enclosure – took place early, but also one which de-industrialised after its worsted industry, constituting one of England's three main wool textile regions, went into rapid decline after 1790. Even within the county there were sharp contrasts between the light soil areas in west Norfolk, the centre of early, easy agricultural improvement (Holkham, Houghton and Raynham were all in this region), and the clay lands of south Norfolk, where soils were difficult to work and upgrade and where estates were small. Similar inter-county disparities existed between Hertfordshire, where estates affected by proximity to London were small with a high turnover of owners, Northamptonshire, a county of big ancient aristocratic estates and houses, and Northumberland, where agrarian improvement came later and the fortunes made in its great coal trade added a new dimension.[50] Nevertheless, the Norfolk example is instructive.

In Georgian England, as the country's roads improved, Norfolk (together with Derbyshire) became an established venue for the growing band of genteel country house visitors. The landscape itself was little draw, even if the Cromer Ridge put the fanciful Lady Beauchamp-Proctor from flat south Norfolk in mind of the Swiss Alps when she made her tour of Norfolk houses in 1764. The majority of gentlemen excursionists came to view the county's lauded farming methods as well as its country houses.[51] Their itinerary is instructive. They only visited half a dozen houses: Holkham, Houghton, Raynham, Wolterton, Blickling and Narford, perhaps occasionally making a detour to Felbrigg and Kimberley. The first three, the homes of recently ennobled peers, came to stand unchallenged at the top of the county's first division of houses. Holkham and Houghton, wonder houses of the second quarter of the eighteenth century, were much visited. Holkham, planned and built over forty years, was the supreme English example of pure neo-Palladian taste on the grand scale; Houghton, a monument to the spoils of government office, was grossly extravagant. It struck the eighteen-year-old Caroline Girle (later Mrs Lybbe Powys), who visited it in 1759, as like Aladdin's cave: interiors 'very superb … it makes the whole what I call magnificently glaringly'.[52] Sir Robert Walpole, bragging to his neighbour Lord Leicester, reckoned that Houghton had cost him £200,000 before he began to burn the bills (Plates 13 and 14).[53] Raynham, an innovative house of the 1620s, had fine William Kent interiors of the 1720s. Beneath these came another dozen or so houses built and extended for the peerage and the wealthier members of the greater gentry. They included the rest of the houses already mentioned as featuring in the Norfolk Tour. There were others, however, whose position shifted in this ranking of first division houses as the fortunes and building activities of families fluctuated across the generations. Melton Constable, the ancient seat of the Astleys, a perfect triple-pile, Pratt-style villa of the 1670s, was deemed old-fashioned by the 1720s.

PLATE 13.   Houghton Hall, Norfolk, under construction. From a drawing by Edmund
Prideaux, *c.* 1725.

PLATE 14.   Houghton Hall, Norfolk (Colen Campbell and James Gibbs, 1721–32). Painting by
J. M. Winckler, 1984.

So increasingly was Blickling. Sylas Neville in 1782 found the north wing (completed by the Ivorys of Norwich between 1765 and 1779) 'very inferior and looks more like an hospital than a nobleman's seat. There is nothing worth notice in the house but the Library'.[54] In the 1740s Gunton Park joined the upper stratum of Norfolk houses. It was built for Sir William Harbord by Matthew Brettingham, who had carried out William Kent and Lord Leicester's designs at Holkham. Gunton was a solid seven- by five-bay affair. But the family was on the up, the rents on its estate of good quality land advancing. Although Robert Adam was invited to submit plans in 1767–68 for enlarging the house (only his designs for the church in the park were carried out), not until the early 1780s, just before Sir William's son was created Baron Suffield in 1786, after representing Norwich in Parliament for over twenty years, was a big, ill-matching new wing added by James and Samuel Wyatt.[55] Similarly, Langley Park was transformed. It was bought in 1739 by a London merchant, George Proctor, from a member of the Norfolk gentry who had ruined himself by building a house beyond his means a decade earlier. Proctor and his nephew and heir, Sir William Beauchamp-Proctor Bt, MP for Middlesex 1747–68, were well-travelled men of fashion. They engaged Matthew Brettingham to alter the house into 'externally an abridged edition of Holkham, in red instead of white brick'.[56] Corner towers and wings were added, the interiors being finished with superb rococo plasterwork by Charles Stanley (Plate 15). Throughout the nineteenth century an increasing number of houses were admitted to this top league of Norfolk houses. Mostly they were built with non-landed sources of income: the original E-plan house at Costessey was, between the 1820s and 1850s, surrounded and dwarfed by great Gothic additions by J. C. Buckler, including a 130-foot high tower for the eighth Lord Stafford, whose rent-roll from his relatively small estate in Norfolk was supplemented by a growing industrial income from his Staffordshire properties (Plate 16). Big extensions to Shadwell Park by Edward Blore and S. S. Teulon were a considerable factor in ruining the Buxtons, long-established south Norfolk landowners, whose income from a large estate on marginal Breckland soils was decimated by the agricultural depression after the 1870s. Lynford Hall, another Breckland estate, was bought with the proceeds of a London mercantile fortune so extensive that its new owner, Lyne Stephens, could expend an incredible £145,000 between 1856 and 1861 on a vast, state-of-the-art Jacobean-style house, designed by the ubiquitous early Victorian country house architect William Burn (Plates 26–28). Even at its peak, the 7000 acre estate produced an annual rental of only £2736. By the early

PLATE 15.   Langley Park, Norfolk. The Beauchamp-Proctor family at Langley, by John
Wooton, 1749.

1890s it was on the market. Shadwell and Lynford illustrate the vulnerability of
houses and estates, both of old and new landowners, to the acute agricultural
depression after 1880. Bylaugh ('Neither Holkham nor Houghton, those Norfolk
wonders, can compare with it for either appearance or comfort', raved the *Norwich
Mercury* on its completion in 1851), Didlington, Sandringham and Sennowe (and
in the Suffolk brecks, on an even more prodigious scale, Elveden and Culford
for the Earls of Iveagh and Cadogan) were similar symbols of the taste and
lifestyles of those Victorian and Edwardian nobles and plutocrats whose predilection to build on the most extensive scale was not constrained by agricultural
rent rolls.[57]

   In the second rank of Norfolk houses there were surprisingly few: some had
pre-1660s origins and were altered, usually in the nineteenth century, like Merton,
Honingham and Great Witchingham; all three were eventually the seats of peers.
Others graduated into the league after their acquisition by aspiring newcomers

PLATE 16. Costessey Hall, Norfolk (demolished). A photograph of 1865 showing the Tudor house with J. C. Buckler's big additions of 1826–55 rising up behind.

to the county. The third Earl of Albemarle bought the Quidenham estate in 1762; the old Jacobean house was refaced and extended, and its interiors altered out of all recognition. Westwick, a lesser gentry house acquired through inheritance by a branch of the Petres, Essex's leading landowners, was similarly enlarged around 1800. Those houses which entered this 'middling' reckoning after 1660 usually did so in periods of marked economic prosperity, often being associated with an architect suddenly fashionable with the county's leading gentry. Matthew Brettingham (1699–1769), who was involved at Holkham for a quarter of a century after 1734, 'so early as the year 1740 ... had a numerous Acquaintance with the Gentlemen of the County'.[58] Gunton and Langley, and alterations to at least three other Norfolk country houses, were clearly the results of his standing with Lord Leicester. In the 1780s, after the American War recession, the young John Soane designed Shotesham Park and Letton Hall, both for up-and-coming gentry families. He also remodelled Ryston, Sir Roger Pratt's own 1670s villa.[59] W. J. Donthorn,

PLATE 17.   Honing Hall, Norfolk. Built in 1748, Soane added the bow window and first floor platband in 1788.

an architect of far less repute than either Brettingham or Soane, nevertheless had a good west Norfolk practice in the late 1820s and 1830s, designing sizeable houses at Hillington, Elmham, South Pickenham, Marham and Cromer.[60]

The majority of the houses of the gentry were on a lesser scale. Many old manor houses, always numerous in Norfolk, were extended and remodelled as their owners prospered and the land attached to them grew. Nationally known architects were not often involved in this updating. At this level of country house building, Norfolk, more insular than the Home Counties, was less influenced by the latest metropolitan fashion. Of the fifty-seven houses of the greater gentry in the early 1870s, no architect is attributed for as many as a score of them. Of these lesser houses, Stradsett Hall in west Norfolk provides a typical example. The house is basically built on an Elizabethan E-plan. Around 1750 it was acquired by Philip Case, who somewhat mysteriously and improbably acquired a vast fortune (the newspapers always reckoned £100,000) from his attorney's business in King's Lynn. He acted for a number of the west Norfolk estates and his daughter and co-heiress (the other revived the Astley fortunes at Melton Constable) married a Bagge, from a family of prominent brewers and ship-owners in Lynn. Case spent little time at Stradsett, although he undertook some minor internal alterations. Only in 1819 was the fenestration altered, the eleven-bay facade rendered and a park and lake planned. Although the house was extensively 'Georgianised', no great sums were expended upon it. Yet by the 1870s it was the centre of a valuable fen-edge 3769 acre estate, and its owner had been MP for West Norfolk for thirty-five years, having been created a baronet in 1867.[61]

New houses, of course, had been built by the gentry after 1660, but the cost of quite stylish houses, like Stanhoe, Ditchingham, Honing and Salle, was not large. The 'case' of Honing Hall, a five-bay, two-and-half storey, red-brick house cost no more than £500 in the late 1740s; finishing the interior probably a little more (Plate 17). Salle Park, a rather larger seven-bay red brick house built between 1763 and 1765, cost £2470, with a further £565 expended on its kitchen garden walls.[62] By the early nineteenth century, when landed incomes rose quite sharply with the advance in agricultural prices during the French wars, especially if owners had benefited from enclosure, there was a good deal of new building by smaller estate owners. It was an activity that continued into the 1830s and was then refuelled by rising rent rolls in the High Farming period from the 1850s through to the mid 1870s. Humphry Repton designed Hoveton Hall in 1809 and Sheringham three years later, at the peak of the wartime boom (Plate 69). The Revd William Gunn, an amateur architect who had undertaken two long continental tours in the mid 1780s and early 1790s, built Sloley Hall for the Cubitts (1815) and Smallburgh Hall for the Postles (1820), both families having clearly prospered during the high-price period.[63]

When these smaller houses are examined, they fit the contemporary dissection of eighteenth-century society revealed by the social tables of King, Massie and Colquhoun (and indeed the tripartite division John Bateman devised in the 1870s to categorise his large landowners). There were quite sharp status divisions within the landed elite. Looking at the entire cross-section of country houses, there does not appear to be a yawning gap between those of the smaller gentry and those of urban grandees. Just as landed incomes at the lower end fused with those of the richer merchants, industrialists and members of the more lucrative professions, so did their houses. Certainly, landed society remained 'aristocratically' cohesive down to the 1870s, but it was not a permanently closed world of impenetrably large owners. Architecturally in Norfolk there is an obvious descent from Houghton and Holkham through the houses of the greater gentry to those of the smaller landowners, the Rolfes of Heacham and the Cubitts of Honing and Sloley. These smaller houses suggest that the county's ruling elite was neither closed nor fossilised. It was possible for newcomers to afford houses and estates like these. Then the ascent could begin. There was an 'openness' that existed at the lower levels of landed society, with obvious close links of material culture between them and the trading and professional elites. Socially, this phenomenon was extremely important in the early stages of Britain's industrialisation, for by and large its landed classes condoned the momentous changes which took place.

Newcomers to landownership tended to build ostentatiously, sometimes provoking the envious censure of the old gentry class. Take Henry Vincent of Buckenham Tofts. An early building developer in London, he bought his west Norfolk estate in the 1690s. Roger North, the amateur architect, country house builder and writer, was scathing about the outcome of the massive £20,000 he reputedly spent on the house, 'the capitall part … was paltry, but kitchen, dairey, brewhouses, etc. for a duke … but his rooms of entertainment … such as a citisen would contrive at Hackney' (Plate 18).[64] A decade later, in 1713, Sir Richard Hoare the banker bought New Hall at Boreham, a great Tudor house which boasted the grandest list of owners of any house in Essex. Neither he nor his second son, Benjamin, for whom he bought the property, appear to have lived there. Between 1727 and 1733 the latter engaged Edward Shepherd to build him a neo-Palladian villa with attached pavilions, three-quarters of a mile away. Lord Oxford was rude about the result five years after its completion, 'such is the fine taste of a banker on Fleet Street. He has laid out about £12,000 and had eight been laid out upon the old house when he first bought it he would have had one of the best houses in England.'[65]

   In 1757 Caroline Girle went to stay with Pemberton Milnes, the richest merchant in Wakefield. He took her father to dine at two West Riding show houses, Wentworth Woodhouse and Nostell Priory. They also visited Mr Birt, 'a gentleman of large fortune' who lived, in contrast to Lord Rockingham and Sir Rowland Winn, almost on top of his coalmines. Reflecting many years later on the ugliness of his surroundings, she wrote, 'but as sinking these pits raised Wenvoe Castle, neither Mr Birt or his family, I dare say, think them odious'. Peter Birt, also

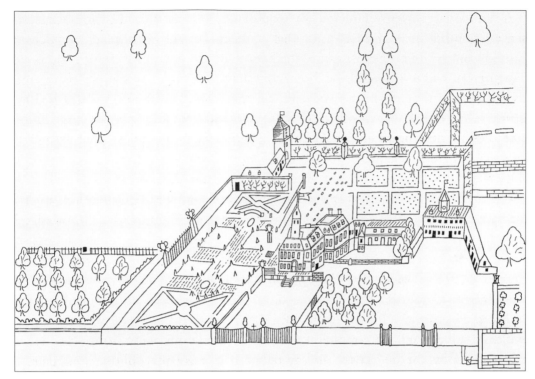

PLATE 18. Buckenham Tofts Hall, Norfolk (demolished). Redrawn from a map *c.* 1700.

involved in farming the highly profitable tolls of the Aire and Calder Navigation, had bought the Wenvoe Castle estate in Glamorganshire in 1775. Immediately, he invited Robert Adam to provide him with a set of plans for rebuilding it. They were not proceeded with, but instead Henry Holland designed a Gothic-style house for him around the end of the decade. John Byng, a jaundiced younger son who approved of little that was new, liked neither the house nor its owner when he visited it in 1787:

> with the air and pomposity of newly acquired wealth ... he desired us to come in, and survey his new-built house, and all his sterling improvements ... forced us about his mansion: it is a single house, with of course an immense front, a gallery from one end to the other towards the cool north, and all the rooms towards the hot south: – which are to be well gilded etc. etc.
>
> It is surrounded by a steep unsloped bank, without any walk or shade, and without any water in view; and, throughout, exhibits a charming effort of bad taste and burgeois-ity: most glad was I to get away from the owner, his vulgarities, slopes etc. etc.[66]

A decade later, Henry Holland was completely rebuilding the Byng's ancestral seat at Southill in Bedfordshire for the younger Samuel Whitbread, the richest London brewer of his generation. Byng's brother, the spendthrift fourth Viscount Torrington, had in 1795 sold the 4300 acre estate to Whitbread's father (who died the following year). Within five years the son had spent some £36,000 on the house – he didn't even bother to obtain an estimate from Henry Holland – although the fine house he had bought with the estate was little more than fifty years old (Plate 19). Southill's furnishings were valued at a further £25,000. But then Whitbread, as extravagant as Lord Torrington, had assets of as much as £750,000. These were sums beyond the dreams of impoverished members of the aristocracy. The result, Christopher Hussey considered, 'must be acknowledged the classic example of the most civilised decade in the whole range of English domestic architecture'.[67] Philip Rundell, George IV's silversmith, possessed even greater accessible wealth than the Whitbreads. When he died in 1827 his personalty was valued at an incredible £1,000,000, an almost unheard of sum in Regency England. His nephew, Joseph Neeld, inheriting two-thirds of his fortune, promptly acquired a large Wiltshire estate at Grittleton (the family were baronets owning 13,812 acres by the late 1870s) and engaged a little-known London architect to

PLATE 19.   Southill Park, Bedfordshire. The painting by Thomas Garrard shows the Isaac Ware house being refronted in 1797.

build him a house in the grand manner – principally to display Neeld's enormous collection of contemporary sculpture. Mark Girouard reckons, 'its setting remains as sensational and spatially ingenious as anything to be found in Victorian design. Gas lighting, fireproof construction, hot-air heating, eleven WCs, no bathroom.' [68]

Henry Vincent, Benjamin Hoare, Peter Birt, Samuel Whitbread and Joseph Neeld were top-flight builders to a man. But were they typical newcomers to landed society? Were newcomers in any case very numerous in the general population of landowners? The latter question is one which has greatly exercised historians evaluating in recent years the nature of English society and the way, curiously at first sight in a pioneering industrial economy, traditional landed values remained dominant at the pinnacles of politics and society until the late nineteenth century. From evidence ranging from 1540 to 1880 and taken from three counties at varying distances from London, Hertfordshire, Northampton-shire and Northumberland, it has been argued that 'the number of people selling property was always relatively small, and the newcomers from trade or business equally small and socially unimportant'. [69] More generally, English landed society remained a closed elite until the end of the nineteenth century. A study of the very rich added an extended coda to this argument. It concluded that those bankers, brewers and industrialists who became millionaires and half-millionaires in increasing numbers, as Britain's prosperity reached new heights in Victorian Britain, tended not to buy land in quantities which would have given them a place in Bateman's collective of landowners owning at least 2000 acres and an income from it of more than £2000. Thus wealthy newcomers from finance, trade and industry made little impact in the world of the established large landowners and a competing bourgeois elite was created and flourished. [70]

This debate is an important one in so far as country house building is concerned, because newcomers obviously brought considerable fortunes with them. As Adam Smith observed, one-time merchants and financiers were the best of all estate improvers; and, more generally, newcomers to landed society, whatever their origins, tended to build. They were out to impress. Two issues about newcomers, however, require clarification – the turnover of land to allow them entry to landed society; and the origins of the newcomers themselves. There does seem to have been a considerable and regular turnover of land. Estates of varying size came onto the land market as families faced serious debt or demographic crisis (which most of them at some stage did). As family fortunes fluctuated, some estates grew as successful owners consolidated their estates by frequent purchase, others declined as their owners sold at least outlying portions of their properties to meet contingencies. Few estates remained static across the generations. Supply and demand factors also shifted over time, varying significantly as distances from London increased. Disraeli maintained in the debate on the repeal of the Corn Laws in 1846 that not less than a third of the land in Buckinghamshire had changed hands in the previous twenty years.[71] In Cambridgeshire Lysons noted as early as 1808 that, out of 235 families recorded as living in the county in 1433, only one was now resident and even its descendant had moved house.[72] Amongst the identifiable families of gentry and squires in Essex, Oxfordshire and Shropshire, the infiltration of newcomers varied somewhat by 1873. In Essex a quarter of them had nineteenth-century origins, with almost a half making their appearance in the eighteenth century; in Oxfordshire the nineteenth-century figure was similar, but fewer, around a third, had originated between 1700 and 1800. In the more remote county of Shropshire, where ancient gentry families were more predominant, one-sixth were of nineteenth-century origin, a quarter founded in the previous century.[73] The figures for Shropshire are not inconsistent with those for the 'aristocratic' counties of Northamptonshire and Northumberland. On all counts, however, significant numbers of newcomers infiltrated landed society after the Restoration. Generally they did not break into the ranks of the largest landowners, whose estates tended to change hands least frequently. Men like Lord Overstone and Lord Londesborough, whose vast mid nineteenth-century estates were founded on banking fortunes, were unusual. More often, newcomers bought small or moderate-sized estates; if a dynasty was established, their descendants built them up on the pattern common amongst successful landed families.

Who were the newcomers? Some of course had connections through family or marriage with the old gentry, especially if their fortunes derived from great achievements in the armed services or law, two regular sources of new wealth at least before the second quarter of the nineteenth century. Nabobs, too, whose riches were derived from the East Indies or those whose fortunes came from lucrative sugar estates in the Caribbean, could again establish themselves readily in county society via a seat in the House of Commons and a good marriage. There were also merchants and financiers in London, prominent in the organisation of government borrowing and City affairs, who made large fortunes across the period especially during times of war, who were often returned as Members of Parliament, and who bought estates usually in the home counties. But what of genuinely 'new' men such as Henry Vincent and Peter Birt, a London property developer on the one hand, a colliery proprietor and toll farmer on the other? The type seems to have been numerous amongst the very richest men in industrial and commercial life for 'down at least to the agricultural depression (1880) most new men of great fortune bought estates'.[74] The vast majority of merchants and industrialists had not the means to buy even a small landed estate and build. This is unsurprising. At most, when times were prosperous, they enjoyed a suburban villa, such as those surrounding London which so delighted Defoe, or 'one of those gaudy scarlet houses we see springing up like mushrooms in the neighbourhood of large manufacturing towns'.[75] Nevertheless each major industry and each major port, town and city (besides London itself, the biggest generator of new wealth) enabled a handful of the most successful men across the two centuries after the Restoration to make fortunes large enough to enable them to buy estates in neighbouring counties. The process of gentrification and aggrandisement could then begin. Often the real breakthrough in the establishment of a landed dynasty came with the second generation. The father provided the means and took the initiative; the son acquired polish, immersed himself in the ways of the landed gentry, and usually ran down the family's business interests. William Milner, immensely wealthy, lived next to his cloth-packing shops and warehouses beside the grimy River Aire in central Leeds for over thirty years after he had bought the Nun Appleton estate in 1709. He rebuilt the great tumbledown mansion, which had reputedly cost the Fairfaxes £30,000, in the next three years, but it was left to his Eton-educated son, created a baronet in 1717 and returned as Member of Parliament for York five years later, to enjoy a landed lifestyle.[76] Thereafter, the latter's most obvious connection with Leeds was to be buried in the parish church with his forbears.

So long as newcomers lived by the unwritten rules of the old landed gentry, enjoyed hunting, shooting and, before the 1770s, cock fighting, were not extreme in politics or religion, so long as they were hospitable, appeared at the local assemblies and race meetings, treated their tenants generously and fairly, educated their children like those of other landowners, generally showed the good manners of polite society, they were soon accepted in the county. Membership of the bench, the appointment as High Sheriff, a commission in the Militia, Volunteers or Yeomanry more or less came along with ownership of a good landed estate. Initially newcomers from trade and industry were never going to meet the social criteria of the closed circle of peerage families, but an expensive education, a good marriage, membership of Parliament and a deep pocket could work wonders in the second and third generations. At the level of county society, acceptance does not therefore appear to have been difficult if its ground rules were sensibly followed. The path of advancement was well sign-posted from the sixteenth century onwards. Building an impressive country seat was high on any new-comer's agenda. A country estate and a fine house was the most obvious way, in a highly wealth-conscious society, by which the affluent could demonstrate their great riches and success to the world.

3

The Inspiration of Travel

'To a man of your taste no part of England is so well worth a visit [as Norfolk], at least none than I have ever seen ... Lord Leicester's [Holkham] alone would pay you the trouble and expense of your journey.'

Charles Lyttelton writing to Sanderson Miller, August, 1758.[1]

'The man who sat beside me [in the coach] pointed out to us the various seats of the nobility and gentry as we passed them by.'

C. P. Moritz, a German traveller in England in 1782.[2]

When Horace Walpole first saw Castle Howard in 1772, even he, the most critical of arbiters of country house architecture, was bowled over: 'the grandest scene of magnificence I ever saw ... the highest rank of palatial dignity'.[3] Its creator, the third Earl of Carlisle, had already been lying snug in Hawksmoor's great mausoleum for almost thirty years, but Walpole's encomia put into words exactly what the earl had set out to achieve in his extraordinary career as builder and landscaper from 1698 to 1738 (Frontispiece).

Charles Howard, a descendant of the dukes of Norfolk, born in 1669 in remote north Cumberland, had succeeded to the Carlisle title in 1692.[4] Possessing estates in three northern counties with an old castle in each, his political career took off in the mid 1690s (very briefly he was First Lord of the Treasury, 1701–2). Earlier he had undertaken the Grand Tour and was well versed in the classical authors and in architecture and antiquities. Although he was a member of a junior branch of the Howards, and his title had been created as recently as 1661, he was immensely proud of his ancestry and deeply steeped in heraldry. In London, where he lived in some state in Soho Square, he absorbed the ambitions of the Whig peerage and envied their great building schemes at Petworth, Boughton, Burley-on-the-Hill, Chatsworth and Kiveton, and in Cumbria, those of his political rivals the Lowthers. The new King, William III, was also spending large sums at Hampton Court and Kensington Palace.

Henderskelfe Castle, the earl's seat on his North Yorkshire estate, was burned down in 1693. On the orbit of country house building in the 1690s and at the peak of the earl's own brief political ascendency, he decided to build on the grandest scale in 1698–99. Castle Howard's historian, Charles Saumarez Smith, maintains that the earl was employing architecture as the language of dynastic ambition: 'the buildings were intended to produce in the mind of the spectator an awareness of the lineage of the Howard family and its place in history'.[5] And for the next forty years Charles Howard built, to the acclaim of his fellow peers, probably the finest private palace. He certainly created the most remarkable landscape in England. Vanbrugh and Hawksmoor, Pelligrini and Marco Ricci, and the best stuccoists and carvers London and York could produce, were engaged and supervised by the earl to create paradise on an unlikely bleak hillside in north Yorkshire. 'Nobody', enthused Horace Walpole, 'had informed me that at one view I should see a palace, a town, a fortified city, temples on high places, woods worthy of being each a metropolis of the Druids, the noblest lawns in the world fenced by half the horizon, and a mausoleum that would tempt one

PLATE 20.   The Mausoleum at Castle Howard, Yorkshire, by Hendrik de Cort (c. 1810).

to be buried alive; in short I have seen gigantic palaces before, but never a sublime one (Plate 20).' [6]

If very few country house builders matched the realisation of Lord Carlisle's vision of 'fantasy and wealth and ostentation', his schemes, encompassing political and familial ambitions, wealth and fashion, underline a number of points about the aspirations of landowners to build.[7] We will now examine more broadly two aspects of their motivation: the purpose of the English country house and what exactly builders were attempting to achieve in their schemes; and the ways in which ideas about architecture and building were formed and communicated across the spectrum of the English peerage and gentry. Underlining both is the manner in which architecture, expressing the dynastic ambitions and fine education of the landowning class, was confined by their means. Building was not simply the cerebral realisation of landowners' aims and dreams, expressed in a set of architect's plans, it was also practically linked to their pockets and the careful management of their projects.

It is necessary, however, to stress at the outset that by no means all landowners after the Restoration built a country house from scratch. It is easy for us now to be carried away by the likes of Sir John Vanbrugh's famous quotation of 1708, 'All the World are running Mad after Building, as far as they can reach', or with the sheer stock of surviving country houses, to imagine that most landowners shared Carlisle's experience.[8] Houses *were* new built of course. But the majority of builders in our period at best remodelled or extended existing houses, usually spurred into action on inheritance, or marriage, at the prospect of a large family, by the frequent incidence of fire, or by a sudden improvement in financial circumstances. Moreover, by the 1700s many existing houses were already a century or more old and thus in need of refurbishment. The architectural enthusiasms of the Elizabethan and Jacobean periods meant, too, that they were overfenestrated for classical tastes, with inconvenient circulation in single-pile ranges. It was these perceived design faults which the post-Restoration generation of gentlemen builders and their neo-Palladian successors began to address. Country houses therefore evolved over the centuries; some little changed, others constantly altered.[9]

It has become fashionable for historians to represent the country house as a symbol of the landowner's power in the countryside.[10] Castle Howard was clearly a token of Lord Carlisle's power as well as a monument to his pride in his

ancestry. The avenues and walls still march over the hills for miles. In 1730 every
tenant and neighbouring landowner must have been astounded by his bold imprint
on the countryside. But displays of power on this scale, most frequently associated
with the prodigy houses built between 1570 and 1620 and the great Whig palaces
erected in the half century after 1680, were quite rare in any county. Not many
landowners could share Lord Leicester's lament about the vastness of the
landscape of power he had created:

> It is a melancholy thing to stand alone in one's own Country. I look around, not a
> house to be seen but my own. I am Giant of Giant's Castle, and have ate up all my
> neighbours – my nearest neighbour is the King of Denmark.[11]

Blatant representations of authority on the scale of Holkham and Castle Howard
were not typical of the large majority of England's landowners. Nevertheless, the
uses of architecture and landscape to embody power was common virtually
amongst them all.

A return to law and order in the countryside had been established primarily
by the growing authority of justices of the peace in the century after 1560. The
basis of their standing in county administration was their estates. After the 1660s
these tended to grow in size and prosperity. Through them the landowner
established his ascendency over a growing number of tenants and employees,
full-time and casual, who were almost entirely dependent upon his decisions.
The country house was the administrative nerve centre of the estate, its offices
and yards servicing and maintaining dozens of farms and cottages. Even the lesser
gentry created their own tiny kingdoms within those villages largely made up of
their properties. And increasingly, by the manipulation of ecclesiastical patronage,
they were able to oversee church life and charitable effort within their parishes.

This delineation of power based upon landownership, employment, control of
church livings and local administration was stamped upon the countryside, especially as estates grew and enclosure, either by private agreement or parliamentary
Act, removed the constraints of communal practices. Every overseer of the poor,
parish constable and rural miscreant certainly understood exactly the basis of a
landowner's rule as he trudged up the drive to the great house for the dispensation
of justice. And the country house as an architectural embodiment of authority
was more widely proclaimed as the literature of counties and regions exploded
in the print revolution of the eighteenth century. Antiquarians traced the descent
of manors and landowners (Burke's and Walford's compilations later providing

full-scale if not always accurate genealogies) and listed the monuments of their families in parish churches; agricultural writers enthused about the efforts of those landowners who engaged in agrarian improvement; artists and print makers produced representations of their houses and parks; map-makers indicated their seats and invariably added names to identify their ownership of them; and directories in the nineteenth century came to include the scale of their ownership in the parish, the number of church livings they controlled, and the offices they held in the county. With all this information, as well as gossip from innkeepers and servants, an increasing number of tourists, bowling along the improved roads of Georgian England, knew exactly who owned what, and how tasteful, extensive and well-maintained each country house was. Thus the instantly recognisable landscape of power – houses, parks, lakes, dovecotes, woods, walls – was revealed to them.

Country houses had other purposes besides the proclamation of power. Above all they were homes which their owners usually enjoyed and from which they dispensed generous hospitality to their extended families, to tenants and employees, and to the wider county community. Their architecture, from the fortified castle of the middle ages to the luxurious country house 'hotels' of Edwardian England, reflected above all social changes in the lifestyles and circumstances of landowners across the centuries.[12] A critical point in their evolution appears to have occurred during the seventeenth century.

During it the power of the old nobility waned. Their great, predominantly male, hierarchial households, which had provided such good training grounds and career prospects for members of their extended families and other genteel young men who served in them, contracted. Before the late sixteenth century the households of the peerage and the great prelates had regularly contained one or two hundred members besides further retainers on call as the occasion arose. Hospitality, when the lord was in residence, especially at Christmas and the major feasts of the church and the family, was dispensed on a massive, stupefying scale. And the greater gentry imitated their state. Inflation after the 1530s, increasing periods spent by the nobility in London at Court and at the law, and the state's growing control of local government and the use of its own courts, meant however that the scale and organisation of feudal-style households became unnecessary. With the need for economy, traditional hospitality and ceremony diminished, and already by the early seventeenth century dismay was being expressed about its erosion.

Although aristocratic patronage long remained significant in men's careers, service in their households did not. The government's business, finance, trade and the professions, training via the grammar school, the Inns of Court, the universities, and the prestigious apprenticeship, became increasingly important as the way upwards. Pepys's diary and career reflects exactly the shifting interplay between favour at Court, the role of aristocratic patronage, and the growing importance of education and business acumen in the accumulation of power and wealth in post-1660 England.[13]

These changes did not take place with a dramatic swiftness following the Civil War. The greatest peers continued to live in considerable state. The Duke of Chandos employed ninety-two servants at Cannons (unusually in England including sixteen musicians) in a precisely defined hierarchy; the Duke of Newcastle, as we have seen, employed sixty-nine, in the early eighteenth century.[14] But these were exceptions: both men were thought to be wildly extravagant, both lived their lives in perpetual debt. Indeed the Duke of Newcastle, with his extensive, old-fashioned hospitality dispensed on his Sussex properties and his complete lack of interest in estate improvement, was seen as a dinosaur in his own lifetime. Nevertheless, there was a tension between those who favoured the old traditions and those who adopted the new social conventions of more exclusive, private forms of entertainment. It certainly underscores Roger North's treatise *On Building*, where he contrasts the extensive Jacobean court house of the old aristocratic world and the compact Pratt-style villa of post-Restoration society. As the proud son of an impoverished peer, and with a brother who was an immensely successful Turkey merchant and Lord Mayor of London, he knew both worlds and the tensions between them well. He abhorred 'the abolishing grandure and statlyness of that sort the former ages affected' and 'wish't that the gentry and nobility would look farther for their invention, than suburb models which may serve a family, in a London expedition, but not in country living, which requires something more like a court'.[15] North's observations (similarly articulated by Ben Jonson in his poem *To Penshurst* eighty years earlier) continued to have resonance throughout the eighteenth century as men of conservative views, wonderfully captured in the travel diaries of John Byng, expressed their dismay, when presented with a particularly opulent new house, at the ways in which the old traditions of generous hospitality and the old social cohesion had been eroded. Wild Twelfth Night revels enjoyed by tenants and neighbours alike were out of place in a Robert Adam dining-room. Politeness had killed them.

Architectural style after the Restoration adapted to these social changes. In the long run, the villa Roger North thought so demeaning to aristocratic traditions and status clearly won out. At first, the grandest peers employed an extravagant court style, as at Chatsworth, Castle Howard, Blenheim and Kimbolton, employing architects from the Office of Works and inspired by William III's building schemes. But these houses were enormously expensive, way beyond the pockets of the gentry. Besides, crowded with dressing-rooms, state beds, ante-rooms, corridors and cabinets to form an axis of honour, they were not particularly convenient. When Philip Yorke visited Chatsworth in 1763, 'the Duke told me himself he had not lodging room in proportion to the size of the house ... the rooms are 24 feet high, very magnificent, and fitted up with fine carving, but of little use but to be walked through.' [16] As early as 1727, Sir John Clerk of Penicuik thought that, besides the first floor saloon at Castle Howard, 'there is not one good apartment in the whole house at least not one which is any way suitable to the grandeur and Expense of the outside'. When he viewed three of Vanbrugh's castellated fantasies overlooking the Thames he was moved to a more general denunciation:

> Sir John was a famouse Architect but of an odd taste. These houses of his consist of great heaps of brick and thick walls but little acomodation within. There's scarce a Room in them above 8 or 10 feet square and some much less. The ornaments are such which the Goths and their successors had to place in castles and prisons use: battlements, round Towers, Little windowes and doors and yet this man was chosen to build Blenheim House for the Duke of Marlborough.

On the other hand he found Wanstead, Colen Campbell's influential neo-Palladian, extended villa of 1714–21, 'one of the best in England', with a commodious ground floor open through to the garden, a particularly fine saloon and dining-room and very good bedrooms on the first floor (Plate 21).[17] Large houses like Wanstead continued to be built, influenced by the publication of the three volumes of *Vitruvius Britannicus* between 1715 and 1725 and the building boom which ran on until the mid 1730s, but eventually a new, smaller-scale house came to be adopted with more emphasis on interior arrangements and decoration as perfected by Robert Adam. By the 1760s the villa form of country house, refined by Isaac Ware, Sir Robert Taylor and Sir William Chambers, had triumphed,

> the idea of the villa is the essential innovation of the [eighteenth] century and ... the development of the country house can most easily be elucidated as a struggle between the great house and the villa in which the villa first achieves the disintegration of the

54   CREATING PARADISE

greater house and then supersedes it, but in doing so becomes something totally different from what it started as.[18]

The majority of the gentry wanted a house, elegant and new furnished, in which they could raise their families, entertain their neighbours and put up their relations and friends for weeks on end. They wanted it built on a good site commanding their park and, if possible, a fine vista. Their precise demands usually ran to three or four sizeable rooms for entertainment, at least half a dozen commodious bedrooms, and accommodation for the dozen or so servants and horses which were essential elements in country house life.[19] It was these requirements which led so many landowners to build, renovate or extend their houses; it was these social considerations which had such a profound impact on country house architecture.

A major influence in the development of the 'social house' appears to have derived from the forms of entertaining, both public and private, in London and

PLATE 21. Wanstead House, Essex (Colen Campbell, c. 1714, demolished), from a watercolour by Charles Catton.

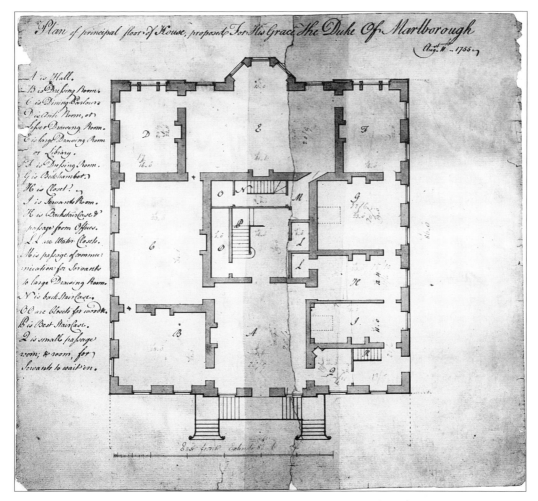

PLATE 22. Langley Park, Buckinghamshire (Stiff Leadbetter, 1755). The plan of the principal floor.

Bath – centres at which the nobility and gentry gathered for increasingly long periods. Owners wanted accommodation for dancing and music making. They also wished to house – the most evident feature of Georgian country house planning – their growing libraries, as literature on every subject which interested them mushroomed; and rooms in which they could display their wealth in the forms of London-purchased furniture, an expanding array of family portraits and often such pictures and mementoes as they had picked up abroad or in the metropolis. The extended villa with its 'parade' of rooms was ideal for these forms of entertainment and show (Plate 22).

Country house visitors are the best witnesses of prevailing tastes. None excel Mrs Lybbe Powys, not as an appraiser of architectural niceties but as a typical representative of the gentry class in the second half of the eighteenth century. She was a tireless country house visitor for more than half a century, both before (as Caroline Girle) and after her marriage to an Oxfordshire squire. London-born, she was fashionable yet sensible, and her diaries reveal exactly what typical owners required of a house to underpin and proclaim their lifestyles. She herself lived at Hardwick Hall overlooking the Thames in the heart of a sociable neighbourhood: 'In this part of our country there are more fine houses near each other than in any I believe in England, nineteen within a morning's airing worth seeing.' There was therefore a constant exchange of dinners between their owners and frequent, grander entertainments. Amateur theatricals were the great vogue in the 1780s, particularly those of the spendthrift Lord Barrymore. After one such performance given by Lord Villiers, she noted that ninety-two sat down to dinner afterwards at the Freemans of Fawley Court. Clearly what was required (she and her husband could never afford to remodel their old-fashioned Tudor house rebuilt in the 1570s) was a fine set of reception rooms. Mr Jones of Langley Park, who had married a daughter of Earl Camden, had, she thought, owned the perfect house. It had 'a large hall, drawing-room, two eating-rooms, library, an inner hall, grand staircase, and some small rooms, many apartments above so spacious and convenient, out of every bed-chamber a large dressing-room' (Plate 23).[20] A house like this exactly fitted her dreams, whereas Wilton she dismissed as 'too grand, too gloomy ... magnificently uncomfortable, the situation bad, the rooms, except one, too small'. In 1771 she visited the Shropshire seat, Court of Hill, of some cousins. It was always full of company and, as their journey was a long one, the Lybbe Powyses stayed three weeks. There was a party of sixteen, all of them relations. Each day it was divided: some went riding, others walking, shooting, reading and drawing. They met up for a vast and extended dinner after four o'clock. Neighbours also often dined; they were entertained by them in turn. This is an early example of a house party, albeit made up entirely of family. The 'social house' had to cater for multifarious leisure needs, especially providing a good eating room, library and space for dancing.

Of course there is a touch of envy in Mrs Lybbe Powys's description of fine sets of reception rooms designed for extensive genteel entertainment. The 'social house' she so approved of remained beyond the reach of many gentry families until the benefits of enclosure and rising rents after 1750 made a marked improvement

PLATE 23.   Langley Park, Buckinghamshire, from a print by J. P. Neale, 1821.

in their finances. Even then, especially in neighbourhoods less fashionable than the Buckinghamshire, Oxfordshire and Berkshire borders, not all landowners envisaged a constant round of large-scale entertainment. Parson Woodforde's Squire Custance of Weston Longville, the son of a Norwich merchant who had married well, built himself a dull five-by-five bay, two-and-a-half storey house in 1781 on a good site ten miles out of Norwich (Plate 24). His architect was Thomas Rawlins, a stonemason better known for his memorial tablets in the city's churches. Indeed Weston Longville was Rawlins's sole venture into country house architecture, although he had already written an architectural guide for country house builders with an impressive title.[21] Woodforde records the squire's regular hospitality to the neighbouring gentry and clergy, besides his putting up his grander Norfolk in-laws, the Beauchamp-Proctors of Langley, the Bacons of Raveningham and the Durrants of Scottow, for weeks on end. But there were no grand routs and dances of the kind Mrs Lybbe Powys so enjoyed. Nor is there much mention of hunting – coursing and shooting were more popular – for arable central Norfolk even by the late eighteenth century was not good fox-hunting

PLATE 24.   Weston Longville Hall, Norfolk (Thomas Rawlins, 1781, demolished).

country. Elsewhere a landowner would probably have put greater stress on a more commodious stable block and possibly kennels for hounds. These were high on many landowners' lists of priorities, along with a good kitchen garden and set of hot-houses – a desideratum Mrs Lybbe Powys sometimes overlooked in her dash to record the lay-out and furnishings of every house she visited. Squire Custance, however, simply wanted a modern house which would comfortably accommodate his large family and from which he could entertain the Norfolk gentry in some style. Most large landowners shared his viewpoint.

A critical feature in shifting country house specifications, besides the growing wealth of landowners from various sources, was the result of improvements in transportation. A series of broad changes seems to have taken place in at least the largest houses. In the mid eighteenth century the social radius of a country house neighbourhood stretched no more than nine or ten miles, a distance limited by a sound pair of coach horses on a moonlit night. When Marchioness Grey and her husband, the Hon. Philip Yorke, returned to the country at Wrest (Bedfordshire) for five months each summer, they found social life quite restricted by the limits of coach travel and bad roads. A journey of twenty miles to visit a distant part of their estate was very difficult to encompass even on a summer's day. Wrest was therefore developed to reflect the needs of the Grey-Yorkes and the limitations arduous travel placed on entertainment. Horace Walpole found it, 'a wretched low bad house built round a small court'. But Brown had 'corrected' the garden and they had made a fine dining-room and there was a good library. It was a house which, with their passion for landscaping, exactly suited their needs. Occasionally they held a public day when as many as thirty sat down in the new dining-room. More often the house was used for family visitors who enjoyed their books and harpsichord, a game of billiards, twice-daily prayers in the chapel, long walks in the park, and tea taken in Thomas Archer's pavilion.[22] Only at Houghton, Wimpole and Wentworth Woodhouse were grander political gatherings or 'congresses' held for politicians.[23] Usually these took place at the London houses and Thames-side villas of the aristocracy during parliamentary sessions. In general, however, mid eighteenth-century *country* social life was confined. Its dimensions depended entirely upon the sociability of a neighbour-hood. In the home counties it could be extensive; in the Lincolnshire fens, the Cumbrian fells and Pennines it was almost non-existent at gentry level. The Grey-Yorkes were the centre of a limited social galaxy; only rarely did they see their only social equals, the Bedfords, in the country. Each October they returned for seven months to their St James Square house and Richmond villa to enjoy the social whirl of the metropolis.

Long-distance travel was transformed by the rapid extension of the turnpike road system after the 1740s and by the invention of the sprung carriage. Times were reduced, services increased and journeys made more comfortable. Whereas it had taken four days to make the trip from London to York and a week to Edinburgh around 1700, by the 1790s, when toll income was at last sufficient to pay for better road foundations, surfaces and regular maintenance, these journeys could be accomplished in a little more than a quarter of the time. For the landowning classes, usually travelling post in their own carriages, the benefits of road improvements were enjoyed to the full. Good roads and post-chaises were vital ingredients in Horace Walpole's recipe for civility and for enlightenment.

Thomas Creevey, the political diarist and socialite, who usually went by regular coach services, wrote in 1824: 'There never was such perfection of travelling. I left London at ½ past 8 on Friday morning, and, without an effort, and in a coach loaded with luggage, I was at Doncaster by 5 the following morning – a distance of 160 miles!'[24] He was *en route* to nearby Cantley to stay for the St Leger meeting. Road travel had been so transformed that, in its brief golden age between 1815 and 1835, Creevey, based in London, enjoyed regular forays to Southill, Petworth and Cassiobury, and further afield to Holkham, Wentworth

Woodhouse, Lowther, Raby and Lambton. In 1821 Charles Greville fitted in eleven country house visits around the autumn race meetings at Newmarket and Doncaster. In the following year he recorded, 'Since I left London for Doncaster Races I have travelled near 1200 miles'. This was a far cry from John Buxton, the gentleman amateur architect, advising his son in London in September 1729 that the roads were so bad to Norfolk that he 'must make very short stages and ought to make three days to Newmarket' (seventy miles from London on the main Norwich road).[25]

After the 1780s Britain was opened up to members of Charles Greville's class. The grander country house had to adapt to the needs of a richer, more mobile aristocracy. At each house, Creevey and Greville met large, primarily political house parties. John Wilson Croker and Wellington's well-connected confidante, Mrs Arbuthnot, listed the same grand world, whether Whig or Tory in complexion, regularly coming together during the Regency period across England.[26] These get-togethers were as large, possibly as frequent and certainly more aristocratic than those assembled in the plutocratic Railway Age, supposedly the golden age of the country house party. Already in the 1820s Mrs Arbuthnot listed large New Year house parties at Apethorpe (Northamptonshire), Belvoir and Burghley. At Belvoir in 1829 the Duke of Rutland's birthday was celebrated by 300 dining at the castle, 'above 30 at the grand table, and the new drawing room was opened for the first time. It is the most magnificent room I ever saw'. At Apethorpe in 1824, in a passage foreshadowing those in Jennifer's Diary, she noted, 'a great party was assembled. The Dukes of York, Rutland and Wellington, Lords Hertford, Anglesey and Winchilsea (all Knights of the Garter, quite a Chapter), Lord and Lady Howe, Lady Lonsdale and a great many other men.' Entertainment of George III's numerous sons, the notorious Royal Dukes, who seem to have been perpetually on the move, was especially demanding in terms of accommodation and organisation, as well as taxing on conversation. A visit of the Duke of Sussex to Cantley in 1822 (not a large house) was typical:

> This Royalty is certainly the very devil ... Sussex arrived on Wednesday between three and four, himself in a very low barouche and pair, and a thundering coach behind with four horses – his staff, Stephenson, a son of Albermarle's, a Gore, servants, groom of the Chambers, a black *valet-de-chambre* and two footmen, clad *en militaires*.[27]

Aristocratic owners built or remodelled their houses to cater for regular entertaining on this scale. The trend was set by the extravagant schemes of the Prince

PLATE 25.   Lowther Castle, Westmorland (Sir Robert Smirke, 1806–11).

Regent at Brighton Pavilion, Buckingham Palace and Windsor Castle. Nothing quite approached those financed by the state at Windsor, but the Grosvenors, Lambtons, Londonderrys, Lonsdales, and above all the Bridgewater–Stafford–Sutherland clan, all of them enjoying enormous, burgeoning non-landed incomes, were building on a scale unknown for a century. The latter's industrial fortunes underwrote Trentham in Staffordshire and Lilleshall in Shropshire, Bridgewater and Stafford (now Lancaster) houses in London, Ashridge in Hertfordshire, Worsley near Manchester and Dunrobin in Sutherland, each models of luxury and comfort (although some visitors to Dunrobin disputed this) on the grandest scale. Mrs Arbuthnot thought Lowther Castle the nearest to perfection of any house she knew (Plate 25):

> I cannot conceive anything finer or more magnificent, as well as comfortable, than the interior of the house. The entrance is like coming into the aisle of a Gothic cathedral, of which the cross or centre forms the staircase, and the apartments branch out from the side aisles. There is a beautiful library, dining-room, saloon and drawing-room, the latter not finished, a billiard room still unfinished, and very comfortable small apartments

for when they are alone. The sleeping apartments are excellent, and it is in all its details the most beautiful Gothic building I ever saw. The staircase is magnificent. I used to think Ashridge beautiful but it is not to be named with this house.[28]

Seasoned guests like Mrs Arbuthnot exaggerated the comfort of these vast new houses, at least in winter. At Knowsley, where the Derbys entertained great house parties of thirty or forty people in the 1820s, a huge new fifty-three by thirty-seven feet dining room was added to accommodate them. In spite of two fireplaces, fifty wax candles and ten great lamps on pedestals, in December 1822 Creevey reported that the cold was 'quite petryfying', that 'two great Gothic church-like doors the whole height of the room' were opened for every pat of butter that came into the room, and circulated the rumour that it was likely to be abandoned 'entirely from the cold'.[29]

The architectural expression of the requirements running, on the one hand, from the likes of Mrs Lybbe Powys and Squire Custance, hankering after a good family house, to those of the Earls of Lonsdale and Derby on the other, ever ready to accommodate royalty and an army of their fellow peers, were represented not only on very different scales but also in different styles after the 1780s: Palladian, Grecian or, increasingly in more Romantic national British forms, Gothic and Jacobethan. Whatever the style preferred, however, the lay-out of houses and the purpose of rooms changed as families grew in size and wealth, and as new forms of leisure and entertainment were devised. A library, increasingly used as the main living room, had become an essential part of any sizeable country house in the second half of the eighteenth century. Eventually other purpose-designated rooms were added as the wealth of individual builders allowed: billiard-rooms, boudoirs, breakfast-rooms, smoking- and gun-rooms, bathrooms, water closets and conservatories. This increasing definition of room usage reflected a growing tendency to isolate gender-specific areas within large houses. The hall, like the dining-room, was common ground. In the better-heated houses of Victorian England it was restored to its old prominence in house plans. A multi-purpose room, it could be used informally for family and visitors. It could also be used for estate and village entertainments which, better regulated and more improving in purpose than those of the medieval and Tudor periods, crept back into fashion as the social responsibility of many of the gentry was activated, first by the fear of revolution after the 1790s, then by the prevailing religiosity and earnestness of the early and mid Victorian periods. One of the architectural consequences of the proliferation of rooms was the movement away from the compact classical villa towards asymmetry in plan and form. This was reinforced by a growing absorption in the picturesque and the desire to return to the more nationalistic idiom of 'olden-times' architecture. These were yet other incentives to rebuild after the Napoleonic wars.

Improved travel increased the number of visits from family and friends but, in what must have been a welcome relief in many cases, reduced the length of time stayed. Victorian visitors' books record an increase in visitor throughput. Guest as well as family accommodation had to be extended and modernised. To cater for their needs more female servants were employed. Servants' quarters were enlarged to accommodate precisely defined divisions of labour and servant hierarchies; they were segregated (as were those of bachelor guests) to conform with Victorian views of morality. Nurseries and schoolrooms, as the size of families reached its peak, became more prominent. Thus the lay-out of even moderately-sized country houses became more complex. Some new houses in the Victorian period, increasingly built from non-landed sources of income, were as large as the key models of the Regency period, Ashridge and Lowther Castle. Houses such as Stoke Rochford, Westonbirt, Bearwood, Lynford (Plates 26–28) and Waterhouse's Eaton Hall were staggering monuments of domestic organisation and regimented comfort.[30] By the 1890s houses like Elveden, the exotic house of the Maharajah Duleep Singh, trebled in size by Lord Iveagh with his enormous Guinness fortune and run with near military precision by a total estate and domestic workforce of almost 400 people, and Sandringham, rebuilt and then continually extended in the three decades after the Prince of Wales's acquisition of the estate in 1862, had become in effect vast *grande luxe* country house hotels providing the best shooting and most sumptuous entertainment in Britain. The Elveden estate was producing annual bags of over 100,000 head of game half-a-dozen years after Lord Iveagh acquired the estate in 1894. Augustus Hare, an ubiquitous member of late Victorian country house parties, found the house 'almost appallingly luxurious, such masses of orchids, electric light everywhere, etc.'[31] The big country house at the outset of the eighteenth century is best seen as a realisation of the power and wealth of the landowning class; by the third quarter of the nineteenth century it had also come to embody the opulence of an infinitely privileged leisured class.

If the country house in England came to represent the power, wealth and leisure of the landowning classes in the two centuries after the Restoration, how did individual members form their tastes and judgements about it? How were

PLATE 26.   Lynford Hall, Norfolk (William Burn, 1856–61).

PLATE 27 (*opposite, top*).   Lynford Hall, Norfolk. The ground floor plan.

PLATE 28 (*opposite, bottom*).   Lynford Hall, Norfolk. The service basement.

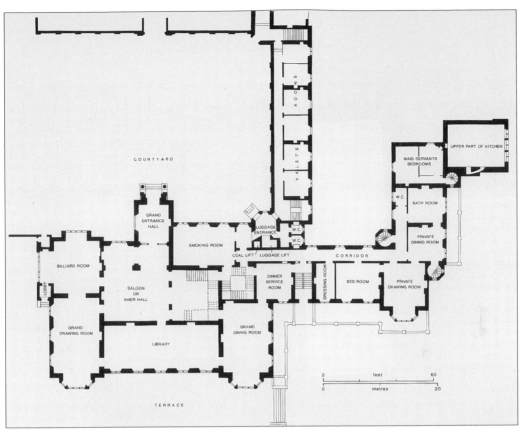

UPPER PART OF KITCHEN

MAID SERVANTS BEDROOMS

V A L E T S R O O M S

COURTYARD

W.C.

BATH ROOM

GRAND ENTRANCE HALL

LUGGAGE ENTRANCE

W.C.

PRIVATE DINING ROOM

SMOKING ROOM

W.C.

COAL LIFT   LUGGAGE LIFT

CORRIDOR

BILLIARD ROOM

DINNER SERVICE ROOM

DRESSING ROOM

BED ROOM

PRIVATE DRAWING ROOM

LOBBY

SALOON OR INNER HALL

GRAND DRAWING ROOM

LIBRARY

GRAND DINING ROOM

TERRACE

| 0 | feet | 60 |
| 0 | metres | 20 |

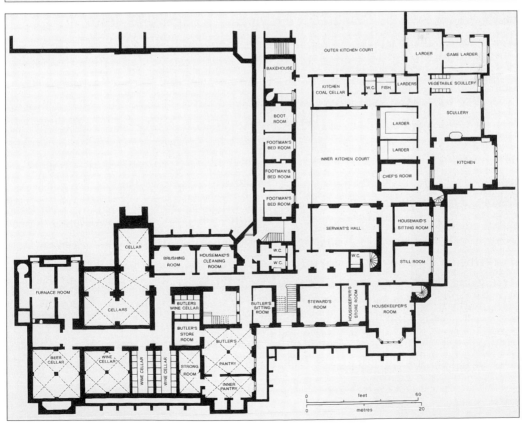

OUTER KITCHEN COURT

LARDER   GAME LARDER

BAKEHOUSE

KITCHEN COAL CELLAR   W.C.   FISH   LARDERS   VEGETABLE SCULLERY

BOOT ROOM

LARDER

SCULLERY

FOOTMAN'S BED ROOM

INNER KITCHEN COURT

LARDER

FOOTMAN'S BED ROOM

KITCHEN

FOOTMAN'S BED ROOM

CHEF'S ROOM

CELLAR

BRUSHING ROOM

HOUSEMAID'S CLEANING ROOM

SERVANT'S HALL

HOUSEMAID'S SITTING ROOM

W.C.

FURNACE ROOM

W.C.

W.C.

STILL ROOM

CELLARS

BUTLER'S WINE CELLAR

BUTLER'S SITTING ROOM

STEWARD'S ROOM

HOUSEKEEPER'S STORE ROOM

HOUSEKEEPER'S ROOM

BUTLER'S STORE ROOM

BEER CELLAR

WINE CELLAR

WINE CELLAR

WINE CELLAR

STRONG ROOM

BUTLER'S

PANTRY

INNER PANTRY

| 0 | feet | 60 |
| 0 | metres | 20 |

ideas about houses communicated amongst their builders? For in a period when the architectural profession was itself slowly evolving, the engagement of the client in the development of the country house was at its height. The rest of this chapter examines the impact of the continental Grand Tour, of extensive sight-seeing tours in England, and of the influence of the metropolis both in the evolution of the country house and in inculcating the constant urge to build.

We know a great deal about the Grand Tour.[32] Young aristocrats, usually between about seventeen and twenty-two years of age, and mostly shackled to an experienced tutor, were enjoined by their parents and guardians, paying several hundred pounds a year for this elite form of finishing, to keep a journal of their continental travels. The accounts which have survived, together with their letters, vary a good deal in content. Essentially the Grand Tour focused upon the major Italian cities, although visits *en route* to the Dutch Netherlands, Paris and Switzerland were of course made. Often tourists returned via Germany; occasionally they made a detour via Vienna; a few travelled further afield for the joy of travel and exploration itself. Nevertheless Italy, the birthplace of Roman civilisation, the study of which was the main plank of a classical education in England, remained the centre-piece of the Grand Tour throughout the eighteenth century (Plate 29).

What did those young men who undertook it learn? They acquired a very varied knowledge of languages, travel, food, architecture, art, political systems, social customs and the Catholic Church. Some attended lectures at universities, especially in Switzerland; some received instruction in horsemanship, dancing and fencing. All supposedly acquired, both from the high-ranking families they were introduced to and from their high-born companions, views and mannerisms which often set them apart when they returned.[33] Their minds were opened; although, given England's intense Protestantism, many impressions were xenophobic. Almost all appreciated England more as the result of their experiences abroad, especially a recognition of the wealth of the English aristocracy in comparison with the droves of impoverished foreign nobility they had encountered everywhere. Mercantilist critics of the Grand Tour deplored that English rentals were being squandered abroad. Others, equally censorious, maintained that, rather than improving themselves, 'tourists' indulged themselves in a positive frenzy of drink, gambling and sex. Far from the parental gaze and congregating in small peer groups of an average age of little more than twenty years, it was hardly surprising that some went off the rails in Paris or in the heat of an Italian carnival.

PLATE 29.   British Connoisseurs in Rome (James Russel, *c.* 1750). 'The quintessential representation of the Grand Tour in Rome'.

On balance, however, it provided the English gentry with a more stimulating education than that supplied by the two universities, then at low points in their history.

Some, however, were serious, intelligent young men who acquiesced in their parents' pressure on them to achieve a knowledge which would stand them in good stead for the rest of their lives. Raised in the classics at home, they were fascinated by the opportunities the Grand Tour gave them to experience, at first hand, Italian opera, architecture, archaeology, sculpture and, above all, Italian painting. They read the numerous printed guides in English produced primarily for them; and they listened to the antiquarians or guides who accompanied them to galleries and to sites. Those with ample purses bought pictures, statuary and curios, imagining where they would place them in the neo-Palladian house they would build when they inherited their family estate back in England. Many, less well-to-do, as the number of tourists increased after the 1750s to include others besides affluent members of the landowning class, had to be content with a few dozen prints and a handful of books. The experience of a Grand Tour formed the tastes of them all.

The multi-faceted experience of foreign cultures which set apart those who had completed the Grand Tour was not the only significant aspect of an extended continental sojourn. Increasingly, it was recognised that the Grand Tour formed the basis of an important network back home. This was of two strands. First, 'tourists' came to know, as well as native ones, those English architects and artists residing in the largest Roman cities for longish periods to complete their training in the best approved manner. On their return to England they commissioned the likes of Robert Adam, Joshua Reynolds and John Soane, and many lesser luminaries, to build their houses and commit their families to posterity. The best-known members of the arts professions, especially after the foundation of the Royal Academy in 1772 gave them a more hierarchically institutional affiliation royally patronised, were generally accepted in London society and welcomed as country house guests. Secondly, those young men who had undertaken the Grand Tour enjoyed, in cities where they spent any length of time, the company of perhaps a dozen or even a score of young Britons of similar age, background and interests. When they returned, they saw each other in London; they visited each others houses in the country to view building and landscaping schemes; and they exchanged views about architecture, archaeology and the joys of collecting. Their tastes and experience having been formed at an early period, they often built upon them across their lifetimes. In the case of the Society of Dilettanti these relationships were formalised.

Founded in 1732, the society, with forty-six members four years later, was restricted to those who had visited Italy.[34] Run on quasi-masonic lines, it met to dine on the first Sunday in each month during the London season (from December to May before 1784; afterwards from February to July), usually in one of the capital's best taverns. Its membership was never entirely restricted to the nobility, even in its most aristocratic phase before the 1780s. There was always a sprinkling of soldiers, diplomats and metropolitan merchant princes and, after the 1750s, a handful of architects and artists. Sometimes there was a strong regional bias in the election of new members. In addition to most of Yorkshire's members of the peerage, Edwin Lascelles, the builder of Harewood, and William Weddell, who remodelled Newby Hall with the aid of Robert Adam to house his collection of statuary, were admitted. In 1775–76 no fewer than five substantial Yorkshire landowners, later mostly Members of Parliament and enthusiastic builders, Lord

PLATE 30. Members of the Society of Dilettanti (Sir Joshua Reynolds, 1777–79). The portrait group shows sitting (*left to right*) Sir Watkin Williams Wynne, Stephen Payne-Gallway, Sir William Hamilton, John Smyth and (standing) Sir John Taylor, Richard Thompson and Walter Spencer-Stanhope.

Mulgrave, John Smyth of Heath Hall, Walter Spencer-Stanhope of Cannon Hall, Henry Peirse of Bedale and Richard Thompson of Escrick Park, were elected to membership of the society (Plate 30). This was indeed an impressive Yorkshire patronage nexus.

Since members were initially young, the society came to have an early reputation for hard-drinking. Horace Walpole dismissed it in 1743: 'the nominal qualification is having been in Italy, and the real one being drunk: the two chiefs are Lord Middlesex [later second Duke of Dorset] and Sir Francis Dashwood, who were seldom sober the whole time they were in Italy'.[35] But in the 1750s the leading members of the well-heeled society began to support a number of expeditions to Italy, Greece and Ionia, and to publish, albeit somewhat slowly, a number of finely illustrated publications which were milestones in the formation of neoclassical design in Britain.[36] Members certainly included all the leading aristocratic connoisseurs of the day and the most innovative and knowledgeable country house builders and landscape enthusiasts: Sir Francis Dashwood, Bubb Dodington, the Earl Temple, the Earl of Leicester and Viscount Harcourt, to name but a few. A view of the membership of the society, and of its sociability and objects, suggest that the Grand Tour was one of the most significant factors in forming the cultural parameters of the English landed classes between the Restoration and the early nineteenth century.

The most interesting exercise concerning the Grand Tour is perhaps to relate its precise influence on the English country house. Of course, even for those most bowled over by the total Italian experience, its impact was softened by the familial and financial circumstances of each individual landowner. The realisation of dreams in Rome and Florence when translated into bricks and mortar in a harsher English climate had to accommodate these more workaday aspects of existence. This interplay between aesthetic ambitions and social and economic restrictions is well-illustrated in the schemes of those builders who undertook the Grand Tour. We have taken the unusually well-documented experiences of three Norfolk landowners (a peer, the first Earl of Leicester, at Holkham; a member of the greater gentry, William Windham, at Felbrigg; and a newcomer to large-scale landownership, Edmund Rolfe, at Heacham) to point up the impact travel abroad had upon their building schemes at home. Although the realisation of their Grand Tour aspirations took different forms, the cross-section of their experiences is not untypical of Georgian landowners more generally.

Thomas Coke (1697–1759), created first Earl of Leicester in 1744 by which title he is usually known, undertook probably the most celebrated of all Grand Tours (1712–18) (Plate 31).[37] First, it was unusually protracted, lasting for almost six years, encompassing travel in France, Italy, Switzerland, Germany, Austria and the Netherlands, Coke having been unusually well-prepared by his tutor, Dr Thomas Hobart, a Fellow of Christ's College, Cambridge. Secondly, much of its detail can be reconstructed from the account book of Coke's principal servant, Edward Jarrett. Thirdly, Coke was ideal Grand Tour material. He was intelligent and well-motivated, although not narrowly academic in his interests. He was also rich. The heir to an estate of £10,000 a year, he was, although still a minor,

PLATE 31.
The first Earl of
Leicester, by
Francesco
Trevisani, 1717.

encouraged by an uncommonly engaged quartet of guardians who had carefully
nurtured his estate from its debt-ridden position at his father's death in 1707. In
Italy he undertook instruction in architecture; he also met up with William Kent,
then undergoing a painter's training, and together they travelled, made notes and
sketches, and collected. He accumulated a large and well-documented array of
pictures and statuary, and, above all – for this was his first love – he made
amazing purchases of manuscripts and books which were to form the basis of
one of the finest private libraries in Britain. Lastly, he in due course built a
near-perfect Palladian palace.

On his return in 1718 he was within a few weeks of his coming of age; a fortnight after which he married. Although inheriting a superb estate and income, he did not immediately replace the Cokes' old north Norfolk manor house, which was totally inappropriate to house his collections. He began, like many builders, by landscaping the park. William Kent transformed the wind-whipped coastal site (Sir Thomas Robinson and Lord Hervey could not understand why he wanted to build there) with woods, water, a kitchen garden, an obelisk, a temple and a triumphal arch, all on the grandest scale.

The house Lord Leicester built was more than equal to his vision for the park (Plate 32). Its designs (building began as late as 1734) are difficult to disentangle, for no fewer than four minds were involved in its design and construction: William Kent; his patron, Lord Burlington, by this time the supreme arbiter of Palladianism in England; the earl himself; and his Norwich-born clerk of works, Matthew Brettingham – who at the end of his life claimed most of the credit for himself. Brettingham, certainly closely involved from the outset, drew out Lord Leicester's schemes. Leicester discussed these early overall designs with Lord Burlington and Kent. The latter also provided much of the interior design work, but it was left to Lord Leicester and Matthew Brettingham (who thanks to Leicester had a flourishing architectural practice himself after 1740) to execute and, in some cases, alter proposals. Certainly, the earl's role was crucial in all stages of the development of the house. Increasingly he was on site to see things finished, 'under my own eye which alone I can trust'. He was part of that architectural *ménage à trois* with the Earls of Burlington and Pembroke that was at the forefront of the promulgation of neo-Palladianism in the second quarter of the eighteenth century. Using as their models the buildings and plans of Palladio and his great English disciple, Inigo Jones, they together pioneered new, intensely academic forms of architecture with their clerks of works-cum-draughtsmen, Roger Morris, Henry Flitcroft, Daniel Garrett, and, above all, with the ebullient, brilliant designer William Kent (they were all eventually architects on their own account). Holkham was its supreme achievement. Thirty years in building, with its four distinctive quadrant wings, its grand suite of gallery (Plate 33) and state rooms, and a spectacular entrance hall, the palace is wonderful testimony to Lord Leicester's learning, vision and persistence. The imprint of the Grand Tour is everywhere. Here its influence on the English country house is at its zenith.

William Windham (1717–1761) was a member of a well-established north Norfolk gentry family.[38] As early as the 1690s his father, Ashe Windham (1673–1749), on his return from the Grand Tour, was reputed to have an income of £4000 a year.

PLATE 32. Holkham Hall, Norfolk (1734–61).

During his sixty-year tenure of the estate he never built on any scale and was but briefly a Member of Parliament. Something of a valetudinarian, living either reclusively at Felbrigg on the collapse of his marriage in 1720 or spending long periods at Bath, Bristol Hotwells or with his relatives, the effects of the low agricultural prices and rentals of the 1710–40 period did not affect him as much as most landowners. He had been to Eton and Cambridge, but his only son received an education which was becoming increasingly uncommon amongst the

PLATE 33.   Holkham Hall, Norfolk. The Statue Gallery.

landed gentry, being tutored entirely at home in preparation for a Grand Tour
of almost five years' duration (1738–42). William Windham was an unusual and
precocious only child, as proficient in languages and science as he was either on
a horse or in the boxing ring. His Grand Tour was mostly spent in Geneva and
Italy. Since his father gave him a good allowance, he was able to buy pictures,
books and prints in Rome and Amsterdam. He accumulated a large circle of
friends abroad; he acted in plays; he undertook an alpine expedition. But the
problem, as with so many young men who had spent a lively few years abroad,
was what to do on his return. Mostly he kicked his heels in London, immersing
himself in the theatre (Garrick was a great friend), hunting in Suffolk, or, to his
old father's dismay, enjoying a succession of mistresses. When in 1749 his father
at last died, the fulfilment of the building schemes he had nurtured for almost a
decade was immediate. So was his marriage to his latest paramour, a forty-year-old
widow six months pregnant, early in 1750.

PLATE 34.   Felbrigg Hall, Norfolk, from the south-west.

Felbrigg was a curious and, by 1750, an old-fashioned and dilapidated house: it combined a 1620s prodigy-house-in-miniature style south range, built in flint and stone, with a starkly contrasting, astylar red-brick west wing of the 1680s and an inadequate service range (Plate 34). Many men of Windham's means would have replaced it with a stylish villa then at the height of fashion. Indeed a cousin had advised him shortly before 'to pull down, build, plant etc. being ambitious to see this ancient Family Seat outshine the clumsy Magnificence of Houghton'.[39] In fact Windham never seems to have contemplated a new house, instead engaging James Paine to remodel the interior of the house extensively in a project which took seven years to complete. He had three objects in view: to provide a good eating room, new domestic offices, and an appropriate setting for the pictures and books he had acquired on the Grand Tour. Paine, under Windham's highly energetic, hands-on supervision, constructed a fine suite of three rooms – eating room, great parlour and cabinet – which were both faithful to the old house, especially in the

PLATE 35.   Felbrigg Hall, Norfolk. The cabinet (James Paine, 1750s).

retention of its splendid ceilings of the 1680s, yet modestly rococo in feeling (Plate 35). Above them a more convenient suite of bedrooms and dressing-rooms was constructed, as well as a Gothic library to replace the great chamber in the 1620s range. A new staircase and new service wing, including two large rooms for Windham's wood-turning and book-binding activities (he also built boats and made fireworks), completed the almost total interior refurbishment of the house. Windham's eye for detail was superb. With Paine and his foreman, he drew out an elaborate hanging scheme for the cabinet (the earliest to survive, Plate 36); and for the six large oils and twenty-six gouaches of Rome and its environs by Busiri, which he had acquired in Rome in 1739–40, and his splendid set of Van der Veldes bought in Amsterdam on the way home, for the great parlour or drawing-room. The results at Felbrigg, one of his Grand Tour cronies thought soon after their completion, were perfect: 'I could cram you with compliments upon your House, Park etc., the Elegance and convenience, the *Utile Dulci*; the freedom

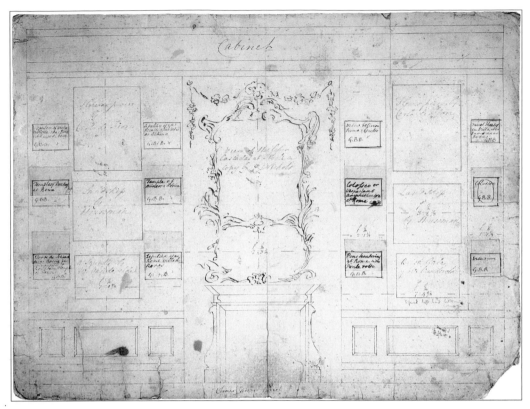

PLATE 36. Felbrigg Hall, Norfolk. Plan for the picture hang on the east wall of the cabinet, by James Paine and William Windham.

and Ease; just enough civility without Ceremony; the various Amusements for the Belly and Head from the Library to the Turning-Wheel.'[40]

The detail of Windham's supervision of transport arrangements, and of London and local workmen as well as of architectural detail, indeed his total immersion in the project, no doubt reflected the fact that he seems to have followed neither of the most regular pursuits of the great gentry – politics and estate improvement. Unusually, he had acquired practical skills himself. But his remodelling of Felbrigg above all expressed the deep impression of his Grand Tour experience (his cabinet is its best surviving articulation in England) and the way in which the group of friends he had formed in Italy fuelled his aesthetic sensibilities during his brief life.

The example of Edmund Rolfe (1738–1817) reveals a tension between the Grand Tour lifestyle he picked up on the Continent and his family background and financial circumstances. (Plate 4)[41] The Rolfes were well-established members of the urban elite in King's Lynn, gradually putting together a landed estate at Heacham. Edmund's father focused all his ambitions on his only son. When an inheritance of £30,000 transformed the family's prospects, Edmund was immediately packed off to Cambridge for a year, then spent three years as a lieutenant in the deranged Lord Orford's West Norfolk militia before embarking upon an extended Grand Tour (1759–62), spent principally in Lausanne and Italy. The journal he wrote is a stilted affair, much influenced by the opinions conventional tourist literature imposed upon his taste. But through its laboured pages a love of Italian opera, Palladio's architecture, the Venetian colourists and the female form emerges, if not shines. Although a liaison in Lausanne produced a son (the family later claimed legitimately when he eventually became the Rolfe heir in the 1830s), he married a neighbouring baronet's daughter. He began to live the life of a minor Norfolk squire. But such was the impact of the Grand Tour that Edmund persuaded his father to lease and in 1771 to buy (for £2500) a house in Wimpole Street where he could entertain the friends he had made on the Grand Tour: the Duke of Roxburgh, John Smyth of Heath and unidentified members of the Dundas and Fox families. Above all, he enjoyed gambling with them. His account books reveal that he bought packs of playing cards four dozen at a time and that 10 per cent of his annual income could be made up or diminished by his luck at the tables. For a decade he led an unsettled life between Heacham, London and Bath waiting for his inheritance. When it came, he immediately extended Heacham by adding a big seven-by-four bays extension (the cellars were dug before his father was buried). No architect appears to have been employed, although it was well-finished with London-bought fittings and furnishings (Plate 5). Built for £4128 during the American war depression, it severely strained Edmund's finances. For almost a decade the family had to reduce its expenditure by a third, living more economically in Bath. Eventually, the sale of a 637 acre farm in 1790 and the hike in agricultural prices after the mid 1790s meant they could return to Heacham and enjoy a rising income.

The effect of the Grand Tour was displayed not so much in Edmund's taste – he seems to have collected little abroad beyond a Battoni portrait of himself – as in the network of friends and the standing it provided him with. Its maintenance was expensive in itself, but to a newcomer anxious to secure recognition in county society this was money well spent. But the Rolfes' income was never sufficient to demonstrate the taste Edmund had acquired in Italy in the building and landscaping he undertook at Heacham. Both ventures in these fields were run-of-the-mill affairs hardly necessitating a three-year continental sojourn. Money was always relatively tight. Besides, he had to invest any surplus in buying more land, in educating his only son at Eton, and in providing a £10,000 dowry for his daughter. In expenditure stretching across these virtually open-ended commitments, features common amongst all landed families, the influence of the Grand Tour upon taste was lessened.

The impact of the Grand Tour declined after the 1790s. Britain was almost continuously at war for almost a quarter of a century after 1793. Not only was much of the Continent closed for years on end, but the wars stimulated the fiercest nationalism and a concentration upon elements more identifiably British in native culture. Patriotism was further encouraged by military victory in 1815 and Britain's increasing industrial leadership of Europe. Of course continental travel soon picked up after 1815 and was immensely stimulated by the coming of the railways. If the Victorian landed gentry travelled abroad more frequently (for almost all Grand Tourists continental travel had been a once in a lifetime event), they did so for much shorter periods. They journeyed *en famille* to sight-see, not to experience an extended education. In the nineteenth century this was provided by the public schools and reformed universities. Much influenced by the novels of Sir Walter Scott, when they built they looked back to native architectural traditions, the glories of the Elizabethan age and beyond to the middle ages. Kenilworth, Warwick, Longleat, Wollaton and Hatfield were their models and inspiration, not Palladian villas or the classical archaeological discoveries of Italy, Greece and Asia Minor.[42] The achievements of the neo-Palladians and neoclassicists were dismissed as ponderous and pompous, their muse derided as unBritish. Moreover, Victorian country house builders did not have to work out architectural solutions themselves as Lords Burlington and Leicester did. They turned to an increasingly reputable architectural profession to carry out their chosen style: Gothic, Jacobethan, something loosely Italianate, or eventually Queen Anne revival. Total immersion in the building process itself was no longer necessary. The architect organised competent, large firms of builders, decorators and furnishers for them.

As war with France raged in the late 1790s, William Mavor developed a bright idea. He would abridge all the better-known travel guides of the British Isles

written in the previous thirty years and publish them in a cheap, six-volume
duodecimo edition (Plate 37). His selections from these authors would thus be
'within reach of every class of subject' available from 'every bookseller in the

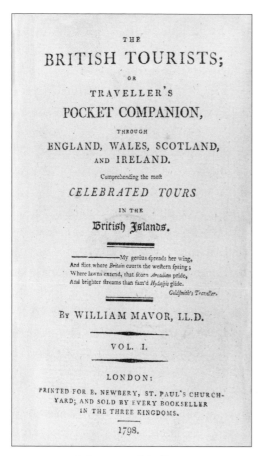

three Kingdoms'. With them his 'most
enlightened countrymen' imbibing
'more patriotic notions than formerly'
would enjoy 'the pleasure and utility of
home travels'. There was much to see,
but journeys would also reveal that the
British Isles were 'the cradle of liberty,
mother of arts and sciences, the nurse of
manufacturers, the mistress of the seas'.[43]
Mavor's aims and sentiments in 1798
were self-evident. His enterprise also reveals how popular travel within the
British Isles had become by the end of
the eighteenth century. It was underwrit-
ten by improvements in roads and inns,
as well as by increasing numbers of
people enjoying the means, education
and leisure to undertake excursions in
the footsteps of those early travel writers.

PLATE 37.   Title page of William Mavor,
The British Tourists (1798).

By the 1790s the beauties of natural
phenomena in the Lake District, the
Pennines and Scotland had come to
dominate British travel literature. Accessible routes were established, 'stations'
fixed from which the best views could be

obtained. Excursionists were encouraged to include the ruins of castles and abbeys
in their itineraries. Readers were enthused by the language of sentiment and the
picturesque. For those who could not wield a pencil and paint-brush themselves,
cheap prints were available everywhere to recapture sensations of the sublime.
Prospects of Derwent Water or Tintern Abbey might be the highlight of a tour
in 1800, but the travel guides also described the states of towns and cathedrals
(not very perceptively before Rickman's classification of the Gothic in 1817),
entertainments at spas, notable industrial projects (a feature in this *genre* going

back to Celia Fiennes and Daniel Defoe) and, above all and often in considerable detail, country houses along the route.

At first glance this extensive noting of country houses is surprising, for the majority were increasingly concealed from sight, surrounded by walls, palings and Brownian-style shelter belts as parks were extended. Yet the quickest perusal of letters and diaries reveals that the majority of the grandest country houses were open to 'genteel' visitors on a regular basis by the late eighteenth century. When she signed her name in the visitor's book at Wilton in August 1776, Mrs Lybbe Powys noted that 2324 people had already done so that year.[44] A handful of great houses possessed printed guides, and for many more lists of pictures at least were available in the general tourist literature to tempt visitors. Those owners of notable houses who declined to open to inspection were castigated. When he was denied access to the interior of Wollaton (Nottinghamshire) in the mid 1770s, William Bray recorded the event in his published tour as 'a piece of gloomy inhospitality'.[45] Owners indeed appear to have been unusually accommodating, at least to members of their own rank. When the de La Rochefoucauld brothers turned up with their tutor at Heveningham ('the only house in Suffolk really worth seeing', François opined) with a note of introduction at 9 a.m., Sir Gerard Vanneck not unnaturally received them 'very coldly'. He kept his hat on and they replaced theirs. Yet he soon warmed, showed them everywhere, rode round the park with them on horses provided from his stable, and entertained them to an 'extra breakfast'.[46] Visitors were inevitably presentable ('polite' in contemporary usage), and prepared to tip generously the servants who showed them round (Plate 38). Bray represented those at Chatsworth, the most assiduous of their species, as surly, avaricious, begging and insolent. One tourist went so far as to suspect that it was the visitors who were paying their wages.[47] The accounts servants relayed of houses, contents and families did not always closely match those printed in travel journals. Sir John Abdy's servants at Albyns in Essex represented to Horace Walpole pictures of Cleopatra and Lucretia as two of Charles II's mistresses. Their confusion was more understandable than that of the housekeeper at Belvoir in 1789: 'pointing to a Picture of the great Duke of Buckingham, she call'd him that Villain Felton; finely confusing the Murder'd with the Murderer!'[48] Costs of pictures, furniture and chimney-pieces were readily, we might think vulgarly, disclosed. The materialistic Mrs Lybbe Powys came away from Heythrop in 1776 marvelling that furniture in the new drawing-room had cost £6000 (the price of a decent country house) and the chimney-piece £1500

PLATE 38.   Castle Howard, Yorkshire. The Orleans Room (Mary Ellen Best, 1832). The housekeeper, waiting here to show visitors around the house, often completed her task at breakneck speed.

(this must have been an exaggeration); at Corsham Court sixty-eight pictures in two rooms were, she was informed, worth £30,000.[49] Providing the family was not in residence, and sometimes when it was, visitors were shown everywhere, taken through state-rooms and bedrooms alike, into stables, kitchen gardens and hot-houses, offered light refreshments and allowed to drive around the park. Visitors – by 1800 including many of the urban elite as well as droves of clergy – loved the experience, their natural nosiness often outdistancing their pursuit of culture.

On the basis of a burgeoning British travel literature, of patriotic opinions such as those held by William Mavor, and of the well-worn routes to the Lake and Peak Districts, through Wales and Scotland, all interspersed with detours to surviving ruins and top rank country houses, it has been argued that the 'British

Tour' had come to form a substitute for the Grand Tour. Certainly for the landowning class this did not happen. The Grand Tour had been a once in a lifetime experience, an essential part of the education and growing-up process of the male gentry. Tours of Britain, however well they might fit late eighteenth-century notions of sentiment, patriotism and the picturesque, and the expositions of recent historians about the commercialisation of leisure, were very different affairs.[50] In any case visits to country houses from the Restoration onwards had long been a part of the culture of landowners. Well aware of building projects within their own county communities, they had, usually when travelling to London or a summer watering place, looked at the more extravagant and archi-tecturally innovative houses and landscapes, as well as old-fashioned models such as Burghley, Wilton, Longleat, Audley End and Hatfield – whose interiors and grounds were themselves subjects for improvement. For them, a century earlier than the growing troop of 'Lakeland' excursionists, admission had been no prob-lem, using letters of introduction and the accepted etiquette of connection and a vast cousinage. The increasing ease of travel and the growing numbers of new and extensively rebuilt country houses after 1700 simply made visits by landowners of all except the Squire Weston variety, sunk in wine, hunting and insularity, a regular and essential part of their experience.

What is interesting, and really has not been attempted by historians, is to examine travel in Georgian Britain as an alternative and complementary cultural experience to the Grand Tour and to consider the overlap between the two. To date, research on the Grand Tour has proceeded quite independently of investigations into the Tour of Britain.[51] In fact there is no shortage of accounts by country house builders of their travels in Britain and the way in which these, together with their reading and perusal of plans and elevations, formed their opinions and tastes. Like those journals and letters of the Grand Tourists, their writings are very variable. Taken together, however, they disclose the impact of foreign travel, a great deal about the world and visions of landowners between the late seventeenth century and the early nineteenth century, and much about those houses, builders, architects and artists which were most influential in the evolution of the country house. Their comments are usually delightfully frank. They can be brutally critical about the architectural achievements and pretensions of their fellow builders. There is none of the sycophancy of patronage here. Those of Sir John Clerk of Penicuik, the second Earl of Oxford and the Honourable Philip Yorke are accounts made by grandees themselves. They provide a wonderful appraisal of the upper reaches of country house building in the half century after 1720 seen from the perspective of three aristocrats, steeped in building, architecture and landscape design through inheritance and interest, on tour in England.

Sir John Clerk of Penicuik (1676–1755), a prominent Scottish improver, builder, antiquarian and anglophile (he was a commissioner for the Union with Scotland, and a Fellow of the Royal Society and the Society of Antiquaries), travelled to London in the spring of 1727 on a two-month jaunt to re-establish his connections in the capital.[52] Although he was engrossed in antiquities, visiting Stonehenge and its great authority, William Stukeley ('as rugh and surly as a bear'), and pictures (he was a cousin of the portraitist, William Aikman, 'a painter of the first rank'), his real interest was in seeing how a house worked in relation to its landscape. On his way to London (the architect William Adam accompanied him after Stamford), he therefore visited the famous landscape John Aislabie was creating at Studley Royal, the gardens at Bramham Park and Wimpole, besides Burghley House. Bramham, 'very indifferent outwardly' (a view shared by Lord Oxford) had too many cascades in its French-style gardens. Wimpole, not a large house in the 1720s although extended by Lord Oxford earlier in the decade, with fine hot houses and a summerhouse whose paintings by Sir James Thornhill were too baroque for Clerk's taste, lacked a good stretch of water, having only some old fish ponds at a considerable distance from the house. From London, he made a special visit to Wilton to see Lord Pembroke's pictures. He was not uncritical of the house's detail, but his real condemnation was reserved for the Duke of Queensbury's house at Amesbury (roofs too low, only one good room, 'no great matter in it') and Lord Cadogan's at Caversham Park. The house and gardens of the latter had been recently laid out at 'vast expense … without either taste or judgement'. The irregular 200-feet front faced a paltry avenue not above twenty feet wide. The garden was otherwise well enough, but its ornaments:

> very bad … His Lordship at a vast expense brought several large marble statues from Holland. There are several Godesses but of such a clumsy make as one may See they were made in a Country where women are welcomed by the pound of A–se.

Clearly, for Clerk, expense did not guarantee correct taste. On the other hand, the considerable detour he made to view Castle Howard was rewarding. Luke-warm at least about the interior of the house, he thought its grounds, especially the walks in Lord Carlisle's famed Ray Wood, very fine.

PLATE 39.
Edward Harley,
second Earl of
Oxford, by
Jonathan
Richardson.

Edward Harley, second Earl of Oxford (1689–1741), although not interested in political office, was a peer of High Tory views, a passionate collector of books and manuscripts, and a great patron of the arts (Plate 39). He was also incredibly extravagant and a shockingly bad businessman. Through his wife, the heiress of the first Duke of Newcastle, he became owner of two great houses, Wimpole and Welbeck, obtaining a colossal dowry package which contemporaries estimated at half a million pounds. It was reckoned at the time that he squandered four-fifths of this through 'indolence, good nature and want of worldly wisdom'.[53] He seems to have enjoyed a tour each year which either he, his protégé George Vertue or his chaplain wrote up. They looked at cathedrals and their libraries, churches and their monumental inscriptions, as well as country houses and his own scattered estates. Lord Oxford clearly inhabited a tiny world of aristocratic grandeur. All but the grandest houses were dismissed. His view of country house building in the 1720s and 1730s is that of a great nobleman, almost alone able to appreciate the achievements of his peers. Parks were appraised by the number of miles they encompassed round them. Narford, the much-acclaimed house of Sir Andrew Fountaine, a famed collector, was 'a fine gimcrack of a house ... all parts are most vilely furnished by all workmen'. The pictures were chiefly copies, the celebrated china room 'a most wretched place', his collection mainly comprising things he had brought to Norfolk having failed to sell them in London. When Lord Oxford was proudly shown portraits of the kings of England in the town-hall at King's Lynn, he pronounced them 'the vilest pictures that probably can be, much worse than any sign post'.

Besides Lord Oxford's ability to dismiss pretension in both houses and men (the architect Colen Campbell was 'an ignorant rascal'; the Bishop of Norwich, 'a most worthless wretch'), two things stand out in the accounts of his tour: the state accorded to a first-rank peer, and the difficulties of travel. In one village in Kent the women strewed mint 'upon the road out of their aprons as my Lord passed along'; at Newcastle the corporation attended him, accompanied by the city music, to view the Tyne from the city barge. Guns were fired from the shore and the river banks lined with crowds to witness the spectacle. Travel, compared with conditions Creevey recorded a century later, was painfully slow on the eve of the turnpike movement. Long days were endured in the coach or sorely in the saddle. Admittedly, Lord Oxford travelled in the style commensurate with his rank: in 1725 it was with ten servants and seventeen horses (fondly he believed he was travelling incognito). Progress, once off major routes, was sometimes at no more than walking pace. Guides were essential. After visiting Castle Howard, one of Lord Carlisle's servants had to accompany Oxford and his party thirty long miles to Thirsk to return them to the Great North Road. Lady Kinnoull's servant was despatched from Perthshire to Northumberland to guide them to Dupplin. Little wonder travel in early Georgian England was largely restricted to the rich or to those on business.

The houses Lord Oxford visited were those belonging to his equals: Belton, Belvoir, Castle Howard, Alnwick, Hornby, Studley Royal, Bramham Park and Wilton. His tour of Suffolk, Norfolk and Cambridgeshire in the September of 1732 (he made a second visit in 1737–38) is especially interesting because it is recorded in his own hand. His object was to view the two great houses of the arch political rivals, and brothers-in-law, Sir Robert Walpole at Houghton and Lord Townshend at nearby Raynham. Oxford approved of Lord Townshend ('he was resolved never to see London again'), and even more of Raynham. The improvements he had made to his estate had added £900 a year to his income; and his park, including a new kitchen garden and orchard, was near perfect. The house, entirely altered within, was pronounced comfortable and well-furnished. Here his Grand Tour learning came into play:

> The rooms are fitted up by Mr Kent, and consequently there is a great deal of gilding; very clumsy over-charged chimney pieces to the great waste of fine marble. Kent has parted the dining-room to make a sort of buffet, by the arch of Severus; surely a most preposterous thing to introduce in a room, which was designed to stand in the street (Plate 40).

At Houghton his Grand Tour evaluation of the newly completed house was

PLATE 40.   Raynham Hall, Norfolk. The buffet in the state dining room (William Kent, c. 1730).

undermined by his detestation of Sir Robert Walpole and the blatant display of
the profits Walpole had made from political office:

> This house at Houghton has made a great deal of noise, but I think it is not deserving
> of it. Some admire it because it belongs to the first Minister; others envy it because it
> is his, and consequently rail at it. These gentlemen's praise and blame are not worth
> anything, because they know nothing of the art of building, or anything about it. I
> think it is neither magnificent nor beautiful, there is a very great expense without
> either judgement or taste.

Sir Robert's famed hunting apartment in the rustic was dismissed as 'low and
being even with the ground one seems to be underground, and it has a very ill
look'. He could only conclude that had the money 'been put into the hands of
a man of taste and understanding, there would have been a much finer house,
and better rooms, and greater'.

Inhabiting the same grand world as Lord Oxford, the Honourable Philip Yorke,
later second Earl of Hardwicke, came from the opposite end of the political
spectrum.[54] At the age of twenty in 1740 he married a great heiress, the Marchioness
Grey, who inherited in the same year the Wrest Park estate of her grandfather,
the Duke of Kent. Yorke, with a powerful father, the long-serving Lord Chancellor, the first Earl of Hardwicke, and three ambitious brothers, was at the centre
of the Whig oligarchy. He himself was retiring and scholarly, a writer, collector of
manuscripts, a Fellow of the Royal Society (at twenty-one) and of the Society
of Antiquaries (at twenty-four). His wife shared his tastes. They centred upon
Wrest, the glory of which was its gardens, laid out over the previous sixty years.
Although he eventually became the master of two great houses, Yorke was a
newcomer to large-scale land ownership (his father only acquiring Wimpole in
1738 from the vastly indebted Lord Oxford). Moreover, he had never undertaken
the Grand Tour himself. Nevertheless, although not a great builder, he soon
acquired a good eye for a country house. To him tours in Britain were an essential
part of his development.

Descriptions of the nine he made between 1744 and 1763 (usually undertaken
with his wife) survive. His accounts of what he saw were invariably succinct. He
appreciated a well-run inn or turnpike and was interested in, if often dismissive
of, the architecture of cathedrals. He pondered the roots of urban prosperity, but
it was the commodiousness and convenience of a great house and its stabling,
the quality of its pictures and, above all, the extent and disposition of its gardens,

water and park (he employed Brown at both Wrest and Wimpole in the late 1750s and 1760s) which enthused him. He could sum up the impact of a country house in a couple of sentences. He liked little that was old. But size was not the sole criterion in impressing him. Vanbrughian vastness made little impact. Chatsworth, a house of grand parade, was inconvenient. He thought the Duke of Norfolk's schemes at Worksop 'so vast and expensive that it is scarcely possible they can be completed'. On the other hand, Holkham, Houghton and Kedleston were reckoned to be paragons of good taste, modernity and convenience. Holkham had the potential to be 'if ever finished perhaps the finest [house] in England'; Houghton was 'fitted up in the most magnificent, convenient and substantial manner in all parts of it'; Kedleston, 'pretty much on the general plan of Holkham ... will certainly be one of the finest houses in Great Britain when completed'. It was for Hagley (Plates 41, 42) that he reserved his real encomia:

> a most excellent house for which Mr Miller of Warwickshire was architect. The hall, salon, eating-room, gallery and drawing room on the first floor are remarkably well-proportioned and pleasant rooms. There are two complete appartments for strangers besides; the attic floor is the best I ever saw; and the rooms in the four towers very good. Lord Lyttelton told me he could make twelve or fourteen *lits de maitres*.

Like Lord Oxford, he seldom visited houses outside the ranks of the grandest aristocracy. Usually, he either stayed or at least dined with their owners (only at Longleat did he get 'a very cold reception'). He empathised with their schemes, although he could be critical about the outcome. At almost all the houses he visited, building work was being undertaken. Often in the 1750s it was to make a house more convenient by adding to, or adapting, existing accommodation to provide a 'great' room for more ambitious entertaining, or, a relatively novel feature, to fit up a purpose-built library. Yorke reveals a world in which building and improving was a way of life, as much a part of the existence of landowners as shaving and dressing.

What do we make of Horace Walpole on the subject of country house tours in England? Through his letters and comments on about four dozen houses in *Journals of Visits to Country Seats*, he is the best-known stately home crawler of the eighteenth century.[55] No other visitor possessed a better eye; no other visitor could dismiss the siting of a house, its architecture or contents more astringently. The sofas in the saloon at Kedleston (which he liked) were 'supported by gilt fishes and Sea Gods, absurdly like the King's coach'; Blenheim (which he hated)

PLATE 41.   Hagley Hall, Worcestershire (Sanderson Miller, 1754–60).

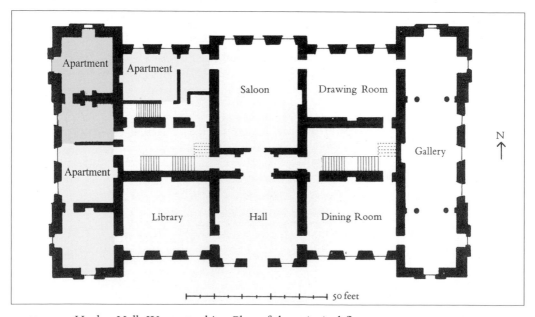

PLATE 42.   Hagley Hall, Worcestershire. Plan of the principal floor.

'looks like the palace of an auctioneer who has been chosen King of Poland, and furnished his apartments with obsolete trophies, rubbish that nobody bid for, and a dozen pictures that he had stolen from the inventories of different families'.[56]

His writings and approach to the country house, like his output generally, are in fact not easy to unpack. Undertaken relatively late with friends and no tutor, his Grand Tour seems to have been a highly charged emotional experience rather than a profound educational and cultural awakening.[57] Eton and King's College, Cambridge, both in terms of their architectural impact and the lifelong network of friends he formed there, were far more important. The other great influence was his father's political career and the mammoth building and collecting schemes at Houghton. Walpole saw the English country house through the visual frame of Houghton. Nothing in England or Italy matched it and its pictures.

Walpole was a third son, even if enjoying a net annual income well in excess of £2000 a year for life from the government places his father had secured for him. He could never build on a grand scale himself. Besides he had no family to provide for, no line to establish. The thought of living in the country appalled him. What he loved was political intrigue in London and the feline world of its grandest dowagers. From an early age he therefore used his eye to describe the dress, houses, entertainments, genealogies and portraits of the *beau monde*. When he travelled each summer with one of his friends into 'squireland', the world of port and parsons (in no sense did he undertake an English Tour: Scotland and the Lakes were avoided; nature for him was confined to the Brownian landscape park and the Thames Valley), he looked at churches, castles, ruins, as well as the country house, in an attempt to reconstruct a fanciful, Gothic past which he could relate to his fantastic London life and building schemes at Twickenham. Ideas were taken back to be drawn out and integrated into the incredible Gothic house he extended over thirty years at Strawberry Hill and which he stuffed with an immense collection of objects which were a parody of his father's at Houghton. In a wonderfully high-camp vignette he received a grand party of two dozen European and English aristocrats 'at the gates of the castle ... dressed in the cravat of Gibbin's carving, and a pair of gloves embroidered up to the elbows that had belonged to James I. The French servants stared and firmly believed this was the dress of English country gentlemen'.[58]

Although Strawberry Hill was a key model in promoting a taste for architectural eclecticism in England, it is also possible to detect beneath the enamel veneer of Walpole's writings a view of country house building which is reconcilable with that of his fellow aristocrats. While a love of irregular forms of architecture and an appreciation for old houses like Drayton (Northamptonshire) and Melbury (Dorset) might be a minority taste in the third quarter of the eighteenth century, he was not indifferent to modern comforts or convenience. He shuddered at houses badly sited 'low in a hole'. He approved of post-Kentian 'naturalism' in landscaping the country house, and he was warm in his appreciation of the great contribution to English architecture of the neo-Palladian school led by Lord Burlington. Moreover, his writings on landscaping, pictures and collecting were influential tracts for the English nobility and gentry. George Montagu paid him an apt tribute when he wrote that Walpole had 'taught the world to treat their kin and their goods and chattels with respect'.[59] For Walpole the proper home for these collections was a noble, Houghton-scale country house, new built or modernised.

The country house tours of Lord Oxford, Philip Yorke and Horace Walpole represent the importance of the experience to the English aristocracy generally. They wanted to see exactly what their friends, rivals and acquaintances were accomplishing. They wanted to extend their own knowledge of architecture and landscaping, to see how the latest fashions in both worked in different situations by examining the best-approved models in the field. It was fine to study Palladio in Italy; but it was also vital to see how well the villa form worked and looked when adapted to the English landscape and climate. As members of a tiny, highly competitive and materialistic group, they also wanted to relate what they saw to the builder's circumstances and pretensions. Horace Walpole was impressed with Kedleston, 'all designed by Adam in best taste but too expensive for his [Lord Scarsdale's] estate' (Plate 43).[60] And when they returned home or gathered in London they discussed eagerly with architects and their own group of friends these latest building ventures, appraising every aspect of design, showiness and cost. Emulation and rivalry were powerful motives in country house building.

The tours of Mrs Lybbe Powys, John Loveday and John Byng show how far down the gentry scale the practice of regular country house visiting and appraisal reached during the eighteenth century. Their journals reveal exactly what the gentry wanted to see and admired and might themselves have contemplated had their circumstances been different. None of the trio seems to have undertaken the Grand Tour. None of them was a builder. It was their travels in England which formed their opinions.

PLATE 43.   Kedleston Hall, Derbyshire, from the north west (attributed to George Cuitt, *c.* 1780).

Mrs Lybbe Powys reveals the tireless, competitive interest of the Georgian gentry in country house building, in landscaping and in picture collecting. We have already seen how well she understood the workings of a 'social house'. From her diaries it can be inferred that, behind the scenes in the seemingly totally dominant male world of country house building, the influence of women insisting upon practicalities of plan and fittings was important. Architectural correctness meant nothing to her beyond the recital of the names of a few fashionable practitioners. Mereworth (Kent), adapted by Colen Campbell from Palladio's Villa Rotunda with only minor changes, she thought was 'not a pleasant house ... in a country so different as ours from Italy, tis a plan, I think, unnecessary to adopt as it seems to make one's residence uncheerful'.[61] She liked things bright and new, gilt furniture and big windows down to the floor. She knew or found out the cost of everything.

John Loveday (1711–1789) was an Oxford-educated, well-connected antiquary of means.[62] He was as inveterate a country house visitor as Mrs Lybbe Powys. The diaries of his many tours after 1729 record visits to around a hundred houses in the country and London. His accounts are careful and prosaic, very different from Walpole's colourful jottings. But it is interesting for a discussion about how ideas were disseminated that a member of the lesser gentry could gain admittance everywhere. Loveday never went to Italy, and never contemplated anything beyond routine repairs to his rambling old house at Caversham in Berkshire, but he was fascinated by contemporary architecture and the vogue for picture collecting. There was clearly a great buzz about both in the 1730s at the gentry level.

The Hon. John Byng (1742–1813) was the William Cobbett of country house visitors, conservative, verbose, deeply opinionated (Plate 44). The accounts of the fourteen tours he made in England and Wales from 1781 to 1794 provide an unparalleled view of the routines of touring, and the whole political economy of country house building, in the critical decade between the American and French Revolutionary wars.[63] Byng was far too cussed ever to follow anything like a standard late eighteenth-century British tour through the Peak District to the Lake District and into Scotland. The picturesque made only a limited impact on him. Suffering from a surfeit of Welsh rain and inns, the gloominess of its hills and the stoniness of its roads, he wrote, 'I do not know a road of more beauty, than that from Biggleswade to Huntingdon', with its prospects of villages, gentlemen's seats, navigable rivers and well-tilled fields.

PLATE 44.   The Hon. John Byng (later fifth Viscount Torrington), by Ozias Humphry, 1796.

With a large family, wayward wife and working as a Commissioner of Stamps, Byng simply wanted to escape London for a month's peace each summer in search of the countryside of his youth and to enjoy the comforts of a good inn, a meal of freshly-caught salmon, new peas and strawberries washed down with a quart of port and half-a-pint of brandy. Perhaps unsurprisingly on this diet, his views became more rose-tinted over the years. Turnpikes had replaced the tree-shaded roads of fifty years earlier to encourage armies of travellers and London habits everywhere; enclosures had brought with them profound social changes highly detrimental to the poor; a great deal of old timber was being cut down by landowners to settle their gambling and building debts; and in some places the quiet of the countryside was being invaded by industries seeking water power.

As a former colonel in the Foot Guards and as the brother of a viscount, Byng was received everywhere as a gentleman of good family – even though travelling unostentatiously for a member of his class on horseback with only a single servant. He often stated what he would have bought and built had his circumstances been different. His house would have been 'nobly Gothic', not 'Cupolaish, Pantheotic, Wyatt-tish', but comfortable with a good library – 'that first of all luxuries'. Nor would he have filled it with imported statuary and Italian pictures – 'filthy, naked or dyeing pictures' – but with Wootons, Van Dykes, Holbeins and Dutch landscapes. The furniture would have been solid, not 'French chairs, festoon'd curtains, and puff'd bell ropes' (some recreations of the National Trust would have troubled him). He deplored the impact of the Grand Tour on the English country house and its owners.

Most recently built houses he dismissed as being too intrusive in the landscape, too tall, and often of 'flaring red brick'. He loved the magnificent oaks at Dunham Massey; but the house he found 'modern, red brick, tasteless ... I had not a wish to enter'. Staunton Harold was almost identically written off, and a whole range of houses that others greatly admired, Hagley, Burghley, Chatsworth, Lyme Park, were summarily dismissed. It is his views of their owners and builders, however, paralleling those of Cobbett on the new-rich clergy and larger farmers of the 1810s and 1820s, which are most revealing. Many houses he found in decay, their owners seldom occupying them for more than a few weeks a year: Grimsthorpe, Wrest, Belvoir, Powis Castle, Boughton, Revesby and Glentworth. On another occasion he noted the Duke of Bedford demolishing superfluous secondary houses as the Woburn estate gobbled up Bedfordshire. At the conclusion of his Midlands tour, in 1789, he wrote, 'almost all we have seen except Clumber, have been aband'd half-finished places'. What was the reason? Sometimes landowners had built beyond their means. Undoubtedly, Byng's views were informed by family experience, since both his grandfather, the first Viscount Torrington, and uncle, the infamous Admiral John Byng, had done so leaving their successors in hopeless debt. Moreover, families were living way beyond their incomes, adopting new codes of metropolitan manners. He thought the Pyms of The Hazells (Bedfordshire) 'would be much happier could they cast off much form and grandeur of living; and adopt an easier stile; permitting the dogs to enter and boots and leathern breeches to sit down to dinner'. At Boughton, 'verging to ruin', the

Scots nobility was blamed, infiltrating English families, their parliamentary boroughs and lands. It was an observation he thought might as easily have been made in Bedfordshire, Yorkshire or even Wales. Above all, landowners were neglecting their country seats to live in London; immured, as Byng imagined, in the terraces or squares of Marylebone, 'immersed in sin and sea coal', 'huddled together on Turkey carpets, before register stoves', 'driving high phaetons up St James's Street'.

Byng's opinions were so strongly held that inevitably they are sometimes contradictory. Some contemporaries maintained landowners increasingly resided in London or Bath with small staffs because it was a cheaper alternative to maintaining estates in the countryside. Yet whichever viewpoint is the more plausible, Byng's impassioned, amateur political economy provides another dimension to the approach of most architectural historians viewing the stylistic evolution of the country house through a succession of pristine key examples: from Coleshill, Belton, Chatsworth, Castle Howard, Wanstead, Holkham and Kedleston to those of the nineteenth century. Byng understood the total context of the country house repertoire around 1790, sizing up the impact of the best-approved houses but also pondering the likes of Powis Castle, with its broken windows, tapestries 'waving in the air', tumble-down terraces and balustrades, boasting a dozen heads of the Roman emperors and other recently imported Italian marbles, yet with not a carpet or comfortable bed in the place.

Perceptions about the country house and its landscape began to change in the forty years between Byng's tours and the coming of the railways. The impact of the picturesque and a fascination with Britain's past increasingly came to dominate the tours of the gentry in Britain. Philip Yorke, Horace Walpole, even John Byng, considered themselves antiquarians, but essentially they were looking at the world their own circle was creating with their burgeoning wealth, their classical houses in many shapes and sizes, their Brownian parks, and their recently formed collections of pictures and statuary. It was a world of patronage and connection they knew intimately, their journeys in England allowing them to appraise progress according to accepted canons of taste. By 1800, however, a much larger band of gentry, scholars with a historical bent, members of the cloth and professional classes, as well as those growing numbers who were making fortunes in industry and trade, became increasingly fascinated with England's past. The majority of them had never seen Europe. But they had perused British tour guides which were deeply imbued with notions of the sublime and picturesque. They also turned increasingly to an expanding diet of historical novels. As a result, they rooted around churches, castles and ruins as well as the entire gamut of English country houses; and, to recreate their settings, they turned from the man-made creations of lakes, temples and green sward to nature itself.[64] Neo-Palladian refinement began to give way to a wilder Gothic fancy. Nowhere is the meaning of this shift for country house builders conveyed better than in the accounts of Sir Richard Colt Hoare's tours, undertaken between 1793 and 1810.[65]

Sir Richard was an antiquarian of distinction, a gifted amateur artist and, as the owner of Stourhead, the guardian of a famous landscape garden and picture collection (Plate 45). He was also thoroughly steeped in the literature of the picturesque. Although he had spent about six years on the Continent, it is evident that the impact of the Grand Tour had begun to recede. Admittedly key houses in the English tour were still appraised, as were picture collections (very critically) wherever he visited. Kedleston, he thought, 'in point of architecture and ornament exceeds any I have yet seen. It bears a foremost rank amongst English country seats'. On the other hand, Harewood was dismissed as everywhere announcing the riches of the Lascelleses, 'a mass of ill-judged expense, a fine suite of rooms fitted up in the most gaudy and expensive style imaginable'. He was also not uncritical of Downton Castle, the creation of one of the high priests of the picturesque, Richard Payne Knight. It was he opined 'neither an ancient castle nor a modern home but a mixture of modern and antique'. The best room in the house appeared to have been copied from the Pantheon at Stourhead; overall the castle was 'not quite adapted to the genius of the place'.

What really fascinated Colt Hoare on his long summer excursions was the landscape – the sublimity of the Parys Mountain mines and Gordale Scar or the beauties of Tintern Abbey. Indeed he approached the prospect of every castle or abbey with an artist's vision. With the landscapes of Salvator Rosa, Nicholas and Gaspard Poussin and Claude in mind, he thought how their settings might be ideally improved. In contrast, those famed landscapes John Aislabie had created at Studley Royal (Fountains Abbey) and Hackforth seventy years earlier were decried. His view of some country houses show how far opinion was similarly shifting. Big brick facades he disliked: 'I have always had the greatest aversion to them and particularly when viewed in a picturesque light. They admit of no variety of tints, no effects of light and shade, and have therefore always a dull and heavy appearance.' His solution, a nice Regency touch, was green blinds and a cream-coloured wash. Lord Bulkeley's house, Baron Hill near Beaumaris,

PLATE 45.
Sir Richard Colt
Hoare and his
son Henry, by
Samuel
Woodforde,
1795–96.

occupied a wonderful site with its views to Mount Snowdon but, 'the elevation of the house, though the work of the celebrated Wyat [Samuel Wyatt, built 1776–79] does not please me: nothing to me is so hideous as a high house crowded with windows. Such a building gives me always the idea of a cotton or silk manufactory, or an hospital. The front of the house has above forty windows' (Plate 46). Colt Hoare possessed a good eye. Few gentry tourists shared his acute sensitivity to landscape and to light, or his antiquarian learning. But a whole

Baron-Hill, *in the Isle of* Anglesey, *the Seat of* Lord Viscount Bulkeley.

PLATE 46. Baron Hill, Anglesey (Samuel Wyatt, 1776–79).

generation of them, through their own reading and journeys in Britain, came to possess similar opinions.

With the railway age, aristocratic tours in England of the kind we have seen came to an end, just as the French wars (1793–1815), for a number of reasons, marked the end of the Grand Tour. The rich increasingly took their leisure sightseeing abroad, yachting off the British coast or holed up in Scotland shooting. As social pursuits shifted, the majority of English country houses were no longer accessible on the terms Sir John Clerk or Colt Hoare had visited them in the century before 1830. In these hundred or more years visits to English country houses had been an important aspect of the leisure and learning of the larger landowners. They travelled widely to see the latest wonder houses and landscapes, the talk of their tiny closed world in London, Bath and the country. They saw what worked in an English climate and landscape; they evaluated changing fashions in the layout and decoration of interiors; they observed how pictures and furniture fitted new and remodelled rooms. They considered how houses matched the purses and pretensions of families. They looked; they compared;

they envied. It is arguable that the widespread habit of country house visiting from the Glorious Revolution onwards was as important as the Grand Tour in enthusing and informing the landowning class about architecture, collecting and landscaping, indeed the whole menu of country house building.

If many of the English gentry in the Georgian period increasingly came to enjoy a summer jaunt, encompassing perhaps visits to a spa and to a handful of country houses and taking in if possible some picturesque scenery *en route*, journeys to London were an even more regular part of their calendar. For the nobility and greater gentry frequently spent as many as seven months, from October to May, in London before improved roads and eventually the railways made more frequent, shorter visits possible. In the eighteenth century it was a comment made by many besides John Byng that landowners were milking their estates to spend the major part of their income in the capital. These long sojourns to enjoy the social whirl of the great wen were an important formative influence on their tastes and lifestyles.

Residence in London was essential to the aristocracy for a variety of reasons: above all they were involved in government, sessions of Parliament (still short, but annual following William III's need to raise money for the wars against Louis XIV), and in Court ceremonies. Many more went to negotiate marriage settlements and to sort out complex business, including financial and legal matters. All endeavoured to enjoy themselves, for this lengthy migration encouraged a whole new demand-led culture of sociability. A perpetual cycle of entertainments, public and private, was put together – breakfasts, dinners, assemblies, routs, balls, plays, operas, exhibitions to provide a dizzying metamorphic social round. In addition the male sex could seek diversion, according to individual predilection, in taverns, coffee houses, social and gambling clubs, whore and molly houses. Little wonder life in the country, the 'squireland' of Horace Walpole, confined to the hunting field and card table, was so frequently represented as dull and visits limited to a few weeks in summer.

The residential needs of the nobility and gentry in London were catered for after the Restoration by the development of the West End over the next two centuries.[66] This housing was at two levels. There were a handful of palaces – not many more than fifty or so – of the richest aristocrats, themselves often the developers of their immensely valuable London estates. But the vast majority of landowners who owned or rented a London residence lived in a terrace house

PLATE 47. Joseph Bonomi's design for the Great Room, Montagu House, 1782.

built everywhere in squares and streets on a common plan – vertically arranged, well-fitted, confined – although varying considerably in size. Both had significant influences in the formation of the tastes of country house builders.

Although the number of great town houses was small, as show houses of the super rich they were invariably trend-setting. From the short-lived Clarendon House of the 1660s to those of millionaires such as the Rothschilds at the end of the period, these palaces, frequently refurbished, were the creations of clients and architects in the van of fashion. Their influence was probably at its height in the thirty years following Robert Adam's breathtaking conquest of the province of architecture and design in the 1760s (Plate 47). Those landowners, old-titled and new rich alike, who saw his wonderfully decorative, spatially ingenious, creations at Shelburne House (Berkeley Square), Wynne House (20 St James's Square), Derby House (Grosvenor Square), the glass drawing-room at Northumberland House (Strand) and Home House (Portland Square) went back to the country

PLATE 48.   Devonshire House, London (demolished).

their minds reeling with schemes, ready to apply at least some element of the
Adam style. Moreover, the aristocracy often kept their best pictures and effects
for display in London. Visitors sometimes found Chatsworth disappointing because the cream of the Duke of Devonshire's collection was housed in London.
An inventory of 1798 reveals that the contents of Devonshire House (Plate 48)
were valued at £29,286, whereas those of Chatsworth were worth £22,322, including a sum of £4762 for farming stock. All these important London houses were
accessible, built to be seen by the whole landowning and plutocratic worlds. At
Northumberland House in 1764 the *London Chronicle* noted '1500 persons of distinction' shoe-horned into its reception rooms; Mrs Montagu entertained 700
people to breakfast when her grand new house, designed by James Stuart in
Portman Square, was finally completed. At the greatest private house in London,
Stafford House, the Sutherlands regularly invited a thousand guests to their
assemblies in the mid nineteenth century (Plate 49).[67] Indeed all the largest London
houses were 'public' in their concept and layout. 'They were not built for domestic
but public life', wrote Sir John Summerson, 'a life of continual entertaining in

PLATE 49.   A reception at Stafford House, London, by Eugène Lami, 1849.

drawing-rooms and ante-rooms and "eating-rooms" where conversation would not be wholly ephemeral, where a sentence might be delivered which would echo round political England, where an introduction might mean the beginning of a career or a deft criticism the dethronement of a policy.'[68]

Even life in the regular terrace house of the West End provided elements which landowners adopted back in the country: neat decoration, good fittings, a whiff of metropolitan fashion, the joys of the 'social' house. Away from the routines of estate business and county administration, they also had time to read the burgeoning architectural literature and to discuss it with its authors, time to talk with printers, sculptors and painters, as well as with the group of like-minded friends whom they saw and entertained.

The Georgian expansion of London was impressive in scale. Yet individual building schemes were often long in completion. Any overall plan was missing. With almost all building being privately and speculatively undertaken, London's development juddered forward, accelerating and braking according to the movement of the building cycle. There was, moreover, a lack of impressive public buildings and royal palaces, a feature all sharp-eyed continentals noted, at least before the surge of building associated with the Prince Regent's vision of an imperial capital and with the great victory of 1815. But for the aristocracy and gentry the metropolitan forcing house of architectural and decorative ideas was not confined within new West End boundaries. They also drew their inspiration from the environs of the capital.

The aristocracy occupied houses not only in one of the recently-built central London squares, they also often had a villa for summer residence in the villages to the west of London, especially along the Thames. Philip Yorke and his wife, the Marchioness Grey, were typical peerage members in owning, besides their Bedfordshire seat, a house in St James's Square and a villa in Richmond. These aristocratic retreats (a central London house was still essential for regular engagements) were quite different from those artisan-designed, neatly executed boxes beloved by city merchants and Defoe. Lord Burlington's Palladian masterpiece at Chiswick, the villa Lord Pembroke designed for the Countess of Suffolk at Marble Hill, and White Lodge, Richmond, were the height of Palladian and metropolitan chic in the mid eighteenth century. And there were other bigger houses around London, Cannons, Gunnersbury, Sir Gregory Page's house at Blackheath, Wanstead, Syon House and Moor Park, which were on the route of every building enthusiast.

The journal of Sir John Clerk of Penicuik provides good evidence of the impact of aristocratic London for a *cognoscente* and builder.[69] Who and what did he see during his six weeks' visit in the spring of 1727? Since the leading collectors of their day kept their best things in town, he visited the houses of Lord Pembroke, the Earl of Hertford and his father the Duke of Somerset, Sir Robert Walpole, Lord Burlington, Lord Malpas, the Duke of Devonshire, Sir Paul Methuen, Sir Hans Sloane ('the greatest collection of things than ever I had seen in my Life, not the Treasure of a Forreign prince cou'd equal them'), and Drs Woodward and Mead. He also saw the three royal palaces, St Pauls, some city churches – greatly admiring Gibbs's portico at St Martins-in-the-Field – and then rode farther afield to look at recent, much talked of building projects. He went with a grand party of Scottish peers to view Wanstead ('this house is one of the best in England'); to Whitton (Middlesex), ten miles from London, where Lord Islay had set out a rather grand garden but not yet built a house as such, simply adding a dining-room and 'three other chambers not yet finished' to his greenhouses; to Sir Gregory Page's at Blackheath, a very large house with 'a floor of state', an Ionic portico to the garden, and wings connected by a colonnade. Sir Gregory, a merchant's son, had a good collection of pictures and the richest furniture Sir John had ever seen. Other Defoe-type villas were noted and dismissed. On the way back from Hampton Court, 'we saw several villas near to Richmond but generally of a very poor sort of Architecture'.

Everywhere Sir John went he spoke of little besides building and collecting. At Burlington House, Lord Burlington showed him his pictures, 'particularly several hundred drawings of Palladio and Inigo Jones'. He even gave him two of the latter's designs for windows made for the Earl of Stafford and issued a coveted invitation to dine at his Chiswick villa (Plate 50). Lord Burlington's 'good taste appeared here in many shapes', but the seventy-foot square building Sir John thought 'rather curious than convenient', the effect of the entry through a portico into a passage about twenty-two feet high and five in breadth particularly puzzling him. When he went to see the Devonshire collection, which he reckoned the best collection of pictures and drawings in England, the duke was 'very obliging pursuant to Strangers. I found him in his Library newly recovered of a fit of the gout.' Sir John was bowled over by London. When he rode north to Scotland on 16 May, his thoughts, like those of the Wise Men leaving Bethlehem, were full of the wonders he had seen.

Sir John recorded none of his expenses beyond simply noting at the end of his

PLATE 50.   Chiswick House, Middlesex (Lord Burlington, *c.* 1725), by Jacques Rigaud.

journal, 'this was a journie merely for curiosity . . . it cost me near £300 including some things I bought' (he mentions only pictures acquired on two occasions). A prime incentive for a visit to London by the country gentry was certainly to shop. Through reading newspapers and journals, looking in book and print shops, visiting warehouses, salerooms, studios and workrooms along the Strand, in Covent Garden and the Bond Street area, and through participation in the emulative social round of the rich, the fires of conspicuous consumption were thoroughly stoked. By these means they picked up notions of style such as the rococo or neoclassical which affected all the arts from furniture to dress, printing to ceramics.[70] The increasing variety and richness of goods available in London was astonishing: textiles, clothing, leather goods, books, furniture, porcelain, enamels, upholstery, paintings, prints and drawings to suit a range of tastes and purchasing power. Designs and prices were discussed face to face with craftsmen; portraits, sculpture and silver plate were commissioned. London-made goods of tip-top design and manufacture carried great cachet in a society obsessed with the price and status of everything. The English country house was therefore filled with them – furniture and upholstery above all, but also metalwares, ceramics, pictures and chimney-pieces. London-carved memorial statuary to announce the family's standing was fixed up in the neighbouring church. It is clear, however, that the capital's wealth of labour-intensive luxury craft trades was not solely under-pinned by the purchasing power of the landowning elite. Their range and breadth also depended upon the trickle-down of aristocratic tastes to a wider, buoyant middle-class base. Nevertheless, the acquisitions of metropolitan goods of every description reached the entire gentry class.

Edmund Rolfe of Heacham was, as we have seen, a marginal member of the gentry.[71] Yet when it came to fitting up and furnishing the extension he made to his father's old manor house in the late 1770s, the range of goods and skills available in London were an important consideration for Edmund and Dorothy Rolfe. A total of £1025 was spent on furniture and furnishings (almost exactly a quarter of his building costs). Most of these were bought in London and transported to King's Lynn by sea. Over £600 in total was paid to upholsterers and drapers. Chintz for curtains, Holland sheets, window shades, painted floor cloths, huckaback, damask fabrics, china and glass were all on the Rolfes' shopping list. Items of mahogany furniture included sideboards, tables, chests of drawers, washstands, bookcases, wardrobes, a shaving-stand and a knife-box. Most attention was lavished on the drawing-room. Joshua Graham of St Paul's Churchyard, London, provided two sofas (£23 10s.) and ten 'stuff back seat chairs in green silk – mixed damask with case covers' (£26 5s.). The curtains and 'hanging papers' matched. Two girandoles, two pier glasses, a pembroke table and a Wilton carpet completed the scheme. Significant sums were spent on coloured marble chimney-pieces: £63 for the drawing-room and £49 for the dining-room. The designs for them were bought from George Richardson, the Adam brothers' top draughtsman, for £1 7s. 6d. and made up by John Hamilton of Duke Street, together with two marble-topped side tables 'with squares of various colours' (£17 7s.).[72] The chimney-pieces were fitted by a London mason who spent four days at Heacham. Kitchen equipment, grates and stoves also came from the capital. Paperhangers and moulders were at work in 1777 and 1778, charging 6d. per mile travelling expenses from London, and a Piccadilly firm supplied the paints and oils. Some furniture, including a sideboard and large mahogany bookcase (14 guineas), was bought from Henry Burcham in King's Lynn, but it was the metropolitan furnishing of Heacham which the north-west Norfolk guests of the Rolfes would have talked about during these final years of the war with America.

One of the more fascinating aspects of provincial newspapers in the eighteenth century is to trace how London-produced goods found their way to retailers in the larger towns. Their advertisements, growing enormously in number across the century as the provincial press took off, disclose the range and regular arrival of goods of every description. It is clear that members of the gentry on their visits to the regional capitals of Georgian England, and to its leading spas, ports and big industrial towns, could increasingly find a range of goods and services, however dimly they mirrored those in London. Their underpinning was of course much wider than the support of the landowning class, for the number of those with middling incomes grew rapidly with industrial and agrarian development. By the early nineteenth century London's influence nevertheless seemed all-pervasive throughout England. Louis Simond, an American visitor wrote of the Lake District in 1810,

> There are no retired places in England, no place where you see only the country and countrymen; you meet, in the country, everywhere town-people elegantly dressed and lodged, having a number of servants, and exchanging invitations. England, in short, seems to be the country-house of London; cultivated for amusement only, and where all is subservient to picturesque luxury and ostentation. Here we are, in a remote corner of the country, among mountains, 278 miles from the capital – a place without commerce or manufacturers, not on any high road; yet everything is much the same as in the neighbourhood of London.[73]

It was London fashions, goods and services which set the pace in the pursuit of luxury consumption. Such journeys as those made by Sir John Clerk in the 1720s, or a century later by those members of the gentry bowling up to town to enjoy the extravagances of Regency London, were clearly as influential as the Grand Tour, and as those endless, inquisitive visits to view country houses, in furnishing landowners with the ideas and stimulus and connections to build.

4

Architect and Patron

'I received from Colonel Moyser a very gentil letter and a plan that I like better than any I have seen yet. I sent him some remarks upon it and I hope to have a second edition. If I state it right my house will be a perfect model of Lord Orford's at Houghton ... but at the same time that I am consulting the Colonel about making a palace, I have taken the liberty to send him an estimate made by one of my workmen that he might cast his eye over it and let me know how far it is to be depended upon. I would wish to have your thoughts and that you would see the second edition of the plan and remember that I want a house to live in, not a house for show.'
      Stephen Thompson, writing to his friend Thomas Grimston, 22 November 1746, on the planning of Kirby Hall. [1]

'Nothing I believe is to be made perfect by any one but the Deity.'
      John Buxton, writing to his son Robert, 13 December 1726. [2]

'Let him therefore who intends to build take the opinion of his friends, as well as of professional men; he may then reasonably hope, to have his doubts and difficulties removed, and to possess all the information that nature, genius, experience and judgement can suggest.' [3] John Soane's advice to gentlemen thinking about a new country house, published in 1788, is a telling comment on practice towards the end of the eighteenth century. Yet whether the aspiring creator of a country house could reasonably expect to have all his worries dismissed was by no means certain. The professional architect was beginning to emerge from the diverse ranks of those who practised the art, but it was to be another fifty years before he generally subscribed to a code of conduct which sought to eliminate potential conflicts of interest with others involved in the construction business. The opinion of friends was therefore of paramount importance to the eighteenth-century gentleman builder, in matters of taste, design and construction.

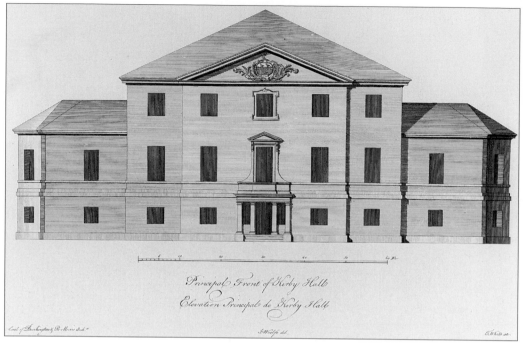

Principal Front of Kirby Hall
Elevation Principale de Kirby Hall

PLATE 51.   Kirby Hall, Yorkshire (elevation attributed to Lord Burlington and Roger Morris, 1747–52, demolished) from *Vitruvius Britannicus* (1767).

The full flowering of this process is illustrated by the experience of Stephen Thompson (1699–1763), who built Kirby Hall in Yorkshire in the 1740s (Plate 51). A Yorkshire and London merchant, Thompson was at the centre of the buzz of building activity in his own county and well abreast of national architectural fashion. He looked at buildings, consulted his network of friends. From them and through gentlemen-disciples, to architects, builders and craftsmen, a stream of advice cascaded from the supreme arbiter of neo-Palladian taste, the third Earl of Burlington (1694–1753).

Thompson felt compelled to rebuild Kirby Hall at Little Ouseburn (Yorkshire) because 'as it happens [the house] now is hardly to be called a dwelling place'.[4] First, he sought the advice of Lord Burlington's Yorkshire disciple and neighbour Colonel James Moyser (c. 1688–1751).[5] Through his patronage of artists, and as an architect in his own right, Burlington promoted the principles of Roman archi-tecture, especially as transmitted through the designs of Palladio and the work of Inigo Jones and John Webb, and played a crucial role in the development of English neoclassicism. Moyser himself returned to Beverley, not far from Burlington's seat at Londesborough, after military service and was active as a 'competent amateur' in the 1730s and 1740s. Espousing Burlington's Palladian cause, he was associated with the building of several Yorkshire houses: Sir William Wentworth's Bretton Hall in about 1730, Sir Rowland Winn's Nostell Priory (where the young James Paine developed his design skills) from *c.*1737, and possibly the Pennyman family's Ormesby Hall in the 1740s (they had Beverley connections).[6] Stephen Thompson's Yorkshire circle was therefore active architecturally and he was aware of house-building further afield. 'My house will be a perfect model of Lord Orford's at Houghton', he grandly informed his Yorkshire friend Thomas Grimston (in the process of buying Kilnwick), though conscious that his mention of this costly exemplar might disconcert him.[7] 'You will think', he continued, 'it will behove me to look out that I don't embark beyond my depth least your tallies go to pot but, at the same time that I am consulting the Colonel about making a palace, I have taken the liberty to send him an estimate made by one of my workmen that he might cast his eye over it and let me know how far it is to be depended upon.' He ended the letter with more reassurance: 'I would wish to have your thoughts ... and remember that I want a house to live in, not a house for show.'

The design was developed with Moyser's help, although it is clear that, while Thompson accepted some advice ('[Moyser] showed me the absurdity of one part of my proposals'), he knew his own mind and persisted with other alterations of the plan in spite of the colonel's disapproval. Thompson did, however, tell Grimston that he would follow Moyser's recommendation to consult Roger Morris, a protégé of the neo-Palladian coterie, although not with an open mind: 'I find these sort of fellows often rather conform to what they find we desire than speak freely and therefore I would lay before him as perfect a plan as I could.'[8] Thompson expected Morris to call at Kirby in May 1747. By this time dreams of Houghton had evaporated. He now envisaged that the final plan would resemble the much smaller Beverley house Colen Campbell had designed for Sir Charles Hotham.[9] The extent of Morris's input is unclear and Thompson was aware that his juggling with advisers might offend: 'Colonel Moyser ... says he is glad I have got a plan I like but says nothing to his opinion. I fancy he thinks I have consulted Morris and therefore won't say anything, but Morris nor no architect but Payne [James Paine] has seen it'.[10] Nevertheless, a contemporary engraving of Kirby Hall is inscribed 'Elevation by R. Morris Architect and the Earl of Burlington: Executed, & the inside furnishings, by J. Carr, Architect. Plans by the Owner, S.T.'[11] Truly, building by committee. The first brick was laid in

September 1747, the roof was watertight by Easter 1750, and the house was ready
for occupation in 1752.

In his turn, Thompson gave advice to another friend, William Gossip, son of
a successful West Riding mercer, who had both inherited and bought estates in
Yorkshire and now faced the challenge of building his own country seat, Thorp
Arch Hall.[12] Gossip knew what he wanted – 'a house of 5 windows and 4 rooms
on a floor with the offices and stables in the wings: to build garden wall and
cellar walls this summer, cover in the next and finish the third' – but he lacked
Thompson's confidence in developing his own design. First, Gossip approached
James Paine through Sir Rowland Winn, who was rebuilding Nostell Priory. When
Paine's responses were delayed by the pressure of other work, he declined his
services (Plates 52–53). Gossip then turned, probably on Thompson's recommendation, to the twenty-six-year-old John Carr, a mason already practising as an
architect. Carr was just the man he needed, for Gossip had 'a very bad opinion
of my own management in building'.[13] His workmen went their own way and

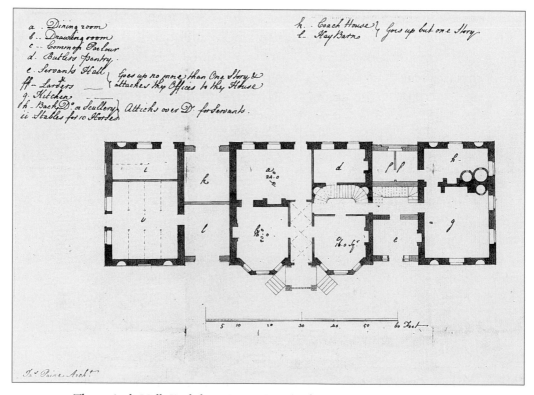

PLATE 52.   Thorp Arch Hall, Yorkshire. James Paine's plan (not executed)

got the better of him in all their dealings so that 'for the sake of my own care, I am obliged to let the boat drive with the Stream'. Gossip's confession came in response to a request for advice from his physician Dr Goddard, on behalf of yet another prospective builder, Lady Dawes. Gossip concluded, 'I am a stranger to

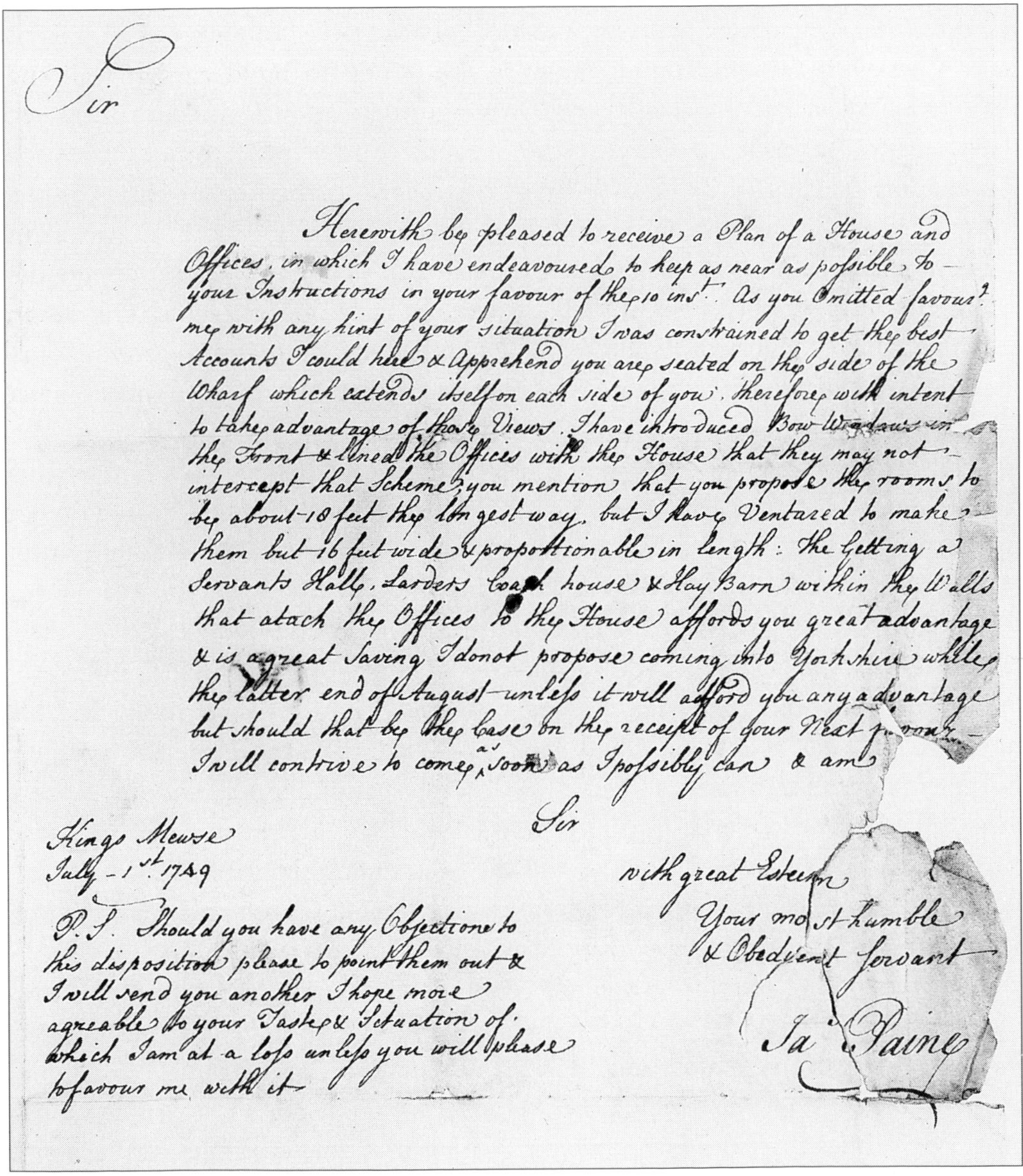

Sir

Herewith be pleased to receive a Plan of a House and Offices, in which I have endeavoured to keep as near as possible to your Instructions in your favour of the 10 inst. As you omitted favour me with any hint of your situation I was constrained to get the best Accounts I could here & Apprehend you are seated on the side of the Wharf which extends itself on each side of you. therefore with intent to take advantage of those Views. I have introduced Bow Windows in the Front & lined the Offices with the House that they may not intercept that Scheme you mention that you propose the rooms to be about 18 feet the longest way, but I have ventured to make them but 16 feet wide & proportionable in length: the getting a Servants Hall, Larders Coach house & Hay Barn within the Walls that attach the Offices to the House affords you great advantage & is a great Saving. I do not propose coming into Yorkshire while the latter end of August unless it will afford you any advantage but should that be the case on the receipt of your Next favour I will contrive to come as soon as I possibly can & am

Sir

Kings Mewse
July 1st 1749

P.S. Should you have any Objections to this disposition please to point them out & I will send you another I hope more agreeable to your Taste & Situation of which I am at a loss unless you will please to favour me with it

with great Esteem
Your most humble
& Obedient Servant

Ja Paine

PLATE 53. Thorp Arch Hall, Yorkshire. James Paine's proposals for a new house for William Gossip, 1749.

the circumstances of the work & the agreements with workmen & therefore can't tell how to proceed further in complying with yr req[ues]t.' [14] The cascade of architectural advice, which had sprung from the Burlington fountain, descending over layers of discipleship, finally trickled down to Gossip. At this level it clearly spent itself. Here there was architectural ambition, but also a demonstrable lack of confidence when faced with the practical problems of building. [15]

Fifty-seven years had separated Lord Burlington's own first practical essay in Palladianism – a garden pavilion in the grounds of Chiswick House – from the Restoration of Charles II. In 1660 there had been no theoretical basis for the study of architecture, nor an organised profession of architects. It is a modern notion that the architect should lead a project team, controlling both design and execution, acting for his client in dealings with the building contractor. The design and planning of the seventeenth- and eighteenth-century country house was empirical and controlled by clients. The relationship between builder and architect was that of patron and servant rather than that of client and professional. The patron secured a design, or a version of his own, and made his own arrangements for building. Moreover, his education fitted him for this leading role. Foreign travel, the study of the arts and architecture, and the collecting of architectural books were inspired by discussions with networks of friends and acquaintances well-versed in 'the Queen of the arts'. [16] Educated aspiring builders derived their knowledge of the classical orders and the rules of proportion from the architectural literature of the mid sixteenth century onwards. They read Vitruvius and his Italian Renaissance followers, Alberti, Serlio, Palladio and Scamozzi, and northern European interpreters such as Vredeman de Vries, in continental editions. Robert Peake's translation of Serlio into English was issued as early as 1611, but from the late 1730s a flood of translations of the classical sources, and practical builders' manuals, disseminated designs for houses and their interiors and methods for applying the classical orders ever more widely. [17]

At the beginning of the seventeenth century the only English examples of the rigorous application of the principles of High Renaissance architecture had derived from Crown patronage after 1615, during the Surveyorship of the Royal Works of Inigo Jones (1573–1652). The Queen's House at Greenwich and the Banqueting House at Whitehall, for example, were rare if inspirational examples for Palladian followers. Leadership of taste then rested with the Court and only its own tiny circle could draw upon the design and architectural expertise of royal servants.

Though the uncertain years of the Interregnum were hardly conducive to country-house building, Jones and his pupil John Webb (1611–72) found gentlemen patrons able to commission new work. Classical alterations to the Earl of Pembroke's Wilton House (Wiltshire), encouraged by Charles I, had begun in 1636, and a project that had started as a grandiose tribute to the monarch continued in the 1640s, on a reduced scale, under Webb, when the fourth Earl was espousing the Parliamentary cause.[18] At Coleshill (Berkshire) in 1650, the London businessman and Parliamentary supporter Sir George Pratt began to build a new house, influenced at least if not designed by Inigo Jones, and completed ten years later under the supervision of Sir George's cousin, Roger Pratt. It provided an influential Palladian model for generations of middling gentry houses.[19] Even some Royalist gentlemen added quietly to their existing seats. Sir Justinian Isham, with an estate impoverished by loans to the King and fines by Parliament, nevertheless celebrated his second marriage in 1653 by engaging John Webb to design additions to his Northamptonshire house, Lamport. He continued to communicate with his building contractor even while imprisoned as an alleged threat to the regime during the summer of 1655.[20]

The late seventeenth-century gentleman whose architectural taste inclined towards Inigo Jones's interpretation of Italian Renaissance models still needed practical help to achieve his building ambitions.[21] Sir Roger Pratt (1620–85) advised:

> get some ingenious gentleman who has seen much of that kind abroad and been somewhat versed in the best authors of Architecture: viz. Palladio, Scamozzi, Serlio, etc. to do it for you, and to give you a design of it in paper, though but roughly drawn, (which will generally fall out better than one which shall be given you by a home-bred Architect for want of a better experience, as is daily seen).[22]

Pratt was one of a small number of gentlemen who specialised in architectural design and support. In addition to his work at Coleshill, he designed the highly influential, if short-lived, Clarendon House (London), Kingston Lacey (Dorset), and another large house with a brief life span, Horseheath (Cambridgeshire).[23] There were other practitioners with similar interests and background: Hugh May (1621–1684), son of a Sussex gentleman, who served the royal court in exile and prospered as a gentleman architect after the Restoration; William Samwell (1628–1676), grandson of Queen Elizabeth's Auditor of the Exchequer; and William Winde (?–1722), another exile with the Stuart Court, who turned to country house architecture after the 1688 Revolution removed his royal patron. But most gentlemen contemplating building thought it unnecessary to consult anyone but a master tradesman. Between 1660 and 1720, a period that was one of the high-water marks of English architectural craftsmanship, the skilled tradesman was artistically self-sufficient, and he was free and able to submit designs for the approval of a patron or his architect.[24] Indeed, the gentlemen architect could hardly have operated without him. But Roger North, the opinionated designer of his own country house in Norfolk, had doubts about dependence on either architect or craftsman:

> For a profest architect is proud, opinionative and troublesome, seldome at hand, and a head workman pretending to the designing part, is full of paultry vulgar contrivances; therefore be your owne architect, or sitt still.[25]

Many men held similar views, echoed by Sarah, Duchess of Marlborough, when she wrote in 1732 that she knew no architects who were not mad or ridiculous (her experience with Vanbrugh at Blenheim was fresh in her mind), and that two gentlemen of her acquaintance with great estates had had their houses built by able workmen without an architect.[26] True, work on some prominent houses of the period is without attribution, including the west front of the Duke of Devonshire's Chatsworth (c. 1700), for example, and the Earl of Nottingham's Burley-on-the-Hill (1695–c. 1705).[27] Sir John Lowther Bt has been described as his own architect at Lowther Castle (Westmorland, 1692–95), as has Lord Conway at Ragley (Warwickshire, 1679–83). Both were content with the results. John Buxton compared the house he built for himself with the published designs of James Gibbs: 'The plan 63 in Gibbs looks too full of windows. The rooms are too small and two of them lost by being thro fares to the offices, the stairs but three foot wide. I like Shadwell better.' While the owners may have made significant contributions to the design of their houses, the apparent lack of surviving evidence of the involvement of an architect is not however a reliable indication that none was employed, for an architect had no protection against the patron who claimed the work as his own.[28] Certainly, in the early years of the eighteenth century, the impact of gifted, educated, amateur architects, such as Talman, Pembroke and Burlington, and of men who moved to architecture from other professions, including the soldier-playwright Vanbrugh and painter Kent, was paramount.

Leadership of taste passed increasingly in Hanoverian England to private landowners. Successive surveys of their building efforts, *Vitruvius Britannicus*, appeared between 1715 and 1725. The editor of these volumes, Colen Campbell, including his own designs and promoting Inigo Jones as the English Palladio, in the process produced a fully-blown neo-Palladian tract. This cause was further promoted by Leoni's English translation of Palladio's *Four Books* (Plate 54), published between 1715 and 1720, and by William Kent's *Designs of Inigo Jones* in 1724. James Gibbs's *Book of Architecture*, of 1728, was the first book of designs by a living British architect.

PLATE 54.
The frontispiece of the first edition of Andrea Palladio's *I Quattrolibri Dell'Architettura* (1570).

The market for such books was extensive. When the second edition of Giacomo Leoni's English translation of Palladio's *Four Books* was published in 1721 – the first complete version of the work in the language – the young Thomas Coke, who had completed his Grand Tour only three years before and had plans for building Holkham already swimming around in his head, was among the 141 subscribers. With him in the list, as well as fellow gentlemen and numerous merchants, were building practitioners: Henry Joynes, the King's clerk of the works at Kensington Palace; the London surveyor James Gould, and his son-in-law, the young mason and aspiring architect George Dance (1695–1768).[29] Other masons, joiners, carpenters and bricklayers also bought the book. If they were to take the initiative in the execution of fashionable designs, they could no longer depend upon knowledge gained by experience, handed down from master to journeyman and apprentice, but had to acquaint themselves with the literary sources and pattern books of the new style. Folio volumes were produced for the gentleman's library. Design details were republished in popular, small-sized manuals for builders, and specialist trade books appeared, such as Francis Price's *Treatise on Carpentry*, William Salmon's *Palladio Londiniensis* and Batty Langley's *The Builder's Jewel*.

In the absence of a formal architectural academy in England, the Office of Works was the key source of systematic training. Christopher Wren, himself a pioneer of the scientific method, developed it as a putative school after 1669. It was a route to professional status for building craftsmen such as the contemporaries Thomas Ripley (*c.* 1683–1758), a carpenter, the joiner Henry Flitcroft (1697–1769) and the mason Roger Morris (1695–1749). They caught the eyes of influential patrons and their careers prospered. Ripley advanced with the protection of Sir Robert Walpole, Flitcroft under the aegis of Lord Burlington, and Morris with Henry Herbert, ninth Earl of Pembroke. Provincial master-craftsmen too, through the execution of the plans of metropolitan designers, had the opportunity to achieve professional independence. With the undoubted advantage of practical experience of building and its organisation, the most successful also had qualities enabling them to deal easily with aristocratic patrons and building workers alike. They included the Smith brothers, William (1661–1724) and Francis (1672–1738), mason and bricklayer respectively and leading Midland master builders, the Norfolk bricklayer Matthew Brettingham (1699–1769), the self-taught Yorkshireman John Carr (1723–1807), and John Johnson (1732–1814), the Leicester-born joiner.

The influence of the Office of Works declined with the dismissal of Wren in 1717 and the death of Vanbrugh in 1726, but it remained a base for influence through the filling of posts by patronage. Furthermore, the imposition of the Palladian 'dictatorship' was greatly helped by Lord Burlington's capture of the Office in the 1730s. With stylistic discipline inherent in building to Palladian models, individual craftsmen became subordinate to a single controlling mind, and from 1730 the architect as a professional design supervisor emerged. Notwithstanding John Webb's training by Inigo Jones, pupillage in an architect's office only developed in the second half of the eighteenth century, becoming usual by the third quarter. James Paine (1717–1789) had introduced the practice from 1756, Sir William Chambers (1723–1796) possibly from 1758, and Sir Robert Taylor (1714–1788) from 1768.[30] Yet the old practices died hard. Sanderson Miller (1716–1780), financially independent at the age of twenty-one and a pioneer of the picturesque Gothic style, demonstrated that the amateur architect, albeit with professional assistance, had by no means disappeared after 1750. Frederick Augustus Hervey (1730–1803), fourth Earl of Bristol and Bishop of Derry, showed that the amateur architect builder also survived, with Ballyscullion, his vast neoclassical Irish house, and Ickworth (Suffolk), largely funded by the income from his Irish see (Plates 85–86).[31]

By the 1770s the character of the architectural profession was changing profoundly, gradually approaching the form we recognise today. With economic expansion and the growth of towns came a wealth of new building opportunities controlled not by individuals but by committees, constructing hospitals, town halls and a whole range of public buildings. Country house building patronage itself also became broader and less exclusive – the old landowning class had already erected its seats and newcomers to its ranks were increasingly prominent among the builders. In parallel, the role of the architect became more closely defined. The architect filled the gaps in the architectural education and taste of these new men. In an expanding market place in which fashion became ever more capricious, architects, hitherto dependent upon patronage, were themselves now courted by clients.

The professional architect increasingly distanced himself from those who had risen through the craftsmen's ranks. The Architects' Club, founded in 1791 at the instigation of James Wyatt, Henry Holland, George Dance and Samuel Pepys Cockerell, was a step on the road to professional organisation. It was also deliberately exclusive.[32] There was the social motive of not wishing to be associated with masons and joiners. For the craftsmen, the particular advantages they had brought to architecture – knowledge of materials, prices and building practice – became less relevant as the building industry crystallised into more specialised and professional elements. By the early nineteenth century the able and ambitious tradesmen, who hitherto might have sought to become architects, were more likely to achieve their entrepreneurial aspirations as general contractors. In this period, the permutation of the range of levels of involvement an architect might have with construction, and with the diverse attitudes, expectations and personalities of the clients, generated a bewildering variety of possibilities for the organisation of building. The architect's responsibility might end with the provision of a design, but he also might supervise building; or even go as far as contracting to erect the structure itself.

In spite of their increasing professional identification, eminent architects paid a variable level of attention to their commissions. James Wyatt (1746–1813) (Plate 55) raised the level of an architect's detachment from his clients to an art form. His nephew Jeffry told Joseph Farington that 'when a commission to build a house ... is proposed to him by a nobleman or gentleman by whom he has never before been employed, he will eagerly attend to it till he has got all the instructions necessary for the commencement of the work, but then he becomes indifferent to it'.[33] Wyatt's practice, the most extensive of its day, is evidence that his notorious irresponsibility and unbusinesslike behaviour were more than adequately balanced by his genius and charm. Nevertheless, complaints could be bitter. The exasperated William Windham of Felbrigg wrote with total candour on 23 November 1793:

> It is near two years since you undertook a business for me neither requiring, nor admitting of, delay; and which you have not done yet. I have written to you no less than five letters desiring to know, whether you meant to do this, or not: and you have returned no answer. You may perhaps think that this is a mark of genius, and the privilege of a man eminent in his profession: but you must give me leave to say, that it must be a profession higher than that of an Architect, and eminence greater than that of Mr Wyatt, that can make one see in this proceeding anything but great impertinence, and a degree of neglect, that may well be called dishonest.[34]

The experience of Sir John Rous of Henham in Suffolk was scarcely more encouraging.[35] Rous knew of Wyatt's work in Suffolk. Indeed, in February 1782, Rous dined at Ickworth with Sir Charles Kent, for whom the architect had worked at Fornham, Sir Gerard Vanneck of Heveningham Hall, the interior of which was regarded as Wyatt's decorative masterpiece, and William Hervey. The editor of the latter's journal commented that 'this party would seem to be a sort of

PLATE 55.
James Wyatt, by
his fellow
architect George
Dance the
younger, 1795.

building committee'.[36] Rous must also have been aware of the less favourable aspects of Wyatt's reputation, for his letters reveal an increasing level of frustration even before building began. In 1791 Rous took desperate measures. He wrote to a friend: 'called yesterday at Mr Wyatt's. The maid said he was out, but seeing his hat, I broke into his office, where I found him ... fighting off going down with me on Monday.'[37] Wyatt, however, knew how to flatter a client and Rous was unable to resist his architect's effusiveness: 'The divisions, dimensions and plans ... I executed and I am much flattered by Mr Wyatt's thinking he cannot make them better nor alter one chimney, door, or window from what I have marked.' There is no evidence that the architect ever visited Henham (Plate 56).

He was paid a commission equivalent to 5 per cent of his estimate of £12,000 for the house (it cost over £21,000 in the event), but neither Wyatt's travelling nor any other expenses are recorded in the meticulous set of accounts which survives.[38]

Wyatt's insouciance was notorious, but generally incompetence amongst architects was not unknown. Yet the increasingly professional practices of architects reveal that clients, a difficult and motley group, could rely upon them for the direction of their building projects to a far greater extent than a century earlier. With a professional practice second only to Wyatt's, the relations of John Soane (1753–1837) (Plate 57) with his clients were as punctilious as Wyatt's were neglectful. His estimates were based on quotations from tradesmen and checked against price books, drawing on his experience of earlier projects and the standardisation of design details.[39] He was a tireless traveller, often journeying by night coach to leave more time for consultation with his clients. He was a young man when he made no fewer than seventeen visits to Ryston Hall (Norfolk), which he remodelled for Edward Pratt in the 1780s; at the end of his career, well in his seventies, he still set himself a punishing schedule, making ten visits to Purney Sillitoe's Pell Wall House (Shropshire), over 150 miles from London, sometimes

PLATE 56.   Henham Hall, Suffolk (James Wyatt, 1792–98, demolished), by J. P. Neale, 1820.

PLATE 57.
Sir John Soane,
by Sir Thomas
Lawrence, 1829.

rising as early as 3.30 a.m.[40] Soane had made the Grand Tour in his youth. John
Carr (1723–1807), the son of a West Riding quarry owner, started life as a stonemason. Self-taught, he became the best-known architect in the north of England
in the second half of the eighteenth century. A disciple of the Burlington-Kent
school somewhat lacking in originality, his complete reliability was a comfort to
his many clients (he was associated with building or altering eighty country houses
in Yorkshire alone) and a towering beacon to the growing number of those
aspiring to the architectural profession in the provinces. Twice Lord Mayor of
York, and a justice of the peace, leaving a massive fortune of £150,000, he acted
for many years as a contractor as well as architect. He also enjoyed commissions

to build the whole range of buildings sanctioned by landed gentry and urban elites alike – assembly rooms, racecourse grandstands, churches, hospitals, asylums and bridges. Appropriately, he was the only provincial architect among the four men invited to become honorary members of the London Architects' Club.[41]

Soane himself in his writings was an outspoken critic of what he regarded as unprofessional conduct. In 1788 he defined the architect's duties:

> The business of an architect is to make the designs and estimates, to direct the works, and to measure and value the different parts; he is the intermediate agent between the employer, whose honour and interest he is to study, and the mechanic, whose rights he is to defend. His position implies great trust; he is responsible for the mistakes, negligences, and ignorance of those he employs; and above all, he is to take care that the workmen's bills do not exceed his own estimates.[42]

Through the example of his own business procedures, his lectures at the Royal Academy as Professor of Architecture and his influence upon his pupils, Soane made a significant impact upon the next generation of architects and a major contribution to the raising of the standards of professional practice.[43] Earlier, James Paine (Plate 58) and John Carr had set more prosaic examples but had nevertheless pursued highly successful careers. As a result their patrons, unlike Roger North or William Blathwayt struggling to build on their own account around 1700, could rest a good deal more easily as their creations rose before them.

Until clients could look to architects for reliable protection against bad workmanship and rapacious contractors, the prospective builder was well advised to gain an understanding not only of architectural aesthetics but also of the intricacies of contracting and construction. There was no shortage of models for the organisation of a building project. Sir Balthazar Gerbier (1592–1663), whilst offering the advice on layout that 'Too many stairs and back-doores (as the old English proverb) makes thieves and whores', was practical in his recommendations. Buy your own materials, he counselled, contract for measured work, and fix a time for completion.[44] Wren weighed the alternative ways of paying building workers in 1681.[45] Paying men by the day revealed when they were lazy, but it was recognised that men thus employed had little incentive to finish the work. William Blathwayt, when frustrated by slow progress at Dyrham (Gloucestershire) in 1703, observed typically of his London joiner, Hunter, that he 'intends never to have finished the work but to linger in the country at my expense'.[46] Wren, in common with most of his contemporaries, preferred building by measure, establishing prices beforehand and valuing work at different stages as building proceeded. It was necessary, however, to employ a skilled and trustworthy measurer. Lastly, it was possible to contract 'by the great', that is agree to a fixed price. In the absence of detailed building specifications and bills of quantities, estimates of cost were generally based on past projects, as nearly comparable as

PLATE 58. James Paine and his son, by Sir Joshua Reynolds.

possible. For planning purposes this could be acceptable but, for anything but
the simplest of projects, the procedure was hardly a reliable basis for contracting.
If a contractor found that he could not do a job for the price he had agreed, he
was likely to skimp on the work; if he used sub-contractors, he would be tempted
to reduce their payments to increase his own profit, creating a situation ripe for
cheeseparing.

Pratt argued that overspending generally followed an owner's lack of providence
or of ignorance. If he had neither skill, time nor patience to superintend building,
he should get an experienced, honest surveyor to do it for him.[47] North thought
such men rare. It was wise to separate the buying of materials from their use.
He preferred working by the great, but recognised the difficulty in making the
bargain because it required a good understanding of building work.[48] First, it was
necessary to calculate all parts of the house, then have a contract which defined
each party's obligations. Pratt would not, for example, pay for the workers'
journeys or the carriage of their tools; scaffolding was also their responsibility.
The distance from which materials were to be carried at the workers' expense
had to be specified. Accounts should be settled at the completion of each floor;
and if new pay rates were agreed for alterations to the original plan, they then
applied only to the new part.

Many landowners entered the world of contracting and building when, performing their roles of justice of the peace or poor law guardian, they became involved
with the maintenance of a county's bridges, or the construction of public buildings
such as prisons, court houses and workhouses.[49] As major contributors to the
poor rates and first in line when loans were needed to carry out public works,
they had an incentive to manage projects effectively and to secure the best possible
bargains. For bridges, for example, the competitive tendering element was a
statutory condition as early as 1739, when justices were required to accept 'the
most reasonable price or prices' after public notice had been given at quarter
sessions.[50] A single contractor was often used for the erection of large public
buildings. Bulcamp House of Industry, one of a series of large innovative institutions built for the relief of the poor in East Anglia in the second half of the
eighteenth century, was built in 1765 on land sold to the directors by John Rous
of Henham. The building contract was agreed after competitive tender but,
characteristically, the tentative nature of the plans and changes made during
construction meant that the final cost of the shell of the workhouse, £11,033, far
exceeded the contract price of £6847 16s. 6d.[51] When Rous's son came to rebuild

the family seat twenty-five years later, his father's experience could hardly have encouraged him to favour competitive tendering or a single contractor. Although a single contract for a lump sum was simpler and offered the apparent attraction of determining the cost beforehand, it had serious disadvantages, as the Leicestershire county surveyor William Parsons pointed out in 1826. He favoured payment by measurement and valuation of work done 'for large buildings of an unusual character and description'. When changes were inevitably made during construction, it was a considerable inconvenience having to change a contract. Measurement and value also assured the contractor that he would be paid fairly for the work he did, whereas a general contract, however carefully the estimates were prepared, would not. Parsons cited the London Custom House, designed by David Laing in 1812 to replace Thomas Ripley's building, which was incommodious and later destroyed by fire in 1814. The lowest tender was accepted: £165,000 for the carcase and foundations and £2050 for additional stone work. Between 1813 and 1829 £435,000 was spent, the climax of the scandal being the collapse of the building itself in 1824–25. Constant additions and improvements meant that the original contract had to be abandoned and the building instead measured and valued. This example of the winning of a contract with a low tender and the exploitation of variations to make a profit could well have applied to any country house project for which the same contracting route was chosen.[52]

Many an estate owner acted as his own builder, directly recruiting craftsmen and labour, and arranging a combination of fixed-price contracts, piece work and day work, according to the nature of the job. The involvement of the architect, if one was used at all, might end with the provision of a design. He might, however, recommend skilled tradesmen and clerks of the works, handle queries related to the execution of the work and pay supervisory visits to the site. When William Blathwayt (?1649–1717), King William III's Secretary at War, rebuilt Dyrham, the new west front begun in 1692 was designed by the obscure Samuel Hauduroy. An agreement made with a London joiner, Robert Barker, stipulated that his instructions were to come from Blathwayt himself, or his clerk John Povey. When Blathwayt continued with the replacement of the east side of the Tudor house, he exercised his prerogative as a senior civil servant to employ an architect from the Office of Works and chose its Comptroller, William Talman (1650–1719) (Plate 59). Talman performed at least a consulting role for the stable block, and provided a design for the new east front. A contract of 12 August 1698 with the carpenter Edward Wilcox (who had worked under Talman at Hampton

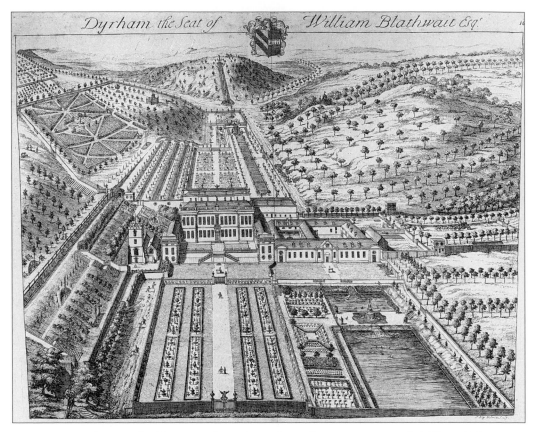

PLATE 59.   Dyrham Park, Gloucestershire (Samuel Hauduroy, 1692–94, and William Talman, 1700–3) by John Kip (paid £6 9s. 0d. by William Blathwayt on 20 September 1710).

Court and Kensington Palace) provided that disputes should be referred to the architect.[53] Talman visited Dyrham in 1698, meriting the provision of half a buck for his entertainment, and was on the list of Blathwayt's 'particular friends' for whom withdrawals of wine from the cellar could be made. But he may have left the execution of the design to Wilcox. The architectural solecism committed in the central archway of the stable block by omitting the entablature of the Tuscan columns and running the abaci together, 'if the result of intention, could only come from Talman, if of ignorance from Wilcox'.[54] On the first floor of the east front, the mason mistook the architect's intentions and placed two of the blind balustrades below the wrong windows.[55]

   Blathwayt chose to manage the rebuilding of Dyrham himself, in spite of the complication of having to do so by letter from London, or even from the

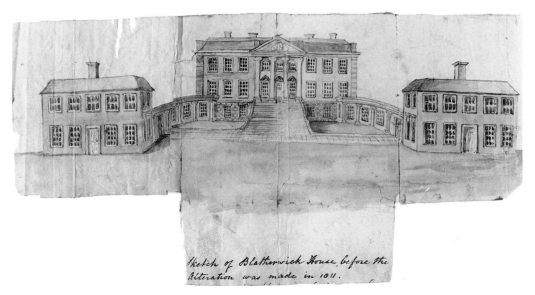

Sketch of Blatherwick House before the
Alteration was made in 1811.

PLATE 60.   Blatherwyke Hall, Northamptonshire. A sketch of the house (Thomas Ripley,
1720–24) made in 1811 before its alteration (demolished).

Netherlands when campaigning with King William III. Henry O'Brien of Blather-
wycke Hall in Northamptonshire preferred the more straightforward route of
employing a local builder to execute his architect's design. O'Brien, a younger
son who had just secured an advantageous marriage to an heiress, contracted
with Richard Wright, a timber merchant of Castor near Peterborough, some
eleven miles distant, to build his new house for a fixed price, 'according to the
plans and designs' of Thomas Ripley (Plate 60). It was one of Ripley's earliest
private commissions. The contract, signed on 26 July 1720, embraced clauses to
protect both client and builder. Wright was to supply materials commonly associated with estate sources – stone, lime and brick. He was allowed to quarry
stone in the park, burn lime there, and extract clay and sand for brick-making.
O'Brien was to buy deals, thus eliminating the middleman's profit if Wright had
supplied them. The responsibility for the cost of changes in plan, a notorious
problem, was defined as O'Brien's, while Wright was to pay for the reinstatement
of unsatisfactory work. The roof was to be covered within fourteen months and
Wright was to be paid in instalments, starting with £500 on account, with further
payments made at defined stages of the work, making a total of £3000 in all.
Each party was protected against default by the other, agreeing to a bond of
£2000. The house cost rather more than the contract price, presumably because

of changes requested by O'Brien. Wright's receipts, including a final payment of
£871 11s. 2d. on 15 April 1727, came to £3838 2s. 5¾d.[56]

Prospective builders sometimes secured more than one design and subjected
the estimates to close scrutiny. In the 1750s the third Earl Fitzwilliam envisaged
the rebuilding of the south front of sixteenth-century Milton House, Northamptonshire. He obtained designs from two architects, Henry Flitcroft and Matthew
Brettingham. Both were costed by a local builder, John Sharman.[57] In sending a
detailed estimate to Lord Fitzwilliam, Sharman disclosed an openness unusual
for his trade: 'I have sent an Estimate of particulars, according to Mr Brettingham's
Draught, Which if it be made publick, I must expect to be condemn'd, both by
Surveyors & Workmen ... for setting forth the Mystrey of every man's Business
in so clear a light ... which I imagine your Lordship will not Obtain, from any of
your Surveyors.'[58] Sharman claimed to have measured every part of the work
and fixed prices that would allow the tradesmen to execute their work in the best
manner. If Lord Fitzwilliam had any suspicion that he would be led to greater
expense, Sharman offered to do the work for the stated price and to employ only
tradesmen approved by Fitzwilliam. The estimates were scrutinised by Lord
Fitzwilliam and he put questions to his steward which he 'thought proper to ask
Mr Sherman'.[59] He inquired, for example, what allowances had been made for
pulling down the kitchen and servants' hall to clear the way for laying the new
foundations, the depth of the foundations, the thickness of the walls, and what
was to happen to the roof on the old part of the building.

The existence of a building contract, however, was no guarantee that the parties
would not fall out. John Stonehouse of Radley House in Berkshire concluded
agreements, dated 28 June 1721 and 20 June 1724, with the masons William
Townsend and Bartholemew Risley to build his house. The division of responsibility for the supply and working of estate materials was defined.[60] Stonehouse
was to find lime, sand, gravel, brick, rubble stone, water, quarried Sunningwell
stone and carriage. The masons were responsible for workmanship, labour,
hoisting [lifting], setting, making mortar, scaffolding and tackle, and the carriage
of stone from a second quarry, Hodington. The business ended in disagreement.
Stonehouse paid them £1200 by 14 September 1724 and then contested a bill for
£49 2s. 5d. He argued that the masons had over-measured some work, and for
some other had charged unreasonably. Moreover, he could not be expected to
pay for surplus stone at the building site – which presumably the masons did
not wish to carry away. The case was still unresolved in January 1726/27, but

the cost of the lawsuit, £35 15s. 5d., approached the sum at issue, including £18 4s. 5d. for witnesses, who were plied with food and drink at the local ale houses, the Blue Boar and the Wheatsheaf.

Nor was the artistic outcome of a local builder's execution of an architect's design always acceptable. We have seen how the result at Dyrham may have been affected by local misinterpretation of the architect's intentions. When Lord Burlington provided his fellow East Riding landowner, Sir William Strickland, with designs for alterations to the south and west fronts of Boynton Hall, the local builder blundered. The amateur architect, Sir Thomas Robinson, related in 1768 how 'Lord Burlington gave him [Strickland] a beautiful design, with a Palladian roof, and an Attic Storey, instead of the old wretched and ugly roof of our Gothick ancestors – when the house was compleated, Sir William went down ... when alas he found the old fashioned roof, and many other material alterations from the plan'.[61]

Notwithstanding Sir William's experience, 'Most provincial centres', as John Summerson wrote, 'at this time had one leading figure, usually a mason who had "left off his apron", who led the way in design, who designed and built the bigger houses in the town and district and whose manner was copied by lesser men.'[62] Usually they could offer the client much closer attention than he could expect from a metropolitan architect and, with the use of favoured craftsmen for one project after another, establish in their localities a reputation for reliability, quality and reasonable cost . Many houses for which no architect can be identified were designed and built by skilled provincial craftsmen, men like Thomas Pritchard of Shrewsbury (1723–1777), who were well-placed to handle the myriad extensions and remodellings which kept country houses roughly and cheaply abreast of metropolitan fashion and developments in domestic design.[63]

Amongst the most celebrated provincial architect-builders were William Smith (1661–1724) and his brother Francis (1672–1738) of Tettenhall, Staffordshire, and later Warwick.[64] They designed and built entire houses and, although providing estimates of cost, preferred to work on a 'cost plus' basis. At Lamport (Northamptonshire), Francis Smith added a library wing in 1732–35 to the north of John Webb's additions of 1654–55. William Smith junior (1705–1747) completed a balancing south wing in the early 1740s.[65] Their patron, Sir Justinian Isham Bt, found all materials, having been provided with an estimate of requirements by the architect. When Francis Smith submitted a bill in 1736, the nature of the prevailing relationship between patron and architect/builder was revealed: 'For my trouble in drawing drafts, measuring and valuing the several workman's bills, I leave my reward to your honour.'[66] Far from securing an extra payment, he received only £306 1s. 3d. in 'full settlement' of an account for £324 4s. 11d. In another letter Smith wrote: 'for all of which trouble I have had no manner of allowance my usual pay from other gentlemen is one shilling in the pounds [5 per cent] but I wholly earn it your honour'.[67] This degree of deference, when set against John Rous's dealings with James Wyatt, is telling comment on the transformation of the client-architect relationship within a period of sixty years.

These provincial men did not work in isolation. Although none of them established building dynasties, they were often followed by others for whom they had provided training or with whom had close business relationships. Working under the Smiths and succeeding them as leading Warwick architect-builders were William Hiorne (1715–1758) and David Hiorne (c. 1712–1776). They built Delbury House (Shropshire) inexpensively in 1751–56 'by the great', subcontracting all work except masonry and joinery.[68] Joseph Pickford (1734–1782), the leading architect in Derbyshire, trained in London as a mason and architectural draughtsman, worked under Hiorne in Derbyshire on Foremark Hall in 1759.[69] Thomas Gardner (c. 1737–1804) of Uttoxeter was a Pickford pupil.[70] He built Strelley Hall (Nottinghamshire) for Thomas Webb Edge from 1789 to 1792. The sixteenth-century hall, which had been the family seat since the 1670s and was itself a replacement for a decayed fourteenth-century house, was rebuilt in 'plain Georgian style'. Gardner's businesslike approach made clear the division of responsibility between himself and his employer. He contracted to build the house for £1656 18s. 0d., exclusive of brick, timber and floor and stair boards already sawn, laths, scaffolding, chimney- pieces, and land carriage for all materials. 'I never include land carriage', Gardner wrote, 'as the party concerned has it in their power to get that done at a less expense', presumably using estate and tenant wagons and labour. He provided an estimate of the quantity of stone required, and wrote that about 5000 cubic feet of oak timber would be needed 'which you desired to be informed of that it might be cut down at the proper season'. He also defined how he wished to be paid: 'In my contracts of late years I find it more convenient to receive the money as expressed – as my foreman may have it at the stated times to pay workmen etc when I am not there.' 'Where there is housekeeping', he added, 'my foreman lives in the house.' The contract allowed for the payment of £1400 on account, in monthly payments of £100, starting in April 1790, with the balance to be paid on or before 1 January 1792 (Plates 130–31).

PLATE 61.   Lilburn Tower, Northumberland (John Dobson for Henry Collingwood Esq., at a
cost of £21,975 excluding stables, 1828), by John Wilson Carmichael.

For all but the grandest country house projects, the local dominance of builder-
architects in the provinces was underlined by the Newcastle architect John Dobson
(1787–1865) in his presidential address to the newly founded Northern Architectural
Association in 1859 (Plate 61).[71] Looking back over half a century to a time when
there was no employment for a professional architect in the counties of Northumberland and Durham, he recalled that 'the duties were performed by builders
alone, who united to their special business the profession of an architect'. An
architect, Dobson maintained, was then a superfluous luxury. 'When a gentleman
wanted a house erected, all he had to do was inform the builder', who would
produce a well-worn copy of James Paine's general plan. Criticising Paine's designs
for failing to provide protection from the cold blasts which 'our friends from the
south find too often occasion to complain of', Dobson observed that even in the
mid nineteenth century there were still men who preferred adherence to these
traditions rather than to the dictates of common sense. Nevertheless, he pointed
proudly to the enrolment of about thirty members in their Society of Architects
'as an unmistakable evidence of our great social and aesthetic progress'. The

professional architect had indeed emerged, even in remotest Northumberland, as successor to the diverse ranks of gentlemen amateurs, others who had received specific training, and promoted tradesmen. It was also, Dobson thought, now easier to answer the question: 'Who is an architect?'. He and his colleagues were anxious to provide a positive response to the further question: 'Do you need an architect?'. Nonetheless, the architect was still only one of the contributors to the building process and we now turn to consider parallel developments in building organisation.

In the first thirty years of the nineteenth century, beyond the world of the country house, the building industry, formed from a large number of small enterprises, was changing. Traditionally, when master-builders contracted for a whole building they directly supervised only members of their own craft, sub-contracting to other master-craftsmen for the rest of the project. Erecting a country house without unreasonable delays required massive expansions of normally small permanent workforces, hence the common practice of the direct recruitment of the scores of men required. Now large building enterprises emerged within which all crafts were managed by a single employer, the general contractor, enabling him to undertake the largest construction projects. In parallel, the roles of the participants in the building business, the architect, the builder and the client, were redefined. Professional specialisation saw the architect distance himself from direct involvement in building, emphasising his design responsibility and concern for the representation of his clients' interests. The traditional measurer was transformed into the professional quantity surveyor. These important developments were to affect the way in which the building of the Victorian country house was organised.

A massive expansion of military building in the French wars, and disquiet about the procedures used to control public expenditure, both for barracks and for the notoriously expensive, semi-publicly funded projects of the Prince Regent at Carlton House, Brighton Pavilion, Windsor Castle and Buckingham Palace, coupled with a general increase in demand for building, public and private, accelerated these changes. Building large barracks in relatively isolated locations posed problems of the organisation and management of men and materials familiar to the country house builder. Whereas an estate owner could provide an administrative infrastructure and resident supervision, however, the public client was often a remote government office in London. The vacuum at the site created an opportunity filled by the large-scale contract builder, employing all the men and arranging the supply of materials. Between 1796 and 1806 the builder Alexander Copland (1774–1834) was paid over £1,300,000 for such work.[72]

The model for the new type of general builder was Thomas Cubitt (1788–1855). As a master-carpenter, he was by 1815 undertaking the construction of whole buildings, typically sub-contracting for work outside his own trade. His experience when building the London Institution, where he faced a penalty if the work was not finished on time, convinced him of the need to eliminate his vulnerability to the performance of sub-contractors by creating a workforce of his own which would include all the building trades. Such an organisation, offering continuity of employment, especially to key foremen and clerks, could not be sustained by contract work alone. Cubitt therefore secured the future of his business by himself undertaking large-scale speculative developments from the 1820s.[73]

The rise of the large general contractor was made possible by a sustained demand for building in favourable economic conditions. It was also facilitated by the increasing preference of both public and private clients for competitive tendering for work to be carried out by one builder at a fixed cost. Large builders with comprehensive workforces and substantial capital resources were better equipped than smaller master craftsmen to contemplate the greater risks and outlay involved. These changes were felt at all levels of building activity.

Competitive fixed-price tendering was not an essential prerequisite for the rise of the general builder, nor did it necessarily mark the end of payment by measure. Alexander Copland was paid by the Barrack-Master-General according to the time-honoured principle of measure and value, prices for the various kinds of work being those current in the locality (witness the frequently revised editions of builders' price books – the bibles of measured work in the eighteenth century).[74] The prevailing assumption was that good work at a fair price was best obtained by adding a customary 15 per cent gross profit to the current cost of labour and materials. Fair perhaps, but when work started the client did not know the precise amounts of either; he therefore had to keep his own detailed sets of accounts. This problem could be eliminated, noted the 1806–7 Commission of Military Inquiry, by contracting for whole buildings at fixed sums. Initially expert opinion was divided. Traditional objections to the placing of a project in the hands of a single undertaker, plus fears of bad workmanship from sub-contractors, persisted. An examination of the Office of Works in 1812–13 found that they too commissioned work on the basis of measurement and value, with the safeguard that they drew up a select list of established tradesmen. Although the commissioners concluded in favour of competitive tendering, however, they still preferred it to be for measured work rather than that undertaken by 'the gross'. Yet lay opinion was shifting significantly. In 1828 the experts consulted by a select committee of the House of Commons scrutinising the Office of Works still argued for contracts by measure and value, although the process was complex and costly and often ended with litigation. The committee concluded, nevertheless, that the public interest might be best served by fixed-price contracting.[75]

Architects in particular had strong reasons for criticising the new system. Some of their number were far better designers than they were managers of building projects. Preparing a credible estimate of building cost when it was not usual practice to provide precise specifications in detail, upon which bills of quantities could be devised, was a source of difficulty for many of them. Yet John Nash, the leading architect of the Regency, was a supporter of contracting in the gross by a single undertaker. As an innovator in his profession, he unsurprisingly provided ammunition for the critics of the procedure by the well-advertised shortcomings in the execution of his design for the new Royal Mews in 1822–25. His plans were ill-prepared, necessitating changes after work had started; the contractor found himself in financial difficulties after pitching his tender too low; and the architect's supervision was inadequate, allowing the use of inferior materials and excessive claims beyond the contract for extras.[76] Nevertheless, such problems could be solved. Architects improved their professional standing by eschewing financial interest in building firms, and so could mediate on behalf of their clients between competing contractors. They also received support from professional quantity surveyors in the preparation of bills of quantities – key documents upon which sound estimates could be founded.

The long-running debate among architects about their role and status culminated in the formation of the Institute of British Architects in 1834. When defining an architect's duties nearly fifty years earlier, Soane had stated: 'If these are the duties of an Architect, with what propriety can his situation, and that of the builder or the contractor, be united?'[77] In expounding the need for an architect to maintain his integrity by avoiding any involvement with building or contracting, Soane in the 1780s was a voice crying in the wilderness. By 1835, when his statement was reprinted in his memoirs, his words were a text for the converted.

Contracting to build for a fixed sum relatively simple and repetitive, if often large buildings – barracks, hospitals, railway stations, or warehouses – was one thing. Building or altering a more complex structure, such as a royal palace or castle, a university college or a church, was quite another. But the elasticity of institutional purses was finite, and for such buildings the new contracting procedures were generally adopted. Designing, estimating and contracting to build country houses for frequently idiosyncratic clients was less straightforward. It is not surprising that the new procedures were accepted more slowly in a field where individualism reigned. Like their established aristocratic and gentry patrons, leading country house architects of the nineteenth century had been schooled in an environment where traditions had firm eighteenth-century roots and died hard. Edward Blore's career covered the years 1816 to 1847, William Burn's the remarkable span of 1814 to 1870, and that of Anthony Salvin from 1825 to 1879. Of the three, only Burn seems to have been a pupil of an established architect – Robert Smirke. Blore's and Salvin's entry into the profession was less formal and the active years of all three overlapped those of the inheritors of the more relaxed standards of the eighteenth century, men like John Nash (active 1777–1830) and Lewis Wyatt (active 1803–33). Minutely defined contracts based on fixed designs, rather than gentlemen's agreements about schemes which continued to evolve during construction, took longer to become the norm. Indeed, some men still had the confidence in a world of increasing professionalism to be their own architects. Charles Hanbury-Tracy, created first Baron Sudeley in 1838, rebuilt decayed Toddington Manor (Gloucestershire) to his own picturesque Gothic design in 1820–35. While attracting the plaudits of contemporary visitors, he had only himself to blame for the enormous expenditure of £150,000.[78] In the agricultural depression of the 1870s, the 24,000 acres held by the family were insufficient to offset the burden of the house and prevent the bankruptcy of his descendant, the fourth Lord Sudeley, in the 1890s.[79] Gregory Gregory (1786–1854), a nineteenth-century continental traveller with the collecting and building enthusiasm of an eighteenth-century Grand Tourist, employed Anthony Salvin in 1831 to turn his long-gestated plans for a new Jacobean mansion at Harlaxton (Lincolnshire) into reality. Building started in the following year but the design continued to evolve during construction. There was a change of architect in 1838, when Burn took over. The interior was decorated by teams of specialist craftsmen, including perhaps some recruited in Bavaria, to execute designs based on seventeenth-century German models which certainly owed more to Gregory than Burn.[80] No general contractor could have undertaken such a commission on a fixed-price contract. Another Salvin client changed his mind during the course of building. The architect's radical reorganisation of Alnwick Castle for the fourth Duke of

Northumberland was well under way when, in 1854, the duke wrote from Rome
directing that the internal decorations for his Edwardian castle were to be in the
Italian style of the fifteenth and sixteenth centuries. Although Salvin publicly
expressed his doubts about the propriety and practicability of this development,
his client's wishes were paramount.[81] Another amateur architect, Thomas Philip,
the second Earl de Grey (1781–1859), after inheriting Wrest Park (Bedfordshire)
in 1833, replaced the dilapidated house in 1834–39 with a Louis XV château designed
by himself.[82]

Others chose to ignore both builders and the contracting process by managing
themselves the execution of their architect's design, putting together a direct
labour force and supervising the construction process in a manner reminiscent
of the eighteenth century. In the case of Bearwood in Berkshire, built by the
proprietor of *The Times*, John Walter, between 1866 and 1874 at the enormous
cost of £130,000, the use of this obsolete procedure led to the familiar consequences
of overspending and a dispute between patron and architect about their precise
contractual relationship (Plate 62).[83] Ironically, it was Robert Kerr, professor of

PLATE 62.   Bearwood, Berkshire (Robert Kerr, 1866–74).

architecture and author of *The Gentleman's House* – a wordy protagonist for the professionalism of architecture, the systematic reorganisation of training and the theoretical exponent of best practice in the 1860s – who crucially failed to establish the basis for his remuneration before undertaking the commission. Kerr, after nearly a decade's work, which he asserted had been to the exclusion of all other, argued that he was entitled to charge 5 per cent on a hypothetical *contract* value of the building: not the actual cost, but one including the assumed cost of materials a contractor would have bought (if one had been employed) instead of using estate materials. Kerr further claimed that he was entitled to charge extra for exceptional trouble in the alteration of the design and drawings throughout the project. There was also the matter of travelling costs and incidental expenses. Furthermore, he argued that he had lost interest charges on deferred payments because the sums he had received had left virtually half his commission (as he calculated it) unpaid for eight or nine years. He concluded that this sorry situation could be rectified by the payment of 2 per cent beyond the usual 5 which 'ought to be satisfactory to both parties'. Surprisingly, Kerr did not know how much had been spent and had no basis for calculating his fee. He wrote to Walter: 'I have no right to enquire into your prime cost ... I am sorry to have to run the risk of overestimating the value of the house which may have been actually built more economically than its appearance when finished would lead one to suppose.' Kerr estimated that the house had cost 'a little under £200,000.'

Walter would have none of this. He had kept the accounts and stated that, in round figures, 'the whole expenditure upon the Mansion and its surrounding for which you are directly or indirectly responsible' came to £120,000, 'though I am happy to say it falls far short of the magnificent though ruinous ideal which you appear to have formed nevertheless it greatly exceeds the sum which I originally contemplated spending upon the work ... it exceeds twice the amount estimated by your surveyor Mr Freeman'. Far from agreeing to an additional commission, Walter believed that, with much greater reason and justice, he was entitled to make a deduction. After all, with no contractor involved, Kerr had escaped all trouble and responsibility in relation to the review of specifications, the estimation of quantities, the measurement of work and the settlement of disputes. Walter would not budge from his position that 5 per cent of £120,000 'in a case like the present one ... is more than an adequate remuneration for [an architect's] services'.

Although building a new house for a fixed sum was never universal practice, the use of general contractors became common. Nevertheless, the career of

PLATE 63.   Thomas Cubitt (unknown artist).

Thomas Cubitt (1788–1855) demonstrates that personal advance could still depend upon old-fashioned recommendation rather than competition (Plate 63). Cubitt's enterprise, competence and integrity was widely recognised, but the recommendation to Prince Albert for his employment from 1845 to 1848 as architect and builder for Osborne House, as a man 'untainted by any position as an official building tradesman', in fact may have come from Lord Lincoln, Chief Commissioner of Woods and Forests.[84] It is likely that, in turn, Prince Albert recommended Cubitt to the Prime Minister, Lord John Russell, to execute Blore's design for the enlargement of Buckingham Palace in 1846–50. Cubitt, basking in the success of completing Osborne to the complete satisfaction of the Queen and the Prince, made clear that, despite the employment of a single contractor being an innovation for royal palaces, he would not enter into competition with other tradesmen on prices. Payments were to be based on the old system of price and measurement. He also expected an assurance that he would be allowed to carry the whole building through to completion and that money would be advanced as the work proceeded.[85] It was Lord de Grey, whose involvement with Buckingham Palace has already been noted, who in turn proposed Cubitt to Lord Harrowby for the rebuilding of Sandon Hall, his Staffordshire house damaged by fire in 1848. Cubitt's London men adapted the local inn, The Dog, for use as a home by the Harrowbys during the six years of reconstruction. In fact, Cubitt's designs for the house were rejected as too old-fashioned. When Harrowby consulted William Burn, Cubitt, declining to be bound by competitive tendering, refused further involvement with the project.[86]

Architects inevitably became associated with particular contractors, just as in the eighteenth century they had continuously employed favoured, highly-skilled craftsmen. Thomas Cubitt and Sir Charles Barry were well acquainted for example, and the contracting firm founded by Thomas's brother William restored Crewe

Hall, badly damaged by fire in 1866, under Barry's son Edward Middleton. George Smith carried out a number of Anthony Salvin's country house commissions, including Dunster Castle, Petworth House and Thoresby Hall. Indeed, the contractor's own house, Paddockhurst in Sussex, was designed by Salvin. Another London contractor who worked with Salvin was George Myers (1803–1875), known as 'Pugin's Builder' because he worked principally for him (Plate 64). In 1851 Myers won in open competition the contract to build the carcase of Mentmore Towers to the design of Sir Joseph Paxton for Baron Mayer de Rothschild. His successful bid

PLATE 64. George Myers, 'Pugin's Builder'.

of £15,472 was just a foretaste of a long and profitable association with the Rothschild family who, by 1873, had paid Myers some £350,000 for building work.[87] From the 1850s it was increasingly common for small as well as large country house works to be placed with London contractors. Whereas Haveringland Hall (Norfolk) had been built in the 1840s in the traditional way by a directly recruited labour force supervised by a clerk of the works, when the house was extended in 1851 by London contractors, Messrs Thomas and William Piper, they worked to an agreed price and completion date. George Trollope and Sons, also London based, were employed in the same decade for alterations to the domestic offices, repairs and redecoration. When relatively modest work was needed in 1890 on the heating and lighting systems in the billiard-room, fixed-price bids were sought from no fewer than four different contractors.[88] Yet another well-known London firm of country house contractors, Holland and Hannen, finished the interior of T. H. Wyatt's Orchardleigh (Somerset) in 1859 for William Duckworth.[89] They secured the contract by competitive tender to rebuild the north-west front of Sir Charles Isham's Lamport Hall (Northamptonshire) under William Burn in 1861–62, extended Deene Park (Northamptonshire) for Lord Cardigan in 1865, again to T. H. Wyatt's designs, and built Shabden (Surrey) to those of E. M. Barry in 1871–73.[90]

Although there appears to have been an increased tendency by top-flight architects to employ London contractors, provincial architects and builders also conformed to the new procedures. They are revealed in the contract to rebuild Backford Hall (Cheshire) in the late 1840s.[91] Captain Edward Holt Glegg's neo-Elizabethan house was designed by John Cunningham; John and William Walter contracted to erect it in just under two years for £10,700, payable in seven instalments, the first six at defined stages of construction, and the last one month after completion. All changes had to be agreed with the architect and the client was protected against unreasonable claims for day-work payments because they would not be entertained unless certified by the clerk of the works in the week in which the claimed work was done. The contractor was responsible for repairs for six months after completion and each party undertook to pay £1000 for non-performance of the contract. The architect prepared drawings and working plans, and specified the work to be done. The schedule of quantities of materials was drawn up by John Faram, a Liverpool civil engineer and surveyor, for a commission of 1¼ per cent, half paid by the contractor. The proposals, when approved by the client, were passed to a clerk of the works for execution by the contractor.

This well-defined arrangement demonstrates that the division of responsibilities between client and contractor must be known if a reported 'building cost' is to be interpreted correctly. In this case Glegg undertook to level and excavate the site. He also supplied stone and paid for the local carriage of materials from the railway station, canal, and sand and gravel pits. On the other hand, the contractor provided labour and the payment of wages and lodgings, workmanship, materials delivered to the local station or canal wharf, sheds and coverings. He was liable for damage or loss of materials. He was also responsible for scaffolding, ladders, ropes, tools, tackle, implements and utensils, and for providing an office for the clerk of the works. The specification of work covered each trade separately. Some old materials were reused, and particular fittings specified: a hot-air apparatus from Walkers of Manchester was installed, designed to achieve a comfortable 65°F in the heated rooms when the outside temperature was a freezing 22°.

Captain Glegg no doubt recognised the advantages of dealing with a single contractor and knew in advance how much he had to pay. His experience was not universal. It might be expected that new recruits to the ranks of the landed gentry and aristocracy from industrial or commercial backgrounds would be more likely to approach building in a businesslike way. However, building aspirations and ample resources were a heady mixture. Business acumen was no guarantee that building costs would be kept within bounds, nor that the outcome would satisfy the client. Among nineteenth-century clients, the degree of architectural education or awareness that was a *sine qua non* for the eighteenth-century gentleman could also no longer be assumed. We have seen how John Walter's relationship with his architect foundered on the rocks of contractual imprecision and design uncertainty. In 1856 William Duckworth (1795–1876), beneficiary of a Lancashire fortune, flushed with the success of securing the Orchardleigh (Somerset) estate for £96,000, obtained a design for a new house from T. H. Wyatt (1807–1880).[92] Tenders for the carcase were obtained from five local builders. Bidding was close, the contract going to a Bradford-on-Avon builder with a bid of £9714, with wrought iron girders specified as having to be obtained from London for an additional £1479. Significantly, the more complex task of finishing the interior was not put out to tender, but given to the ubiquitous London contractors Holland and Hannen. Wyatt estimated that the cost would be three-fifths of the carcase cost, that is £6681. Thus the expected total for the house was £17,824. In the event, although the contractor kept to his price for the shell of the house, by 1864 extras had taken Duckworth's bill to £34,592, almost exactly twice Wyatt's original costings.[93]

At least Duckworth had chosen an experienced architect. Other clients ventured into the unknown. Samuel Jones Loyd (1796–1883), elevated to the peerage as Lord Overstone in 1850, was born into a banking family and possessed one of the largest fortunes of his day. From the 1830s he began to look forward to his retirement, reducing his dependence upon income derived from finance by buying large landed estates.[94] In the 1870s he enjoyed a rental income of over £58,000 per annum from nearly 31,000 acres, of which half were in Northamptonshire.[95] There he was persuaded by his wife to build a new house, Overstone Hall, in 1861–62 (Plate 65). For reasons best known to himself, he chose an obscure young architect, W. M. Teulon, brother of the better-known Samuel. Loyd's enormously successful background in business was no guarantee that his country house building project would proceed smoothly. It was not the cost of the house that concerned him but its design and execution. He bemoaned:

> The New House I regret to say, is the cause of unmitigated disappointment and vexation. It is an utter failure – We have fallen into the hands of an architect in whom incapacity is his smallest fault. The House tho' very large and full of pretension – has

PLATE 65.   Overstone Hall, Northamptonshire (W. M. Teulon, 1861–62), from *The Builder*, 1862.

neither taste, comfort nor convenience. I am utterly ashamed of it ... the principal rooms are literally uninhabitable – I shall never fit them up ... I grieve to think that I shall hand such an abortion to my successors.[96]

There were of course reliable architects and contractors in plenty. Successful commissions were achieved through the patronage of young talent. Country houses were, however, complex creations. Predicting the outcome of a building programme was not always possible. Certainly, the new contracting procedures did not remove all uncertainty. Soane's statement of the duties of an architect had touched on a crucial issue for the client. How would his project be executed and what control would he have over expenditure?

5

A Pleasure Not to be Envied

'The immediate and most obvious advantages of building are, employing many ingenious artificers, many industrious workmen and labourers of various kinds; converting materials of little value into the most stately productions of human skill; beautifying the face of countries; multiplying the conveniences and comforts of life.'

Sir William Chambers, writing in 1791.[1]

'How very little, since things were made,
Things have altered in the building trade.'

Rudyard Kipling, 'A Truthful Song'.[2]

However beguiling the prospect of creating a new house, or altering an existing one, the building of a country house was always a complex task in terms of planning, financing and management. The undertaking in reality was a formidable one. Often builders were rueful about the experience. '[There are] those who say, that a wise man never ought to put his finger into mortar', wrote Sir Balthazar Gerbier in 1662.[3] Daniel Finch, second Earl of Nottingham, the builder of Burley-on-the-Hill, was hardly more encouraging in 1701 when he advised Lord Normanby: 'Building ... is a pleasure your lordship will not envy me once you have tried it.'[4] Although more than a century later Sir Thomas Cullum, of Hardwick House in Suffolk, wisely took himself off to Rome while his house was being remodelled, he could not escape the warning to him conveyed by his banker, in the words of Miss Westrup (was she Sir Thomas's housekeeper?) amidst the turmoil at Hardwick: 'Pray sir, don't think of building, you can't tell the misery of it.'[5]

The prudent country house builder was therefore meticulous in the development of his plans. Whether it was the country squire desiring a comfortable but modish home for his family, the territorial magnate anxious to make a grand architectural statement about his political and social position, or the newcomer keen to display his wealth, talking to friends, consulting experts, looking at buildings, reading books, and considering the financial implications of the venture, was the route to perfection. Yet however carefully plans were laid, at the point of departure upon usually the biggest enterprise of his life, the country house builder ventured into potentially uncharted territory. As Henry Wilson of Stowlangtoft Hall in Suffolk wrote in the 1860s to Sir Thomas Fremantle, after completing his own house and anticipating Sir Thomas's undertaking: 'I rejoice at your determination, though I should be still better pleased if, like myself, you were stepping out of the mire instead of stepping into it.'[6] Plans themselves were not easy to formulate and, of course, they took years to execute. But it was the cost and management of projects which caused the most prolonged headaches for builders over the years. In the absence of reliable cost-estimating procedures, the drain on a builder's purse was difficult to predict.[7] They also found themselves engaging large, diverse workforces which lacked the customary discipline of their own estate employees. Large quantities of materials had to be secured from a wide range of sources and made available on site when needed. Assistance and support from someone well-versed in the reading of sets of architects' plans and detailed drawings, building techniques, man-management and the keeping of accounts was therefore essential. A key figure in building the country house, ideally combining all these talents, was the clerk of the works.

There were established precedents for the organisation of building projects, both large and small. In the king's service, the clerk of the works emerged as a specialist administrator during the course of Edward III's great building programme of the mid fourteenth century.[8] The clerks were distinguishable from the master craftsmen responsible for the technical direction of the work. They were not specifically trained for their role, but were increasingly drawn from the growing body of king's clerks, who moved from one royal duty to another. For men such as William of Wykeham, the appointment proved to be a stepping-stone for further advancement. Geoffrey Chaucer was another notable clerk of the works.[9]

The clerk's essential duty was to account for his expenditure, although it was a difficult process without the benefit of a regular system of estimates on the one hand and some predetermined allocation of money on the other. The clerks had other responsibilities. They organised the craftsmen, labourers, materials and transport necessary for the undertaking. They paid the workforce and maintained its discipline; they ensured the security of the building materials and oversaw the disposal of any surpluses. The clerk's role developed to embrace inspection of the works as well as accountancy, the title 'surveyor' being coupled with that of clerk in the patents of employment from 1421 onwards. In the sixteenth century it was to become the sole designation. Early in that century came the appointment of men who spent their whole career in the service of the king's works and, with the engagement of the master carpenter James Nedeham in 1532, a significant shift to the employment of technically qualified men.[10]

The scale of royal building led to increased differentiation of roles. Lay surveyors, not trained in writing and book-keeping, needed a staff of professional clerks. A purveyor acquired materials; a tallyman checked their arrival and looked after their security; another clerk oversaw the workmen and kept the books. When specialist knowledge was needed, craftsmen were deputed to inspect materials and fix rates for contracts. Progress clerks watched the pace of building so that targets were met.

Country house builders were aware of the importance of these tasks undertaken by the royal clerks-surveyors, but finding one man who could perform them all effectively was difficult. Gentlemen builders of the seventeenth and eighteenth centuries, for whom architecture was a polite accomplishment rather than a professional qualification, might have the knowledge, interest and time to cover much of the ground themselves. Sir Roger Pratt (1620–1685), 'The Ingenious Gentleman Architect', recognised the danger of overspending, and argued that it chiefly proceeded from a lack of providence or the ignorance of the builder. He recommended that: 'If estate owners have neither skill, time or patience to superintend building, better get an experienced honest surveyor.'[11] His near contemporary, Roger North (1653–1734), a builder himself and an intelligent and astringent commentator on current architectural practice, recommended that project supervision should not be delegated: 'if he leaves the affair to his surveyor ... he shall be miserably disappointed in charge as well as convenience'. North therefore envisaged that gentlemen should keep close personal control of their building projects.[12] Epitomising this approach, Thomas Worsley was his own architect and builder in the construction of Hovingham Hall from 1751 to 1778.[13] Similarly, John Buxton, the Norfolk amateur architect, remodelled his 1560s house, Channonz Hall, and designed and built two other villas for himself, Earsham Hall and Shadwell Lodge. Of the latter he wrote in 1727: 'The building goes forward very well, and I thank God I've yet strength enough to be with the workmen six or seven hours in the day and find much occation to be there not knowing how to depend upon the surveyor, who is often absent and as often when there liable to blunder.'[14] Few, however, are likely to have exceeded the total commitment of William Wrightson in the 1740s, an old man who daily directed the building of Cusworth Hall, on a bleak hillside overlooking Doncaster, from a bo'sun's chair fixed to the scaffolding.[15]

There were many owners who had neither the time nor inclination to involve themselves on the scale of Worsley, Buxton and Wrightson. Some were non-resident for years on end, some deeply immersed in government business. Also, as the roads improved, the gentry went up to London and Bath more frequently. Therefore, in the late seventeenth and early eighteenth centuries, when an increasing number of houses were either being rebuilt or remodelled, it was common for estate stewards to act as clerks of the works.[16] Their particular assets were local knowledge of the estate and the surrounding region. They were also deemed trustworthy, as members of the master's 'family' and administrators of estate income.

Given a competent steward, a master's absence was certainly no bar to his detailed involvement in building construction and maintenance. The letters that frequently passed between Lord Fitzwilliam and Francis Guybon, his steward at Milton in Northamptonshire, show that, although Fitzwilliam did not once set foot in Milton during the twelve years covered by the correspondence, the able Guybon kept his master well informed about all aspects of estate activity, and Fitzwilliam could effectively manage Milton affairs from the capital.[17] Guybon engaged, supervised and paid building craftsmen, although the responsibility for reports on Milton House and discussions with the architect William Talman, who inspected Milton in 1688, were passed to Fitzwilliam's chaplain, the Revd Jeremiah Pendleton. In the 1720s to 1740s, Daniel Eaton, steward at Deene in Northamptonshire for the third and fourth Earls of Cardigan, was well-versed in surveying, building technology and brickmaking.[18] He prepared estimates of cost for building work, and was additionally enrolled in the Court of Common Pleas as an attorney. Such skills would have been of particular value in negotiations with farm and building labourers and craftsmen, for it was Lord Cardigan's practice to employ few regular full-time men, instead contracting for nearly all work 'by the great', a fixed price being agreed with individuals or groups of men.

William Blathwayt had considerably less confidence in his estate staff when he rebuilt Dyrham in Gloucestershire from 1692 to 1703. Although he was deeply involved in the planning and execution of the project, his duties as Secretary at

War to William III, and his attendance upon the King during his summer campaigns in Flanders from 1692 to 1701, meant that building operations were conducted by correspondence. Building was supervised by local men acting as clerks of the works, with his agent, Charles Watkins, supplementing the clerks' reports with his own statements of progress. Blathwayt's clerks of the works managed the workforce and oversaw the acquisition and movement of materials, but they seem to have lacked technical knowledge of building. His acknowledged administrative skills in fact proved to be no guarantee that the notoriously difficult task of supervising building workers would be accomplished without problems. Unwilling to delegate authority, he forced his diffident and easily confused staff to refer the smallest details for his decision.[19]

It is not surprising that the additional responsibilities associated with a major building project were sometimes accepted with reluctance.[20] Indeed, it is difficult to see how a full-time steward could also perform the onerous duties of a clerk of the works. It might be possible where the relatively small scale of the project, or the desired rate of progress, meant that the work could be handled by the estate workforce or a small number of trusted master-craftsmen.

When clerks of the works were employed, they might come from a number of different backgrounds, with many of the non-professionals doing the job only once. They might be clerics, estate tenants, stewards or craftsmen, independent craftsmen, or pupil architects. In exceptional cases, like that of Thomas Ripley, the role shaded into that of executant architect (Plate 66). A London-based master carpenter and, most importantly, a protégé of Sir Robert Walpole, Ripley held a string of official positions in the King's Works from 1716. He was already architect of the London Custom House (1718), and probably that at Liverpool, before he began supervising the construction of Houghton Hall in Norfolk for Sir Robert in 1721. Not only was he responsible for the superb quality of the

PLATE 66. Thomas Ripley, by Joseph Highmore, 1746.

execution of Colen Campbell's designs during the house's construction between
1721 and 1735, he also seems to have adapted them, especially those of the stables;
to the extent that Isaac Ware, admittedly an apprentice of Ripley's, claimed in
1735 that Ripley was the architect of Houghton. He was certainly responsible for
nearby Wolterton and for alterations at Raynham in the 1720s.[21] Gaining experience
of architectural design and construction through the position of clerk of the works,
thereby attracting a patron's eye, was important to other able young men from
craft backgrounds: William Etty at Castle Howard, James Paine at Nostell Priory,
John Carr at Kirby Hall, William Thornton at Beningborough Hall and Samuel
Wyatt at Kedleston Hall, for example.[22] On the other hand, when Edmund Rolfe
greatly extended Heacham Hall in Norfolk in the 1770s, probably never employing
more than two dozen men on site at any one time, the work was supervised by
Charles Hay, a small farmer who seems to have managed the estate.[23] It was
unlikely, however, that anyone other than a full-time clerk of the works, thoroughly
trained in building practices, could have effectively supervised big projects involv-
ing a sizeable workforce of directly-recruited men, which, as we shall see later,
constantly altered in composition not only because tasks changed as a project
proceeded but also because of the transitory nature of building workers.

At Henham Hall, entirely rebuilt in the 1790s for Sir John Rous, the clerk of
the works was the estate carpenter, Rufus Marsden.[24] At peak periods in the
construction of the house he was supervising eighty men. Unusually, the weekly
statements or pay-bills he prepared have almost all survived, covering the period
of building from March 1792 to early 1800. They take a form familiar for most
big building projects throughout the period, listing the names of workers, the
number of days they were employed, and their wage-rates, earnings and expenses
(Plate 67). The men are usually grouped by trade, although in the Henham case
this is rarely stated explicitly.

It is the recording of other payments which throws further light on the key
organisational role of the clerk of the works beyond the supervision of labour.
Marsden travelled to Yarmouth where he bought deals, battens, scaffold poles
and mahogany veneers. He arranged the transport of the goods to the building
site, and the movement of considerable quantities of timber from the estate's
woods. He paid the contractors, leisurely in the mode of the eighteenth century,
with sums advanced by Rous or his agent. In all, Marsden accounted for the
payment of some £17,200 over seven years, more than 80 per cent of the money
spent building the house passing through his hands.

£ s D

January 24th Brought forward — — — 124-12-10

Thomas Rowe 5 Days — — — 0-6-8

Thomas Skipper 5 Days — — — 0-6-8

James Loddimore 5 Days — — — 0-6-8

William Bens 5 Days — — — 0-4-2

to alowance for Bear of 72-17-2 in this Bill at 2/ ⅌ Pound 7-17-8

14th January 1795 Paid mr Hurray of yarmouth for Deels } 120-19-0
these Deels bought 27th august 1794 — —

Elizabth Marsde Expences of Iorney to yarmouth to pay } 0-3-0
mr Hurrays Bill and to Buy a bed for Greenhous —

January 7th Paid David Cparman for the frigth of 2 Logs } 0-16-6
of mohogeney Recid these 2 Logs Octobr 17th 1794 —

Ditto Paid John Seger for the frigth of 2 Logs of mohogany } 0-13-0
these 2 Logs Recivd november 11th 1794 — —

January 9th Paid David Cparman for the frigth wharf } 6-1-8
and Sufrige of 10 Tun of Slate Recivd these Slats
august 15th 1794 — —

Paid for garding the Buiding 4 Sundays at 1/ ⅌ Sund 0-4-0

Paid for a Letter from mr Grifis the Slater — — 0-0-6

to 4 lb of Candels to Cellors — — 0-2-8

£ 262-15-0

Jaady 24 1795 Recd the Contents by Payment of Mr Dressed

Rufus marsden

PLATE 68.   Eshton Hall, Yorkshire (George Webster, 1825–27 and 1830s).

In the absence of a suitable candidate from his estate or, increasingly, a recommendation from an architect, the prospective builder of a country house might have recourse to his friends, or a business acquaintance. Mathew Wilson of Eshton (Plate 68) in Yorkshire recorded in his day book in 1824 that his supplier of timber, 'John Settle of Skipton, recommended me to one Mawson, a joiner and house carpenter. Agreed with him for 35s. per week until my house finished if he conducts himself well, very strongly recommended.' In the margin of the book Wilson scribbled 'To be a foreman'.[25]

For clients with no architectural or building knowledge, however, and who had no suitable estate servant to call upon, it was not enough simply to recruit a clerk of the works. It was necessary to define his responsibilities and determine to whom he reported. Was he the client's agent or, if an architect was involved, was he his man? If this was unclear, the position of the clerk of the works as 'pig in the middle' could be very uncomfortable and the consequences serious. Building was an activity, inherently difficult to manage, which often led to friction between the parties involved. It does not necessarily follow that enterprises were always beset by problems, despite the frequency of cries of anguish from disgruntled clients. The architect Henry Holland (1745–1806) was complimented in 1801 by Samuel Whitbread, for whom he built Southill, for the 'very handsome manner in which you have treated me throughout the whole business', adding that never had he transacted any that had given him such pleasure and satisfaction.[26] Conflict, especially when litigation was envisaged and where papers survive, is inevitably better documented than amity. Nevertheless, apart from the recital of difficulties, the study of problem projects reveals much about the changing expectations of clients, and business patterns across our period.

When Humphry Repton was engaged by George Freke Evans to make alterations to Laxton Hall (Northamptonshire) in the 1800s, problems soon arose concerning the clerk of the works.[27] Their crux was supervision. Repton provided the first clerk, John Collett, whom Freke Evans, already wary of Repton's delays and his expense claims, believed to be incompetent from the start. Repton, with no training yet perhaps the wordiest member of the architectural profession, shrugged off the matter, blaming jealousies and ignorance among the tradesmen. Eighteen months later, Freke Evans himself seems to have attempted to find a replacement through the master carpenter on the site. As the latter explained, it was not easy, for he reckoned that out of forty workmen it was rare to find more than one who was fitted to act as clerk of the works. A man might be a tip-top carpenter but useless at keeping accounts and directing a large, assorted workforce. At this point Repton employed the fifty-seven year old, and presumably vastly experienced, Uriah Woolcot. He proved to be no more acceptable. Repton, increasingly exasperated by his exacting client, sought to distance himself from the problem. His view was that Evans clearly knew what was going on from day to day, whereas he, not receiving copies of Woolcot's report to Evans, had no intelligence about detail and progress until the clerk of the works was in serious trouble. Somewhat nonchalantly, Repton claimed that (as far as he was concerned) no news was good news. He expected that if they were not covered by the architect's plans, points of detail could be settled on site between the clerk and the client. This clearly left the latter in a vulnerable position.

Generally, it was a matter of judgement how much detailed support the clerk needed from the architect. However, if the former was not up to the job – and was reporting to a client with little experience of building – trouble ensued if he was not well supervised. At Sheringham (Norfolk), built in the 1810s again to

Repton's designs (Plate 69), the first clerk of the works, the local workhouse master, a man diligent to a fault according to the enthusiastic client, Abbot Upcher, allowed the premature removal of wooden arches supporting the cellar roof after incessant rain.[28] To everyone's surprise and dismay it caved in. Who was to blame? The unfortunate clerk of works, the workmen, Upcher himself or the ever-voluble Repton? Or was it the impossibility of closely supervising an inexperienced clerk of the works one hundred and thirty miles away from Repton's base at Hare Street near Romford?

Also in the early nineteenth century, when the architectural profession faced criticism of its inability to control costs, and agonised about its relationship with general building contractors, two well-documented examples from the career of Lewis Wyatt are especially revealing on the subject of building supervision and the relationship between client, architect and clerk of the works.[29] By the 1820s he was an architect of considerable experience both public (he held positions in

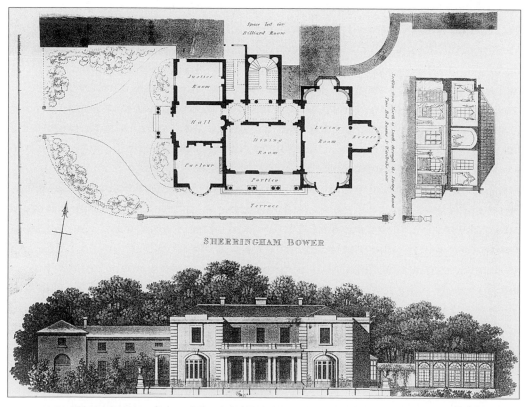

PLATE 69.   Sheringham Hall, Norfolk (Humphry and John Adey Repton, 1813–17, completed 1838–40) plan and elevation.

PLATE 70.   Sherborne Hall, Gloucestershire (Lewis Wyatt, 1829–34).

the Office of Works for over thirty years) and private (he inherited the flourishing Cheshire practice of his uncle Samuel in 1807).[30] Lord Sherborne commissioned him to rebuild his eponymous Gloucestershire house (Plate 70), insisting it should preserve something of the spirit of its predecessor.[31]

Before building began in 1829 Wyatt had discussed the management of the project with his client. A curiously fragmented structure was devised. John Roberts, already employed at Sherborne, would agree contracts for the supply of materials and take charge of masons, bricklayers, slaters and quarrymen, whilst George Beedham, who had worked under Wyatt's direction at Stoke Hall (Nottinghamshire), would supervise the carpenters and joiners. In addition, a general accountant-supervisor was 'to conduct the whole and prevent jealousies'. A faint hope. Wyatt's opinion of Roberts was soon qualified, although he admitted that the burden of supervising a great number of men seven days a week was a heavy one. When Lord Sherborne's agent, George Newmarch, timidly complained 'that matters do not quite go on satisfactorily', Wyatt recognised the folly of divided responsibility which had fuelled both jealousies and costs. When Beedham left in some haste on the discovery of dry rot in the spring of 1835, Lord Sherborne's patience snapped. Having spent upwards of £40,000, he wrote to Newmarch: 'Considering that I was dealing with a gentleman I had no written agreement with Mr Wyatt, therefore I can only complain generally that he never paid the attention to the works which according to our understanding he was bound to do ... I might as well have saved all the percentage [Wyatt's 5 per cent commission] for a common builder could not have done worse.' Wishing to avoid litigation, both parties sought advice and arbitration between 1835 and 1837. Lord Sherborne pressed for Wyatt to be made liable for the cost of putting the house in order, and an award for negligence of £996 was made against him.[32] In the end, Anthony Salvin was brought in to complete the interior between 1841 and 1842.[33]

In 1826 Wyatt was invited by Gibbs Antrobus to submit plans to extend Eaton-by-Congleton Hall in Cheshire.[34] Antrobus had very recently inherited the house from an uncle who had been a partner in Coutts Bank. The client initially contemplated the extension of the existing house but, uneasy about the balance between old and new accommodation, then proposed rebuilding on a new site, whilst stressing that his income was fixed and the estate entailed. Wyatt, almost doubling the cost of the project in prospect, persuaded the Antrobuses to build their house in 'new' Elizabethan style, although Mrs Antrobus 'was glad ... to find that the style of architecture you gave us was not so much more expensive than the Grecian' (Plate 71). These were early days.

In encouraging his clients to accept his plans and remuneration, rather than those of Thomas Lee, his former clerk of the works, Wyatt explained the basis of professional practice around 1830. After thirty years in the business, he knew what was expected of a clerk of the works:

> The usual [architect's] charge being 5 per cent on the expenditure of the building when executed from the necessary working drawings and under the superintendence of a regular Clerk of the Works whose duty it is to communicate with, and to report his proceedings to the architect. He is also to order and look into the proper materials, to keep a regular weekly building account, and to hire and pay the workmen's wages. The tradesmen's and merchants' bills, after being certified by him are either paid by the Gentleman or his Steward, who is usually appointed to keep a proper cash and building account.
>
> The Clerk of the Works being in fact the builder will be a proper person to ... look out the timber, deals, wainscots and laths, to see what oak timber, bricks, lime, sand or any old materials the estate can furnish, to look into and make contracts for proper

PLATE 71. Eaton-by-Congleton Hall, Cheshire (Lewis Wyatt, 1829–31, demolished), garden front. Watercolour 1827 from a collection of Lewis Wyatt plans for the house.

supplies of stone, slate, lime, lead, or any other building materials, and for the carriage and delivery of the same. He is also employed to look into and hire at the customary wages of the country all workmen viz masons, bricklayers, carpenters, joiners, sawyers, slaters, labourers or any other he can employ with advantage and of them he is to keep a regular account of their time, to pay them all the wages they are hired at and with a proper check or assistant to see them on and off their daily work and to control the time allowed for their meals.[35]

Wyatt's description of the clerk of the works as 'the builder', under his supervision, is instructive. He went on to explain to Antrobus that he himself would not get tied up with general building contractors. If Antrobus employed, as he proposed, his late uncle's builder, that would be unacceptable to Wyatt, and the clerk of the works would be employed by and report to Antrobus alone. Antrobus might well have been confused which route to choose. In the end, he relied on Wyatt. His final bill for a 'plain and heavy' house was £23,000 – the cost had escalated from a first estimate of £10–12,000 for extensions. Wyatt's fee was £1150.[36]

As the nineteenth century went on, there is evidence of an increasingly professional approach to the appointment of a clerk of the works and the performance
of the role. At Haveringland in Norfolk in the 1840s, Edward Blore designed a
new house for Edward Fellowes.[37] The clerk of the works was Richard Armstrong.
He was neither an estate employee nor a local tradesman; and, although he does
not appear in lists of Blore's pupils, he was practising in London as an architect
in his own right by the 1850s. Indeed, he reappeared at Haveringland in the 1850s
and 1860s to design extensions and garden buildings. He was also responsible for
alterations of 1856–60 to Englefield House, Berkshire, the seat of Edward Fellowes's
brother, Richard Benyon, besides restoring churches for the family.

The layout of Armstrong's weekly reports to Fellowes was essentially the same
as those prepared at Henham fifty years before. They show that he visited Bristol
and Bath in 1839, at the start of the project, to arrange the supply of Bath stone.
He obtained competitive bids from Norwich haulage contractors for the movement of building materials from Great Yarmouth and Norwich to Haveringland.
Dissatisfied with the performance of the Haveringland brickmaker, Armstrong
dismissed him and supervised production himself. Some estate owners involved
themselves in the details of such disputes with building workers. Immersed up
to his ears in government business, William Blathwayt never hesitated to settle
a squabble with the Dyrham workforce, although his messages from London and
the Netherlands lost something of their force by the time their contents were
made known to the miscreants on site. For many, however, to be shielded by
their clerk of the works from such problems was very welcome.

It is clear from his attitude to wages and expenses that clerks of the works like
Armstrong could achieve savings of the order Wyatt claimed. The purse-strings
at Haveringland were indeed tightly controlled. Neither in his detailed reports
nor in Edward Fellowes's own ledgers is there any trace of the expense of the
traditional roof-raising ceremony, or the sniff of a barrel of beer, during the four
years the accounts run.[38] In the teeth of the worst depression of the nineteenth
century (1837–42), Armstrong managed to employ men at Haveringland at rates
20 per cent or more below those of similar projects in the same county.[39] When
Armstrong closed his accounts, Fellowes was evidently so satisfied with his
performance that he was given a £50 gratuity, the equivalent of sixteen weeks'
salary. It marked a project very differently concluded from James Wyatt's at
Henham, costing some 70 per cent over the estimate, or from the litigation
surrounding his nephew's work at Sherborne.

Oddly, the remuneration of good clerks of the works does not seem to have matched their usefulness. It was variable, but often little in advance of the skilled workmen on site.[40] Hay at Heacham in the 1770s was paid a guinea a week, whereas the London-based mason who came to fix two statuary marble fireplaces was paid 3s. a day (with 1s. a week lodging allowance) and the better-paid joiners and bricklayers 2s. to 2s. 3d. Marsden at Henham, a local man again, received 3s. 6d., no more than the other highest-paid men on site, the bricklayers and joiners James Wyatt had sent from London. During the inflationary period of the French wars, when skilled labour was scarce, Humphry Repton recommended a clerk of the works at Laxton in 1806 at 2 guineas per week, little more than his estimate of 7s. per day for top tradesmen, although he may have exaggerated the latter, as he did most things, to push the clerk of the works he proposed.[41] By the 1840s the real contribution of clerks of the works was being recognised by thoroughly competent architects like Edward Blore. Armstrong at Haveringland was clearly distinguished from the other workers there. He received 3 guineas a week, or over 10s. per working day, when the highest-paid tradesman received only 3s. 6d. per day, a rate no higher than that paid at Henham fifty years earlier. Armstrong's total remuneration, as the man on the spot, masterminding the smooth running of the whole project and effecting significant economies, was £778 – not far short of the £894 fee earned by the architect. Richard Armstrong received much more support from Edward Blore, a conscientious attender at Haveringland, than did Rufus Marsden at Henham. The latter was paid far less for a more difficult job. It is doubtful whether James Wyatt, notorious for his neglect, ever visited the site. Lewis Wyatt, although criticised for neglect at Sherborne, was there on ten occasions.

The increasing professionalisation of architects, and their more regular site inspections which improvements in transport allowed, made the tasks of the clerk of the works easier and better defined. A good clerk of the works clearly saved considerable sums of money for his client. He ensured that men paid by the day did not spin out the work, that piece-work was not skimped, and that materials were of good quality, reasonably priced and delivered on time. By good management, the clerk of the works also relieved the client, and his steward, of time-consuming and stressful involvement in the resolution of disputes. He was also in a position of considerable trust, with a high proportion of the cost of building a house passing through his hands. In a labour-intensive activity like building, in addition to keeping labour costs down, maintaining the productivity of the workforce alone offered considerable potential savings. Completion on time, and the avoidance of subsequent repairs due to the use of poor materials or faulty construction, constituted other obvious advantages for a country house builder who employed a skilled clerk of the works. Given the expenditure on a house of the equivalent of five or more year's rental income, saving 10 per cent of the cost would keep a six months' portion of this sum in the builder's pocket.

Around the middle of the nineteenth century, the clerk of the works's traditional role disappears from estate accounts, with the emergence of the general contractor and of building to a fixed price.[42] The function of course survived within contractors' organisations, with their clerks 'expected to be fully competent to fulfil the several duties of architect, builder and artizan, to be thorough draughtsmen and accountants and yet be practically acquainted with work'.[43] Thomas Cubitt trained men as clerks of the works, his pupils paying a premium of 300 guineas for the privilege. For the country house owner, the focus of the supervisory role performed on his behalf shifted from the customary involvement with labour and the acquisition of materials to the overall supervision of the contractor's performance, under the guidance of the architect.[44] The client's interests, once the contract was signed, were less concerned with cost (unless he indulged in the expensive business of changing his mind) and more with the design and quality of the building. The nature of the professional support he required therefore changed.

When Stephen Thompson was building Kirby Hall in the late 1740s, he wrote somewhat discouragingly to his friend, Thomas Grimston, who was similarly engaged in the building of Kilnwick Hall: 'I have bricklayers, joiners, carpenters, glaziers, upholsterers, and smiths at work, from all of which the Lord soon deliver me.'[45] Thompson could have added labourers, masons, roofers, plumbers, painters, even thatchers if new walls had to be capped to protect them from frost damage. Clients were only too aware of the multifarious activities, the dirt and the disruption associated with building. The prospect of the management and payment of scores of workmen for years on end must sometimes have daunted even the most determined builder (Plate 72).[46]

Country house workforces were not only diverse in composition but also of course varied considerably in size. Lord Carlisle had nearly 200 men at work at Castle Howard in the summer of 1703 when construction of the central block was in full swing.[47] Five hundred men are said to have been drafted by James Wyatt from Windsor Castle to Fonthill Abbey in 1799 to complete the Gothic

PLATE 72. Building tradesmen photographed in 1856 during the construction of Orchardleigh, Somerset.

extravaganza he was building for William Beckford.[48] Massive alterations to Alnwick Castle, costing in all some £320,000 between 1854 and 1865, employed 800 workmen at their peak.[49] At Westonbirt (Gloucestershire), a huge Victorian house, there were 250 to 300 men on the site for long periods in the 1860s.[50] For the exceptional building activity of the crazy Duke of Portland, above and below ground at Welbeck from 1854 to 1872 – spending £100,000 a year for eighteen years – '1500 workpeople of all classes were constantly employed in carrying out his instructions'.[51] At the other end of the scale, every granite stone in the walls of Castle Drogo was seemingly placed by one of two masons who toiled there for twenty years from 1911, although the accounts show that the builder, Lewis Bearne, had 100 men on site continually for the first four years and forty other men worked in the estate's quarry, sand and gravel pits and on the roads.[52] These are extreme examples. The construction of eight south Yorkshire houses in the eighteenth century, including the vast Wentworth Woodhouse, generated employment for between thirty-five and ninety men.[53] Snapshots of the number of men on site conceal important temporal changes in the composition of the workforce, however, and are a poor guide to the numbers of men of different occupations employed.

Whether a house was built in a new location, on an old site or involved the remodelling of an existing structure, the pattern of employment was much the same. Labourers were most numerous when clearing and levelling the site, digging foundations and drains, and moving materials into position for the start of construction. There was often an old house to pull down and materials to be recovered and cleaned for reuse. Saw-pits had to be dug and, as at Wolterton (Norfolk) in 1727, sheds erected for the sawyers, bricklayers, carpenters and masons, and a forge for the smith.[54] Robert Rose of Wolterton and 'his company', as many as a dozen men in summer and as few as four in winter, were clearly a cheap and highly flexible workforce (whatever their propensity for absenteeism and drunkenness), unloading the brick kiln, making preparations for the kitchen – and clearing up everywhere. In 1741–42, although the house was complete, as many as sixty labourers were digging new stew ponds, raising a terrace round them and planting trees, probably more men than had worked on the house at any time.[55] Before the nineteenth century, however, demand for building labour in the countryside had always to be matched with the needs of the farming calendar. Robert Rose's gang worked on the farm at Wolterton as well as on the house, hoeing turnips and making the hay and the corn harvests. Building Shadwell Lodge, John Buxton wrote in the summer of 1728: 'No thing is begun about the yards or outhouses. Our labourers are so taken up with the husbandry affairs that I can't yet spare them.'[56]

There was work on the building site for some labourers throughout a project, to fetch and carry for the craftsmen and keep the place tidy, but the number of bricklayers and masons grew as the walls were raised, with carpenters erecting the structural timber and making forms for the turning of arches. In due course, when tilers and plumbers had covered the carcase of the house, interior work proceeded, with structural carpentry succeeded by the finer joinery of floors, doorcases and windows. Plasterers and glaziers turned up, and lastly painters, upholsterers, and specialists to fit kitchens, stoves, bells and other internal equipment. Blacksmiths were employed at some sites as permanent members of the workforce; at others local men worked on a job by job basis. But at all sites the sharpening and repair of tools, and farrier's work, were essential.

The character of the workforce across an entire building project is well illustrated by the example of Haveringland Hall (Norfolk). This substantial Italianate seat of the Fellowes family had stood for little more than a century before it was demolished in 1946. In its lifetime it attracted little attention beyond the mere listing of its existence.[57] The house is given a posthumous significance, however, by the survival of Richard Armstrong's meticulously prepared building statements, Edward Fellowes's own account books and the architect Edward Blore's drawings. Blore's conservative approach to building – he eschewed the increasingly common practice of building to a fixed price by general contract – meant the use of directly-recruited day labour. It was the last house of any size built in the region before the railway reached Norwich and transformed the movement of men and materials. Therefore it is possible to reconstruct the building operation and quantify aspects of a traditional form of project organisation, managed in a thoroughly professional way.

In each of the four years of building, from 1839 to 1842, the workforce peaked successively at eighty-seven, sixty-seven, seventy-one and sixty-eight. Numbers of the various tradesmen reached a maximum at different times during the house's construction (see Table 1).

Table 1. *Peak numbers of men employed building Haveringland Hall, 1839–42* [58]

Year	Labourers	Sawyers	Carpenters/ Joiners	Bricklayers	Masons	Plumbers	Painters	Plasterers	Glaziers
1839	37	4	12	21	5				
1840	26	2	18	12	15	1	1	3	
1841	26	2	26	10	8	1	1	8	1
1842	16	2	31	4	5	6	7	12	1

Total of different men within each occupation:

	103	6	52	44	17	9*		18	

* Plumbers, painters and glaziers, some men covering more than one trade.

Two hundred and forty-nine different men were employed, most of them for short periods. Only thirty-two of the men (13.2 per cent) were on site for more than half the building period and 114 men (46.9 per cent) were there for less than 10 per cent of the time. Some tradesmen were of course only needed for a short time, but employment generally was casual; and when men left, after a period of work, most did not come back.

The pattern for Henham, fifty years earlier, is even more striking. The workforce peaked at sixty-four in the summer of the fourth year of the eight-year project.

But no fewer than 407 different day-workers, and some additional piece-workers, were involved. Only eleven men (2.7 per cent) worked for more than half the project's duration and 310 (76.1 per cent) for less than 10 per cent of the time. Thus the casual and unpredictable nature of employment for building workers, typical of the Tudor and Jacobean periods, persisted through the eighteenth and nineteenth centuries.[59]

Haveringland and Henham Halls were built when and where labour was plentiful, indeed the former was constructed during the most acute economic depression in the nineteenth century, and was supervised by a clerk of the works intent upon keeping costs down. Where labour was short, the rate of turnover of men is likely to have been lower, but there are few projects for which surviving documents permit an equivalent analysis. East Carlton (Northamptonshire), a smaller house than either Haveringland or Henham, built for Sir John Palmer Bt in the 1770s by the Leicestershire-born architect John Johnson, is one (Plate 73). In the course of just over three years the number of men on site peaked at

PLATE 73.   East Carlton Hall, Northamptonshire (John Johnson, 1777–81, enlarged 1823 and rebuilt 1870) by George Clarke, c. 1840.

thirty-eight, with eighty-seven different men being employed overall, indicating a more stable workforce.[60]

There was a long-term scarcity of building labour in the sixteenth century, even of masons in stone-producing areas.[61] Such problems persisted into our period. Daniel Finch, second Earl of Nottingham, building Burley-on-the-Hill, wrote in 1696 that progress was delayed because his master masons were unable to procure enough freemasons to work and prepare the stone.[62] The earl's contemporary, William Blathwayt, faced a similar problem at Dyrham in Gloucestershire. In 1698 his agent visited nearby quarries with the clerk of the works but found that all the masons were fully engaged for the summer.[63] His master mason, Philip West of Corsham, scoured the countryside up to a radius of thirty or forty miles looking for men in 1701, reporting to Blathwayt that they were very scarce. In such circumstances it was difficult enough to prevent men leaving, let alone find more. A century later, in 1808–9, skilled workmen were hard to obtain at Parnham (Dorset). Then, during the French wars, country house builders had to compete with the state for men – dockyards alone drew in thousands of carpenters – and it was found necessary to 'advertise' to attract labour. Soldiers were borrowed from Lord Hinton's regiment at Weymouth to supplement the workforce.[64]

The fluctuating demands of the Crown, backed by the power of impressment, therefore had an effect, as did 'public' construction work during an economic boom, as in 1824–25. Local competition between private builders had also to be faced. Another factor was the seasonality of building, which concentrated the call for labour in the summer months, when the hay and corn harvests also demanded men and waggons. In winter, bad weather and poor roads combined to prevent the movement of materials, frost ruled out the laying of brick and stone, and short days reduced the productivity of day labour. Obviously, men were more attracted to sites which offered the prospect of winter employment, being willing to work by the piece rather than the day in winter to secure it.[65] During the eighteenth century, however, the seasonal character of building appears to have become less marked. Transport improvements played a part, but also better organisation and supervision – ensuring that materials were available in good time; moving quickly to get a roof on under which work could be maintained in all weathers; and continuing appropriate and preparatory work in winter, by candlelight if necessary. Substantial numbers of men were employed at Henham and Haveringland throughout the year. At Henham the number of men on site fell to ten in the first January, picking up rapidly from mid February. In later years there were forty to fifty men working even in the depth of winter. At Haveringland, a similar sized workforce was employed each winter throughout the project.

There is no hint of any problem recruiting labour in the well-documented cases of East Carlton, Henham or Haveringland. Even there, however, it was not possible to find enough men nearby to maintain the desired rate of building progress and there were often local shortages of particular skills. Masons were understandably scarce in East Anglia, a region almost without native building stone.[66] But high quality joinery, carving and interior decoration, and the fitting of equipment bought from the metropolis, everywhere demanded imported skills. Workforces were, therefore, necessarily a mixture of local men, itinerant workers, and others recruited from a distance.

A multiplicity of labour markets, with agricultural and general labourers' wages differing widely between regions, was to some extent modified from the mid nineteenth century by the practice of tramping and the contribution of the railways in facilitating personal mobility.[67] Fast-growing rural populations after 1780, however, with landlords and farmers content to maintain a surplus of labour upon which they could draw at harvest time, depressed wages. These set the level for country house building labourers. Itinerant workers were more attracted by the availability of work than pay differentials, so building projects did not necessarily disturb local market rates. Where he wished to attract highly skilled specialists, however, a builder had to match wage rates elsewhere, pay travelling expenses, and arrange accommodation or pay an allowance for it.[68] Never willing to pay higher wages than he had to, William Blathwayt was nevertheless shocked when he found that the London joiner Robert Barker expected a massive 5s. per day (and 3s. for his men) to attract him to Dyrham, whereas local carpenters were paid only 1s. 4d. per day, advanced to 2s. if they assisted the London craftsmen.[69] In the same decade at other country houses, local carpenters were paid 2s. at Levens, near Kendal (Westmorland), 2s. 6d. at Milton (Northamptonshire), 1s. 3d. at Burley-on-the-Hill (Rutland), and 1s. 2d. at Mapperton (Dorset).[70] Clearly, large premiums had to be paid to attract skilled men from London.

Such direct comparisons between wage rates are not often possible because specialist craftsmen were usually paid by the piece, especially those at the apex of the craft pyramid, the decorative artists. Post-Restoration royal patronage of woodcarvers and Italian and French painters and decorators was emulated by the fashion-conscious builders and remodellers of grand houses in the late seventeenth century. Sought-after artist-craftsmen moved from one great house to another. Antonio Verrio and his assistants worked for the Earl of Exeter at Burghley from 1687 to 1697, for his brother-in-law at Chatsworth, and at Lowther Castle.[71] Louis Laguerre and his team painted walls and ceilings at Chatsworth, where Jean Tijou provided the metal balustrade for the staircase for £250 in 1688–89.[72] The French Huguenot carver Nadauld also worked at Chatsworth in 1700–1, having previously been employed at Hampton Court. In 1705 he arrived at Castle Howard, where he spent four and a half years executing much of the vigorous decoration which so enlivened both the inside and outside of Lord Carlisle's house. He was paid a massive £863 13s., presumably including board and lodging and possibly payments to assistants.[73] Such specialists worked on a foundation laid by skilled local craftsmen. At Castle Howard in 1709, for example, joiners and carpenters from York were followed by the Italian mural painters Giovanni Antonio Pellegrini and Marco Ricci, who also worked on Lord Manchester's London house and at Kimbolton (Plate 74).[74] The engagement of such artists was as much a business arrangement as was the recruitment of lesser tradesmen. The architect of the Mausoleum at Castle Howard, Nicholas Hawksmoor, discussed terms with the Venetian painter Giacomo Amicomi in 1731, covering payments for painting, the extent to which he or his assistants would execute the work, responsibility for the cost of materials, and travelling and board expenses. Amicomi promoted himself with the assertion that Pellegrini would charge more. Hawksmoor subsequently negotiated with Pellegrini, advising Lord Carlisle of Pellegrini's favourable painting rate of £2 per yard, compared with the £3 charged by Sir James Thornhill at Greenwich Hospital.[75] In the end, the Mausoleum was not painted.

Private clients, whose taste shifted from the iconographic deployment on walls and ceilings of mythical deities, earthly rulers and their triumphs to the more disciplined schemes of the Palladians, nevertheless maintained the demand for elite carvers, stuccoists and decorative artists, exemplified by William Kent's contributions at Houghton and Holkham. In due course, the formers of taste turned to the flowing asymmetry of the rococo style, and the employment of Italian *stuccatori* and their English counterparts working in plaster and wood. From the 1760s the neoclassical revival reached its artistic climax with Robert Adam. At Harewood, provincial craftsmen laid the base for Adam's artists: Biagio Rebecca depicted classical themes in the library and gallery; Antonio Zucchi worked in the music room, and on ceilings there; wall insets in the gallery were

PLATE 74.   Castle Howard, Yorkshire (Sir John Vanbrugh, 1701–12). The doorway of the High
Saloon with decorative surrounds attributed to Giovanni Bagutti, giving a view of the balcony
of the Great Hall beyond.

painted by Angelika Kauffmann. John Devall, George III's master-mason, executed marble chimney-pieces. Adam paid these artists directly. How much his bill for them added to the £37,000 that Lascelles's accounts reveal was spent on the house, excluding its furnishings and the park, is not disclosed.[76]

Even when ambition did not demand, or the depth of the builder's purse precluded, the more expensive forms of interior decoration, it was still necessary to bring to rural building sites skilled men from the metropolis or from a major regional centre like Bristol or York. Architects' favoured craftsmen followed their patron from one project to another. The growth of James Paine's practice from the late 1740s, and his foreshadowing of Robert Adam's complete control over interior design, employing native craftsmen, introduced the Yorkshire plasterers Joseph Rose and Thomas Perritt, and their families, to a wider clientele.[77]

At Henham, on the evidence of the payment of expenses for travelling or accommodation, thirty men of the 400 or so who worked there (7.5 per cent) were specially recruited.[78] London men were paid for the two days it took them to travel to Henham, their coach fare, and the expense of transporting their tools. The cost to a London man of the round trip to Henham was the equivalent of fourteen days' wages, so the importance of these payments is clear. Because such men worked continuously for relatively long periods, they accounted for a higher proportion of the man-days worked (19.3 per cent) than their numbers would suggest. Their share of the wage bill was even greater (30 per cent), because they were the highest paid men on site. The total was therefore significantly influenced by metropolitan rates.

Building remained a labour-intensive activity relatively untouched by technological change. The application of levers and block and tackle had long been employed at quayside, quarry and building site for moving and lifting heavy objects, and hand- or horse-driven (and, eventually, steam-powered) machines were used to raise the heavy weights to be dropped for pile-driving.[79] But craftsmen's tools changed little and what advances there were tended to be offsite in the development of continuous brick-making, for example, and the application of steam power to the sawing of wood, repetitive joinery, and even, by the mid nineteenth century, the copying of carved work.[80] As John Crace wrote to Lord Crewe in 1869, having visited Cubitt's works in London to inspect work done for the restoration of Crewe Hall:

[I had] pointed out to me the various works now in progress for Crewe Hall. I cannot but express to your Lordship how much I was delighted with the perfection of the workmanship and the beauty and great variety of the designs. The application of ingenious machinery has enabled work to be accomplished which would not have been expected some years ago ... the surfaces of the woodwork are so even and the mouldings and mitreings so exactly true.[81]

Even without improved technology, substantial increases in productivity could be achieved within the wasteful and archaic nature of the building industry by better organisation.[82] The professionalisation of architecture, project administration and supervision played a part, but the better organisation of labour was the key.

Progress and discipline could be a problem, especially when the employer was absent. 'The work rises slowly without I'm here often', bemoaned John Buxton of Shadwell Lodge in 1727.[83] The celebration of 'St Monday' and overindulgence at traditional fairs and feasts persisted. William Blathwayt's agent at Dyrham despaired of getting things done in July 1702 when a great part of the workforce was drunk and incapable. He lost more of the men a week later after celebrations at Box. News reached William Denison in Leeds that his foreman and labourers at Ossington (Nottinghamshire) had spent all day drinking at Sutton feast and 'put down both his own and their labour to my account'.[84]

At Dyrham, Blathwayt generally had a poor opinion of his workforce and believed in keeping wages back: 'These people want stirring up roundly and not to be overfed with money'. And he instructed his agent: 'You must not be too liberal if you want the work to go on.' Men were fined for lateness or slacking, but the stick was ineffective at times of labour shortage or when particular skills and experience were at a premium.[85] Unsurprisingly, the men themselves were not happy. 'Sir we are in great want of money', wrote the masons Thomas Simpson and Richard Broad desperately in 1703 when they saw what big reductions had been made to the bill they had submitted. The mason Philip West threatened to stop work unless more money was received; and men from Chippenham had to be given the hope of a pay rise as an inducement to stay. Attempts were made to prevent those deemed to have left unreasonably from working elsewhere. Blathwayt was incensed when the London joiner Alexander Hunter left Dyrham to do some work in Bristol and instructed his agent to speak to the other employer about it, but Hunter made it clear to the Dyrham clerk of the works that he would not return to a master who sought to bar him from all other work. At Parnham (Dorset) in 1808 Stephen Peach, the labourers' foreman, was paid 6s. 6d. expenses for a journey to Chard to summon back men who had left their work.

The ultimate sanction was recorded in the building accounts three weeks later: 'Paid the town cryer for crying a man who had absented himself from his work. 1s.'[86]

Organised labour disputes seem not, in fact, to have affected country house building to any great extent. Combinations in the building trades were virtually unknown before the end of the eighteenth century and craftsmen's strikes were an urban phenomenon.[87] As the nineteenth century progressed the strength of organised labour increased but men on an isolated site in the country were in a weak bargaining position and clerks of the works tried not to employ potentially disruptive London workmen.[88] However, after a strike of union members in 1839 at Merevale Hall (Warwickshire) all were sacked and replaced by a more compliant workforce. James Firth, who was supervising alterations at Everingham (Yorkshire, East Riding) in 1846, had to travel to York to deal with joiners who were demanding an increase in wages.[89] At Hemsted House (Kent) in 1859, men dissatisfied with the food they were given worked noisily through the foundation ceremony conducted by the parson, and struck for higher wages in the following year. In August 1860, at Ickworth (Suffolk), the London contractor R. J. Waller, anxious to relate some good news since his men had mistakenly clad the west wing with scaffolding when they should have been working on the east wing, wrote to Lord Bristol that a general strike by metropolitan building workers was imminent but that their country work would not be affected in any way.[90] Some masons, bricklayers and scaffolders walked out at Westonbirt (Gloucestershire) in 1865, after seeking an extra 6d. per day, but the clerk of the works believed that it was principally the travelling union men who caused trouble and that, with winter coming on, all were well aware of the difficulty of getting work elsewhere, and that therefore the best policy was to resist demands.[91]

The disciplinary prospect of unemployment and the wielding of the employer's stick were sometimes balanced by the constructive use of the carrot. Generous amounts of food and drink were provided at key stages of construction. Fifty men sat down to dinner in February 1826, for example, to celebrate the raising of the roof at Eshton (Yorkshire, West Riding). They were entertained by two musicians from Skipton and drank twenty-six-and-a-half bottles of rum and sixteen gallons of strong ale. At this stage the majority of them must have been totally incapable for the steward had bought a whole hogshead (fifty-four gallons). 'An error in [his] calculations', recorded Mathew Wilson primly, revealing that poor predictions were not restricted to building costs.[92] The Duke of Northumberland entertained his workmen at Alnwick with a dinner every November at a cost of 4s. 6d. per head.[93] Favoured tradesmen might receive bonuses from time to time or leaving presents. John Rous at Henham rewarded his London men, and Sir William Oglander Bt gave his foreman at Parnham (Dorset) one guinea as a Christmas present in 1808.[94]

With many different trades represented on the country house building site, with a range of skills within each occupation, and with some men recruited locally and others travelling long distances, the pattern of wage rates was complex. The evidence of day labour payments alone provides an incomplete picture. It is seldom practicable to deduce equivalent day rates from the payments made to piece-workers. Their earnings depended not only on pay rates but on the speed at which they were able to or chose to work. Where the piece-workers were the more skilled men on site, a study only of day rates will fail to represent the prevailing earnings for the most proficient craftsmen.[95] From those projects where day labour was the rule, but occasional references made to day rates paid to craftsmen who usually worked by the piece, an overall view can be obtained. The picture is more involved, however, than the relatively orderly series of wage rates over seven centuries derived for a typical southern English location.[96] Beyond Oxford, the main source of the published data, there were considerable regional differences, and the pattern of wage rates became less clear when the labour market was moving and new engagements were made at rising marginal prices. Nevertheless, the ratio of craftsmen's to labourers' wage was remarkably stable at 3:2, although other work has indicated that it was 2:1. There also appear to have been shifts in the proportion in the towns of northern England between 1450 and 1750.[97] There the evidence supports both views, with the 3:2 ratio widening in some towns from the mid seventeenth century, when craftsmen's rates advanced rapidly to at least double the pay of the labourers, although the latter made up some ground in the early eighteenth century. Within the three hundred year period, northern labourers and building craftsmen were always paid less than their London counterparts, but more than southern men outside the metropolis.

Country house building projects were large impositions on rural labour markets. Whereas unskilled men might be hired without disturbing local rates, a marginal demand price was more likely to apply to craftsmen, especially at times of peak activity. Country house projects do not therefore offer a simple basis for regional comparisons and, given the engagement of men from both rural and urban locations, differentials were significantly wider than in a stable labour market.

Within each trade there were groups of men of different origins paid on different scales. They reflected levels of skill – master, journeyman, labourer, apprentice – and also local market rates for some, besides the higher wages needed to attract skilled itinerant craftsmen.[98] Moreover, there were seasonal wage variations. These seem to have depended upon local practice in relation to the length of the working day, and upon the need to match harvest earnings when labour was scarce. At Dyrham in the 1690s William Blathwayt's labourers received 8*d*. per day in December and January, advancing to 10*d*. after Candlemas and to 1*s*. from late June for the harvest.[99] Those labourers who worked temporarily as carpenters experienced similar wage variations. Their high summer rate (1*s*. 6*d*.) and evidence elsewhere in the accounts suggests a local market rate for carpenters in south Gloucestershire of close to the 1*s*. 6*d*. rising by 1710 to 1*s*. 8*d*., which has been shown to be the general rate for building craftsmen in southern England around 1700.[100] At any period, however, between 1660 and 1870 the most significant feature which leaps out from the building accounts was the different payments rewarding different skills. In the 1720s at Crowcombe in Somerset the masons were the most highly paid, at 2*s*. 6*d*. per day, with joiners 2*s*., carpenters 1*s*. 6*d*. and labourers 1*s*.[101] Wolterton (Plate 75) labourers in 1738 were also paid 1*s*. per day (1*s*. 2*d*. in the garden), but even the general run of craftsmen were paid as much as 90 per cent more than the labourers: in 1738 the Wolterton carpenter was paid 1*s*. 10*d*. and his man 1*s*. 8*d*.; a bricklayer and his labourer were given 3*s*. per day together. But masons and carvers skilled in working marble could command much higher pay. William Roberts, paid the large sums of £75 for carving the chimney-piece in the saloon (Plate 76) and £60 for that in the south-west corner room at Wolterton, received a guinea a week (3*s*. 6*d*. per day) for 'setting up fruit and

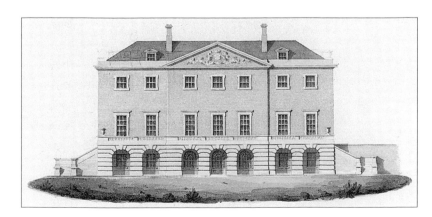

PLATE 75.
Wolterton Hall,
Norfolk (Thomas
Ripley, 1727–41).

PLATE 76.
Wolterton Hall,
Norfolk. The
saloon
chimney-piece.

foliage in middle room East'. Thomas Yeoman, a mason, received £28 12s. for polishing and fixing the saloon chimney-piece, and 2s. 6d. (and his labourer 1s. 8d.) when paid by the day.

By the last quarter of the eighteenth century most general rates had advanced somewhat. At East Carlton (Northamptonshire), although two masons were paid 2s. 6d., the same as at Crowcombe fifty years earlier, two carpenters received 2s. 8d., and a bricklayer (probably including his labourer) as much as 3s. 6d. to 4s. The general rate for all three trades was 2s. Labourers wages varied seasonally from 1s. per day in winter to as much as 2s. at harvest time.[102] At Henham in the 1790s, London bricklayers and joiners were paid 3s. 6d. per day plus 1s. per week lodging allowance, masons 3s. 3d. and plasterers 3s. 0d. per week. Local bricklayers and carpenters were paid 2s., with the prevailing rate for labourers being 1s. 4d.[103]

Significant wartime inflation in the 1790s and 1800s led to widespread wage increases. At Parnham (Dorset) in 1807–9, when, as we have seen, recruitment was a problem, labourers received 1s. 6d. per day for digging sand, digging clay for brickmaking and loading furze for use as fuel. Masons were paid from 2s. 7d. to 3s. 6d. But of four London carpenters who arrived in March 1809, one was paid 4s. 8d. per day, and three 4s. 6d., plus 2s. per week lodging allowance. Benson, the clerk of the works, was paid 6s. per day.[104]

Then followed a catastrophic decline of wages.[105] The rates at Haveringland from 1839 were hardly higher than those at Henham fifty years earlier, and those for the London men employed there were over 20 per cent lower than had been paid at Parnham in the 1800s. These reflected the economic transition from wartime boom to acute depression between 1837 and 1842, and the weakness of labour's position in the face of the emergence of general contractors operating within tight cost limits, although the practice was not yet dominant in country house building. The highest-paid masons, carpenters, plasterers and plumbers were all paid 3s. 6d. per day, the lowest-paid receiving 1s., 1s. 6d. and 3s. respectively. Bricklayers were paid in the range 1s. 6d. to 2s. 8d.

The likely interpretation of the distribution of wage rates at Haveringland is that the bricklayers were paid neighbouring market rates, the relatively high rate of turnover of these tradesmen also indicating that they were local men. Other trades contained a proportion of highly-skilled itinerant men, including masons from the west country and a small number of higher-paid London joiners fitting out the house. The general rate for adult labourers was 1s. 9d. throughout the year, reflecting the prevailing rate for agricultural labourers in Norfolk.[106] Remarkably, craftsmen were attracted from London for only twice the wage paid to Norfolk farm workers, evidence of the dramatic impact of the depression of the early 1840s on employment prospects generally.[107]

By the 1870s building workers had achieved significant improvements in their working conditions – a nine-hour working day, a half day on Saturdays, payment by the hour – as well as higher wages. There was a rise of about 50 per cent in the prosperous mid Victorian period 1850–74 with the main gains coming in the 1860s.[108] For the country house client employing a London contractor the rise in cost was substantial. Messrs Holland and Hannen worked under the architect William Burn at Lamport (Northamptonshire) in 1861–62.[109] They charged 13s. 1d. per day for a plumber and his man, 8s. for a bellhanger, 7s. 2d. for bricklayers, masons, carpenters and plasterers, and as much as 4s. 8d. for a labourer. Ten shillings per day was charged for the foreman. These men may have had to find their own food and accommodation but the contrast with either the 3s. 6d. per day assumed for a carpenter's time in an 1869 repair bill or the rates paid at Haveringland twenty years earlier is striking.[110]

The appearance of women on building sites is rarely documented. At Wolterton in 1738 two women were paid 6d. per day to clean through the near-completed house, a penny less than Elizabeth Fosque [?] and 'her company of weeders' (four in all) working in the gardens.[111] At Henham between August 1796 and May 1797 women scrubbed the floors in the new house to prepare it for occupation, receiving from 10d. to 1s. per day.[112] At Parnham (Dorset) two women were each paid 10d. per day in 1807 to clear up the brickmaking yard, and in October 1808 Martha Peach received 6d. per day for airing rooms in the new house.[113] It is common for the surnames of such women to be the same as men working regularly on the same project. Otherwise, building workers' families are almost invisible in the archives. The final settlement of master-slater Peter Westcott's account for work done at Kimberley (Norfolk) from 1755 to 1757 was made with his widow.[114] T. Kippes, a carpenter who worked at Parnham for at least twelve months in 1807–8, and was paid 4s. 6d. per day plus 2s. per week lodging allowance, arranged for his wife in London to receive part of his pay, one guinea every fortnight, from the architect John Nash – a rare reference to such a provision.[115]

The evidence of the building accounts is that itinerant building workers spent lengthy periods of time away from their families. Lodgings for those unable to walk often long distances to work were either in the village or, especially in winter, uncomfortably on site in out of the way places far from ale house or taverns. The obsessional William Blathwayt objected to any houses of entertainment near his Dyrham seat. He was also well aware of the propensity of workmen to seek out clean and dry accommodation wherever they could. His agreement with the carver John Harvey for the erection of a monument in Dyrham church after his death stipulated that Harvey's men were 'not to ly in any part of the house or outhouses'.[116] The two masons lodged in a nearby cottage in 1701 must have considered themselves fortunate indeed, even given the owner's injunction that they must not 'smoke tobacco up in the chambers, the thatch of the roof lyeth pretty low'.[117] Little wonder that workmen are sometimes recorded drunk at neighbouring fairs and feasts. Nor do training practices merit much of a mention, although clearly country house projects provided a superb grounding for apprentices as well as opportunities to catch an influential patron's eye.

The building of country houses undoubtedly employed large numbers, but only for a favoured few was there any continuity of either architect's or builder's patronage. Some fortunate craftsmen, like those attached to John Carr or James Paine – architects with large country house practices – moved from one site to another. Craft dynasties were founded, such as the Rose family of plasterers. Others stepped from the craft ranks to the professional status of architects, at least before the late eighteenth century. For these a good living was possible. The highest skills were well rewarded. In contrast, the reality for the majority employed was uncertainty and an increasing loss of craft autonomy: in the field of design, with the professionalisation of architecture in the eighteenth century; and in terms of employment, with the rise of the general contractor in the nineteenth. Moreover, it is not possible to calculate their rewards over time because although we can trace the movement of wages we cannot deduce annual earnings from them. The number of days an individual worked beyond the rare well-documented project is unrecoverable. Evidence suggests that, unless there was a pattern of activity sparked off by a major house in a region or the building cycle was near its peak, employment was, except for the most highly regarded, irregular.

The wide differentials and high cost of skilled workmen makes the assertion that England's country houses were invariably monuments to cheap labour difficult to sustain. Clearly labourers were cheap (which is why work in parks and gardens was *relatively* inexpensive), but the most highly-paid craftsmen could be three or more times as costly as local men. The finest skilled work was fearfully expensive. By the late eighteenth century statuary marble chimney-pieces were costing as much as £300 each. The de La Rochefoucauld brothers wrote in 1785: 'And the luxury of their furnishings, decorations and above all of their country houses, is infinitely superior to ours ... the chimney-pieces in the saloons of their country houses are objects of luxury on a ruinous scale.'[118] The material and labour costs of their sumptuousness were inevitably expensive. And, of course, the wages bill made up a high proportion of the total cost in a labour-intensive enterprise like country house building.

Having marshalled a costly labour force, it was essential for the smooth execution of a building scheme that sufficient materials were delivered to the building site on time. Building materials were heavy and cumbersome so that the delivered price of goods could easily double if they had to be transported over a relatively short distance. Addressing gentlemen and builders in the 1750s in his *Complete Body of Architecture*, Isaac Ware considered the question of choosing the ideal location for a house. Surprisingly to us, one of the more important factors he stressed was accessibility to a navigable waterway.[119] Yet not one of his readers would have doubted this, for movement by road of bulky, low-value building materials – brick, stone, slate and timber – was both difficult and expensive. The use of walling stone, for example, was uneconomical beyond a very short distance from a quarry, little more than a mile when building small houses and cottages, although good quality freestone might be carted further for grander structures if builders were willing to meet the high costs of road carriage.[120]

Of course, roads did improve during the period. The development of the turnpike toll system accelerated rapidly after the mid eighteenth century and was essentially complete by 1810. Construction and maintenance methods continued to improve with, for instance, Macadam's surface construction methods.[121] The county reports of the Board of Agriculture, compiled in the 1790s, maintained that great improvements had been made in the previous half century. While travellers' comments about the quality of the roads varied considerably, these were by the Regency period on balance favourable, especially when compared with continental experiences. Seasonality in travel had been all but eliminated, the risk of loss or accident much diminished, and the cost of carriage of both goods and passengers reduced (Plate 77). Significant savings in journey times for passengers were undeniable.

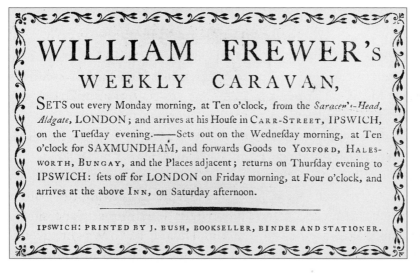

WILLIAM FREWER's WEEKLY CARAVAN,

SETS out every Monday morning, at Ten o'clock, from the *Saracen's-Head*, *Aldgate*, LONDON; and arrives at his House in CARR-STREET, IPSWICH, on the Tuesday evening.——Sets out on the Wednesday morning, at Ten o'clock for SAXMUNDHAM, and forwards Goods to YOXFORD, HALES-WORTH, BUNGAY, and the Places adjacent; returns on Thursday evening to IPSWICH: sets off for LONDON on Friday morning, at Four o'clock, and arrives at the above INN, on Saturday afternoon.

IPSWICH: PRINTED BY J. BUSH, BOOKSELLER, BINDER AND STATIONER.

PLATE 77.
The East Anglian carrier William Frewer's trade card, 1790s.

Road transport, however, was still unable to compete with water for the movement of heavy, relatively low-value goods. At the turn of the seventeenth century, each of William Blathwayt's mules carried only two to three hundred-weight of building materials, such as deals, the twelve miles from Bristol to Dyrham; and his waggons, drawn by oxen, and limited to use in the summer months by the condition of the roads, were restricted by statute to carrying no more than thirty hundredweight. Heavy rain could make even the summer movement of building materials difficult, as Francis Guybon, steward of Milton in a low-lying part of Northamptonshire, reported in June 1703 to Lord Fitzwilliam in London. Nevertheless, in reply, the latter stated he was very much against the uneconomic carriage of half-loads of stone, anxious though he was for building work on his estate to continue.[122] The permitted load of waggons increased to three tons in 1741 and six tons in 1765, although a team of four or six horses would have been needed to haul the bigger load. A single horse, on the other hand, could tow a loaded boat of up to thirty tons along a river or as much as fifty tons along a well-constructed canal towpath. Differences in cost between the two systems were significant. In the early eighteenth century the cost of waterborne carriage might be as low as 1d. per ton per mile (the average was nearer 2½d.), whereas transport by road was around five times higher at 1s.[123]

The development of the railway network from the 1830s brought food, fuel and raw materials at lower cost to centres of industry and population, but it came relatively late to the service of country house builders in rural locations. Rail complemented rather than replaced established means of carriage. Even when an estate had a nearby station or halt, the last leg of the journey was necessarily by horse-drawn waggon, and the frequent handling of goods, perhaps from rail to coastal vessel, back to rail and then to road, inevitably added to costs. The railway was considered in 1863 for the transport of stone from Filey (Yorkshire) to Brandon (Norfolk) for use at Didlington Hall, but the quotation of 14s. 6d. per ton was higher than the alternative of coastwise shipping to King's Lynn and onwards by river.[124] The risk of damage to goods had also to be considered. Robert Ketton, a Norwich architect, wrote to William Amhurst at Didlington in 1867 to report that a truckload of bricks was ready for despatch but that he feared for the safety of moulded bricks unless great care was taken moving them from truck to waggon.[125] For the supply of building materials from one inland site to another, however, rail might be the only option. Thus T. & G. Wright, quality brick manufacturers of Woolpit (Suffolk), sent a sample of their best white brick to Sir Thomas Fremantle, who was building at Swanbourne (Buckinghamshire) in the 1860s. They quoted a price of 58s. per 1000, delivered in London by the Great Eastern Railway (already much more expensive than the 40s. 6d. paid by Henry Wilson of Stowlangtoft Hall, five miles from the brickworks), and with the cost of transport from London to Buckinghamshire still to be added.[126]

Waterborne transport therefore offered advantages throughout the period. Stone from Yorkshire, Dorset, and the south west, slate from Wales and the north west, and timber imported from north-west Europe and north America, was moved around the British Isles by coaster, and far inland by river navigation and canal, to build the English country house. In 1693 four hundred deals for Dyrham were shipped 124 miles up the River Thames from London to Lechlade, still forty miles by land from the house. For this first leg of the journey carriage and supervision alone added £10 to goods costing £40.[127] Baltic timber for Harewood from the 1750s was imported through Hull and transported about sixty miles along the rivers Humber, Ouse and Wharfe to Tadcaster, within eleven miles of the house.[128] By the time Eshton Hall in the West Riding of Yorkshire was built, in the 1820s, the east and west coast river navigations inland from the ports of Hull and Liverpool had been finally linked by the Leeds and Liverpool Canal in 1816. Close to the canal at Gargrave, Eshton was built from waterborne material conveyed from both directions: slate from Hull; other slate and marble from Westmorland via Liverpool; timber and plaster from Liverpool and Manchester.[129] From the east coast, goods flowed through King's Lynn and the smaller Wash ports like Boston via long-established river navigations to the east Midlands, Norfolk and Suffolk. Norwegian deals from Christiania and marble chimney-pieces from London were shipped along the Fossdyke, linking the rivers Witham and Trent, to Burley-on-the-Hill, built between 1694 and 1708 for Daniel Finch, second Earl of Nottingham.[130] South from King's Lynn, building materials were transported deep into East Anglia. In the eighteenth century the firm of De Carle conveyed stone to Bury St Edmunds, and used the ports of Ipswich (Suffolk) and Mistley (Essex) to serve the south of the region.[131] From Great Yarmouth came Baltic timber for Henham in the 1790s, via the Waveney navigation to Beccles, and for Haveringland in the 1840s, by the Yare to Norwich. Even smaller ports were used: Southwold (Suffolk), for example, to unload Portland stone for Henham; and Aldeburgh for miscellaneous goods from London. Given a firm beach, even the lack of a staithe was no obstacle to the use of water transport. In favourable weather, barges from King's Lynn were unloaded on the beach at

Heacham (Norfolk) when the hall was extended in the 1770s. Waggons were sent down to the shore, only two miles from the house, when the vessels were sighted.[132] The advent of the railway had much less impact on the cost of building materials at destinations with good access to water than at inland destinations where there was none. In 1856 Bath (Coombe Down) stone cost 7½d. per cubic foot loaded into trucks at the quarry, and 9½d. f.o.b. at Bristol. The cost delivered to Great Yarmouth was 1s. 7½d. by sea and an even heftier 2s. 3d. by rail.[133] The flow of materials to the Henham building site in the 1790s, by coastal ship, inland waterway and by road, is shown in Figure 1.

Even if navigable water was not far away, a few extra miles by road to the building site from the nearest port, wharf or staithe could add significantly to the cost of the millions of bricks, thousands of tons of stone and the hundreds of loads of timber required to build a country house. Local carriers might be hired, but generally waggons, draught animals, and men drawn from the estate handled the work. The engagement of a carter for the duration of a project was often justified. Waggoner Jonathan Freek agreed to serve Thomas Carew at Crowcombe (Somerset) from July 1724 for £6 per year wages, plus 3s. 6d. per week board wages when there was 'no housekeeping at Crowcombe'.[134] For tasks such as carting sand, furze or bricks, men paid labourer's wages received more when they provided a horse as well; and on occasions horses were hired without their owners.[135] Reliance upon local resources meant that without careful planning, especially before road improvements reduced the seasonality of building, waggons and men could be scarce at hay and corn harvest times. In late July 1698 William Blathwayt was advised by his agent at Dyrham that the estate waggons were fully stretched carting stone from the quarry and bringing timber to the site; and that it was essential immediately to charter as much carriage as possible, before the corn harvest made the hire of horses and carts impossible. Blathwayt had no alternative but to agree, 'everything must be brought home before winter, whatever the cost'.[136] Right at the end of the period, the loss of men to the harvest could still be a problem. In 1873 Jackaman, a Bury St Edmunds builder, excused delays in laying new drains at Ickworth – which, fearing cholera, worried Lord Bristol – because he could not obtain enough hands until after harvest.[137]

The security of goods in transit or on the building site was also of concern (Plate 78). Blathwayt's Cornish tiles at Bristol, awaiting carriage to the building site, were stored in a secure cellar, and deals stacked on the quayside were policed by a man paid 6d. per night.[138] Watchmen were employed to guard building sites

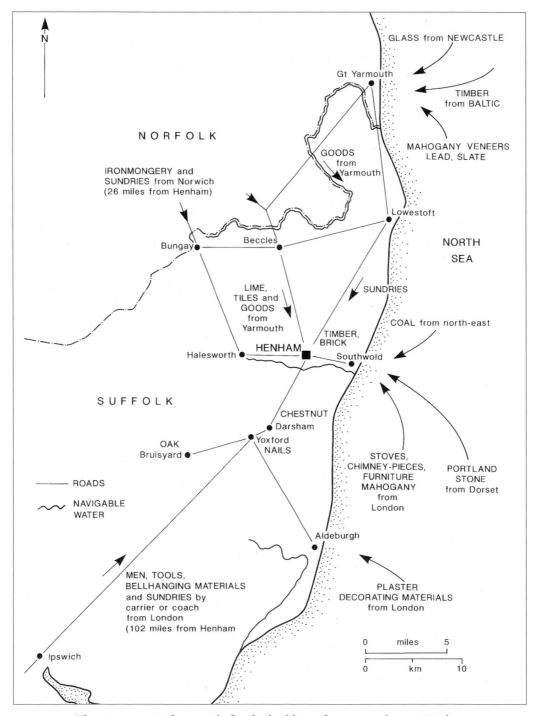

FIGURE I.   The movement of materials for the building of a country house: Henham, 1792–98.

PLATE 78.   A building site in the 1850s: Orchardleigh Park, Somerset.

on Sundays. At Henham John Rous paid a man 1s. for looking after the site on the Sabbath, and thought it necessary to pay him an extra 4d. in May 1797 to patrol the nearly finished house 'while the gypsies were in Henham'.[139]

Given the importance of keeping the men on site supplied with materials, architects and contractors advised builders on the nature and quantity of goods that they would need. Thomas Ripley, anticipating Horatio Walpole's intention to rebuild Wolterton Hall in Norfolk, wrote in 1724: 'It surely will be right ... to order Earth to be thrown up for as many bricks as possibly can be made the next season, and to buy any oak that is fitt for building.'[140] We have already seen that Thomas Gardner estimated the quantities of stone and oak timber that Thomas Webb Edge would need for Strelley Hall in the 1790s. Lewis Wyatt, in providing Gibbs Antrobus with an estimate of cost for building at Eaton-by-Congleton, included a list of materials with the injunction: 'The greater part of these materials should be ... provided for conveniently on the premises before the works are begun.'[141] When Lowther Castle in Westmorland was rebuilt from

1806, 'the necessary materials of stone and timber [had] been collected for the purpose previously by the first Earl'.[142]

Notwithstanding that preparations were made in advance for the supply of materials, not least for those from distant sources such as Baltic timber, stone and slate, stockpiling does not seem to have been the rule. While concern about the security of goods on site, and the desire to minimise the number of times they had to be moved, may have played a part, there appears to have been sufficient confidence in the transport system in this period to plan for the arrival of materials throughout the building period. Delays, the consequence of its shortcomings in the pre-railway age, were nevertheless legion. Of course, the builder himself controlled the provision of materials from his estate, although, as William Blathwayt discovered at Dyrham, this was no guarantee of an adequate rate of supply, the men at his quarry failing to cut stone fast enough to keep the masons at the house continuously employed.[143]

Building materials were purchased from producers or through dealers. The general builder's merchant did not exist until well into the nineteenth century, presaged by the ambition of Thomas Cubitt to control all aspects of his speculative building and contracting activities. It was the comprehensive stocks at Cubitt's London works, established in 1815, which enabled him to supply other smaller businesses.[144] Country house builders might engage tradesmen for the supply of materials as well as labour, more often in the case of specialists such as glaziers, plumbers and upholsterers than with the basic masonry or woodworking trades. The opportunity to benefit from the supply of materials at a profit was attractive to tradesmen, but their customers were aware of the possibility that by these means they might end up paying too much. Edward Wood, an upholsterer recommended by Stephen Thompson to his friend William Gossip at Thorp Arch (Yorkshire) in the 1750s, volunteered the information that Thompson had saved 30 per cent of the cost of materials by buying direct from the London factors who served the upholsterers.[145] With the increasingly professional management of building projects from the early nineteenth century, the separation of functions and the advent of general contracting, the supply of materials by individual trades-men working on major projects became rare. The link between materials and labour remained, however, for the most specialised of fixtures and furnishings. London upholsterers, furniture suppliers and kitchen equipment manufacturers, for example, would send their own men, often for weeks on end, to install their wares in country houses.

The economic incentive to maximise the use of materials available on the estate itself was obvious. A builder's first thought, if he was demolishing an old house, was the prospect of reusing old materials. They might only be suitable for use where not visible but they nevertheless had an appreciable value. Stone and brick were cleaned for building internal walls, and glass refixed in the domestic offices. The use of recycled timber, however, was more problematic. Old hardwood was difficult to cut, its attractiveness reduced if much reworking had to be undertaken. In any case timber was inherently less durable than brick or stone, less likely to survive a fire than other materials.

John Rous paid labourers 1s. 2d. per 1000 to clean over 150,000 bricks from his Elizabethan house (burnt down nearly twenty years earlier) to supplement nearly two million fired for the construction of his new house at Henham in the 1790s.[146] Edmund Rolfe at Heacham bought some 'wreck timber', perhaps providing justification for the popular myth about the reuse of ship's timbers, although the purchase could have been of a stranded cargo.[147]

Contractors were obliged to make as much use as possible of recovered materials. Stylishness and wealth were no bar to their employment. When Brodsworth Hall (Yorkshire) was built in the 1860s, the specification drawn up by the executant architect, Philip Wilkinson, required the London contractor, Longmire and Burge, to make extensive use of materials from the old, mid eighteenth-century house. Recovered stone was to be employed for the north wall of the new building, the external walls of the domestic offices, basement walls, the foundations to the terrace and the portico columns, and for inside walls where brick had not been specified. The old material was equal in neither quality nor quantity to the job. The original contract price was £17,609 12s. 0d., but, of the additional £2903 0s. 10d. charged for extras and omissions, £1338 14s. 7d. was justified by 'Deficiency of stone in old mansion'.[148] A great variety of other goods was also reused: no fewer than twenty chimney-pieces for example, including a marble statuary one prominently refixed in the dining-room. The carpenters and joiners were expected to adapt the timbers of the old roofs, to reuse the whole of the old floors, skirtings and dados, and the roofers were to recover old tiles. Sinks, dressers and shelves from the old kitchen were to be refitted, and iron stair panels, ballusters and a mahogany handrail were to find their way to secondary staircases. Even the sound and feel of the previous house was not destroyed entirely. The old dinner bell was rehung and four lavatory seats were specified for reuse in the nursery, school-room and servants quarters. The survival of such detailed specifications is rare; the reuse of a great variety of materials was not.

Brick, stone, lime, sand and timber were the building materials most likely to be found on an estate. The manufacture of brick on the spot was universal where suitable brick-earth was available. Nathaniel Kent, a well-known land agent and agricultural writer, wrote in the late eighteenth century:

> Upon most estates of any considerable size, brick-earth or clay may be met with and, where this is the case, they may always be made and burnt on clamps for one-third less than they can be bought at the kilns and equally good in quality. I have had a great many burnt in this manner, from eleven to fourteen shillings a thousand ... the medium price is twelve shillings a thousand where fuel is reasonable. Besides the difference in price, there is generally a great saving in carriage.[149]

Brickmaking was largely a manual process following long-established patterns (Plate 79). Mechanisation before the second half of the nineteenth century was minimal. The horse-powered pug mill for working the clay had been introduced towards the end of the seventeenth century, and was steam-driven from the early nineteenth century. The Hoffman continuous kiln, however, was only invented in 1858.[150] Many estates had experience of brickmaking, meeting their own needs and sometimes supplying a wider market, but usually, when the big house was rebuilt and a new kitchen garden walled, production had to be increased beyond the capacity of any permanent kilns. Then temporary kilns or clamps, if possible close to the building site, had to be brought into use. Clamps were stacks of

PLATE 79.   Moving newly made bricks in an early nineteenth-century brickyard.

dried bricks, interspersed with layers of fuel, often faggots, made from local brushwood, furze (gorse), or tree and hedge cuttings. At Crowcombe (Somerset) in the 1720s, as many as nineteen labourers were employed at any one time from mid May to the end of the year, cutting and carting furze for use as fuel.[151] The outside of the clamp was cased with burnt bricks and sealed with clay, leaving a number of openings through which the fuel could be ignited, depending upon the direction of the wind. The brick-earth was dug late in the year and left to weather during the winter. Brickmaking proper started in March, continuing until the early autumn. The clay was puddled with water if necessary to remove foreign matter such as flints and pebbles, and to produce a smooth dough. The water was then drained from the resulting slurry and, when dry, the clay was mixed, churned, cut into pieces and moulded into 'green' bricks. They were stacked to dry for several weeks, then fired for about seven days, or even some weeks. Using such methods it was difficult to judge the correct amount of heat required, and it was usual for some imperfect bricks to be produced. Many of these were used for concealed work and rubble infilling.[152]

Excellent results could be achieved with high-quality estate brick. That at Holkham has presented an immaculate face to the north Norfolk winds for over 250 years. Nevertheless, the brickmaking process was not without its problems. Indeed, Sir Balthazar Gerbier wrote in 1662 that there was little to choose in terms of cost between making and buying 20,000 bricks.[153] That might be true, if all of the things that could go wrong went wrong together. It was common, for example, for local labour to be supervised by a peripatetic brickmaker in spite of their generally poor reputation. Roger North was blunt about them: 'The brickmakers are a bad, and thievish sort of men, so are not to be trusted with advance.' John Buxton, denouncing them with a biblical roundness, hoped that 'they have not so good an intrest in Heaven as those who made Pharaoh's bricks. They are an vile generation of people.'[154] Their views were echoed in the 1740s: 'The Brick-Maker's Business is by some not reckoned a very reputable employment.'[155] The problem was that the occupation was seasonal and hours worked in summer were incredibly long. Absenteeism and heavy drinking were endemic. William Earle Bulwer's brickmaker at Heydon (Norfolk) was discharged for cheating him of £18.[156] Richard Armstrong, the clerk of the works at Haveringland, was unhappy with the performance of his from the first clamp he fired, 'the man appears to be quite honest but fit for anything but a Brick yard'.[157] He was dismissed after the ninth clamp was fired, and Armstrong thereafter supervised brickmaking himself. In all, about 1,800,000 bricks were produced at Haveringland in four seasons: individual clamps contained up to about 100,000 bricks each, with a wastage rate of about 10 per cent in firing. The size of the workforce at the brickyard varied, men being transferred from housebuilding as and when required. Four moulders were employed at the start of the 1841 season and three in 1842, with a fourth man dividing his time between moulding and clamping. Extra labour was used from time to time to turn the brick-earth, for loading and unloading, and for tidying up the brickyard.

Landowners sought advice from one another. When John Rous at Henham was dissatisfied with his brickmaker, he wrote to Rufus Marsden, his clerk of the works, that Mr Coke (of Holkham) said that it was impossible to burn a fine white brick with a coal fire.[158] A little later Rous wrote:

> In spite of what Marsden and the brickmaker say, I shall bring down a couple of Mr Coke's bricks which will make them ashamed of their ware, though my earth is much superior to the present Holkham earth, which is now so indifferent that they make a mixture of two or three sorts before it will burn white at all. Mr Pelham [of Brocklesby] has the same earth as mine, and never made an handsome brick till Coke sent him a brickmaker, and now Pelham's bricks exceed Coke's.[159]

The overall performance of estate brickmakers is difficult to assess because of different accounting practices, doubts about the efficiency of the use of different fuels, and the absence of information about wastage rates. The literature is confusing on the subject of labour productivity. Presumably it was higher in commercial brickyards employing seasoned gangs.[160] Cost data are more accessible. In 1680, at Ebbisham (Surrey), 7s. per 1000 was quoted for 'making and burning', with 'wood fuel' at 3s. per 1000, an additional 43 per cent on the brickmaker's charge. The selling price was 13s. to 14s. per 1000, a mark-up of 30 to 40 per cent.[161] Estate accounts can, however, give the impression that locally-made bricks were cheaper than they actually were. It was common, for example, to record only labour costs. In the 1733 contract between John Ingleby of Ripley Castle (Yorkshire) and John Davis, a Hunslet brickmaker, Ingleby provided materials, and tools (except spades), and built the kiln. Payments on account were to be made when all the clay had been dug, at each of two turnings of the clay, the balance being settled when all the bricks had been produced.[162] Brickyard men were paid labourers' wages, but the cost of competing fuels varied, depending on estate-sourced supplies and the price of delivered coal. When only the labour cost for making brick is known, it would be reasonable to add half as much again for the cost of the fuel. At Cusworth (Yorkshire) in 1741, eighty chaldrons of coal were consumed in producing 411,000 bricks, and thirty-one chaldrons for 114,000 in the following year, adding 31.4 and 44.4 per cent respectively to the 6s. 6d. per 1000 paid to Samuel Brooksbank, the brickmaker.[163] In the same year, at Langley (Norfolk), £51 18s. 6d. was paid for making bricks and tiles, and a further £26 19s. (51.9 per cent) for burning them.[164] The cost of producing 1,800,000 bricks at Haveringland (excluding duty) was £687 3s. 8d. and the bill for coal and faggots £406 4s. 0d., (59.1 per cent).[165] The savings, compared with the purchase of brick and its transport to the site, were substantial.[166] The price for commercially produced white brick delivered to Haveringland, based on samples received in 1839, was expected to be between £3 2s. 0d. and £3 6s. 0d. per 1000, well over three times the cost of the estate-produced red brick. Estimates of the cost of making brick are given in Table 2.

Table 2. *The cost of making brick (per 1000)*

	Labour + fuel ('home-made' = production cost)	Ex-kiln (Including profit + rent on brickmaking)
1670–1710	5s. 6d.	9s. 0d.
1750	7s. 0d.	11s. 0d.
1790	12s. 6d.	18s. 0d.

Source: Linda Clarke, *Building Capitalism* (London, 1992), p. 138.

It is clear that the avoidance of the commercial brickmaker's profit and high carriage costs made estate brickmaking, even with problems of quality control, potentially very attractive.

The use of stone from an estate quarry, or one nearby which could be rented or from which stone could be bought, was equally advantageous. Few builders were as fortunate as Lord Anglesey at Plas Newydd with 'stone quarries on the very spot where the house is built'.[167] Lord Nottingham obtained stone for the external walls of Burley-on-the-Hill from Clipsham, a few miles away, and Ketton stone was transported ten miles for the colonnades on the flanks of the house.[168] His contemporary, William Blathwayt, had his own quarry for supplying Dyrham, as did Lord Carlisle at Castle Howard and Thomas Worsley at nearby Hovingham, although complaints from the masons working at Dyrham that stone was not being delivered quickly enough illustrate that having an estate source of

supply was no guarantee that materials would be available on time.[169] Quality
was also a consideration. The detailing of the local stone from which Harewood
was built in the 1760s is still sharp, whereas the limestone employed at Brodsworth
over one hundred years later has long since decayed. Matching existing stone
when remodelling a house posed particular problems. New work by the London
contractor Holland and Hannen at Lamport (Northamptonshire) in 1869 deteriorated quickly. Although the stone was thought to have come from the same
quarry, on closer inspection it was found that Bath stone had been employed.
Remedial work was carried out in the preferred local Ancaster stone.[170]

The expense of the handling and carriage of stone even from a local quarry
was no small consideration. In an estimate of the cost of building at Milton
(Northamptonshire) in 1754, it was expected that for Ketton stone, priced £300 at
the quarry, an additional £150 would have to be paid to transport it eleven miles
to the house.[171] Small quantities of stone supplied to Oulton Park (Cheshire) in
the 1820s doubled in price although carried only three miles.[172] The market for
stone was, however, increased by the improvement of river navigations and the
construction of canals. After the opening of the Kennet and Avon canal in 1810,
the cost of Bath stone in London fell to 1s. 11d. per cubic foot – one-third of that
carried long distances by road.[173] Mathew Wilson's ashlar for Eshton in the 1820s
was brought about ten miles from Keighley by canal, being delivered to Raybridge
staithe at Gargrave for 1s. 1d. per cubic foot. Wharfage at Gargrave cost a further
2d. and the stone still had to be carted to the house.[174] But builders remote from
sources of supply paid much more for their stone. The vast sums spent by Sir
Robert Walpole when deploying the fruits of government service on the building
of Houghton Hall are unquantifiable, since he burnt his bills when removed from
office, but they included the cost of bringing stone from near Whitby, Yorkshire,
to the north coast of Norfolk and carting it a dozen miles overland to the building
site. Even the relatively impecunious John Rous of Henham, who removed from
the plans of his architect James Wyatt 'columns and unnecessary stonework by
which there will be a saving of £500', nevertheless indulged in the expensive
business of bringing stone to East Anglia in the 1790s. For decorative details on
his brick-built house he had 358½ tons of stone brought from Portland to Reydon
quay at Southwold, in eight separate shipments. The prime cost of the stone was
£292 15s. 6d., but sea freight, land carriage for the five miles to Henham, handling
costs and duty more than doubled this to £714 10s. 8½d., equivalent to over 30d.
per cubic foot.[175] For Haveringland Hall in the 1840s, the clerk of the works

travelled to Bath at the start of the project to arrange the supply of stone. 1015 tons were shipped to Great Yarmouth in nine consignments, transported by wherry to Norwich and the final twelve miles to Haveringland by waggon. The cost of the stone f.o.b. Bristol was 15s. 8d. per ton. Sea freight added 16s. 3d. to this, and Yarmouth-Haveringland carriage 9s., making the delivered cost £2 0s. 11d. per ton (over 30d. per cubic foot), two and a half times the cost at Bristol. Best York stone for the same project, shipped out of the Humber direct to Norwich, cost £1 18s. 1d. per ton f.o.b., and £3 0s. 5d. at Haveringland (45d. per cubic foot).

Westmorland slate was an expensive but much favoured roofing material. Sir Armine Wodehouse's contract with his slater, Peter Westcott, for work at Kimberley (Norfolk) in the 1750s, reveals not only details of prices and carriage arrangements, but the problem of synchronising deliveries with the availability of slaters on site and the forwardness of the building. Slaters met the ship at Great Yarmouth, assisting with the transfer of the slate to a wherry for the river voyage to Norwich and the loading of the waggons for carting ten miles to Kimberley. When the slate arrived before Thomas Prowse's four corner towers were completed, the slaters (an unknown breed in Norfolk in the 1750s) returned to London. For the domestic wing, two metropolitan slaters kicked their heels for twelve days in Great Yarmouth waiting for the ship to arrive, fondly imagining Sir Armine would meet their expenses. A slater travelled with the vessel bringing the next consignment, but again roofs were not ready and the slaters went home. Sir Armine paid their wages only from the time of arrival of the slate at the port and refused to pay the man who had travelled with the ship.[176] In the 1770s, Westmorland slate delivered to the coast at Ulverston for 40s. per ton could be shipped to King's Lynn for an additional 15s.[177] With good sea and canal connections, the cost of delivery of slate from Ulverston (costing 52s. per ton at the quarry) to Eshton in 1838 was 6s. 6d. per ton to the Leeds and Liverpool canal terminal, then 17s. per ton for canal freight.[178]

Timber was usually the single most expensive material employed in housebuilding. An estate might furnish much of the material itself, but the use of imported hardwoods and softwoods was common. The greater suitability of foreign wood for specific purposes, its cheapness and accessibility, meant that imports rose steadily throughout the eighteenth century.[179] Deals from the Baltic states, oak from Flanders, and exotic woods from the Americas, flooded onto English building sites. The quantities needed for one project might justify the engagement of an overseas agent and the delivery of complete shiploads to the nearest port. For Burley-on-the-Hill in 1696, the supply of deals from Dram and Christiania was organised by John Landsdell, a London merchant, shiploads being consigned to a Spalding dealer for onward carriage on Lord Nottingham's behalf.[180] Delivery of Swedish deals was arranged for William Blathwayt at Dyrham in 1701 by Dr John Robinson, Minister to Sweden. A Swedish ship brought the cargo to London for conveyance by coaster to Bristol. Blathwayt also imported Flanders oak for doors and window shutters, Virginian walnut for the staircase built in the first phase of construction, and American cedar for the later 'best' staircase.[181] Baltic softwoods for Harewood came through the port of Hull. The selection, measurement and checking of both local and imported timber proved such an exacting and time-consuming job that Edwin Lascelles engaged an agent, William Smith of Leeds, to handle the business. He took charge of all arrangements and travelled to Amsterdam and Norway in the course of his duties.[182]

It was more usual for timber supplies to be arranged by the clerk of the works, selecting, felling and transporting timber from the estate's woods or yards, or buying from a dealer located at a port or on navigable water inland. Thus Rufus Marsden organised the movement of over 400 loads of *estate* timber to Henham, some from as far as twelve miles away, at a cost ranging from 2s. 4d. to 5s. per load. But he also bought imported timber in Great Yarmouth, at auction or from dealers. The distinction between material cost and freight is not always clear in the accounts but, for timber costing £1379 in Yarmouth, an additional £164 was spent carrying it to Beccles by water and a further eight miles by road to Henham. Edward Fellowes spent £2416 14s. 3d. on imported timber for Haveringland, mainly from a Norwich dealer, James Steward; the value of the estate timber used was £679 10s. 0d., the two sums amounting to 14.5 per cent of the cost of the house.

Lime was made wherever limestone or chalk suitable for burning was available. Appreciating their aesthetic impact as much as their economic importance, Mrs Philip Lybbe Powys in 1771 found that the kilns of The Hills, her Shropshire cousins, had 'a very pretty effect from the house in a dark evening'.[183] More prosaically, the Heacham accounts give some indication of their cost and scale. In 1775 Edmund Rolfe used 4800 bricks to make a new lime kiln. Constructing and running it for one year cost £46 2s. 0d., including £17 2s. 0d. for fourteen chaldrons of coal and £8 12s. 0d. for the lime-burner. It produced eighty-six chaldrons of lime, charged at 10s. each to the building account.[184] The quicklime from the kiln was slaked with water for making mortar and some plasters, although for the highest quality of external rendering or internal work special grades might have to be bought in. John Rous at Henham had lime available at nearby Reydon, but it seems not to have been of building quality and he bought lime for 12s. per chaldron delivered at Beccles and spent a further 5s. per chaldron transporting it eight miles to the building site. Another six tons or more of materials for the finer plaster work came from London through the port of Aldeburgh.[185] Sand for mixing with lime to make mortar was usually dug locally; with typically three parts sand mixed with every part of lime, hundreds of loads were required.

Lead was used for covering flat or low-pitched roofs, valleys between ridges, chimney flashings, and for gutters and downpipes, internal plumbing and glazing. It was expensive, and costly to transport from the few available sources, mainly in Derbyshire and the Mendip Hills. Hopeful that he could discover a valuable estate resource, William Blathwayt engaged miners in 1698 to look for lead ore on his Gloucestershire estate, but without success.[186] Lead was often supplied by the plumbers themselves, charging for the material by weight and casting it into sheets at the building site. For a modest house in Warwickshire in 1720, the cost of lead and its carriage came to £162 out of a total expenditure of £860.[187] This seems to have been an extreme case. Indeed, if the figure for lead is correct, the total building costs may be understated, but the frequent inclusion of the cost of lead and its carriage in the total cost of plumbing (sometimes including glazing as well) complicates the analysis of bills. When building John Carr's Denton Hall (Yorkshire) in the 1770s, £310 2s. 0d. was spent on lead, 3.3 per cent of £9459 11s. 7d., the total cost of the house.[188] John Davidson, the Henham plumber, charged £1442 18s. 11d. for labour and materials (6.7 per cent of the cost of the house), of which only £158 was for wages.[189]

For two hundred and fifty years, the River Tyne was the most important centre of the English glassmaking industry, sited there through the availability of cheap coal. For glazing, superior quality crown glass was usually chosen, although the size of pane that could be cut was limited by the diameter (forty-eight to sixty inches) of the circular 'table' produced by the process, and the restriction of a 'bull's eye' in the centre. William Blathwayt's glass for Dyrham was supplied by his glazier from London, whereas John Rous had glass for Henham shipped direct from the north east to Great Yarmouth, where it was transferred to another vessel for conveyance to Beccles. The glass completed its hazardous journey by road and, not surprisingly, Rous complained to the North Glass Company in Newcastle about breakages en route.[190] His glazier charged 5s. per piece of 22¾ by 18¾ inches. For Eshton in 1825 Mathew Wilson bought 340 sheets of much more expensive polished plate glass (15⅝ by 11⅝ inches) from a London company for 10s. 3d. each.[191] For larger windows, glass had to be imported from the Continent, although supplies were interrupted during the French wars and it was not until the 1830s that imports, backed by superior technology, made a marked impression. House builders benefited from the removal of excise duty on glass in 1845. Factory prices were cut by more than a half and manufacture on the Tyne collapsed in the face of competition from Lancashire companies better placed to profit from the tax change with new sheet glass processes.[192] By about 1850 it was possible to buy vast fourteen-by-eight-feet glass sheets at less than one-tenth of the cost of their eighteenth-century equivalents.[193] Large plate-glass sashes then became common. George Gilbert Scott's Kelham Hall (Nottinghamshire, 1858–61), a providential commission after the original house had burned down (he had, ironically, been inserting plate-glass windows), embodied sheets as much as ten feet high in its Gothic design (Plate 80).[194] Spectacular glasshouses

PLATE 80.   Kelham Hall, Nottinghamshire (George Gilbert Scott, 1858–61).

proliferated. The Duke of Devonshire's gardener, Joseph Paxton, had in 1836–40 crowned a series for his master at Chatsworth with the monumental glass and cast-iron 'Great Stove', 277 by 123 feet, and 67 feet high.[195] Similarly ambitious but less affluent patrons took advantage of the later fall in prices to reglaze their windows and erect extensive conservatories.

The fabrication of those iron components needed in the building process – nails, securing ties and cramps, door and window catches and fire-bars for example – was a specialised manufacturing rather than a building-site activity. Nevertheless, the blacksmith was an important member of the workforce. A forge was sometimes established on the building site, as at Henham in the 1790s, where raw material in the form of iron bars and rods was bought for the smith (and action taken against rats knawing his bellows); or the services of a nearby tradesman might be called upon when required.[196] Workmen's tools had to be repaired and sharpened, and components made for the construction and repair of barrows and carts, and a farrier would be occupied keeping the horses in working condition. But a widening range of ironmongery, and non-ferrous goods within the province of the whitesmith, was bought from local dealers, in nearby towns, and in London – nails, sieves, buckets, brushes, tools, hinges, locks, candles, and transparent paper for covering window openings before they were glazed. By the second half of the eighteenth century, Birmingham had established a dominant position for the manufacture of door furniture. Iron girders were increasingly used in the structures of houses as the nineteenth century progressed. The most expensive fixtures were heating stoves and kitchen ranges. The vast cast-iron installations in the new country-house kitchens of the nineteenth century, with smoke- and mechanically-driven jacks to turn the roasting spits, backed by stoves, boilers, and hot-cupboards, reflected the quickening advance of technology into the country house from the late eighteenth century (Plate 81). Owners and their cooks saw them on display in the warehouses of specialist suppliers in London and the larger provincial cities.[197] When houses were modernised or new-built owners, like the servant-keeping classes in general, eagerly installed them.[198] From the 1840s gas-making plant for lighting and cooking was also installed. Such equipment was invariably fitted by the supplier's own men, or under their direct supervision.

The final internal decoration of a new house could not be rushed. Servants moved in as early as possible to light fires to dry out the building. Stone houses were notoriously slow to respond, as Lord Nottingham was advised when

PLATE 81.   Holkham Hall, Norfolk. The old kitchen with its huge cast iron range.

considering the construction of Burley-on-the-Hill: 'stone work ripens by so slow degrees in comparison to brick, that the one in a year or two may afford a tolerable habitation, while the other in thrice the time will continue green, moist, cold and unfit to dwell in'.[199] In reality the equally massive brick-built houses also took a long time to dry. For several years winter residence in either must have been spine-chilling. Thomas Cubitt advised his clients to live 'under builder's finish' for two years to prevent expensive decoration from being spoiled.[200] Nevertheless, the final stages of building were often completed with the family already in residence.

Decorative schemes were carefully specified by house owners but, surprisingly, painters often did not themselves supply materials, even essential tools like brushes. Long lists of colours and oils occur in building accounts: Prussian Blue, Roman Ochre, Naples Red and Turkey Umber were among the colours shipped from London to John Rous at Henham in 1798 (over a year after servants had moved into the house), together with linseed oil, turpentine, pummice stone, emery and glass paper, two dozen brushes and one dozen camel-hair pencils (fine brushes).[201] Half a century later, Haveringland Hall, although built with a directly-recruited labour force, was painted and decorated by a London contractor, Thomas Fairs. His bill for work done in 1844–45 (construction was completed in 1842) added £1150 to the £21,380 spent building the house.

The payment of the final bill from the decorators signalled the end of the country house building process, if not spending, because elaborate furnishings and upholstery, especially of hangings, might still have to be completed. A building project could merge into one of remodelling because some patrons had a perpetual itch to build and improve. Moreover, craftsmen were retained to make sure a house worked. A remarkable thirty-five-page bill detailing the efforts of John Langwith, a self-employed joiner who worked at Syston Park (Lincolnshire) almost continuously between 1766 and 1773, has survived. Langwith was the Figaro of the site. He undertook journeys to Newark, Nottingham, Boston, Sleaford, Collyweston and Buxton to secure materials; he made barrows, ladders, scaffolding, 'rammel' carts (prototype skips) and moulds in the quiet winter period; he surrounded the house with a fence (it needed constant repair); he protected chimney-pieces and columns with slips; he cleared snow 'off ye house'; he even made a bedstead for one workman. Not only did he ensure that the whole building project ran easily in assisting masons, carvers, plumbers and upholsterers in all their fine work, he also ensured that everything operated smoothly in the new house, easing doors and windows, 'try[ing] ye chimneys', making a seat for the servants hall, even fixing the door of the hen-roost and 'putting up a seat against a tree in ye park'. Every feature of a country house functioned so well because there were craftsmen like John Langwith to ensure that no detail was overlooked.[202]

The conclusion of a project can nevertheless usually be identified. Its success depended upon the efficient deployment of considerable resources of men and materials. The faith of many builders in the satisfactory outcome of their great enterprise was often sorely tested and the journey could be a long one. As we saw in the previous chapter, building contracts with specified completion dates were evident early in our period, and the carcase of a straightforward house might be completed within two years. Its finishing, however, could take much longer and very large houses sometimes took decades to complete. Philip Yorke noted in 1755 that Hopetoun House (West Lothian, Scotland) 'was begun by this Lord's father in 1698, and has been in a state of alteration and addition ever since and is not yet completed'.[203] That might be the builder's choice, matching the rate of his expenditure with his income, but many must have wondered if they were ever to be free of the disruption of building and the unceasing drain on their income, echoing William Blathwayt's cry at Dyrham, or Philip Yorke's that Holkham, *if ever completed*, would be the finest house in England.[204]

6

The Pattern of Building

'And All the World are running Mad after Building, as far as they can reach.'
Sir John Vanbrugh in 1708, writing to the Earl of Manchester.[1]

'It surprized me a good deal to find that in so large a County as Suffolk and so near the Metropolis, not a single Gentleman's Seat that I saw or heard of, except the Duke of Grafton's at Euston, had been improved in the modern taste.'
Charles Lyttelton to Sanderson Miller, August 1758.[2]

In the summer of 1758, Charles Lyttelton (1714–1768), Dean of Exeter and later Bishop of Carlisle, set out from London for East Anglia on a country house jaunt. He rode through Essex, Suffolk and Norfolk, and stayed the weekend with the Bishop of Norwich, writing to the architect Sanderson Miller that the bishop had 'expended much money on his house and gardens, so that it may justly be considered the best Episcopal mansion within any City in the Kingdom' (an opinion not generally shared).[3] The bishop's hospitality stood out in a county where inns, as Lyttelton bemoaned, were generally bad, 'which would be the less felt, if gentlemen were more hospitable, but you will allow me to say that Hospitality does not remarkably flourish in Norfolk ... I was not offered the least refreshment, but a glass of wine at Lord Leicester's, at any house I visited in the whole County.'[4] Lyttelton added, however, that in contrast to the absence of new building in the neighbouring county of Suffolk, 'It is well for the County of Norfolk that three or four Noblemen, etc., have done so much to their Places, else very few strangers would visit a Country that has so few natural Beautys to attract them.'[5]

Lyttelton was a dependable observer. The architectural excitement of the years in which Vanbrugh's world was 'running Mad after Building' had left little mark in Suffolk, the rising tide of Palladianism largely passing it by. Had Lyttelton on the other hand travelled through Yorkshire, he would have reached a different conclusion. Not only might he have appreciated Lord Carlisle's Castle Howard, but also the endeavours of a number of less-exalted gentry, Thomas Duncombe at Duncombe Park, John Brewster at Aldby, John Bourchier at Beningborough and Lord Fairfax at Gilling Castle, following Carlisle's example in the immediate vicinity. Seventeen Yorkshire landowners were among the subscribers to James Gibbs's *A Book of Architecture* (1728), and at least nine of them were building in the 1720s and 1730s.[6] And Lyttelton could hardly have missed the extension of this boom into the 1740s and 1750s as James Paine's and John Carr's careers began to flourish. Above all, the concentration of aristocratic estates in south Yorkshire 'unrivalled in any full county except Rutland', witnessed a surge of building activity, spurred on by the almost megalomaniac intra-family building rivalry of the Wentworths, with the Earl of Strafford and the Marquess of Rockingham competing with successive large additions to Wentworth Castle and Wentworth Woodhouse respectively. Sir John Bland, a notorious gambler, enlarged Kippax Park around 1750 so that its thirty-seven bays encouraged him to wager a bet with Lord Rockingham that Kippax was larger than Wentworth Woodhouse. Although a staggering 600 feet in extent, he narrowly lost (Plate 82).[7] This uneven distribution of housebuilding activity, both chronologically and spatially, had many implications, defining the population of country houses that can be used to examine the link between building and landownership. In this chapter we have explored the differences in the character of county gentry populations and their building experiences in the two centuries after 1660, across the predominantly agricultural, coastal counties of East Anglia, through Midland Northamptonshire, to Yorkshire with its industrial development, into Cheshire and Gloucestershire, both close to flourishing west-coast ports.

PLATE 82.   Wentworth Woodhouse, Yorkshire. The design for the east front, 606 ft long (Ralph Tunnicliffe, 1734, developed by Henry Flitcroft).

When, forty years ago, Sir John Summerson posed the key questions about the number of country houses, their chronology and their distribution, he arranged 148 large country houses erected in England between 1710 and 1740 in chronological order of building.[8] Acknowledging the inadequate basis of the assessment, and the approximate dating of some of the houses, he observed a startling onset of activity in 1720–24 and suspected a latent stylistic factor at the beginning of this boom with the desire to build augmented by the urge to employ the new Palladian style. Who was building in these thirty years? More than 75 per cent of the houses were built on the site of an old house on inherited property. A minority were new owners who rebuilt; the incentive to replace Tudor and Stuart manor houses with ones in the modern taste was obvious. In 120 documented cases, of twenty-seven peers and ninety-three commoners building, fifty-four were at one time or another MPs. They represented 58 per cent over the thirty-year period, and 71 per cent in the first fifteen years (1710–25), suggesting a close connection between political activity and architectural enterprise.

The distribution of the houses Sir John discussed was remarkably even throughout the English counties, which was unsurprising since the main object was to enhance the owner's prestige in his neighbourhood and sphere of political influence. He acknowledged that it was easier to list without serious error houses designed by top-flight architects with Court connections – members of the Office of Works – than those built by contracting masons or bricklayers (an architectural distinction of importance until after 1780), the list of which is likely to be seriously incomplete. His analysis may therefore give undue weight to metropolitan influence and politically active or well-connected men. The even distribution of building activity across the country then merely reflects the distribution of constituencies and says little about possible variations between counties and regions.

More recent studies, reviewed in the Appendix, have revealed significant regional differences in the number of country houses and their building chronology. Conclusions are dependant upon the choice of sample. Concentration upon a landowning elite, for example, leads to the understatement of the building activity of those, especially in the nineteenth century, less concerned with owning a large estate. The definition of what constitutes a new building also presents problems. The boundary between the radical remodelling of a house and a complete rebuild is sometimes blurred; deciding what is a significant alteration introduces further subjectivity; and there is a bias in the availability of data towards the later years in any study period. Notwithstanding these reservations, some interesting differences between counties have emerged. Two major building periods have been pointed up, the first extending from 1660 until 1730, the second from the 1790s until well into the nineteenth century.[9] But this template does not neatly fit all counties: general patterns hide a multitude of differences. Aristocratic building on the larger English estates (10,000 acres or more) was always buoyant in both new construction and remodelling until about 1830, then fell away. The character of the country house builder was changing, with successful industrial entrepreneurs and their bankers increasingly evident in the ranks of the nineteenth-century builders, displacing the established landed families as creators of new country houses.

Our main focus is upon the house-building activity of the landed classes – the owners of significant estates whose houses qualify as family seats performing the roles of local power bases and status symbols, 'country houses' rather than simply large houses in the country. The distinction is not of course clear-cut. Especially from the late eighteenth century, the most successful bankers and industrialists bought large estates and founded landed dynasties, members of which in the course of one or two generations acquired educations, leisure pursuits, outlooks and sometimes titles to match those of long-established landed lines. But for the later entrants into the ranks of the great landowners, the estate as the centre of a paternalistic agricultural economy, the source of local or national political influence and the focus of generations of dynastic pride, was likely to be of lesser significance.

The New Domesday survey of landownership in the early 1870s provides the best starting point for an examination of building activity on landed estates. Bateman's analysis of this great inquiry is a reasonably accurate listing of the owners of more than 3000 acres of land and an income of at least £3000 per annum.[10] For these estates we have identified seats and their building histories. These histories do not necessarily relate to a particular family. Many estates did remain the property of one family throughout the period, but others changed hands, a process sometimes concealed by a new owner's adoption of the old family name. Rankings of estates by size were not constant, as estates grew at different rates through the absorption of others by inheritance, marriage and purchase. Therefore our classification based on the 1870s will not necessarily apply in earlier years, with possibly greater divergence the further back in time one goes. If building activity has been missed by our study it will have been on smaller estates because in the process of estate enlargement in our period it was rare for the largest estates to disappear. If they lost their separate identity before their houses were rebuilt (increasingly likely the further one gets from the 1870s), their absence from our list is unimportant. Some of the houses on estates which lost their separate identity became secondary seats and have been included. We have also looked at the estates of the squirearchy, with estates of 1000 to 3000 acres, for which the starting points are the county lists in the New Domesday.[11] It is not, however, possible to define this group with the same precision. The distinction between the estates of the squirearchy, the larger farmers, the owners of areas of relatively unproductive land, and those estate-owners who drew most of their income from non-landed activities is unclear simply from a perusal of the columns of acreages in the New Domesday, and the documentation of the building history of their houses, even when they can be identified, is often incomplete.

We have studied in detail country house building in the counties of Cheshire, Gloucestershire, Norfolk, Northamptonshire and Suffolk, and the West Riding of Yorkshire. Our analysis has benefited from the availability of published surveys of the country houses of Cheshire and Gloucestershire, and the work of the RCHME in Northamptonshire.[12] Coverage by county histories, however, is uneven. Northamptonshire, for example, has two major early histories, whereas Suffolk has no similar parish by parish equivalent.[13] Progress in publishing the Victoria County Histories is equally variable: the East Riding of Yorkshire is well surveyed in modern volumes; Norfolk and Suffolk possess none at all.[14] Therefore, although the county studies have been pursued as far as possible on a comparable basis, some areas remain better documented than others. Excepting the West Riding, the counties were predominately rural and escaped massive industrialisation in the nineteenth century. They nevertheless vary in character, from mainly arable East Anglia to the more pastoral Cheshire and Gloucestershire. East Anglia had, as observed, few local sources of freestone for building whereas the limestone of Northamptonshire and Gloucestershire is revealed in many of their houses. These counties were too far from London to be attractive to those working merchants and financiers able to afford a country estate, yet the influence of Bristol, Hull and Liverpool, and the impact on neighbouring Cheshire of the burgeoning industrial activity of Lancashire, and of the woollen-textile industry in the West Riding of Yorkshire, was considerable. The pattern of landownership is summarised in Table 3.

Table 3. *Pattern of landownership:*
percentage of county acreages owned by categories of landowner

County	'Aristocratic' estates[a] 10,000 a. +	Greater Gentry[b] 3–10,000 a.	Squirearchy[c] 1000–3000 a.
Cheshire	35	16	11
Gloucestershire	16	21	12
Norfolk	19	22	15
Northamptonshire	30	17	9
Suffolk	22	17	12
Weighted averages	23.1	19.1	12.3
Yorkshire[d]	28	18	12
England	24	17	12.4

Notes:

[a] Thompson, *English Landed Society*, p. 32, classified owners of estates above 10,000 a. as 'landed aristocracy', although not all were titled, to distinguish them from the greater gentry.

[b] Ibid., p. 114.

[c] Ibid., p. 115.

[d] Percentages for the individual Ridings were not given.

The distribution of the estates of peers, and to a lesser extent those of the greater land-owners, is not the same as the distribution of their seats, because some land was held in counties where they were not resident. Thompson, *English Landed Society*, p. 31.

Cheshire and Northamptonshire stand out as having the highest proportion of large estates, and the greatest density of country seats. The greater gentry were relatively more prominent in Gloucestershire and Norfolk, and Yorkshire was the least densely populated with seats. Overall, the sum of the these counties is close to the English average.

Figure 2 shows the chronology of building from the 1660s to 1880 for 353 seats in the study counties on the estates of the owners of at least 3000 acres nationally. The use of the term 'new' house embraces not only the completely new house constructed on a fresh site but also those (the majority) completely rebuilt or substantially reconstructed on the same site. In some instances existing fabric may have been incorporated in the new structure, but the criterion for inclusion in the list is the thoroughgoing rebuilding of the body of the house, not simply its fashionable recasing. The data are broken down by county in Table 4. Building

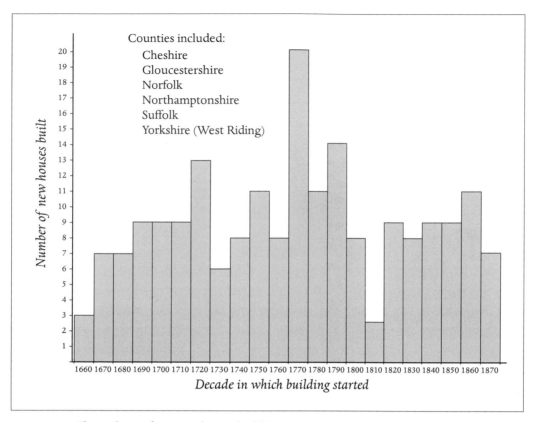

FIGURE 2. Chronology of country house building, 1660–1880

activity grew steadily after the Restoration and peaked in the 1720s. After a pause, it recovered in the 1750s. The 1770s saw activity rise sharply to its highest level. Building continued through the 1790s but collapsed with the French wars, resuming again in the 1820s. A steady level was maintained through the nineteenth century, until a precipitous fall in the 1880s coincided with the onset of agricultural crisis. Almost one-third of the total population, 113 houses, were never completely rebuilt in the period.

CREATING PARADISE

Table 4. *Building chronology, 1660s to 1870s:*
new and rebuilt houses in each decade by county for owners of more than
3000 acres nationally

	Cheshire	Gloucs.	Norfolk	Northants.	Suffolk	Yorks WR	Total
Seats	43	55	82	39	48	86	353
Pre-1660 houses not rebuilt	12	18	23	26	11	23	113
1660	—	—	2	—	1	—	3
1670	1	2	—	1	—	3	7
1680	—	1	2	1	—	3	7
1690	1	4	2	—	1	1	9
1700	—	2	2	1	1	3	9
1710	3	2	2	—	—	2	9
1720	1	—	6	3	—	3	13
1730	1	1	2	—	—	2	6
1740	1	1	1	2	1	2	8
1750	1	—	2	1	—	7	11
1760	2	2	1	—	1	2	8
1770	4	3	4	2	5	2	20
1780	2+1[a]	1	3	—	3	1	10+1[a]
1790	—	2	4	1	6	1	14
1800	1	2	1	—	1	3	8
1810	1	1	2	—	—	—	4
1820	3	3	1+1[a]	—	—	1	8+1[a]
1830	2	1+1[a]	1[a]	—	3	—	6+2[a]
1840	1	2	1	—	2	1+2[a]	7+2[a]
1850	—	1+1[a]	4+2[a]	—	1[a]	1	6+3[a]
1860	1	2[a]	1[a]	1+1[a]	3	1+1[a]	6+5[a]
1870	1	1+1[a]	2+2[a]	—	—	—	4+3[a]
Imprecise dates:							
C17th	1	—	—	—	—	—	1
Late C17th	2	—	1	—	—	2	3
Early C18th	—	—	1	—	2	—	3
Mid C18th	1	—	—	—	—	—	1
C18th	—	—	3	—	3	7	6

Mid Georgian	—	—	—	—	1	1	1
Late Georgian	—	—	3	—	—	1	3
Georgian	—	—	1	—	—	1	1
Early C19th	—	—	1	—	1	—	2
C19th	—	—	1	—	—	—	1
No date	—	5	4	—	2	12	11

Note: [a] Second rebuilding of house after 1660.

The periods of heightened building activity in these six counties are close to those identified by the studies reviewed in the Appendix, with an earlier start for the late eighteenth-century boom, and a distinct pause in the first two decades of the nineteenth century.[16] There are, however, marked divergences from the average picture at county level: 64 per cent of pre-1660 houses in Northampton-shire survived without complete rebuilding (Plate 83); whereas the figure for Suffolk was barely 21 per cent.[17] Although Suffolk had the highest proportion of

PLATE 83. Dingley Hall, Northamptonshire. A representative of the county's durable early houses. A sixteenth-century stone house with major later additions but never completely rebuilt.

houses rebuilt, however, there was very little new building before the 1770s, while
in Gloucestershire and Norfolk there was considerable activity in the late seventeenth and early eighteenth centuries. The boom of the 1750s is almost entirely
attributable to new construction in the West Riding. Northamptonshire is noteworthy for the very low level of new building in the nineteenth century. Table 5
compares the percentages of houses built before 1800, revealing that the differences
between counties are clear cut.

Table 5. *Percentage of datable houses built before 1800*

	For all estates	Estate size (thousand acres)		
		10+	5+	3+
Cheshire	76.7	77.8	75.0	76.9
Gloucestershire	68.0	77.3	87.5	60.0
Norfolk	74.4	80.6	76.9	71.4
Northamptonshire	94.9	88.2	100.0	100.0
Suffolk	78.3	80.0	78.6	66.7
Yorkshire, W. Riding	85.1	92.0	80.0	84.2

Note: Houses built before 1660, and those with imprecise dates which can nevertheless be assigned to a century, have been included.

The relative lack of building in Northamptonshire after 1800 is noteworthy.
Early houses also predominate in the West Riding, especially on the larger estates.
Gloucestershire has the highest proportion of nineteenth-century houses. In all
the counties, however, the majority of houses on these estates at the end of the
1870s had been built before 1800. For this range of estate size, houses on the
largest estates tend to be earlier than those on the smaller ones.[18]

The character of building in each of the counties becomes clearer if three
periods of heightened activity identified in Table 4 are considered in more detail –
the 1690s to 1720s, 1770s to 1790s, and the 1850s to 1870s. Table 6 gives a breakdown
for the first period. The proportion of seats in Northamptonshire rebuilt in the
years 1660–1880 was relatively low and of these more than a quarter were built
in the forty years after 1690. Three of the four houses were rebuilt after a change
of owner or head of family. The situation in Suffolk diverged sharply from that
in Northamptonshire. As Lyttelton observed on his travels, very few new houses
were built in this period, and those were on small estates – both being resold in
the eighteenth century. Dr Simon Patrick, Bishop of Ely, bought Dalham Hall

Table 6. *The building of new houses, 1690–1729*

	Total	Estate size, thousand acres			Percentage of all new builds, 1660–1879
		10+	5+	3+	
Cheshire	5	3	2	0	15.6
Gloucestershire	8	4	1	3	21.6
Norfolk	12	6	4	2	19.7
Northampton	4	1	3	0	28.6
Suffolk	2	0	0	2	5.6
Yorkshire, W. Riding	9	6	2	1	16.7
Total	40	20	12	8	17.1

in 1702 and rebuilt it, but after his death in 1707 the estate was sold to John Affleck, a Baltic merchant, whose descendants held the property until 1901.[19] Worlingham Hall was rebuilt at the end of the seventeenth century and sold in 1755.[20] In contrast, all of the Cheshire houses were built on the estates of long-established families and they remained in the same family or descended by marriage until at least the 1870s. In Gloucestershire new owners were prominent among the builders at Dyrham and Barnsley Park (both acquired by marriage, and where decayed manor houses were rebuilt), and at Witcombe Park and Sandywell Park. Both William Blathwayt at Dyrham and Edward Southwell at King's Weston deployed the profits of public office. Two of the three houses built on 3000–5000 acre estates did not last long. Sir Richard Cocks inherited Dumbleton from his grandfather in 1684 and shortly afterwards built a new house. His and the next generation failed to produce a male heir and the estate passed to a relative who had no use for the house. It was abandoned by the 1770s.[21] Henry Brett bought Sandywell in 1704, but by 1708 had mortgaged the property, perhaps to finance the completion of his new house, which he sold outright in 1712.[22] The new owner, Lord Conway, soon enlarged it. In Norfolk, Sir Robert Walpole built Houghton and his brother Horatio built at Wolterton on his newly-acquired estate. There were new owners at North Elmham and Narford (where the fruits of office financed building, as they had at Houghton). Some of the smaller estates soon changed hands: West Harling before the new house was even finished and Cranmer Hall in 1751. Four more of the 3000–5000 acre estates changed hands in the nineteenth century. In Yorkshire, Thomas, Duke of Leeds, built at Kiveton in the 1690s, but the use of new money was also evident. John Aislabie, whose fortune survived the condemnation of Parliament for using the office of Chancellor of the Exchequer to profit from the South Sea Bubble, retired to build Studley Royal. Robert Benson, first Lord Bingley, whose father had prospered under the Commonwealth, also did well out of South Sea speculation. He created Bramham. The York merchant, Sir William Robinson, built Newby (now Baldersby) Park from 1718, of architectural significance as 'the first Palladian villa in England' (Plate 84).[23]

With few new houses being built in any one county, the identification of trends is difficult, but whereas in the whole period 1660 to 1879 the distribution of new or rebuilt houses between estates closely matches the proportion of each size of estate in the sample, in 1690 to 1729 there was a slight bias towards building on the larger estates.[24] The small estates were more likely to change hands later, although the tempting conclusion that indebtedness as a result of building was generally a factor is difficult to substantiate. Some counties were more favoured by (or accessible to) new men than others, and in some counties there was almost no new building at all. Neighbouring counties, for example Suffolk and Norfolk, had quite different building profiles in these years.

The greatest concentration of new building in the whole study period ran from the 1770s to the 1790s. Twenty houses were started in the 1770s alone, half as many again as in the most active decade outside this thirty-year period. Table 7 shows the pattern of construction in these years.

Table 7. *The building of new houses, 1770–99*

	Total	Estate size, thousand acres			Percentage of all new builds, 1660–1879
		10+	5+	3+	
Cheshire	7	3	1	3	21.9
Gloucestershire	6	0	4	2	16.2
Norfolk	11	5	5	1	18.0
Northampton	3	1	0	2	21.4
Suffolk	14	8	3	3	38.9
Yorkshire, W. Riding	4	1	3	0	7.4
Total	45	18	16	11	19.2

Suffolk stands out as enjoying a remarkable building boom in this period, as

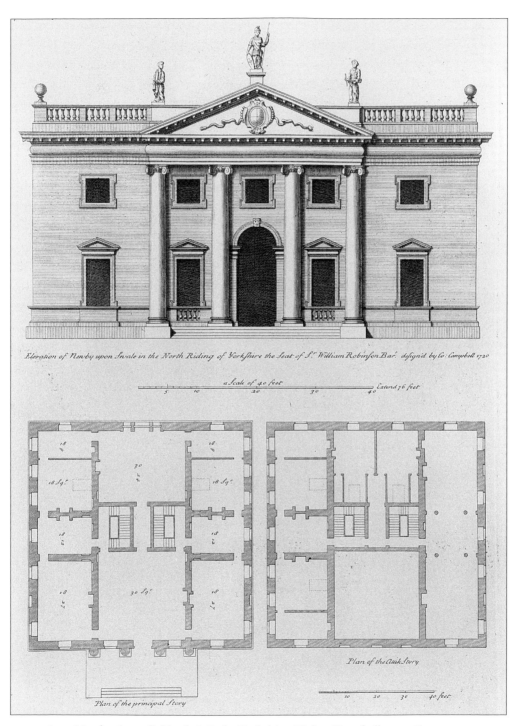

Elevation of Newby upon Swale in the North Riding of Yorkshire the Seat of S.ʳ William Robinson Bar.ᵗ design't by Co: Campbell 1720

a Scale of 40 feet

Extend 76 feet

Plan of the principal Story

Plan of the Attik Story

PLATE 84. Newby (now Baldersby) Park, Yorkshire (Colen Campbell, 1720–8).

PLATE 85.   Ickworth, Suffolk (Francis Sandys from a design by Mario Asprucci, 1795–1803, completed 1824–29).

PLATE 86.   Belle Isle, Westmorland (John Plaw, 1775). A small circular house which inspired the design of Ballyscullion, Londonderry, the precursor of the fourth Earl of Bristol, Bishop of Derry's Ickworth.

if a demand for new houses, latent earlier in the century, was at last satisfied. Over one-third of all the houses built between 1660 and 1880 were constructed in these thirty years. There was certainly ground to make up, and the lead was taken by the county's largest landowners. The Herveys, whose social position in the county qualified them to inspire a fashion for building earlier in the century, but whose financial circumstances led to them being conspicuously under-housed, at last started to rebuild Ickworth, when the fourth Earl of Bristol's income from his extensive English estates was supplemented by those of his Irish bishopric of Derry (Plates 85–86). Rather earlier, a cluster of Suffolk gentlemen, Philip Broke, Sir Charles Kent, Sir John Rous, Sir Gerard Vanneck and Sir Richard Wallace, all patronised the eminently fashionable James Wyatt. Long-established families, like the Herveys and Rouses, and the Bacons who engaged James Paine to rebuild Shrubland Park, were matched by those new to the county such as Vanneck at Heveningham (Plates 87–88), Berners (who bought Woolver-stone around 1773 and then rebuilt), and Viscount Keppel at Elveden. Most of the estates remained in the same family for generations, although Sir Charles

PLATE 87.   Heveningham Hall, Suffolk. The early eighteenth-century house showing the central block incorporated in the rebuilding of the 1770s.

PLATE 88.   Heveningham Hall, Suffolk (Sir Robert Taylor and James Wyatt, 1778–84).

Kent's estate at Fornham St Genevieve, with its new house, was sold as early as 1789.

In Cheshire, too, a group of houses appeared to the designs of a single architect: no fewer than five by James Wyatt's elder brother Samuel. Emulation, as in Suffolk with its knot of James Wyatt houses, was probably a factor. The emergence of professional architects in the later eighteenth century may also have encouraged building by landowners who lacked the architectural knowledge and self-confidence of gentlemen earlier in the century. Four long-established Cheshire families built and at least three of the county's builders had just succeeded to their estates.[25] In Norfolk, four old families and one new purchaser were among the builders.[26] In contrast, the great landowners in Gloucestershire at this stage were inactive. One new purchaser, a Quaker banker from Bristol, built Blaise Castle. Dilapidated Estcourt Park was also rebuilt by Thomas Estcourt, who secured a private Act to permit the sale of settled London property to pay for the work. Likewise there was little activity in Northamptonshire. Lord John Cavendish, son of the Duke of Devonshire, rebuilt Billing Hall after buying it in 1776 from George, Earl of Egremont, who had inherited the estate from an uncle;

PLATE 89.   Heath Hall, Yorkshire (remodelled by John Carr from *c.* 1754). Described thirty years later as 'an elegant composition in architecture' although 'not exactly conformable to the present taste'.

and, in turn, Cavendish's heir resold.[27] Courteenhall Hall, owned by the Wake family since 1672, was rebuilt when it became the main seat of a new heir. East Carlton Hall, in the Palmer family since the fifteenth century, was demolished, to be replaced by a new house to the design of John Johnson by the fifth Baronet, a decade after he succeeded to the estate in 1765 (Plate 73).

Whereas in the 1750s the level of building activity in the West Riding had outstripped the pace in the other counties, in this period it was relatively low. As we have seen, building in the Palladian manner was then in full flow, rapidly advancing the careers of the young John Carr, engaged at Kirby, Thorp Arch, Heath Hall (Plate 89) and Harewood, and James Paine at Nostell Priory, St Ives (Bingley) and Stockeld. Carr was still designing in a conservative style into the first years of the nineteenth century, his clients including numerous west Yorkshire merchants who, as the eighteenth century progressed, increasingly looked to the acquisition of a country house. While many invested part of their fortune in land, few commanded sufficient acreage to qualify for our list of landed proprietors.

From the 1770s to the 1790s, as in the early eighteenth century, the owners of the larger estates (5000 acres and above) were more prominent among the builders than would be expected from the proportion of the sample they represented, suggesting that country house building booms tended to be led by the larger landowners.

Building activity was much lower in the first two decades of the nineteenth century than it had been in the preceding thirty years. From the 1820s there was a resurgence of construction which lasted until the sharp decline of the 1880s. The pattern of building in the years 1850–79 is shown in Table 8.

Table 8. *The building of new houses, 1850–79*

	Total	Estate size, thousand acres			Percentage of all new builds, 1660–1879
		10+	5+	3+	
Cheshire	2	0	1	1	6.2
Gloucestershire	6	2	1	3	14.3
Norfolk	10	4	2	4	15.4
Northampton	2	2	0	0	14.3
Suffolk	4	1	2	0	10.5
Yorkshire, W. Riding	3	1	1	1	5.6
Total	27	10	7	10	11.5

Although the total number of new houses built in this period was much lower than in the 1770s to 1790s, there are again differences in the distribution between counties. The number of new houses built in Gloucestershire, six, was the same in both periods, and the number in Norfolk was similarly balanced, ten from 1850–79 compared with eleven in the 1770s to 1790s. The number of new houses in the other counties was much lower in the later period. Both well-established families and 'new' men replaced old houses which could not satisfy Victorian needs. Houses originally built in the seventeenth century – Alderley House, Colesbourne Park, Eyford Park, Lydney Park and Rendcomb Park – finally succumbed to Gloucestershire demolition men. Only the last-named was for a new wealthy owner, the bullion broker Sir Francis Goldsmid. He bought the estate in 1864 and rebuilt the house to the designs of Philip Hardwick. A nineteenth-century fortune also backed the replacement of Westonbirt, then only forty years old, where R. S. Holford (brother-in-law of Robert Blagden Hale who rebuilt Alderley House) built a new house in the 1860s with money derived from the New River Company which supplied London's water.

The geographical distribution of new building in Norfolk showed a marked bias with spending on completely rebuilt (and remodelled) houses concentrated, on the one hand, on sporting estates in the west of the county, and on the other hand, smaller estates around Norwich. The Prince of Wales's Sandringham House, rebuilt in the 1860s, was a notable social magnet. His sporting companion, Edward Green, deploying an industrial fortune made from his father's invention of the 'Green's Economizer' for steam engines, moved to nearby Snettisham from Wakefield, building Ken Hill in the 1870s to the designs of the young London architect, J. J. Stevenson. In the south west of the county, Lyne Stephens bought the Lynford estate in 1856 and immediately replaced the house, remodelled as recently as 1827, with a Jacobethan mansion to the designs of William Burn. Epitomising a new purchaser's interest in 'a place in the country' with sporting rather than agricultural prospects, Stephens, heir to a Lisbon merchant's fortune, 'gave £133,000 for Lynford and Tofts 7,770 acres – rental said to be about £1,800 per ann.' [28] This was, if Lord Walsingham's information was correct, a staggering eighty-four years' purchase. He then spent a reported £145,000 on the house. Long-established families, the Hares at Stow Bardolph and a kinsman at Docking, were also rebuilding in west Norfolk. Cockley Cley and Congham were other new houses in this western group. Close to Norwich, old families rebuilt at Dunston (taking the house away from the newly-laid London railway) and Taverham, and John Gurney of the Norfolk banking family completed Sprowston Hall in the 1870s, soon after his marriage.

Just one of the four Suffolk houses built in this period, High House, Campsea Ashe, built to the designs of Anthony Salvin for John Sheppard, was for a long-established family. Rebuilding was precipitated by the destruction of an earlier house by fire. This was also the spur at Brandeston, when the Elizabethan house bought by Charles Austin in the 1830s (it had declined into use as a farmhouse) burnt down during restoration in the 1860s. It was replaced by a house designed by the Ipswich architect R. M. Phipson. Henry Wilson of Stowlangtoft Hall was also a new owner, buying the estate in 1825 and rebuilding in 1859 to designs by John Henry Hakewill. The family of the fifth Lord Rendlesham, who rebuilt Rendlesham Hall to William Burn's designs in 1868–71, was well-established in Suffolk, the property having been bought by his great-grandfather, Peter Thellusson (d. 1797), a London banker and West Indian merchant of Swiss origin.

The fortune which supported Lord Rendlesham's building programme derived from his share of Peter Thellusson's fortune, in trust since 1797 and finally divided with his second cousin, Charles Sabine Augustus Thellusson of Brodsworth (Yorkshire), the other 'eldest male lineal descendent' under the terms of the notorious Thellusson will.[29]

There was little building in Cheshire and Northamptonshire by owners of more than 3000 acres in this period. Sir Philip de Grey Egerton rebuilt Broxton Hall in 1873 as a dower house for the Oulton Park estate but otherwise 'new' money was again prominent. The successful railway contractor Thomas Brassey built Bulkeley Grange on the family's ancestral acres in Cheshire in the 1860s, although his holdings in the county were modest; the family's main seat being at Normanhurst (Sussex), rebuilt by his son. The only major new house in Northamptonshire was Lord Overstone's Overstone Hall of the 1860s, the other qualifying house of these years being Whittlebury Lodge owned by the Loder family in the 1870s and built by Lord Southampton a decade earlier.

Only in this last period were the owners of 3000–5000 acre estates relatively more active builders than their counterparts on the larger properties. As we have seen for earlier decades, county patterns of building were quite dissimilar. Mercantile and industrial money was more conspicuous in the later years, and the changing role of the country house can be seen, for example, in building on the sporting estates of west Norfolk. But 'new' money did not contribute to a major surge in building on the larger estates. In Yorkshire, for instance, there was relatively little new building on them in the 1850–80 period. Charles Thellusson ploughed his share of the Thellusson inheritance into the rebuilding of Brodsworth Hall, the recreational Malham Tarn House was built on the Pennine moors, and the worsted manufacturer James Lund built Malsis House at Sutton-in-Craven. At first sight, therefore, there may appear to be some substance in references to a mythical Victorian building boom, and also the assertion that the number of extremely wealthy entrepreneurs who purchased land on a large scale after 1780 was very small indeed.[30] However, these conclusions have been challenged because not only was a high threshold of land purchase assumed (2000 or, occasionally, 5000 acres as the criterion), which meant that many wealthy newcomers were not counted, but also it was important to include the descendants of wealth creators as well as the fortune-makers themselves.[31] Taking descendants into account, 90 per cent of the forty millionaires who died between 1809 and 1879 had bought land; 80 per cent had succeeded in founding landed families, with estates measured in thousands of acres. Of 150 half-millionaires, it appeared that about half entered the landed ranks. Some of these men will not have been counted by Bateman but, even if all the hundred or so men involved had built houses, those who had larger estates were not concentrated in one area. Whereas, for example, thirty-nine Lancashire cotton masters achieved at least minor gentry status in the nineteenth century, by acquiring a minimum of 1000 acres of land, for the majority who wished to maintain close connections with their businesses, the limited amount of land available meant that they had to be content with country houses on small acreages. Consequently, the larger the estate they obtained, the farther from Lancashire it was likely to be.[32] The immensely-rich Leeds merchant William Denison left seven estates scattered across four counties when he died in 1782. The banker Lewis Loyd, holding land in eleven counties, chose to settle in Northamptonshire; the engineer William Dalziel Mackenzie bought nearly 28,000 acres in eight counties; the Halifax carpet-weaving fortune of Francis Crossley was sunk into the Somerleyton estate in Suffolk, bought from another entrepreneur, the railway and civil-engineering contractor Samuel Morton Peto. On the other hand, some, like the son of the Bradford industrialist Titus Salt, built within sight of the source of the family's wealth: Milner Field, described in *Building News* as in 'twelfth century medieval' style, was built in the early 1870s only one mile from Salt's mill at Saltaire. At county level, however, the rich emigrants were thinly spread. An Overstone house in Northamptonshire, or a Goldsmid one in Gloucestershire, did not make a construction boom. And large estates, until the late nineteenth-century agricultural depression, were more difficult to buy anyway. Given that land was relatively unattractive as an economic investment, it was rational to buy sufficient land and acquire a house to confer status and social and recreational opportunities.[33] In Cheshire especially, as will be seen below, many 'houses in the country' were built with new money, but the builders either did not want much land or it was not available.

For all the attention paid to the building of country houses, the construction of a new house was in fact a rare experience for the head of a landed family. Table 4 lists 257 new builds on 353 estates in a period of 240 years. Assuming the average length of a generation to be thirty years, there were 2824 heads of families of whom only 9.1 per cent – less than one in ten – actually built a new house. The aggregated figures for six counties show that on average just one new house was started in each year and at the level of the individual county there were long periods when no new houses at all were built. This is less surprising when the

cost of a new house in relation to rental income is remembered. Neither was
building usually a young man's game. A long wait to inherit might dampen
building enthusiasm, even given the resources, although an heir could find his
hand forced by succession to a house neglected by an aged predecessor. Outside
the ranks of those blessed with inherited disposable wealth or access to the choicest
dowries, it took time to make a fortune. John Byng commented in 1783 that 'men
do not make fortunes before they are fifty years of age, when they are harrass'd
and worn out; and then should buy a place ready cut, and dryd'.[34] He wrote of
the folly of men who built new houses, only soon to die, 'leaving their heirs
encumber'd with great houses – and inadequate estates'. He cited the example of
his grandfather, Admiral Sir George Byng, first Viscount Torrington (1663–1733),
who erected Southill House 'in an open field; and had to plant trees, to dig canals,
to make mounts, and to throw away his money in vile taste' (Plate 90). Byng's
cri de coeur was deeply personal, but his opinion was probably quite widely shared.

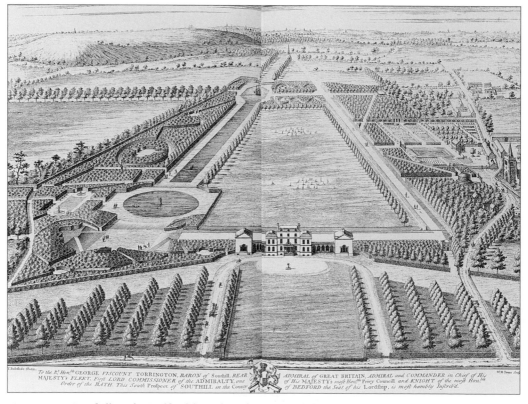

PLATE 90.   Southill Park, Bedfordshire, by Thomas Badeslade *c.* 1739.

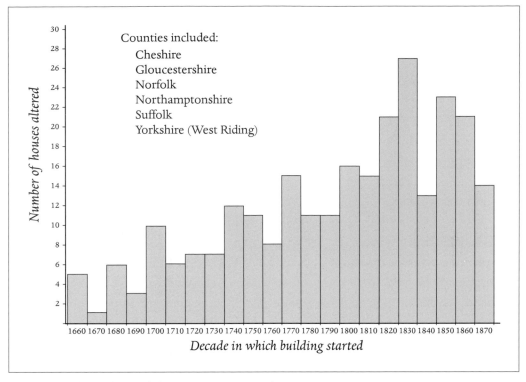

FIGURE 3. Chronology of alterations to country houses, 1660–1880.

No picture of building activity is complete without considering the alteration of existing houses. Although nearly one-third of the houses studied survived from before 1660 without ever being completely rebuilt, the majority felt the hand of the remodeller, and the new houses of our period were also subsequently altered and extended by their owners.[35] The pattern of remodelling activity is shown in Figure 3. However, the resulting picture of a generally increasing level of activity with an early nineteenth-century peak, a fall in the 1840s, and renewed activity from the 1850s to 1870s, is misleading. Even with the application of consistent criteria about what constitutes a significant building event, the range of activity is wide. Combining such disparate projects as the addition of a new dining-room to a small house and the almost complete rebuilding of a large one reduces the value of the sum of events as a comparative indication of total building activity.

There is a more fundamental problem with the availability of data. Much less is known about the building histories of the older houses, or indeed any pre-decessor of a house rebuilt in our period. The results for Northamptonshire are revealing. They form a higher than expected proportion of building events for the seventeenth century and well into the eighteenth simply because the structural surveys of the RCHME have generated information lacking for the other counties. The picture of remodelling activity therefore remains an impressionistic one. There may well have been periods of heightened activity, when economic conditions were especially favourable, the demands of fashion pressing or new comforts in the Victorian period irresistible. Nevertheless, because the scale of remodelling and its cost could, in theory at least, be matched more reliably to the builder's income than the greater and equally elastic cost of a new house, their piecemeal alteration and modernisation was a continuous process.

One characteristic shared by all landowners was their enjoyment of rental income. The obvious question is then whether there was a relationship between building activity and the level of rents.[36] The investigation is not straightforward. Across the counties, the pattern of forms of tenure was complex, and archaic forms survived, so the real value of a holding was often not reflected in the actual rents paid. Average figures for a county are more or less meaningless, when rents varied even for the same class of land, let alone for differences in soil type and land use. Until the nineteenth century, before the railway network broke down regional distinctions, and industrialisation itself had a major impact, rents tended to fall with increasing distance from London. Rents in broadly pastoral counties tended to be lower than those in arable areas but by 1850 they were rising faster than those in counties where grain was predominant, although not finally catching up until after 1875 when cereal prices dramatically collapsed.

The national pattern of rents shows a doubling between 1690 and 1730, with a further doubling by 1750. This throws doubt upon the concept of a general agricultural depression in the second quarter of the eighteenth century, although corn prices fell in the 1730s and 1740s compared with the 1720s, and depression affected some regions but not others. After a slightly upward trend from 1750 to about 1790, rents rose sharply, nearly trebling by 1810–15. This coincided with the first period of serious and sustained inflation to hit the British economy since the sixteenth century. Prospective builders were certainly aware of rising costs. Lord Cadogan, in writing to the second Lord Walsingham about replacing or remodelling the latter's seat at Merton (Norfolk) in 1804, referred to the doubling of building costs since an earlier undated consideration of such an enterprise (Plate 91).

PLATE 91. Merton Hall, Norfolk. An unadopted proposal of the 1800s to add a new wing to the early seventeenth-century house.

Whether they were as well aware of the real increase, having taken into account the rises in their rents, is less clear.[37] Rents fell again immediately after the French wars and remained roughly constant from 1815 to about 1850. From 1850 they rose steadily, gaining 30 per cent by 1880. They then plummeted: by the late 1890s they had returned to the levels of fifty or sixty years before, or even to the levels of a century earlier on the hardest-hit arable estates.

The relevant measure of the landowner's income is the rent actually received. Trends in arrears 'may act like a thermometer to gauge the general health of agriculture'.[38] Accumulated arrears could not easily be separated from those accruing in a particular year, however, and there were large variations from estate to estate. Just as consideration of rents on a national basis tended to smooth out the evidence of a depression in the second quarter of the eighteenth century, in both magnitude and longevity, the post-1815 depression did not stand out particularly forcefully either.

In the first half of the eighteenth century rents grew faster than output, so landlords did relatively better than tenants. The economic climate for landowners might then be interpreted as favourable for building. In the second half of the

century, however, rents increased more slowly than output, so the landlords'
share of agricultural income fell. Land prices dropped sharply in 1778–83, and yet
the 1770s to 1790s were the peak years for building. In the first half of the nineteenth
century the trend reversed, with the landlords' share of output increasing, but in
the second half of the century the landlords' real share declined again, as it had
a hundred years earlier, when they shouldered the burden of the fearsome
post-1875 depression.

For the purpose of interpreting levels of construction activity, a national rent
index is too generalised and there is no relationship between the general level
of rents and the chronology of building country houses revealed by Table 4.
Concepts of 'recession' or 'boom' may also be unhelpful when they are regionally
specific. Nevertheless, awareness of the prevailing mood about agriculture –
optimism or pessimism (and the attraction of alternative investments) – may have
been among the factors influencing decisions to build or not. Landowners were
obviously aware of marked shifts in rents and therefore a rent index may suggest
the way in which general sentiments about agriculture changed.

Equally, a comparison between the returns on land and yields derived from
the funds does not seem to have been a significant factor. The margin was never
greater than plus or minus 2 per cent, although this could be significant when
top yields seldom exceeded 5 per cent. Until 1770 the yield from land was greater,
and again in 1825–65, but at other times, including the building boom of the 1770s
to 1790s, the funds were clearly a better investment, especially during the French
wars. Certainly, potential builders could and did make the necessary comparisons.
John Rous of Henham, whose country house had burned down in 1773 and had
not yet been rebuilt, calculated in 1788:

> I consider land as a certain loss, when it is not situated so as to be an object to look
> at, or to sport upon: £100,000 in money will produce in these days £4500 a year, and
> the same sum laid out in land at 26 years purchase, after paying taxes and repairs will
> bring about £3400.[39]

Nevertheless, Rous could not resist adding a farm to the core of his estate, and
was prepared to pay thirty years' purchase to prevent it falling into the hands of
others. Moreover, within two years he began to build a new mansion. He well
knew that land was a relatively poor investment in terms of short-term yields,
but he and his peer group took a longer view. Land was more than an economic
investment, its returns never totally calculable in percentage terms. It provided

a long-term secure primary income as well as conferring political and social benefits. Moreover, nothing provided better security in raising loans.

The paradox of building activity peaking when, in economic terms, it was relatively least attractive to hold land is matched by contemporary comment about the desertion of their estates by landowners at the very time when it appears they were most likely to build. Rudder commented in 1779 on the desertion of gentlemen's seats in Gloucestershire and, ten years later, John Byng on a tour of the Midlands concluded that noblemen and gentlemen had almost abandoned the country.[40] Byng returned to the theme in 1792 when he wrote that Staffordshire had once been studded with spacious parks and noble mansions where the nobility lived and dispensed hospitality, 'before operas were known; or that it became necessary to huddle all together, in miserable, mean lodging-houses in London; there to pay extravagantly for what is brought, or stolen from their own lands! But the ladies command.'[41] In reality, it was the magnet of Parliament – composed of the country gentry – that was fundamental.[42] By 1715 annual sessions of several months' duration had become essential and by the late 1720s they ran from mid January to late May. From the late 1770s the session often opened in November and ran until mid June and by the 1790s summer pleasures had extended the season until August. The great political magnates were essentially metropolitan figures, retreating from time to time to one of their country seats for relaxation or to foster their political interest in the locality. Goods and services might flow from the country to the town – servants, food, specialities – and increasingly the country house might be seen from the outset simply as a recreational retreat, with sport as the main lure.[43] At the other end of the spectrum, country houses remained the permanent homes of country squires, although they too, increasingly with their families, moved to London or Bath for comparatively brief sojourns in rented houses.

The conservative Byng, describing in 1793 the melancholy state of even grand Boughton House (Northamptonshire) as 'the residence of the former Dukes of Montagu; now, with many other grand houses, verging to ruin, neglected, and left to desolation', could indeed conclude that the landscape was being swept clean of houses by men who no longer respected the traditions of the countryside, eliminating places surplus to requirements as their estates increased in size.[44] The process of destruction, much publicised in the 1970s by the listing of 1116 country houses demolished between 1875 and 1974 (of which 595 had gone since 1945) was certainly not a new one.[45] In Hertfordshire the rate of loss of country houses was at its peak in the period 1790 to 1829. Men who had several seats but no use for a sixteenth- or seventeenth-century house pulled it down. The process of dilapidation was accelerated by the absence of owners in London. Growing antiquarian interest in the 1830s helped to halt the destruction of old houses. Another important factor was demographic luck. In the absence of a son and heir, the passing of a house to a relative, already well-seated, could lead to the loss of a house. There were also regional differences. The survival rate of houses in Northamptonshire, for example, was much higher than in Hertfordshire. A stone house could be repaired after many years of disuse. Althorp, for example, was restored for family occupation and encased by Henry Holland in 1786 after being abandoned for forty years. Superfluous houses in the county were more likely to be simply neglected or allowed to decline into farmhouses than to be razed to the ground.

Fashion, too, played its part. In Cambridgeshire, 'Charles I's personal interest in reclaiming the fen; his intention of establishing a new town, Charlemont, near Mepal; his visits to Newmarket; and his sojourns, while under the custody of Cromwell, at Childerley Hall and Chippenham Park, helped bring a new consequence to the county.'[46] This seems to have been reflected in the construction of a series of seventeenth-century houses: Inigo Jones's Prince's Lodging House at Newmarket, Wisbech Castle and Thorney Abbey; and Roger Pratt's Horseheath Hall of the 1660s (Plate 92) and Cheveley Park of the 1670s. The eighteenth century, in contrast, was a time of demolition rather than construction, when the county lost its attraction as a place to live. Losses in other counties, too, can be obscured by concentrating on the building of grand houses. In Bedfordshire, for example, between 1714 and 1830, twelve country houses were built and a further nine remodelled, yet three of the five largest houses existing in 1671 were demolished without replacement and a fourth severely reduced in size.[47] The Duke of Bedford was among those castigated by John Byng in 1793 as a great landowner who 'tosses down old manor houses' as a 'baneful' consequence of the monopoly of the land by a few large owners.[48] Over sixty years later the architect George Gilbert Scott made the same point: 'It is a great misfortune to our country that the landed gentry are in many districts so reduced in numbers. The prodigious accumulation of land in the hands of the few is, perhaps, as injurious as its extreme subdivision.'[49]

Northamptonshire appears to be a county of durable houses; indeed, of the counties surveyed in our study, it had by far the lowest proportion of rebuilt major seats after 1660. However, the county's eighteenth- and nineteenth-century

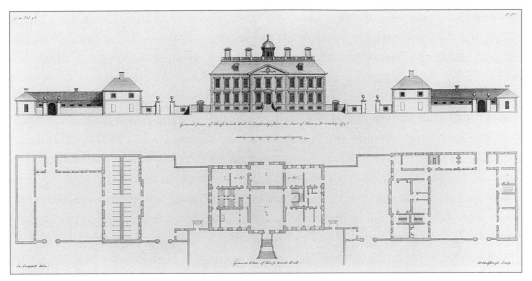

PLATE 92.   Horseheath Hall, Cambridgeshire (Roger Pratt, 1663–65, demolished).

historians, Bridges and Baker, reveal a picture of extensive losses lower down the
gentry scale, in the 120 parishes in the south west of the county where their
works overlap.[50] By the late nineteenth century this area contained twenty-three
seats of resident owners of estates of at least 1000 acres. But Bridges and Baker
identify at least sixty-three houses as having been lost, or as being in a ruinous
state, by the early nineteenth century. In addition, thirty-two houses had declined
into farmhouses or tenements. The estate of the Spencers of Althorp, for example,
embraced eight parishes by the late nineteenth century. They retained their main
seat and one other house for family use, but at least four manor houses had gone
and a fifth had been reduced to a farmhouse. Considering, in addition to the
Spencers, the major landowning families Knightley of Fawsley, Fermor-Hesketh
of Easton Neston, Grafton of Wakefield Lodge and Overstone of Overstone,
covering thirty-three parishes of southern Northamptonshire, eight main seats
and other family houses survived to the late nineteenth century, but twenty-two
other houses had been demolished or had declined to farmhouses or tenements.
For every house retained or rebuilt, three were lost as gentry houses. In Cheshire
between 1580 and 1820, about 130 houses declined into farmhouses or disappeared
altogether.[51] No county escaped the process. When David Elisha Davy, the Suffolk
antiquary, made his notes on the county in the second quarter of the nineteenth
century, he recorded some melancholy losses, including Crowfield Hall, pulled

down when its owners, the Middletons, moved to another family seat, Shrubland Hall.[52] With some grounds John Byng could lament: 'Poor old England! Where are thy Halls, thy Manor Houses, thy Castles, thy Religious Houses? What, all destroy'd?'[53]

House building did indeed run in parallel with house destruction. The answer to the paradox of the coincidence of peak building activity, relatively poor returns from land and a perceived flight from the countryside, rests in the continuing political, social and recreational advantages of owning a country seat, even if it was one that was occupied for shorter and shorter periods.

The 3000-acre estate qualification for entry into the population of country houses, imposed by the availability of Bateman's analysis, is convenient, but many genuine country seats are thereby excluded. Whereas in the Victorian period two thousand acres or more might have been required by a country gentleman to support his lifestyle on agricultural rents alone, the possession of non-landed wealth meant that acceptance into gentry society was possible with much less land.[54] In the six counties represented in Table 4, there were 318 peers and great landowners owning more than 3000 acres in the 1870s. They were outnumbered by the 404 owners with between 1000 and 3000 acres. Reference has already been made to the problem of stating precisely what proportion of the latter group can be regarded as gentry. Within their ranks, however, we find long-established but less affluent landowners whose building activities reflected relatively straitened circumstances, together with a greater number of newcomers to landownership than on the larger estates. The latter, men whose aims in the ownership of a country house were essentially recreational rather than dynastic, seem to have been more conspicuous builders in the early and mid Victorian periods. The results for Norfolk and Suffolk confirm this pattern of later building on the smallest estates. For estates between 2000 and 2999 acres in size, exactly half of the new houses built in Norfolk and 38.1 per cent of those in Suffolk, were built after 1800. An even higher proportion of the new houses on estates between 1000 and 1999 acres in size were erected after 1800: 55.6 per cent in Norfolk and 40.0 per cent in Suffolk. Table 5 shows that on the larger estates the post-1800 houses were a much smaller proportion, accounting for 25.6 per cent of the total in Norfolk and a mere 21.7 per cent in Suffolk.

Excellent published surveys of the country houses of Gloucestershire and Cheshire permit close examination of the building patterns on the smaller estates in those counties.[55] The authors cast their nets wide. In Gloucestershire seventy-seven 'major' houses are covered for the period 1660–1830 (thirty-two on estates of over 3000 acres) with eighty-five 'smaller houses' (of which only seven satisfy the 3000 acre qualification). For Cheshire forty-five houses are described as 'the most interesting and representative in the county' (twenty-one of these were on 3000 acre estates and another three were important secondary seats). No fewer than 233 houses appear in a second list of 'all other architecturally significant country houses' in the county. Just sixteen of these were on 3000 acre estates. These numbers are a dramatic reminder of the elasticity of the term 'country house' and the fact that populations must be carefully defined if comparisons are made of builders and building chronologies.

Among the forty-five 'major' houses in Gloucestershire not embraced by the 3000 acre criterion, seventeen are datable houses on estates of 1000 to 3000 acres in size. Eight were built before the end of the seventeenth century and not rebuilt; six were eighteenth-century houses; and only three were built in the nineteenth century. There are rather more nineteenth-century builds in the list of 'smaller houses', but again eighteenth-century houses predominate.[56] Some 40 per cent of the major building campaigns in Gloucestershire were by men who had purchased the estates on which they built – creating that most important category of new house, the 'House of Arrival'.

Purchasers with resources to rebuild before about 1730 were mainly established gentry families, or else London lawyers and government placemen, such as William Blathwayt and Edward Southwell, investing career profits. After 1730 the availability of alternative investment opportunities seems to have reduced the transfer of fortunes to land. London men were certainly much less prominent. They faced competition from established local landowners enlarging their estates, and from newly-made local fortunes, either from the cloth trade or Bristol mercantile profits, invested in small estates for the construction of a fashionable villa. Bristol's mason-architects like the Paty family, and from the 1760s Anthony Keck, prospered, serving the county community, until London-based professional architects took the major commissions from the early nineteenth century (Plate 93). Overseas money was also prominent. Three East Indian fortunes were expended in the county in the 1780s and 1790s: Warren Hastings at Daylesford; Colonel John Cockerell at Sezincote; and General Sir Henry Cosby, who bought land at Tiddenham for the building of Sedbury Park. Industrial money from the Stroud Valley textile industry continued to be spent upon small estates and house building until the credit crisis of the mid 1820s stemmed the flow. By this time,

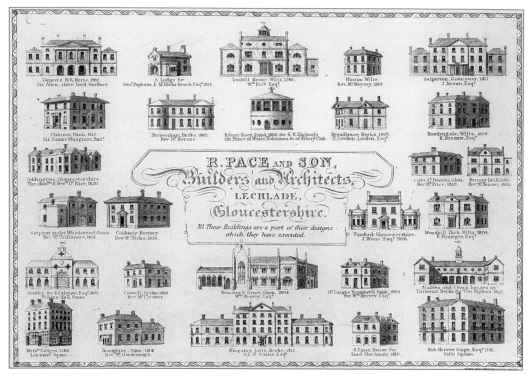

PLATE 93. The Lechlade Gloucestershire architect Richard Pace's trade card indicating the extent of his practice in the Regency period.

competition from the West Riding woollen-textile industry had forced the resale of many properties. The Querns at Cirencester, built in 1825 for a local solicitor, was typical of these houses, erected on what was effectively a single large field. On these smaller Gloucestershire properties, Humphry Repton found ample scope for the application of his skill in landscaping to give the impression of their commanding much more land than the small estate actually encompassed.

From a building chronology based on 376 closely dated building campaigns in Gloucestershire between 1660 and 1830, covering without distinction all sizes of estate, three decades of exceptional activity can be identified.[57] The busiest was 1821 to 1830, within a very active period 1791 to 1830, followed by 1711 to 1720 and then 1691 to 1700. There was a minor peak in the 1750s. Looking at only the larger estates (Table 4) confirms the 1690s as the most active decade, and the 1820s too stand out, but there was also marked activity before the peaks found by Kingsley – for example in the 1760s and 1770s, suggesting that building, at least in the eighteenth century, tended to be led by the larger landowners. The majority of builders were men who had inherited their houses. Once a family had 'arrived', fashion was the main drive to build, money the main constraint. Windfalls and sudden increases in wealth were necessary to impel most men. Few Gloucestershire estates benefited from mineral income, although one or two possessed coal measures. Kingsley concluded that rising agricultural incomes after 1770, and the general prosperity of the local cloth industry from the 1780s to the 1820s, were reflected in greater building activity. The causes of the 1690s and 1750s bursts of activity are less clear.

Cheshire was a more aristocratic county than Gloucestershire, with a greater concentration of gentry seats. It also had some significant absentee landlords: Viscount Combermere, whose main base was in Shropshire, the Earl of Derby in Lancashire, the Earl of Kilmorey in Market Drayton, the Earl of Shrewsbury in Staffordshire, and Lord Vernon and the Earl of Harrington in Derbyshire. [57] The county also had a great legacy of small manor houses. One of the high-water marks of Cheshire country house building, the sixteenth century, predates our period. There was also a boom in the early and middle years of the nineteenth century, when new money of urban businessmen, especially from nearby Lancashire, invaded the county. At least forty-eight of the houses in the secondary list in *Cheshire Country Houses* were built with industrial or other new money. The new breed of owner might enter the landed ranks: Robert Barbour, a Manchester businessman, bought Bolesworth Castle in 1856 from George Walmesley, who had ruined himself attempting to match more wealthy neighbours in rebuilding the house. By the 1870s Barbour had expanded his estate to 4250 acres. With Brereton Hall, an Elizabethan mansion altered in the early nineteenth century by John Howard of Hyde, went an estate of 1912 acres. George Holland Ackers, who at the age of twenty-four inherited Great Moreton Hall in 1836, and had it rebuilt by Edward Blore, enjoyed a family fortune which originated from fustian manufacture in Bolton and land speculation in Manchester. By the 1870s it was surrounded by 1524 acres. Among twenty-two resident owners of Cheshire estates of between 1000 and 2999 acres who can be named from the New Domesday survey, however, only three are identifiable as men with new money. Nevertheless, seventeen of these houses were rebuilt in the nineteenth century, in stark contrast to the Gloucestershire pattern. The majority of new men building in the nineteenth century owned even smaller estates. Sir James Watts, for example, partner in the largest wholesale drapery business in Manchester, completed opulent Abney Hall in the 1850s (the house started by Alfred Orrell, a prominent cotton spinner). Sir James's architects, Travis and Mangall, engaged the renowned London decorators J. G. Crace & Son, who worked to drawings by Pugin. Yet Sir James's estate extended to a mere seventy acres. The industrialist Sir William Jackson's Claughton Manor built in 1864 was surrounded by little more, some 113 acres.

The chronology of country house building, viewed nationally, clearly shows periods of heightened activity, and other times when relatively few new houses were constructed. At county level there are many deviations from the average pattern. Overall, one-third of the seats of the greater and aristocratic landowners were not rebuilt after 1660, but alteration was a continuing process. National factors had some influence upon decisions to build – the renewal of confidence among landowners after the Restoration and their increasing political power after the Glorious Revolution, coupled with the excitement of new architectural styles emanating from metropolitan leadership. Individual factors, however, were crucial. The vagaries of inheritance and succession, the timing and financial consequences of marriage, the condition of a landed estate, and personal inclination, combined in a complex equation to determine whether or not a new house was built. Large landowners tended to build before smaller ones, and once a family had established itself in a new seat it generally did not rebuild, instead extending and remodelling it to meet their changing needs and the dictates of fashion. 'New' men and money were to be found among house-builders in all periods, but their relative importance much increased as the nineteenth century progressed. They are nevertheless under-represented in the ranks of the owners of estates over three thousand acres in size, partly because of the lack of availability of such estates on the market, but mainly because the desire for 'a house in the country' could be satisfied without extensive acres or consideration of land as an agricultural investment. Indeed, while the means to build obviously had to be available, the level of house-building activity does not correlate with either the level of rents or the returns realisable from alternative investment opportunities. The social and political advantages that accrued from the ownership of a seat on a landed estate overrode considerations of return on investment.

7

The Cost of the Country House

'When I began this work, I intended only fifteen designs for small edifices, from £200 to £700 value, but by the advices of some friends who approv'd of what I had begun, I have added to them sixteen more: the value of the largest of which does not exced £6000.'

William Halfpenny, 1749.[1]

'It is well known that architects' estimates are generally mistrusted.'

Robert Kerr, 1871.[2]

When Robert Fellowes (1742–1829) moved his large young family into his new house, Shotesham Park, in the summer of 1791, one of the first things he did was compile a catalogue of his books. The library, the best room in the Soane-designed house, was clearly his pride and joy. In part, the books he arranged reflected the family's history. Shotesham had been bought by Robert's grandfather, William Fellowes, in the early 1720s. Since the estate was acquired for his third son it was not large, 871 acres of scattered land with a rambling *c.* 1600 manor house. But the Felloweses, landowners with no previous Norfolk connection, were wealthy. William was a senior master in Chancery whose mother was heiress to an East India Company director; his younger brother, Sir John Fellowes, a bachelor, was Sub-Governor of the South Sea Company. Most likely the property was a haven for South Sea spoils. Amongst the books catalogued two generations later therefore were a fair number of tomes on political arithmetic and the law, and a splendid set of pamphlets pertaining to the controversies surrounding his great-uncle's company in 1720. When William's son, another William (1705–75), succeeded to Shotesham at the age of nineteen, the books he purchased were those typical of a mid eighteenth-century Norfolk squire: novels, plays and history, works on gardening and agrarian improvement, and books and pamphlets chiefly on the Poor Law, reflecting his role as a justice of the peace. Two interests were more unusual. Books on trade and travel, the Felloweses' old activities, were still purchased; he also bought a number relating to medicine. His interest in the latter led him to set up an infirmary at Shotesham (possibly England's earliest cottage hospital) before becoming the driving force in the establishment of the Norfolk and Norwich Hospital in 1771.[3]

The Shotesham library was not entirely functional, simply displaying the Felloweses' shift from trade to land and county administration. There was a corpus of literature, again to be found in the libraries of all the better-read gentry, which historians now categorise as 'polite'. It provided the perfect diet to prepare Robert Fellowes as a gentleman of cultural tastes. Since both he and his father were Wykehamists there was a good stock of the classics. They also bought books which would allow them to form an appreciation of the arts, to cultivate in Joseph Addison's famous phrase 'the pleasures of the imagination'. Therefore when Robert turned to building a new house, as soon as the economy picked up in the mid 1780s after the disastrous War of American Independence, he could thumb through Isaac Ware's edition of Palladio's *Four Books of Architecture* (1738), Colen Campbell's *Vitruvius Britannicus* (1715–25), Antoine Desgodetz's *Les édifices antiques de Rome* (1682) and Batty Langley's *The London Prices of Bricklayers' Materials and Works* (1750). Although there were few books relating to painting, and no mention of music manuscripts, the literature of eighteenth-century politeness was well represented, Robert possessing the collected works of John Locke, Henry St John Viscount Bolingbroke and David Hume. Their writings, together with those of Addison and Steele in the *Spectator* and *Tatler*, were much-read texts attempting to turn their readers away from the old pre-1715 preoccupation with conflict and party strife to a more rational system of conduct, a world of sociability resting upon the cultivation of politeness, conversation and harmony.

The contents of the library at Shotesham in the 1790s show a neat balance between the literature of polite culture and the practices of agrarian improvements in their widest sense. In this it was entirely typical of the Georgian gentry, supporting the two main planks of their existence. The building of his new house allowed Robert Fellowes to enjoy 'the pleasures of the imagination' to the full. Almost a mile from the original house, it was built on a fine site in the lee of a slope protecting it from the biting east winds of Norfolk. It was a restrained, nicely detailed but not extravagant house, with a good kitchen garden and stable block, overlooking a newly landscaped park running down to the River Tas. The new house was full of light, ideal for family life, social entertainment, display, study and, with a justice's room, county administration (Plate 94). In its contrast

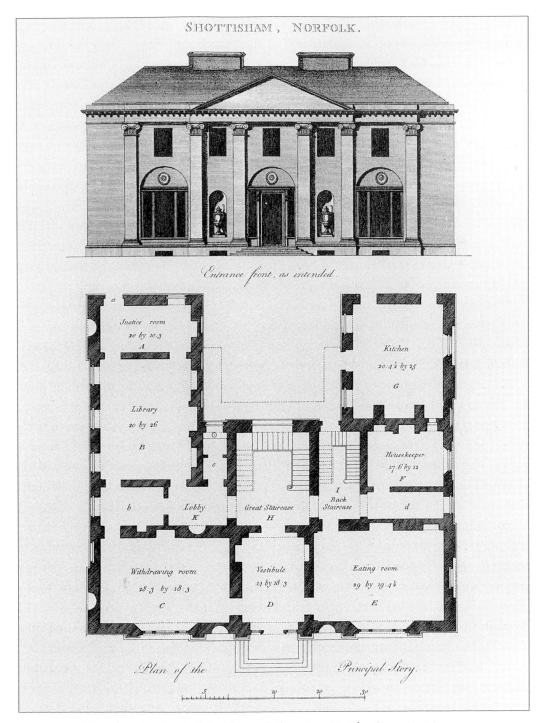

PLATE 94. Shotesham Park, Norfolk. Plan and elevation, Sir John Soane (1785).

with the old, moat-surrounded, dark manor house it epitomised in bricks and mortar the goals of polite society.[4]

Yet underpinning the building of the house to the canons of elite taste was a deep commercialism. For Robert Fellowes's architectural and cultural visions (as an MP he had to participate in the social rounds of Norwich and London) were sustained by agricultural improvement. The library contained all the classics of agrarian literature from Walter Blith's *The English Improver Improved* (1652) onwards. The recent outpourings of Arthur Young were much in evidence. And they were put to use. Indeed the new house and park were made possible by the enclosure of Shotesham in 1781. Moreover, the estate grew impressively in size. The Felloweses at least initially possessed non-landed sources of wealth, but Robert Fellowes by improvement and restraint in spending (the service wing and stable block were simplified), like all the possessors of the estate, sensibly and assiduously bought land. By 1872 it ran to 7758 acres, a nine times expansion across a century and a half. The bills for Shotesham, a house subsequently very little altered, have not survived. The house was insured for only £2000 on its completion in 1792. More plausibly, Robert Fellowes had spent as much as £10,000 on his house, stables and kitchen garden.[5]

Throughout England in the eighteenth and nineteenth centuries a similar process of country house building was taking place. Sometimes, as at Shotesham, new houses were built; just as often old ones were remodelled, frequently several times, across two centuries. But everywhere decisions about scale and architectural styles, the dictates of fashion, and the pursuit of elite social lifestyles had to be sustained by agrarian and other forms of non-landed income. Building ambitions and means were necessarily equated. This chapter looks at the cost implications of this equation.

Recently historians have built up a picture of post-Restoration society as one driven by conspicuous consumption. Elites, landed and mercantile alike, and finely defined by many shadings of rank and wealth, were highly emulative social structures. Contemporaries represent them spending to the limit, and beyond, of their incomes on building, entertainment, dress and (increasingly) leisure activities. Given that the landed elite was small, and operated within tightly integrated county communities linked in financial and administrative terms with leading merchants and attorneys in the neighbourhood, knowledge about the monetary affairs of individual members – details of a family's mortgages, marriage portions, trusteeships and legacies – was widely known amongst them. Sir Edward Turner, writing a chirpy letter of condolence to Sanderson Miller on the death of his father-in-law, hoped he had received a good legacy and concluded: 'I never imagined I should have been obliged to pump for intelligence of this kind; I rather expected it would have been voluntarily spouted forth.'[6] The profits of Court and government office were of course well advertised. Indeed, since they were so fiercely contested, the entire fruits of the patronage system, both lay and ecclesiastical, were accurately computed. Calculations of landed income were also easily made from acreages, the value of estates readily estimated. By the late seventeenth century the more eligible members of the landowning and mercantile classes went round with price tags attached to them. Heiresses and widows appeared in London and Bath and the assemblies of county towns known to be worth a certain sum; landed gentlemen went through life labelled as possessing estates of so much per annum. The rapidly expanding number of newspapers in the eighteenth century openly published these details at marriage and death. When Sir James Ibbetson of Denton Hall (Yorkshire) married, at the age of twenty-two in 1768, Jenny Caygill, the sole heiress of Halifax's wealthiest merchant, the whole of the West Riding was treated to a discussion of their combined incomes. The Denton estate was worth £1100 a year (he had been left even more valuable Leeds property from his father, a one-time merchant, a decade earlier); Lady Ibbetson had a marriage portion of £5000, property settled upon her producing £1250 a year and, eventually, the prospect of inheriting the Essex estate, Down Hall, from her maternal uncle, Charles Selwin. Given the nature of the latter, the *Leeds Intelligencer*, unusually, could not put a precise sum upon her 'immense fortune'. Two years later the young couple were commissioning John Carr to build a new £10,000 house (it was one of his best according to Pevsner) for them at Denton.[7] The cost of the house was broken down in a contemporary account, shown in Table 9.

Table 9. *The cost of building Denton Hall, Yorkshire, in the 1770s*

'An Account of the Several Sums Expended in the New House at Denton'		£	s.	d.
Masons	full account	2105	18	2½
Brick Makers	do	658	4	9[a]
Cowell Slater	do	29	11	2
Bradley Carpenter	do	338	17	8

John Dodgon	Bricklayer	229	1	8
William Rigg	Slate Merchant	187	3	0
Jonathan Cawood	Nail Maker	276	0	0
Maude	Timber Merchant	410	14	0
Summers	Lead do	246	2	0
Clay	do	64	0	0
Robinson	Stone getter	728	2	9
Wilfred Skirrow	Lime	350	0	0
Rothwell	Plaisterer	837	15	0
Sutcliffe	Bricklayer	76	3	5
Mr Carr	Architect	630	0	0 [b]
Mr Wade	Carver	112	16	10
Boynton's and Kemp	Painters	235	0	0
Yeoman	do	38	18	0
Camm	for the best staircase rails	33	0	0
Fentons	for the lights	19	8	3
Thomas Dodgson	for Iron acc	173	14	3
Dixon and Moxon	for Timber	237	10	0
Wilkinson	for Ropes	50	1	9½
Hudson	for Digging for the Cellars	18	17	10½
Newland	Joiner	1407	0	0
Cowell junior	Slater	45	0	2½
Robert Rhodes	Marble Chimney-pieces	20	10	9
TOTAL		9459	11	7

'An Account of Money Expended on Furniture for the New House at Denton'

Chippendale	Bill	551	0	0
Gillows	do	220	12	0
Scholes	do	206	17	0
Ryby	do	9	0	0
Hacker	do	9	0	0
Moore	do	25	0	0
Howard	do	8	0	0
Bulkledge	do	5	3	0
Calthrop	do	22	4	0
Ellis	do	4	15	0

Mayhew and Ince	do		18	0	0
Starkie	do		2	16	0
TOTAL			1082	7	0

Notes:

[a] This sum appears to be £658 4s. 9d. in the original but was read as £558 4s. 9d. by the creator of the account in calculating the total expenditure.

[b] It is rare for a summary account of expenditure in this form to survive. John Carr the architect charged 5 per cent plus expenses. Presumably Mr Wade as well as Robert Rhodes provided chimney-pieces.

Source: J. W. Goodchild collection.

It was knowledge of events like these which fired fierce emulation and consumerism. Status reflected spending. Therefore details about sums poured into houses, coaches, entertainments and dress, as well as knowledge of incomes, were eagerly shared amongst this tiny world of country house builders.

If newspapers and gossip in London, Bath and the larger provincial centres broadcast details about incomes, legacies and marriage settlements throughout the county elites, diaries and letters suggest that the urge to know the price of everything was part of the everyday assessment of country houses, their contents and owners. The growing band of genteel country house visitors in the eighteenth and nineteenth centuries also frequently noted how much a house had cost to build and often evaluated it on this information. We have seen that Lord Oxford in 1738, for example, was dismissive of Benjamin Hoare's new £12,000 house in Essex. When Mrs Lybbe Powys came away from the scores of larger houses she visited her head must have been reeling with details of the cost of wallpapers, chimney-pieces, grates, pictures, books, even panes of plate glass. At Fawley Court (Buckinghamshire), where she stayed a week, she seems to have been given a virtual list of prices that made up the £8000 spent fitting out the interior.[8] She noted them all down, not because she was rushing to buy similarly priced articles, but because they allowed her to evaluate the precise status and fashionability of owners and houses she visited and to share her knowledge of them with her great circle of relations and friends. This totally materialistic appraisal was universal. Both Fonthills drew gasps from every visitor. Warner summed up these impressions after visiting the Wyatt house in 1800: '[it is] where expence has reached its utmost limits in furniture and ornaments; where every room is a gold mine, and every apartment a picture gallery, where in fact every thing bespeaks the presence of unbounded wealth and expensive ideas'.[9]

The same worldliness certainly imbued Parson Woodforde's backwoods social circle in Norfolk. The second time he went to dine with a neighbouring grandee, the Hon. Charles Townshend MP (later first Lord Bayning) at Honingham Hall in 1781, he noted the magnificent furniture in the silk-hung drawing-room, 'the grate is the finest I ever saw, all of steel and most highly polished – it cost nineteen Guineas'. On his next visit, two years later, he was regaled with more details about the contents of the room, amongst them the 'looking glass which was the finest and largest I ever saw, cost at second hand £150. The Height of the Plate was seven feet and half, and the breadth of it was five feet and half, one single Plate of glass only.' Shortly afterwards, at another dinner of the Norfolk gentry, he was treated to a more personal itemisation of his host's and fellow guests' wealth: 'Mr Micklethwaite had in his Shoes a Pair of Silver Buckles which cost between 7 and 8 pounds. Miles Branthwaite had a pair that cost 5 guineas.'[10] Woodforde might well have marvelled. Four guineas was the yearly wage of his cook-maid. In London meanwhile, Joseph Farington, 'the dictator of the Royal Academy', assiduously noted down the conversations of top-flight painters, sculptors and architects who formed the art world of the metropolis in the 1790–1820 period. In his entries there is the same preoccupation with the costs of pictures, statuary and the building and fitting up of houses in London and the country for their patrons. Of course, some owners bragged. Byng wrote of the proprietor of Much Wenlock, 'he bounced in thirties: Mr F. had 30,000 per annum: his foxes ran 30 [miles]'.[11] Nevertheless, the detailed discussion of prices was universal and usually accurate.

Long before the nineteenth-century sociologist Thorstein Veblen analysed the relationship between emulation and consumption in *The Theory of the Leisure Class* (1899), material goods were coming to represent exactly the status of their owners. Landed society clearly read the precise standing of fellow members from knowledge about the cost of their shoe-buckles, looking glasses and seat furniture. But it was the country house itself, the theatre for all this display, which was the most important item of expenditure in the working out of social position. A great country house symbolised many things: wealth, political clout, taste, genealogical respectability. Owners, assiduously pursuing county rivalries in all these areas, were therefore eager to expend large sums on their houses. For most it was certainly the biggest item of expenditure in their lives and one that preoccupied their thoughts for many years. With all this attention paid to conspicuous display, it is unsurprising that the costs of building and remodelling their houses were widely known across the landed community.

How can we categorise the observations about cost of the likes of Mrs Lybbe Powys, Lord Oxford and Horace Walpole, or those the architectural and building journals began to disclose from the 1830s? In this fashion the costs of many country houses between 1660 and 1880 are clearly revealed. Hundreds of examples might be cited. Sometimes the total given is improbable; sometimes different figures are quoted for the same house. The largest expenditures are well known: the gargantuan £600,000 expended by the first Duke of Westminster on Alfred Waterhouse's extraordinary rebuilding of Eaton Hall; Blenheim (£300,000); Fonthill (£240,000 on Alderman Beckford's replica of Houghton, Fonthill Splendens; and £270,000 on his son William's crazy Gothic folly (Plate 95). The cost of great Victorian houses almost matched these sums: Thoresby Hall (£198,993), Westonbirt (c. £125,000) and Bearwood (£129,524); as did the Regency extravaganzas Wynyard Park (£102,098), Conishead Priory (c. £149,000) and Eastnor Castle (£85,924). Those of a handful of famed eighteenth-century examples are again

PLATE 95. Fonthill Abbey, Wiltshire (James Wyatt, 1794–1807, demolished). John Rutter, 1823.

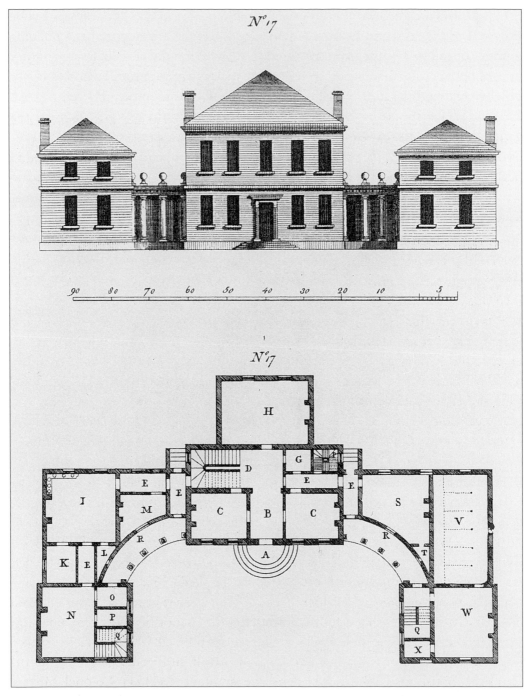

PLATE 96.   Plan and elevation for a country seat by William Halfpenny, 1749. The estimated cost of the house was £1534 and the offices £765, giving a total of £2299.

familiar: Holkham (£92,000), Moor Park (£86,000), Wentworth Woodhouse (£80,000), Castle Howard (£78,000), Kedleston (£70,000) and Harewood (£37,000).[12] But these houses were exceptional, bywords of style and lavishness in their respective counties. The general run of country house costs was much lower, even in the Victorian period, when their size was greatest.

William Halfpenny and Robert Morris in the 1740s were the first architectural designers to attach costs to the plans they published of country houses (Plate 96). The cheapest variants were around £2000 to £2500.[13] It is possible to argue that these costings were little more than confidence tricks tempting susceptible land-owners into building at bargain basement prices unrealisable in practice. Writing in 1768, Thomas Rawlins thought that their estimates had not been well-thought out and had led to 'Contests between Owners and Builders'.[14] After Morris very few architects costed their published plans, although the literature of architectural design continued to grow. Nevertheless, it seems new country houses were being built during the first half of the eighteenth century for around the costs indicated. We have seen that Honing Hall, built in 1748 for a Norwich worsted weaver and looking like a Norwich villa in the east Norfolk countryside, cost little more than £1000. Salle Park (1763–65), a rather larger Norfolk house, cost £2470. At neither house is an architect recorded, but these were recognisable country mansions, later the centres of large estates. Nor were Honing and Salle exceptional. The 'case' of Cole Green Park in Hertfordshire (the precursor of Panshanger), a nine-bay seventy-five by forty-three feet house, was built in 1710–12 for William Cowper, Lord Chancellor and first Earl Cowper, for £1720. Newby (later Baldersby) Park, 'the first Palladian villa in England, [was] built between 1718 and 1721 to Colen Campbell's designs for a tight-fisted York merchant and MP, Sir William Robinson Bart, for a total [which] can hardly have exceeded £2000'.[15] Also in Yorkshire, William Gossip, a newcomer to the county's gentry, engaged John Carr to build him a new house at Thorp Arch between 1749 and 1756. The hall was a plain five-bay villa, four rooms to a floor, flanked by two attached, three-bay wings; it was well-finished by highly skilled craftsmen whom Carr had engaged in York. Gossip noted that the 1074 acre estate and manor had cost him a bargain £8725 in the 1740s. The house was built for around £3480, a sum close to that for Ormesby Hall, another five-bay, two-and-a-half storeyed ashlar-faced north Yorkshire house probably designed by the amateur architect Colonel Moyser around 1750. Slightly earlier, Crowcombe Court (Somerset), a larger house with fine interiors, for which detailed bills exist, was built in two phases for its owner,

PLATE 97.   Crowcombe Court, Somerset (Thomas Parker 1724–28 and Nathaniel Ireson
1736–46). The south front from the church tower.

Thomas Carew (Plate 97). Work between 1724 and 1728 to the designs of Thomas
Parker cost £4182. The final settlement, after completion by Nathaniel Ireson
between 1736 and 1746, reveals a total bill for the house of £5913.[16] At a grander
level, Matthew Brettingham the elder claimed that he and Lord Leicester were
compiling in the 1750s a volume (it was never published) of 'plans of houses from
ten to fifty thousand pounds expense, and some others of less value'. In 1806
John Loudon was still defining a very large job in country house building as one
costing more than £10,000.[17]

   Building costs rose sharply, perhaps as much as doubling between the late 1780s
and 1810s. Two estimates of Peter Atkinson the younger, who carried on Carr's
famed York architectural practice, provide instructive examples about inflation
and the cost of smaller country houses. In 1812 Sydney Smith, the clerical wit
who moved in grand Whig circles, went to Atkinson for plans of a new rectory

at Foston, when he was required to reside there permanently. The architect, matching client and house, produced ones estimated to cost £3000. Even at the height of wartime prices and for a good living worth £600 a year this was expensive. Sixty years earlier new rectories were built for £500 to £600; in the 1810s with the growth of clergy incomes and social pretensions, as well as the increase in building prices, most were built within the £1500-£2000 range. Smith believed that to execute Atkinson's designs would 'have ruined me. I made him my bow. "You build for glory, Sir; I for use". I returned him his plans, with five-and-twenty pounds, and sat down in my thinking chair, and in a few hours Mrs Sydney and I concocted a plan which has produced what I call the model of parsonage houses.' In comparison, when Atkinson built a country house, Brockfield Hall near York, with offices, farmyard and garden walls, for a marginal member of the Yorkshire gentry between 1804 and 1822, the final cost was £8239 (Plate 98).[18] Costing almost three times his estimate for the well above average rectory he had proposed to build a few miles away for Sydney Smith, Brockfield

PLATE 98. Brockfield Hall, Yorkshire (Peter Atkinson the younger, 1804–22).

was smaller than Thorp Arch or Ormesby – both built for less than half its cost in the 1750s.

By the mid nineteenth century the newly-established architectural and building journals were disclosing detailed plans and sometimes costs of country houses. Anthony Salvin, a member of the County Durham gentry, had a large country house practice both in new building and remodelling. Cost data extracted from Jill Allibone's study of his career are presented in Table 10, together with information from Jill Franklin's survey of 380 plans of country houses built between 1835 and 1914 (costs were disclosed for sixty-four).

Table 10. *The cost of English country houses, c.1830–1914*

	Under £10,000	*£10,000– £20,000*	*£20,000– £50,000*	*above £50,000*
New houses designed by Anthony Salvin 1828–75	6	7	2	3
New and almost entirely rebuilt houses included in Franklin's *Gentleman's Country House*	9	15	17	23

Note: The figures are not totalled because Franklin includes some of Salvin's work in her appendix. The cost (£40,000) cited by Allibone for Moreby Hall, Yorkshire, is included but it probably cost less than half that figure.

Sources: Allibone, *Anthony Salvin*; Franklin, *Gentleman's Country House*, pp. 255–69.

Franklin's sample, based upon houses which surfaced in the periodical literature, is wider but more skewed. Increasingly, as the nineteenth century wore on, many of those included were not country houses linked to recognisable landed estates, but ones built by the growing number of plutocrats whose wealth was derived from non-landed sources. She reckoned that by the mid nineteenth century 'the lowest cost of a proper country house was about £7000 to £10,000'.[19]

Comparisons of the costs of houses are instructive. The range of cost embracing Blenheim and its near contemporary Crowcombe is fifty times; that of Castle Howard with Thorp Arch and Ormesby twenty-three times. These huge variations reflect the social and economic gap between their builders rather than a chasm in architectural understanding between Lord Carlisle and William Gossip. Of course Blenheim and Castle Howard were exceptional houses in the early eighteenth century, as were Eaton Hall, Westonbirt and Bearwood almost 150 years later. More usually, a difference of costs of up to ten times between country houses would have encompassed all but the very grandest of new-built houses in any county.

Although a wealth of cost data survives, ranging from the rough guess to figures based upon hundreds of pages of accounts and letters, it is odd that historians of landownership have hardly used it beyond citing a few untypical examples to suggest that costs were impressive, occasionally ruinous; and that, in comparison with the construction of industrial premises and most public buildings before the nineteenth century, country houses were far larger consumers of capital and labour.[20] Architectural historians also remain largely uninterested, choosing to look at the detailed bills of craftsmen and architects to fix changing styles and fashions with precision rather than examining them in the context of the economic and social circumstances of the builders themselves. Take Hagley Hall, enormously admired in the second half of the eighteenth century, for example. Sir George Lyttelton set out, soon after his inheritance of the estate, to build a well-planned house estimated to cost around £8000. 'We are', he stated in 1752, 'pretty indifferent about the outside, it is enough if there be nothing offensive to the eye.' When the house, offices, gardens and park were near completion in 1760, £25,823 had been spent, more than three times the amount he had envisaged at the outset. It was not that estimates had been hopelessly miscalculated, or that the friends on his 'Building Committee', John Chute, Thomas Prowse and Sanderson Miller, all amateur architects of distinction and all closely involved in the plans for Hagley, had in their enthusiasm pushed him into schemes he had not originally contemplated. Simply, he had become Cofferer in 1754 ('a good £2000 per annum, all taxes deducted') and Chancellor of the Exchequer in 1756, the same year he was raised to the peerage. Sir George's means had improved beyond his wildest dreams. The building of Hagley fully reflected his changed financial circumstances.[21]

The figures quoted above, showing the cost of new-built country houses running from a few thousand to hundreds of thousands of pounds, suggest a clear division between the grandest houses built out of peerage incomes (at least before the flood of new money by the mid nineteenth century) and those erected or remodelled by thrusting small squires across the face of England. They also support the view that houses became more expensive over the two centuries after the Restoration, not necessarily because building costs surged inexorably upwards (they didn't except during the French wars and between the 1850s and early 1870s), but because landed incomes increased faster and the general run of country houses became larger. An influx of non-landed wealth after the 1830s also meant that country house building was no longer largely linked to the course of estate rentals. New men bought estates, often for sporting purposes, and built large houses which the land attached to them alone could not support.

These observations are well-known, but they are an insecure foundation for the construction of a picture of overall spending on country houses or the interpretation of expenditure on particular projects. Even apparently well-founded figures say nothing about the scope of a project, the division of responsibility between owner and his builder for the provision and carriage of materials, including reuse, or hidden subsidies from the employment of estate labour and facilities. What is more instructive in the pursuit of landowners and the building of their houses is to interpret more fully those sets of detailed accounts, far rarer than statements of overall cost, which have survived. At the outset it has to be acknowledged that few houses provide accounts and correspondence sufficiently full to provide a complete record of their construction and alteration over the centuries. Most landowners, even when they undertook what was almost invariably the biggest expenditure in their lives, were also not good accountants even by the standards of their day. Merchants had to learn double-entry book-keeping; neither landowners nor their agents (where they employed them) did. Very few indeed struck an account at the end of each year. What the country house builder did at best was jot down in his pocket books or on scraps of paper items of expenditure and income, often introducing capital transactions into either reckoning so that invariably these compilations are difficult to disentangle. Certainly, other sets of accounts exist from which they made up their entries, principally those of their clerks of the works, architects, surveyors or principal tradesmen, each of them presenting or checking various items of expenditure on services and travel, labour and materials. Yet even with a best-practice architect like Sir John Soane, who kept a plethora of account books, notebooks, day books, journals, measurement books, estimate and bill books, ledgers, books of agreement and precedents, it is almost impossible to form a precise view of any of his building projects because nowhere are the transactions these record drawn together in a rational accounting system.[22] Because many building ventures were, to our eyes, a curious mixture of day work, measured work and partial contracts, total precision about the apportionment of costs is in any case elusive.

Occasionally near-complete sets of accounts have survived allowing us to state precisely the specification of costs apportioned between labour and materials, and whether most of both were locally or London purchased; the amounts expended on constructing the 'case' or 'shell' of a house and its finish; whether projects were built within estimate; the extent to which costs changed over time; and the grounds on which landowners based their decision to rebuild or remodel; and to speculate about the economies they might have practised. The accounts for Haveringland in Norfolk, sadly accompanied by little correspondence, are one of the completest sets for any country house to survive.[23] They allow us to draw out in more detail some of the above issues. Our analysis of accounts for other projects permits a more general picture to emerge.[24]

Edward Fellowes, the builder of Haveringland, was a rich young man, an officer in the 15th Hussars. At the age of twenty-eight he succeeded his father in 1837 becoming MP for Huntingdonshire in the same year. A senior branch of the Felloweses of Shotesham, his family had in the course of the eighteenth century acquired estates centred on Ramsey in Huntingdonshire and Haveringland. By 1873 these were very sizeable indeed – some 16,000 acres of rich fenland and 4000 acres of lighter land in Norfolk – well able to sustain Edward Fellowes's dignity when, after forty-three years in the House of Commons, he was created Baron de Ramsey a decade later.

Neither of his houses in 1837 were modish. That at Ramsey, on the edge of the little Fenland town, had originated in the Lady chapel of the great abbey and had after the 1530s become the home of the Cromwell family. Sir John Soane had extensively modernised and extended it (the work cost £19,000) between 1806 and 1808.[25] The house at Haveringland, a smaller affair of around 1710, although in the socially smarter county, seems to have been little altered. For a young bachelor, Fellowes was a zealous and decisive builder. Immediately on his succession, Edward Blore was summoned to Ramsey to disguise Soane's external work in Gothic dress and make considerable changes in the principal rooms. These improvements, a new stable block, and furniture, cost £17,976 between 1838 and 1845. Early in 1838 Blore was advising about the proposed site of a new house at Haveringland, sending a set of rough drawings to Fellowes a fortnight later.

Fellowes's choice of Blore was sensible if unimaginative. Possessing a large country house practice, Blore had a reputation (the grand Lady Gower had dismissed him as 'the cheap architect' a few years earlier) for building houses well and on estimate.[26] Haveringland, a two-and-a-half storey, seven-by-five bay house with a large service court, was built, unusually for Blore, in an Italianate

PLATE 99.   Haveringland Hall, Norfolk (Edward Blore, 1839–43, demolished).

style (Plate 99). Even more unusually for a Norfolk house, its three main elevations were faced in Bath stone. For a secondary house, used principally for shooting, it was an expensive affair. Built in just under four years after the foundations were dug in April 1839, Fellowes spent over £21,000 on the house and stables and a further £10,600 on its fittings and furnishings. In the 1850s a conservatory, an additional chamber storey added to the east wing, and a balancing 'observatory' tower at its northern end, cost around £6000. Similar sums are recorded as having been spent in the next thirty years, including the creation of a billiard-room and gasworks. There was nothing unusual in this updating, but the sheer detail of the returns of Fellowes's clerk of the works, Richard Armstrong, a protégé of Blore and later an architect on his own account, was. As a result Haveringland represents best-practice country house building before the coming of the railways. Blore himself was assiduous, visiting the site a dozen times in all. Unusually, both for Blore's practice and building methods more generally by the 1840s, the house was built almost entirely by day labour. Consequently, with Armstrong carrying out Blore's instructions to the letter, daily statements were made of the workforce's time and precise recordings of the work done and materials used. Certified weekly statements were then passed by Armstrong to Fellowes, residing either at Ramsey or at his secondary Norfolk house, Felthorpe Hall (the old house at Haveringland lodging some of the labour force before its demolition in April 1842).

The old-fashioned form of organisation at Haveringland and the richness of its documentation make it possible to reconstruct the cost of building with a confidence unknown for almost all country house building projects. The sum spent is broken down and classified in Table 11. Wages, salaries, expenses and commissions accounted for just over half the cost of the house (51.8 per cent), materials for rather more than one-third (36.8 per cent), and carriage for the balance (11.4 per cent). Wages alone amounted to 42.3 per cent. Timber was the single most expensive material, 14.5 per cent of total expenditure. The delivered cost of stone contributed 9.7 per cent, and brick, excluding the carting of estate-produced brick, 6.8 per cent.

Precise quantification of the savings resulting from keeping up a workforce's labour productivity by an effective clerk of the works is not possible. Lewis Wyatt, however, assured one of his clients that the employment of a good clerk of the works could result in a cost saving of 10 to 15 per cent with 'more satisfactory and better work done'.[27] It is also striking that the number of man-days required to build Haveringland was significantly less than for Henham Hall in Suffolk, fifty years earlier. The two houses were comparable in size, and there seem to be no grounds for supposing that Henham was more difficult to build or more extravagant in its finish. Certainly, Haveringland was more efficiently supervised, requiring only 64,000 man-days in less than four years compared with 87,000 in five to six years at Henham.[28] Richard Armstrong's efficiency and Edward Blore's superiority as a well-organised architect, in comparison with the colourful James Wyatt, who never visited Henham, may therefore be represented as a saving of over 20 per cent in labour time or over £1500 in the wages bill. Since Haveringland was built during a severe recession and low-priced labour was superabundant in Norfolk, the house was built cheaply. A 20 per cent increase in labour time plus the same percentage increase in wage rates would have raised the cost of the house by over £3500. Those country house builders fortunate enough to build when the trade cycle forced a downward pressure in wages, and enjoyed the services of an architect and clerk of the works who could organise a workforce efficiently, obviously saved considerable sums of money.

Table 11. *The cost of building Haveringland Hall, Norfolk, 1839–42*

	£	s.	d.	per cent
Wages, salaries, expenses and commissions				
Architect	1105	4	0	5.17
Clerk of works	929	13	10	4.35
Labour	1687	17	5	7.90
Tradesmen:				
Carpenters	2809	5	6	13.14
Masons	1465	4	2	6.85
Bricklayers	969	13	7	4.54
Plumbers/painters/glaziers	293	16	6	1.37
Plasterers	713	19	4	3.34
Sawyers	272	8	0	1.27
Slaters	345	13	0	1.62
Smiths	198	11	6	0.93
Wheelwrights	11	6	6	0.05
Turners	4	10	8	0.02
Jobbing accounts	262	16	1	1.23
Sub-total	11,070	0	1	51.78
Materials				
Stone: Bath	797	2	6	
York	317	16	0	
Total for stone	1114	18	6	5.21
Brick: Estate	1172	10	4	5.48
Purchased	287	15	2	1.35
Total for brick	1460	5	6	6.83
Timber: Estate	679	10	0	3.25
Purchased	2416	14	3	11.23
Total for timber	3096	4	3	14.48
Lead and glass	644	17	4	
Lime	438	9	6	
Fuel	406	4	0	10.29
Ironmongery	356	2	6	

	£	s.	d.	per cent
Other materials	354	2	5	
Sub-total	7871	4	0	36.81
Carriage				
Sea freight	959	4	10	4.49
Wherry and land carriage	683	13	11	3.20
Carthorse keep	332	17	0	1.56
Other carriage costs	462	11	0	2.16
Sub-total	2438	6	9	11.41
TOTAL	21,379	10	10	100.00

Source: Norfolk RO, MS 8595 20B, boxes 1 and 2 (architect's account, clerk of the works's pay bills, and client's cash books).

All builders were keen to utilise the produce of their estates in terms of labour, transport and materials. Fellowes was no exception. But the Haveringland accounts allow us to put a more precise figure on its contribution. In most projects it is an item almost impossible to disentangle. The cost of purchased brick depended very much on the distance it had to be transported, but Edward Blore's accounts for Merton (Norfolk), also dating from the early 1840s, offer a direct comparison. There brick from the nearby kilns at Thompson cost 32s. per 1000, 19s. more than the cost of producing brick at Haveringland, which would have represented a difference in cost of £1710 for the 1,800,000 bricks required at the latter. The value placed on estate timber was about 1s. per cubic foot compared with 3s. for purchased timber. Had it been bought on the open market, the £680 account for estate timber would have been increased by no less than £1300. Therefore savings attributable to effective supervision and to the use of estate materials were of the order of £6500. Of course, higher costs resulted from the use of 1015 tons of Bath stone, especially at a site so remote from its source of supply. Had white brick facings been employed instead, more and better quality bricks would have had to be produced or bought. Since eight expensive masons had to be recruited from the west country and the cost of transporting the stone was £1281, the decision to face the house in stone was, as with stone-built houses generally, an expensive one. Most owners, whether remodelling or rebuilding, were anxious to reuse as many materials from their old houses as possible. Oddly, perhaps because the early eighteenth-century house at Haveringland was decrepit or its fixtures out of place in an Italianate one of 1840, very little reuse of them was made. The only reference to them concerns the glazing of a 'small square at the back of the house' and some small sales totalling a few pounds.

At the end of 1842 Blore handed over the completed house for fitting-out, furnishing and decorating. In three years this added a further £10,359 (48.5 per cent) to the cost of the house. A few items were external works, but most money was spent on fitting out the domestic offices and furnishing the main rooms. The £162 spent on marble chimney-pieces, £31 on scagliola, and a more generous £264 on gilding, seem modest in comparison with sums spent on these items a century earlier at nearly Wolterton, for example, and no well-paid carvers or plasterers emerge from the accounts. However, William Caldecott of Great Russell Street, Bloomsbury, who had earlier refurnished Ramsey Abbey, supplied furniture at a cost of £3400 (three of his men spent nineteen weeks fitting curtains and uphol-stery); and a London contractor, Thomas Fairs of 2 Hanover Street, decorated the house for £1126. Other items were also London-purchased, although John Clements of Norwich furnished the secondary rooms for a not inconsiderable £1360.

Edward Fellowes inherited an established park at Haveringland, but major alterations to the garden – the new house was sited 500 yards from the old – seem to have waited almost a decade before a conservatory, summer-house or 'museum', a vinery, terrace and balustrade, and a grand new set of park gates, were erected in the 1850s. This was somewhat unusual because most landowners set about reorganising their gardens and parks at the same time and sometimes before they began building operations. Money was no problem; building the new house was his great priority. When the house was completed, Edward Fellowes married the daughter of the fourth Lord Sondes from nearby North Elmham in July 1845. She must have found, both at Ramsey and Haveringland, little to exercise any talents she might have had for architecture or interior decoration.

From the start of building in 1839 to 1857 at least £38,596 was spent at Have-ringland. Within twenty years, therefore, total expenditure was nearly double the sum spent building the original house (Plate 100). It is a reminder that the cost of building a house often represented just the start of an expensive programme of furnishing and updating house and garden alike. It is reasonable to conclude that at least two-thirds of the building expenditure was of direct benefit to the local economy.[29] Once the house was built, however, the local share of the

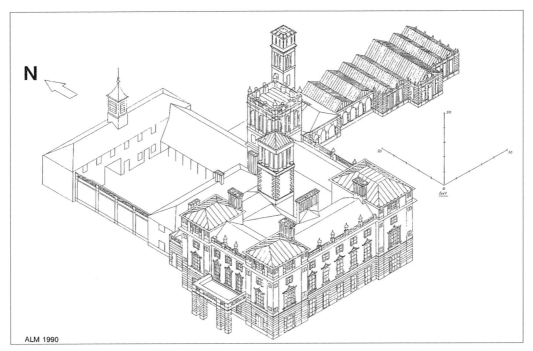

N

ALM 1990

PLATE 100.   Haveringland Hall, Norfolk. Axonometric drawing showing the relationship of the courtyard offices to the main house, the upper floor and observatory tower added to the east wing in the 1850s, and a service wing to the east proposed in 1860 but not built.

benefits of Edward Fellowes's spending was very much less. London contractors and retailers met the bulk of his needs in furnishing the house and remodelling both it and the gardens later in the nineteenth century.

If the detail of the Haveringland accounts provide a greater precision about the stages of building a country house, more partial ones which survive for other houses allow a general picture to emerge of the key elements underpinning the costs of country house building. The most important one was the unchanging apportionment of labour and material costs. By its very nature the construction of a large house required a large amount of labour. And because improvements in building techniques between 1660 and 1880 were minimal (the better organisation of workforces and the move to fixed-priced contacts were more important), the high percentage cost of labour in projects appears to have remained constant. Whatever the scale of the project, the generalisation that labour costs accounted for at least half of a house's cost appears to hold good (Table 12).

Table 12. *The percentage cost of labour, materials and carriage in the construction of country houses, 1670–1875*

House and dates of completion	architect(s)	cost of project to nearest £	labour[a]	materials	carriage	misc.
Ryston Hall (Norfolk), 1669–72	Sir Roger Pratt	2800	63.3	36.7	—	—
Cusworth (Yorkshire), 1737–48	George Platt James Paine	3734	53.8	40.5	4.1	1.8
Kimberley Hall[b] (Norfolk), remodelled 1755–59	Thomas Prowse	9730	67.2	28.5	4.0	0.3
Denton Hall (Yorkshire), 1770s[c]	John Carr	9460	64.5	35.5	—	—
Heacham Hall (Norfolk), 1774–80	Unknown	4082	52.7	41.4	5.9	—
Henham Hall (Suffolk), 1792–97	James Wyatt	21,373	58.8	34.9	5.6	0.7
Sheringham Hall (Norfolk), 1815–17[d]	Humphry & John Adey Repton	6600	51.7	45.3	3.0	—
Eshton Hall (Yorkshire), 1825–30	George Webster	13,906	56.7	40.6	2.7	—
Haveringland Hall (Norfolk), 1839–42	Edward Blore	21,380	51.8	36.8	11.4	—
Bearwood House (Berkshire), 1866–74	Robert Kerr	129,524	55.6	44.4	—	—

Notes:

[a] Includes payments to architects and clerks of the works.

[b] The figures for the remodelling of Kimberley illustrates the point contemporaries made that alterations were often finicky tasks requiring a great deal of skilled labour.

[c] The figures relating to Denton are the least detailed, being summaries of costs under various headings. The labour element probably contains some material costs (see Table 9).

[d] The house was left unfinished for this cost on the death of Abbot Upcher its builder in 1817. It was completed in the late 1830s at a total estimated cost of £12,618.

Sources: Ryston: Gunther, *Roger Pratt*, p. 14; Cusworth: West Yorkshire Archives Service, Leeds, BW/A/159, box 3; A/25–26, 30–32; Kimberley: Norfolk RO, 14/205/1–54; Denton: personal communication from Mr J. W. Goodchild, Wakefield; Heacham: Norfolk RO, HEA 480, 256 x 3; HEA 488, 256 x 4; HEA 489, 256 x 4; Henham: Suffolk RO, Ipswich, HA11, Rous Papers, C7/1/32, 37–40; C7/2/1–5; Sheringham: Norfolk RO, UPC 37, 640 x 4; Eshton: West Yorkshire Archives Service, Leeds, MD 335, box 18; Haveringland: Norfolk RO, MS 8595 20B, boxes 1 and 2; Bearwood: Berkshire RO, D/E Wal E 12.

It is clear that high labour costs, whether a house was built in brick or stone and whatever its price range, were unavoidable. Some estate workers might be used for labouring tasks, but the major part of a workforce was recruited on the local market. Even when labour costs were at rock bottom, as at Cusworth, Sheringham and Haveringland, they never fell below half the cost. Moreover, most projects seem to have entailed the use of expensive craftsmen, recruited from London or regional centres such as York, Warwick and Bristol, for carving, joinery and plasterwork. Even one of the most economical of provincial architects, John Johnson, who built a number of cheap houses at or below estimate in the 1760s and 1770s, always used some London-based labour.[30] Similarly, when John Soane built a smaller version of Shotesham for £3000 at Gunthorpe (Norfolk) between 1789 and 1791, although the house was merely a three-bay brick affair never employing more than a score of men, the principal craftsmen seem to have been London men.[31] Although interior finishes became less elaborate after 1800, the ornamental brickwork and complex roofs and gables of the typical Victorian country house, and sharply rising wage rates after the early 1850s, meant that there was no relief for country house builders from labour costs.

Big, expensive workforces always requiring careful supervision and direction, the better craftsmen well aware of their worth, were the invariable prospect for country house builders. They absorbed this feature when they began to form some idea of the total expenditure involved. In the seventeenth century, Sir William Petty recommended that 'A man of estate ought not in England to build an house [out] of above one and a half years revenue (in Ireland but of one) and to bestow two-thirds in the furniture'.[32] The guide line in the mid nineteenth century seems to have been that the cost of building a country house should not exceed twice annual income.[33] Yet few landowners, imagining that they could build slowly out of income or with a windfall of one sort or another in their pockets, followed prudent guide-lines, especially before 1800. And there were always builders who were sufficiently wealthy to ignore them completely.

If most landowners related the cost of building houses to income in some rough way, a more precise idea of them was worked out with mason, joiner or architect, and often discussed with friends. As we have already seen, Sir John Soane recommended that in order to remove 'doubts and difficulties', prospective builders should talk to friends and professional men, 'to possess all the information that nature, genius, experience and judgement can suggest'.[34] More prosaically, calculations of cost were formed upon the number of rooms required, an

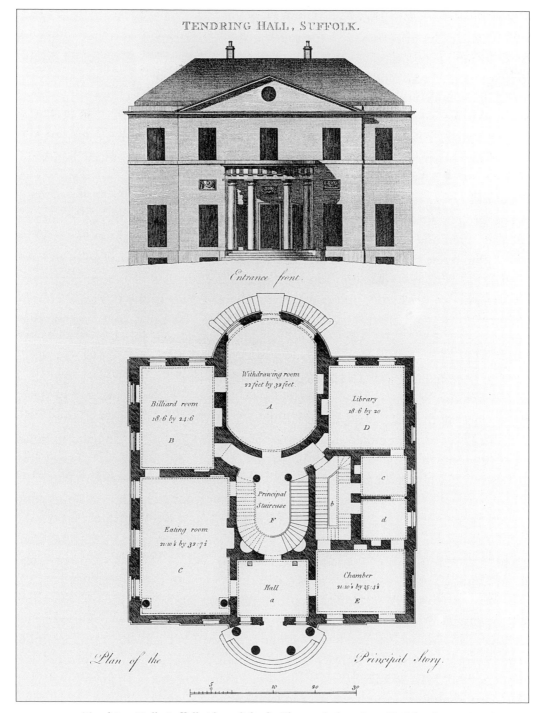

TENDRING HALL, SUFFOLK.

Entrance front.

Plan of the *Principal Story.*

PLATE 101.   Tendring Hall, Suffolk (demolished). Plan and elevation, Sir John Soane (1784).

approximation of the cubical contents of the house, or its ground plan worked out in hundreds of square feet ('the square'). By the 1740s some architectural guides began to produce plans with actual costs, usually expressed in pounds per hundred square feet, which gave landowners an approximate idea of the expenditure they were undertaking. *The Modern Builder's Assistant* (1742) produced plans of houses with estimates attached ranging from around £2000 to as much as £17,000. The cheapest houses worked out at as little as £90 per square: that is, for example, £2160 for a 55 × 43 feet (twenty-four squares of one hundred square feet) house of basically four rooms to a floor, two storeys over a cellar-cum-office basement. On the other hand, a 'country seat', employing the Corinthian order and finished with a balustrade and vases, had a 'body' of sixty-two squares estimated at £200 each with detached offices and a linking colonnade totalling fifty-four squares at £80 per square. The vogue by 1750 was to install domestic offices and stables in separate wings. Usually they were quoted at a more modest £35 per square.[35] Many landowners must have embarked upon building on similar calculations.

The building of Tendring Hall, Suffolk (1784–88), a replacement of a Tudor house for Admiral Sir Joshua Rowley, shows that John Soane arrived at his estimate exactly in this way (Plate 101). Although there is no correspondence, a good deal of evidence about its cost has survived because Soane, most unusually in his country house practice, was the building contractor as well as the architect, and in the process fell foul of the trustees of the Rowley settled estates. As a consequence, the estimates and final building costs were gone over with a fine toothcomb by three other architects, John Johnson, George Dance junior, and Richard Norris. They are set out in Table 13 below.

This method of quotation by the square was only a rough method of estimation. It appears, nevertheless, to have remained common currency to the end of our period. Kerr, with his estimates of the costs of houses from farmhouse, rectory and villa through to the £60,000 plus mansion, was still making his calculations on the basis of the ten feet square or hundred. He also set out costs per cubic foot (reckoned on those in 'the locality of London'), ranging from the cheapest stable at 4d. to the most expensively finished main house at 15d.[36] Certainly, Richard Armstrong, the clerk of works at Haveringland, was producing estimates (£4618 plus reused materials from the old house, Mortimer Lodge) in the mid 1880s for a secondary house on the Berkshire estate of Richard Benyon at Englefield. The house was to contain 171,616 cubic feet with a stable (including

Table 13. *The cost of building Tendring Hall (Suffolk), 1784–88 (to nearest £)*

	Soane's estimate of 1784	Less use of old materials	Estimated costs in 1784	Final costs agreed in 1792
Building and finishing house. 4750 square feet at £150 per hundred square feet	7125	327	6798	7524
Kitchen court and offices 2050 square feet at £60 per hundred square feet	1230	230	1148	1178
Plus small additions	148			
Stable block 3600 square feet at £50 per hundred square feet	1800	350	1665	1780
Saddle room/loose box	215			
Kitchen garden and hot house	659	—	659	831
Lodges	250	—	250	375
Carriage and site costs	—	—	—	730
TOTAL	11,427	907	10,520	12,418

Note: The clients appear to have paid Soane £10,968. The reused materials were finally valued at £1725 (13.6 per cent of final costs), making a total of £12,693. The original estimate also made provision for a park paling (£1130) and a set of farm buildings (£400). Either these were not proceeded with or built by others. Soane appears to have made a loss of £834 on the venture and may never have received his fee.

Source: Soane Museum, Tendring bill book; measurement book 12/NB17; precedent book (SM, vol. 41), p. 22; cash journal no. 1, 7 August 1789, 2 June 1792.

some domestic offices) of 84,986. His estimate was 5*d*. per cubic foot for the house and 3*d*. for the stable. Building costs in 1886–88 were considerably lower than when Kerr made his compilations at the height of the mid Victorian boom. Armstrong reckoned these prices 'very moderate indeed'. Not only did the Ecclesiastical Commissioners usually allow 6*d*. a cubic foot even for farmhouses, but the price of a house he was building in Worcestershire, where he was employing one of the 'best provincial builders' who had 'put the prices very low', was also near 6*d*. per cubic foot.[37]

By the 1870s estimates were generally better prepared. Since 'it [is] now the almost universal custom in England to build by contract', they were also more accurate, being based on a bill of quantities calculated by a surveyor.[38] Providing a client kept a minimum 10 per cent contingency for afterthoughts, he had a good indication of the costs of his building venture. On the other hand, in the late seventeenth and eighteenth centuries, estimates possessed a greater degree of flexibility. Once clients had made their choice about the size of house appropriate to their means and requirements, whether it was to be built in brick or stone, slated or tiled, constructed by day labour or by craftsmen paid for measured work or by contract, the architect or mason produced two estimates. These observed the practice of dividing the construction of the country house into two parts. Therefore one estimate covered the 'case' 'carcase' or 'shell' of the house (foundations, cellars, walls, floors, chimneys and roof) and the other its 'finish' (doors, panelling, chimney-pieces, plastering and carving, brassware and iron-mongery, plumbing, decorating and fitting out domestic offices). Convention seems to have been that the cost of the case of the house somewhat exceeded its finish, although an expensive stone-faced carcase or an especially elaborate finish could easily bend this rule of thumb. Some examples are given in Table 14 (page 263).

Building at or around estimate for the case of a house was more achievable than for its finish, simply because owners and architects were anxious to get a protective roof on the house as soon as possible, whereas they planned its finish, seldom if ever finalised at the outset, less hurriedly. Drawings for interiors and the selection of fittings went on being discussed between architect, builder and client right up to the point of completion.

Work at Stoneleigh Abbey (Warwickshire) provides a good example. There the third Lord Leigh had, on the completion of his Grand Tour, obtained plans from Francis Smith to refront the west wing of his great old house in 1714. These were not put into execution until between 1720 and 1726, by which latter date the interiors were only partly finished. More work was undertaken in the 1740s, but the Leighs had a tendency to get into debt, to die or to go mad at crucial periods during building. It was not until the 1760s, when the carcase of the west wing had been up for forty years, that the hall (later the saloon) was finished to the designs of Timothy Lightoler and William Hiorne and by the stuccoists Robert Moore and Francesco Vassalli (Plate 102). The incomplete accounts suggest that large sums (over £2000) were spent. Its famous Hercules-theme decorations, if old-fashioned by the mid 1760s, were 'perhaps the supreme masterpiece of Baroque stucco sculpture in England'.[39] Little of this could have been envisaged by Lord Leigh or Smith in the 1720s, either in their plans or estimates, for 'despite the intermittent efforts of half-a-dozen owners and at least as many architects,

PLATE 102.   Stoneleigh Abbey, Warwickshire. The hall, later the saloon.

Table 14. *Estimates for the cases and finishing of country houses, 1748–1856*

House and date of estimate		architect	cost of case	% of total	cost of finishing	% of total	total cost
Milton (North-amptonshire), 1748	first estimate	Matthew Brettingham Snr	3717	56.8	2824	43.2	6541
	alternative estimate		4125	52.6	3724	47.4	7849
Cusworth (Yorkshire), 1748–49. Library and chapel wings	first estimate	James Paine	313	49.7	316	50.3	629
	alternative estimate		548	57.9	347	42.1	895
Sherborne (Gloucester-shire), c. 1775		William Donn	3290	44.9	4207	56.1	7497
Dunninald (Scotland), 1795		Sir John Soane	10,528	63.7	6003	36.3	16,531
Pell Wall (Staffordshire) 1822–28	original estimate 1822	Sir John Soane	3661	47.7	4009	52.3	7670
	final cost 1828		8006	49.5	8158	50.5	16,164
Orchardleigh (Somerset), 1856		T. H. Wyatt	11,143	62.5	6681	37.5	17,824

Note: The plans and estimates for Milton, Sherborne and Dunninald were not proceeded with.

Sources: Milton: Northamptonshire RO, Milton plans, 97 and 98; Cusworth: West Yorkshire Archives Service, Leeds, BW/A/22, box 1; Sherborne: Gloucestershire RO, D678/311; Dunninald: Soane Museum, estimate book, 1789–99, pp. 6, 14; Pell Wall: Soane Museum, bill book; correspondence J/8/2, 17 June 1822; Orchardleigh: Somerset RO, DD/DV.

Stoneleigh never has been finished as any one of them seems to have proposed ... its collection of false starts and rejected advances is representative of processes that were going on in houses across the country'.

At Shotesham Park, a far simpler commission than Stoneleigh, a telescoped version of this kind of consultation about plans and designs was certainly taking place throughout the construction of the house. Soane first visited the site in September 1784. Designs, plans and estimates between client and architect, presumably for case and finish as at contemporaneous Tendring, were passed between Norfolk and London for the next twenty-one months. Fellowes, conscious of cost, seems to have pressed for at least simplified domestic offices and stables, and not before July 1786 is there reference to the despatch of detailed plans. Ones for the diggers of the basement were sent on 1 December 1786. Thereafter a stream of working drawings were forwarded by the Norwich mail coach through to the summer of 1789: plans for the garrets (unusually Mrs Fellowes, something of a blue-stocking, had an attic study); more detailed ones for the 'best rooms'; even those for a three-seater 'necessary-house' with a nine-inch air-flue for the servants (two family water closets were fitted in the house). Plans for alterations to the eating room were indeed still afoot in October 1792, well over a year after the Felloweses had moved into the house. Robert Fellowes was consulted at every stage. A careful, even overwatchful client, he had views on the smallest details, sending Soane sketches and long lists of points he thought required alteration. Frequently, he made requests for revised working drawings. Unfortunately, no building accounts have survived so that it is impossible to know the extent to which the original estimate was exceeded by these processes of discussion.[40]

If Stoneleigh illustrates how long drawn out the process of finishing an elaborately remodelled great house could be, and Shotesham the ways in which even a new-built house with plain interiors seems in some respects to have been planned on the hoof, Cusworth (west Yorkshire) provides a classic specimen of how plans of finishing evolved and expenditures mushroomed. The traditional provision of estimates by case and finish seems to have encouraged the latter.

In 1737 George Platt, the Rotherham mason-cum-architect, provided two costings for William Wrightson for a new five-bay, four-storey house near Doncaster. One, with two fronts in ashlar and with a finer set of chimney-pieces, was for £1485; the second, entirely in brick, £1035. In both cases, Wrightson was to find most of the materials and pay for their carriage. In the event a seven-bay house was built in stone; by its completion in 1744 a total of £3784 had been expended. Four years later, and then a very old man, William Wrightson decided to add library and chapel wings (Plate 103). Platt had died in 1743 so he turned to the up and coming local architect, James Paine. Paine again provided two estimates of £629 and £895, depending upon the extent to which Wrightson supplied the materials: one was for the case of the wings, either £313 or £548, and for finishing them either £316 or £347. Explaining the higher estimate of £895, Paine wrote:

> I am afraid you will think the Amount is high, indeed its more than from a Coussory View I coud have expected, but I thought I was best to give you the whole Charge ... but I believe a Considerable deal may be saved; In that estimate I have designed to finish the Chaple in a very Gentiel taste viz Columns inserted in the wall, supporting

PLATE 103. Cusworth Hall, Yorkshire (George Platt, 1740–48 and James Paine, 1749–53) by Thomas Malton, 1788.

a Entablature Adorn'd with Gentill enrichments: & Above the entablature a hansom cove with a few Gentiel Ornaments in it. I propose the Alter table to stand within the Bow which being supported with Columns Also will Produce a fine effect; the Library, I have Proposed to finish in a Plainer manner, but yet neat, with ... Wainscote, Floors, & a Slab marble Chimney Piece.

I hope the Design will Please you & if the expense rises higher than you Propose I can lessen it by finishing it Plainer.

Although Wrightson was a careful and well-seasoned client, Paine's pursuit of the genteel must have persuaded him to loosen his purse-strings, for the original upper estimate was exceeded by no less than 77.4 per cent. The accounts show that it was in the finish of the two wings that it was chiefly surpassed: Joseph Rose's bill for plasterwork at £226 was well over twice the original costing, Samuel Wale and Francis Hayman's decorative panels in the chapel were fifteen times over estimate and the carver's work almost ten times.[41] Yet, however much he might have bemoaned the increased costs, for the last few years of his life Wrightson must have greatly enjoyed his reading and worship in Paine's fine new rooms (Plate 104).

PLATE 104.   Cusworth Hall, Yorkshire. The chapel (James Paine).

It was natural that architects, both in their books of designs and approximate costs, should have attempted to attract custom by suggesting costings which were unrealisable on the building site. Such practices seem to have been part of the everyday currency of large-scale construction before 1830 at least. In the infancy of civil engineering, most rivers were improved and canals and docks built way over estimate. The proprietors of the Pocklington canal, a nine-mile long affair cut in flat country, placed their gratitude on record in 1818 that their engineer had completed the waterway on estimate, making it a very rare exception in this respect.[42] Both the construction of public buildings and country houses seem to have observed a similar pattern.

However a client reached an estimate of his costs, whether by 'the square', by cubic volume or by the seemingly more precise measured calculations for case and finish, the final cost was often well adrift of the figures he had endorsed several years earlier. Why was this? Most architects, from Sir Roger Pratt in the 1660s to Robert Kerr two centuries later, would have replied that it was because the owner changed his mind so frequently. Few were as vacillating as Lord Elgin, of Marbles fame, who commissioned designs for the completion of Broomhall in Fife from no fewer than fourteen architects between 1796 and 1828.[43] Indecision, however, if not to the same degree as Lord Elgin's wavering, was common. Pratt wrote around 1672: 'But then must we be sure not to vary from our first design, which many men doing, either out of lightness of humour, or ignorance of what is right, have not only disfigured their optional [original?] undertaking, but have also taken away all certainty of the expense, and given to their workmen the desired opportunity to unreasonably deal with them.'[44] 'A cheap house' (one built to estimate) was defined by Kerr as 'one for which the owner has stipulated to accept good average workmanship, neither less nor more, with strictly econ-omical administration, having chosen a skilful architect and a trustworthy builder, and having for his own part taken great pains beforehand to comprehend the plan, and equal pains during execution to avoid altering it'.[45] In one note Pratt advocated a 25 per cent contingency fund to cover defective materials and changes in plan; in another, he wrote, 'after you have once laid one stone never to alter your design ... for if you be once irresolute in that, your alterations may charge to you half as much as your whole building'.[46] Kerr suggested that a 10 per cent allowance for extras was viable for the afterthoughts of both architect and client as the plan evolved. Since Kerr's client, John Walter, owner of *The Times*, main-tained the cost of Bearwood (£129,000) 'greatly exceeds the sum which I originally contemplated spending upon the work ... it exceeds twice the amount estimated by your own surveyor Mr Freeman', his contingency proposal seems modest indeed. The Bearwood example is not unique.[47] When Lord Crewe restored Crewe Hall, after a disastrous fire in 1866, Edward M. Barry's estimate was for £35,000 (six-sevenths was secured from the insurers). But Lord Crewe decided to introduce new features and make further alterations so that a year later Barry was advising his client that costs would now be not less than double his original estimate (Plate 105). Although Lord Crewe sought to control the rate of expendi-ture, by May 1868 it had risen to £85,000. Fifteen months later, with the contractor estimating further work at £26,742, Barry was writing to his client: 'In a work like Crewe Hall I do not think it would have been possible to have obtained at the beginning a close and binding estimate. The work is so peculiar and so many improvements have been suggested by yourself as well as by me during the works that the estimate if it had been given could not possibly have been kept to.' Everything was of superlative quality: John Crace and William Caldecott supplied

PLATE 105.   Crewe Hall, Cheshire (restored by Edward M. Barry 1866–71 after a fire), from the
lake *c.* 1895.

upholstery and furniture; and Lord Crewe paid no less than £123,341 to the
contractors, William Cubitt & Co., between 1866 and 1871. It was a settlement
very different from Barry's original costings.[48]

Of course houses were completed on estimate, but they would seem to have
been in a minority. The reputations of provincial architects, such as John Johnson
and Thomas Pritchard of Shrewsbury, derided by Horace Walpole and members
of the Society of Dilettanti, were based upon the modest, economical commissions
of the smaller gentry, both new and old.[49] Some better-known nineteenth-century
architects, including Blore and Salvin, also possessed good names for delivering
projects on estimate. The latter was sought to design a palace for the newly-created
see of Ripon because it was understood he 'never exceeded his first estimate of
expences which in this case was of the first consideration'.[50] Yet even at the end
of our period, when the growing professionalism of architects and surveyors and
the near universality of contracting ensured firmer price controls, everything still
depended on the client not changing his mind. The likes of the Sutherlands, Lord

Crewe and the super-rich could afford to do so on whim. But most accounts, for houses of every size, suggest that, whether owners had a major change of mind or not, estimates crept upwards. Examples are legion. At Tendring, where Soane was contractor as well as architect and whose every voucher was checked by anxious trustees, his final bill, after the presentation of a thirty-eight page account of extras and alterations, was 18 per cent over costs. In 1802 Sir George Beaumont commissioned George Dance to produce schemes for a new £8000 house at Cole Orton in Leicestershire. By the time the house, a picturesque but not large affair, had been completed in 1809, Dance reckoned the cost without furnishing to be £15,000. Strelley Hall (Nottinghamshire) was the plainest seven by five bays two-and-a-half storey house wrapped round an older core in less than eighteen months in 1790–91. Its designer, Thomas Gardner, submitted a contract for £1656 designating that the owner, Thomas Webb Edge, supply most of the materials and pay for local carriage, chimney-pieces, and the fitting up of the domestic offices with 'dressers, shelves, cupboards, presses etc. etc.' In addition, a good deal of material was reused. Clearly Strelley was an economy job. Nevertheless, Gardner's final account was for £2784, which was 68 per cent over his original costs. Webb Edge, as so often, had allowed alterations and extras along the way. The building of Strelley, even where the accounts are full, is also a reminder that, with the owner himself finding most of the materials and reusing others from the old house, it is difficult to arrive at its true final total cost.[51]

The question of final costs often far exceeding the original intentions of owners was the result of other influences besides the predilection to change their minds. Contracts with suppliers, builders and other craftsmen were badly drawn up; careful supervision in practice was often lacking; some architects were not capable managers of projects. Therefore the country house builder was open to many forms of deception. The notebooks of Sir Roger Pratt and Roger North, and the practical guides to measurement, building and carpentry which flooded the building market after 1720, certainly encouraged total commitment so that the builder should, even when employing a proficient clerk of the works, not only oversee every stage of the building process, but also possess a competent knowledge of measurement and materials. Some owners, at every level of a project, followed these best practice guidelines – from William Wrightson at Cusworth, Thomas Worsley at Hovingham and Sir Christopher Sykes at Sledmere, to Lord Leicester at Holkham. The involvement of these and like-minded owners is nicely encapsulated in a romantic-period tinged vignette of Lord Grantham, later Foreign

Secretary in Shelburne's ministry, modernising Baldersby Park in north Yorkshire in 1780: he 'spent half the day overlooking the workmen, played with the Child as often as he could, and at night scrawled little plans and sketches of architecture'.[52] Yet much of the architectural literature tended to pull owners in an opposing direction to the functional. However practically minded they were, perhaps the majority would have found it hard to follow to the letter Pratt's advice or the practical guides on building, especially the interminable sections on measurement. Their preference must have been to thumb through the pages of Palladio and Serlio, and, after the 1720s, the tomes of Gibbs, Ware, Langley, Crunden, Chambers, Soane and their like, which filled their heads and those of their wives with beguiling designs of room interiors, chimney-pieces, temples, bridges and gate-piers – besides page after page of facades and ground plans. This burgeoning literature on country house building was, especially given the practice of presenting estimates by case and finish (the latter always somewhat flexible), an invitation to overspend.

The other aspect encouraging owners to be both imprecise about and to exceed estimates was the habit of at least notionally building out of income. While their timing in deciding to rebuild or remodel houses was usually underpinned by inheritance or marriage, if spending exceeded this initial tranche, houses were often completed out of regular income. Building the house itself was also only one aspect of an owner's plans. Frequently, he might also be building stables, walling round a kitchen garden, altering his park and garden, buying land or improving his farms. With these open-ended commitments, finances were often straitened, especially during periods of recession. The only way to proceed was to borrow in order to spread expenditure over a longer period than originally anticipated.

To build houses stylishly but also soundly and on estimate was the aim of almost all architects from Pratt to Kerr. That the last objective was seldom achieved was, they maintained, because clients and their wives never knew their own minds. For owners, however deeply involved in the building process, were also anxious to immortalise their taste and wealth in bricks and mortar. The wealthier members of the aristocracy and gentry were therefore often carried away in their schemes by the competing projects of their peer group and by the blandishments of architects and designers set out in an increasing array of persuasive literature. Original estimates of cost were often knocked off course. Pratt's advice to owners was difficult to follow in practice:

Let them consider well what the strength of their present stock is, and the superfluity of their income, and according to the efficiency of these, let their undertaking be no more than what they can buy materials for the first year, build the second, finish the third, and at most furnish the fourth one, all which things will very well fall out in their most proper season.[53]

Completion of large country houses took years, illogically defying demographic realities, especially in the century of high death rates after 1660. Savings were depleted; debts mounted; a large proportion of income was consumed for years on end. That owners triumphed in creating the glories of the English country house is remarkable testimony to their vision, tenacity and prodigality.

The decision, increasingly facing owners in the two centuries after 1660, whether to rebuild or remodel the principal house on their estates, was not an easy one. Economic and aesthetic considerations had to be balanced and, in many cases, a more personal analysis made about the degree of attachment to the house already standing. Action at some stage was unavoidable. Even the stoutest built houses were not impermeable. Even those owners most reluctant to spend, those most unmoved by shifts in architectural styles and fashion more generally, and those deafest to the entreaties of their wives, had to undertake major renovations every hundred years or so simply because roofs, walls and woodwork were not indestructible. Almost every country house with a long history was at some stage or other in its existence noted as being in serious disrepair and ripe for refurbishment. Inventories of contents capture the general condition of houses, revealing with precision room arrangements and furnishings.[54] Providing vivid snapshots, Horace Walpole's writings and John Byng's diaries are filled with examples of 'ruinous', 'indifferent' and 'decayed' great houses. The woeful state of Hatfield, Wrest, Boughton, Grimsthorpe, Belvoir, Revesby Abbey and Powis Castle now leap from their pages. The manor houses of the gentry observed the same cycle of order and neglect as family circumstances ebbed and flowed. Some houses of course became so decrepit, so incommodious, so old-fashioned that a new one seemed the only solution. At Wrest, Earl de Grey built a new French-styled house in 1834–39 (Plates 106–107):

For many years before [1833, when he inherited], I had felt the utter impossibility of doing anything to or with the old house. It was very old, but it had neither antiquarian or architectural value. It was not essentially out of repair, but it was of very bad

PLATE 106.   Wrest Park, Bedfordshire. The partly demolished house in *c.* 1838, drawn by
J. C. Buckler.

construction (much of it nothing but lath and plaster), very extensive without a possibility of concentration, utterly impossible to warm, and with no suite of appartments
upon any floor.[55]

In general owners, tossing up considerations about site, condition, convenience,
architectural fashion and costs, pondered long and hard before they demolished
their family seat. What guided an owner, when circumstances were right, to
decide whether to rebuild or to remodel his house? The reasons were many. On
the side of a decision to remodel affection for the old family seat was an important
consideration, especially if it was large and in reasonable order. Age in a house
proclaimed a family's longevity of tenure and association. Lord Sherborne embarked on Lewis Wyatt's disastrously expensive scheme to remodel Sherborne
because he wished to retain much of the exterior of the house and its internal
feel. William Windham was similarly involved at Felbrigg in the 1750s. Sensitively
remodelling the interior, leaving the outside basically intact, his resolution, ap-
pealing to us now but then flying in the face of Palladian fashionability, was bold.

PLATE 107.   Wrest Park, Bedfordshire. The new house of 1834–39, in *c.* 1900.

If large old houses survived into the nineteenth century, with a shift to national styles – Gothic and Jacobethan – they then stood a better chance of pulling through, but not Palladian villas difficult to trick out in Victorian dress. Even architects of great repute, such as Salvin, restored far more houses than they built new ones.[56] Indeed by the mid nineteenth century it was difficult for owners, with increasing rent rolls at their disposal, to resist the blandishments of architects stressing the need to adapt old houses to conform to changes in country house life. Few owners of pre-1830 houses, had they read Robert Kerr's *The Gentleman's House*, could have countered his stress upon the need for Privacy, Comfort, Convenience, Spaciousness, Compactness, Light, Air and Salubrity, Aspect and Prospect.

Economy was perhaps the most important factor in an owner's decision to remodel rather than to rebuild from scratch. Houses could be given a periodic face-lift or extension, and their interior-spaces rearranged. In comparison with the costs of new houses, this could often be achieved quite cheaply. In 1763 at Wrest, John Smith, clerk of the works at Kensington Palace (1761–82), converted the great parlour into the south drawing-room for an estimated £429. Stapleford Park, the Earl of Harborough's Leicestershire seat, was pronounced uninhabitable in 1767. The third Earl, married four times, had failed to produce an heir, and his brother, the eventual successor to the title, was attempting to force him, through the court of Chancery under the terms of an earlier will, to put the house in order. Christopher Staveley, a Leicestershire architect and builder, produced an estimate of £2200 9s. 9½d. for repairs, including work to the park entrance, drive and palings. Almost a decade later further internal improvements were made. But a rebuild of the irregular old house of the Sherards, variously dating from about 1500, the 1630s, and around the 1680s, was never considered.[57] Rather earlier at the other end of the county on the Northamptonshire borders, Stanford Hall, a large William Smith house of 1697–1700, was remodelled by his brother Francis in 1730–31. The bill was for £1171 10s. 11d.: work on the great staircase cost £300; fifty-six sash windows in the 'middle and hall stories'

PLATE 108.   Stanford Hall, Leicestershire (William and Francis Smith). The east front (1690s) and the stable block (1737).

PLATE 109.   Shipton Hall, Shropshire. A Tudor house remodelled by Thomas Pritchard in the 1760s.

cost £318 7s. 3½d. When later in the 1730s he remodelled the east front and built the stable and office blocks, 'a large pile of building, consisting of two quadrangles' which dominated the prospect from the east, his account for the work, submitted in 1738, was for £2881 6s. 10d. (Plate 108).[58] Visitors to Euston in Suffolk as various as Lord Oxford, Horace Walpole and Sir Thomas Robinson had dismissed the house (but not the park) as indifferent, indeed badly built. Between 1750 and 1756 Matthew Brettingham the elder refaced the house for the second Duke of Grafton in red brick with stone dressings, inserted new windows, and remodelled the corner towers à la Holkham for around £6000. For an eighteenth-century duke this was indeed modest.[59] The mid Georgian gentry of Shropshire were similarly moved to update their houses while keeping a grip on their purse-strings. The county was not one of great or grand completely new-built houses. Thomas Pritchard, the Shrewsbury joiner-cum-architect, for example specialised in conversions and extensions: 'He carried [them] out in a sympathetic and economic way and this last factor is probably the one that could account most for his very busy period during the 1760s and early 1770s' (Plate 109).[60]

Remodelling had the additional attraction that it allowed a considerable reuse of old materials and also that, since it was usually a cheaper solution than rebuilding, it could more readily be paid out of income. Edward Pratt engaged John Soane to remodel Sir Roger Pratt's famed 1670s villa two years after he inherited the Norfolk estate of Ryston in 1784 – they had met earlier in Italy on Pratt's Grand Tour (Plate 110). From the beginning of 1786 they drew up plans to rearrange the interior, raise the one-storey side wings of Sir Roger's house, link them to new pavilions containing the domestic offices, and roof the whole in Westmorland slate. Soane's account, finally cleared in 1794, consisted of £335 17s. 4d. for his travel (he visited the site sixteen times) and fees, the latter reckoned at 5 per cent on costs of £3365 plus the large sum of £1239, the estimated value of reused materials (25 per cent of the whole project). Ryston was thoroughly updated by Soane for a net cost of £3704, a considerably cheaper solution than building a new house. Edward Pratt had married a King's Lynn heiress in 1786, some of the proceeds of her dowry most likely paying for the house's refurbishment.[61] Often frequent alterations could be met out of income. Thomas Barrett-Lennard (1717–80), later seventeenth Lord Dacre, an amateur architect and antiquary, very gradually Gothicised in the Strawberry Hill manner his old Tudor

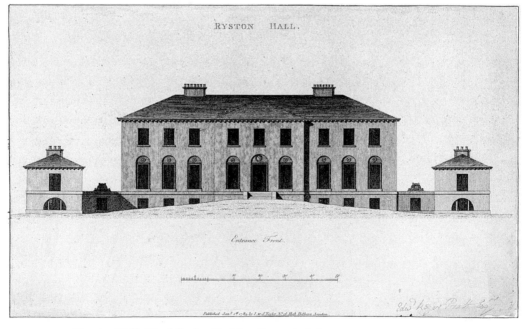

PLATE 110.   Ryston Hall, Norfolk, by Sir John Soane (1789).

house of Belhus in Essex in the fifteen years after the '45 (Plate 134). At the outset of his refurbishment, he wrote to Sanderson Miller,

> I have resolved to fit up my new Hall and Staircase and make that end of the House habitable forthwith, the stucco men being to come down for that purpose next week; indeed both Mrs Barrett and myself are quite weary of living in the way we have done, it being extremely inconvenient to us to have half our House shut up so that we have but three spare beds at present to put our Friends in. The two great rooms however we shall leave till the next year.

Neither the continual mess nor his depressive nature ('the blew devils') stopped him, with Miller's aid, altering room after room in the house, refacing it, and improving the park into the 1760s, eventually engaging Capability Brown. Frequently, he mentions the deterrent of cost, but he belonged to that smart set of *cognoscenti* which gravitated around Sanderson Miller. He was determined to remodel the big Tudor house however slowly his income allowed it. He would have been gratified had he known Horace Walpole approved of his pretty 'Good King James the First Gothic' embellishments, even though they failed to match the 'perfection' of Strawberry Hill.[62] On a larger scale, Sir Roger Newdigate (1719–1807) took over half a century to transform Arbury Hall in Warwickshire, his big courtyard house of monastic origins, into the most remarkable Gothic house in Georgian England. Principally his own architect, he copied with increasing conviction late medieval decorations to make his alterations conform to what he imagined the earlier priory had been. Antiquarianism and modernity were balanced with Georgian good sense. Even though cloisters were inserted in the 1780s, a late eighteenth-century feel for space and ease was created. The entrance was shifted and a sequence of four splendid rooms, saloon, drawing-room, dining-room and library, was formed from the previous higgledy-piggledy arrangement of apartments. Sir Roger was rich, enjoying an income of £15,000 a year by the 1780s, but he chose to remodel his house slowly and painstakingly from it.[63]

The remodelling of Belhus and Arbury had allowed their owners to retain some of the fabric of their homes, to introduce Georgian comforts and to impose their sense of the past. Many owners, as their circumstances allowed, simply added to their houses and knocked them about to incorporate some of the latest fashions in architecture. Sometimes the process of remodelling, as at Trewithen in Cornwall, seems perpetual. The estate was purchased in 1715 by Philip Hawkins, a wealthy attorney. He created pleasure grounds and by 1730 had largely rebuilt the old house to plans (based upon designs of James Gibbs) of Thomas Edwards, a London architect. The work appears to have been incomplete on Hawkins's death in 1738, but his trustees and heir completed the house and undertook further landscaping in the 1740s. A long description of the house in 1757 indicates that it was a large one, faced with Portland stone on three sides and with ten rooms on a floor with a big saloon and 'very large hall'. Already, however, the east front was being taken down 'to be built in a modern tast[e] with bow-windows' and the existing service wing matched by a brick stable block. Less than a decade later in 1763–64, Sir Robert Taylor was rebuilding the south front (although in 1757 it had been described as looking 'as white and clean as if newly erected') and making alterations to the interior. The younger Matthew Brettingham's designs for further alterations in the 1790s were not executed.[64]

The predisposition of owners like the Hawkinses of Trewithen to alter and extend their house was dictated by considerations of architectural fashion, family need and social change. It probably also reflects the fact that most estates were settled. Restricted about their disposition, owners could and did borrow freely on their rent rolls. Provision was also made in settlements for the different generations of families – mothers, siblings and children. In turn, the realisation of these usually initiated a cycle of annual payments in the form of interest charges on these specified sums. Extensive house building might very easily add to these debt burdens. The general run of country house builders were therefore nudged by economic circumstances into remodelling, and into doing so irregularly as ownership of estates passed from one generation to another observing only the random chronology of birth and death. Gibbs Antrobus stressed this aspect of settlements in his discussions with Lewis Wyatt about rebuilding Eaton-by-Congleton Hall in Cheshire in 1827–28. At first he planned the extension of his existing house. The architect's rough estimates, in the way of the Wyatts, unfortunately tended to inflate: £10,000-£12,000 soon became £12,000-£14,000. Whilst liking Wyatt's proposals, Antrobus injected a note of caution:

> with a fixed income and an entailed property I do not feel disposed, I might say justified, in laying out so large a sum, as you seem to think the building would require. £12,000 or £14,000 would swell to £20,000 before the house was finished and furnished even if it went no higher ... on this account I have been endeavouring to find how the expense might be reduced.[65]

In the end, Antrobus, of well-to-do banking stock, was persuaded to build a new house costing over £23,000. Many owners, without his non-landed sources of income, proceeded only to remodel their houses either because they were anxious not to stoke the fires of indebtedness or their incomes were relatively circumscribed anyway.

With these constraints in mind, many country houses were updated, entrances turned round, facades refenestrated, rooms added and interiors reshaped. Although these solutions were usually a much cheaper alternative to building on a new site (the Antrobuses' experience makes the point nicely), in practice costs, from a lower base, could just as easily escalate in remodelling. Once work was underway, further problems were uncovered, work was slower and more troublesome – and landowners, as always, went on changing their minds. Robert Kerr was eloquent about these difficulties:

> No other work of building, treacherous as all building is proverbially, is so charged with hidden danger to the pocket as what is called 'pulling' about an old house; indeed, as a maxim, wherever addition externally can be had, reconstruction internally is generally to be avoided.[66]

This opinion of Kerr, a Scot somewhat given to exaggeration, was, as we have seen, the experience of Lords Sherborne and Crewe. Equally, at the lower end of the scale, remodelling could run owners into far more expense than they had anticipated. Richard Norris, a London surveyor and architect, altered Broke Hall in Suffolk for Philip Bowes Broke in the mid 1770s. His contract amounted to £3374, excluding expenses, the value of reused materials, and with the client finding all timber, bricks and scaffolding. Norris's final account well exceeded his original one. Broke sourly annotated it, 'with labour, papering, painting made this affair cost near £8000'. The work was also unsatisfactory. The house was virtually rebuilt for Broke by James Wyatt in 1791–92.[67]

More generally, the problem with remodelling was that results were often unacceptable in terms of convenience and aesthetic appearance. Arbury was exceptional, although alterations at Burghley in the early eighteenth century and those at Longleat by Wyatville were also widely applauded.[68] Certainly most country house architects, in spite of most of them earning the major part of their living from alterations, were anxious to establish their reputations with their own novel designs. Not surprisingly, they argued against remodelling. Kerr set out a twenty-page supplement, 'Notes on the Alteration of Existing Houses', in *The Gentleman's House*, in which he insisted that the apparent economy of alteration of the old had to be carefully weighed against the convenience of the new upon which it was difficult to put a price.[69] Few old houses would have survived had his strictures about the problems of remodelling and the advantages of a new house been observed to the letter. Similar arguments, put equally forcibly and more concisely, are to be found in the writings of Sir Roger Pratt two centuries earlier:

> But be sure not to be wrought upon either to patch up an old house, at any great expense, or to make an addition to it especially if the place where it stands be not extremely pleasant, for besides that the charge will be little less to build a new one (where much of the materials of the old may very well serve) the old one after all the trouble and expense, will neither answer them, nor anyone's expectations, but look patched and irregular without, and within very little convenience, with low ceilings, and unequal floors, and many things else of the like ungracefulness, neither ever be persuaded to set your house in a hole or the like being induced there unto by the neighbourhood of good out housing there as they call it, for this according to the proverb is to spoil a custard to save an egg, and yet a thing much practised amongst us.

Roger North expressed similar views. Richard Neve stressed the point with biblical simplicity: 'He that alters an old House is tyed as a Translator to the Original, and is confined to the Fancy of the first Builder.'[70]

These views held by architects were fully shared by their clients. Many of them were knowledgeable from their reading about architectural styles; many of them developed a good eye from frequent country house visiting. When he assessed Henry Flitcroft's alterations at Woburn in the 1740s, Horace Walpole was highly critical of the outcome. The work had cost the enormous sum of 'above £40,000', yet the result was 'much spoiled, partly by adhering to the old proportions, and partly by the Duke's persisting to save the grotto, and some old parts at the angles, which had been added by Inigo Jones'. The gallery he thought 'extremely narrow, and is in reality only the Corridor shut up'. The final impression was a riot of styles, Gothic, Chinese, French and Roman. The result of far simpler and popular solutions, the addition of a large room or two, might be equally mis-judged. Donington in Leicestershire was 'a miserable house, small and placed in a hole. Two tawdry rooms like assembly rooms at Blackheath added by the Countess Dowager [of Huntingdon]' (Plate III). But his severest strictures about the lapses of taste that owners often made in remodelling were reserved for Horton House. The old house was bad, but the new facade added as disguise was an incredible muddle.

PLATE III. Donington Hall, Leicestershire. Drawn by Humphry Repton before William Wilkins rebuilt the house in Gothic style during the 1790s. The 'two tawdry rooms like assembly rooms at Blackheath' are on the right.

George, the last Earl of Halifax, was persuaded to new front and alter it, by one Garrett, who finished one end for him with a pediment top. This Earl added a fine but too narrow portico of six stone columns, and added the other end after the design of Wright, but with a round top, and so totally unlike the other side of the portico, that the latter must be pulled down; at present, the Incongruity is ridiculous. Two other ends like the new one are to be added. If they are, according to the intended plan, the whole will be heavy and ugly.[71]

Walpole was a perceptive if unpredictable critic. But even casual country house visitors could discern with precision the defects of houses remodelled after this fashion. Sylas Neville 'went in a post-chaise to see Goodwood – was struck on coming in sight of the house, but not with its magnificence – no – for a Duke's seat it is the meanest I ever saw. The front represents two or three old houses joined together without order or design – but it may be said the offices make amends'.[72] Heveningham Hall, the twenty-three-bay house Sir Robert Taylor and James Wyatt designed for Sir Gerard Vanneck, was the grandest house in Suffolk.

Yet when the young de La Rochefoucauld brothers saw it near completion in 1784, they commented that the old house had been gutted to form Wyatt's 'extremely noble hall'. It was '72 feet by 24, with columns and great altitude', in fact it cut 'the house completely in two, so that one wing has no communication with the other'. Moreover, immediately behind the house was 'an almost vertical slope', which restricted views and was 'so close that it must spread a lot of damp through the house'. They thought it would have been far better to have chosen a fresh site on the other side of the valley.[73]

At Heveningham, the de La Rochefoucaulds hit on the two principal reasons which tilted the balance in favour of rebuilding: the problem of being tied to the original; and the problem of a site which no longer fitted eighteenth- and nineteenth-century concepts of light and landscape. Changing views about the siting of houses were important. Robert Burton had opined, in *The Anatomy of Melancholy* (1621), that whilst foreigners 'build on high hills, in hot countries, for more air ... We build in bottoms for warmth'. This predilection of English builders was supposedly overturned in the course of the seventeenth century.[74] Although the one area in which every prospective builder felt confidence was the selection of a site, increasingly architects and landscape gardeners gave advice about sites, aspects and prospects ('aspect first, prospect second' went the adage), approaches, salubrity, water supplies and drainage. In fact, classical landscape styles from the Restoration to the 1720s and beyond, with their axial avenues and parterres set out with geometrical precision, were entirely compatible with flat, 'bottoms for warmth' locations. It was only with the gradual shift to the more informal styles of the picturesque landscape that once-celebrated houses and gardens such as Boughton, Kimbolton and Wrest were dismissed by the Georgian tourist trade as being sited in low, miserable situations.

The new emphasis was on aspect, approach, large irregular stretches of water and prolific shelter-belt planting. Within the confines of their properties, often themselves being extended and consolidated by purchases, enclosure and road closure, owners were encouraged by architectural and landscape literature and practice to shift the site of their houses when they rebuilt. When they were of a mind and position to afford a good new house, they often moved the site a few hundred yards to create a fashionably ordered whole – a better aspect and prospect, a kitchen garden out of sight, an informal landscape and scenic approach. Sometimes the shift in site was minimal. At Houghton, Sir Robert Walpole's new house of the 1720s was sited only a few yards from the old. This had recently been twice remodelled, in about 1706 and in about 1716, and was already the focus of Sir Robert's ventures into landscaping on a grand scale, the creation of French-style gardens dominated by trees, grass and gravel.[75] This was in flat Norfolk. In Essex, Benjamin Mildmay (1672–1756) pursued a similar, if more cautious, course. A younger son, he followed an unremarkable career, being Commissioner of the Salt Duties from 1714 to 1720, and Commissioner of Excise from 1720 to 1728. Remaining a bachelor until he was fifty-one, he eventually married Frederica Darcy, the thirty-six year-old widow of the fifth Earl of Holderness. Her fortune and connections with the royal family transformed his economic and social prospects, which were further enhanced when he succeeded his brother as Earl Fitzwalter in 1728. Immediately he bought the family seat, Moulsham Hall, from his brother's widow, and engaged Giacomo Leoni to design its replacement. He decided, however, to rebuild slowly on the site of the sixteenth-century house, demolishing it wing by wing as the new house rose on the old foundations. The total cost of the house was around £17,000, but it was spent over a period of twenty-one years, at a rate kept within the means of the prudent earl. Unlike many younger contemporaries, he lived to see the completion of his project.[76] Other builders positioned their houses with enormous care. The new house John Buxton built was sited with much thought. His family's old seat, Channonz Hall, was a 1560s house in the dullest, heavy land area of south Norfolk. With a perpetual itch to build, he modernised it; but, with a large, young family, he was also anxious to build a dozen miles away on his healthier Breckland estate near Thetford. The situation for the new house, Shadwell Lodge, was chosen with the utmost attention in respect of prospect, aspect, soil and water. He turned the house to the south to provide a cheerful vista from the common parlour and study: 'I have taken notice that during November, December and January the sun comes very little upon the east or west side and then so faint at rising or setting that scarce yields and warmth or spirit. The south then must be courted in our scheme.' As building proceeded in 1727 he was 'every day more charmed with the situation, and see ... where new schemes may be put in execution in their order as time and opportunity will give us leave'.[77] At Harewood, Edwin Lascelles built his new house a few hundred yards from the old manor house, which was in a damp hollow besides a tiny tributary of the River Wharfe. This new site, on the southern slope of Harewood bank, and commanding fine views, was made famous by a whole battalion of Romantic water colourists led by Turner (Plate 112). Lascelles built a stable block between the two houses and eventually,

PLATE 112.   Harewood House, Yorkshire. The south front by J. M. W. Turner, *c.* 1800. The lake covers the site of the old house, Gawthorp Hall.

after dismantling the old house (its chimney-pieces were reused in the basement of the new house), its site was submerged in the lake which was the centrepiece of Capability Brown's great park.[78] At Wrest, Earl de Grey's new house of 1834–39 occupied a site the Duke of Kent had selected for a house he had intended to build in the 1710s. The move, the earl maintained, was to escape the old one, a magnet for damp mists and 'the clouds of gnats which used to eat us up'.[79]

Landowners carefully weighed the pros and cons of remodelling. It was popular because it could be achieved piecemeal over the years, a couple of rooms here, a new front there. Many an Elizabethan and Jacobean house, however extensively pulled about by subsequent generations, survived to the present because remodelling was a cheaper solution. It also preserved affection for the old and familiar. But in aesthetic terms contemporaries were often critical about the outcome. Time has now in many cases lent appeal. On the other hand, a new house possessed the advantages of convenience, fitting the latest fashions in architecture and landscaping, and meeting the latest requirements of country house life. In the end, money was probably the deciding factor. The proceeds of a good marriage settlement, a big inheritance, burgeoning income, and new money were the mainstays of the rebuilt country house market.

So far as costs were concerned, Lawrence and Jeanne Stone, in their study of the size and number of country houses in Hertfordshire, Northamptonshire and Northumberland from 1540 to 1800, identified three problems. They noted the difficulty of establishing the costs of different levels of interior finishing of comparable dimensions; the cost of a house as part of a total package of expenditure, including stables, kitchen gardens, park walls and palings, and landscaping more generally; and the problem of adjusting the average cost of the square across three centuries to take into account the increase in building costs.[80] The first problem was abandoned as impossible. For the second, a somewhat unnecessary preoccupation since the measurement and cost of the house was the prime and more easily ascertainable element in expenditure, they fell back upon Robert Kerr's comments. This was that the provision of a stable block and landscaping was reckoned to add around one-third to total costs. Presumably this was not a figure plucked from the air, but one which architects and owners alike used as a rule of thumb for a new house, outbuildings and landscaping which was, *tout court*, an unusual event. In addressing their third problem, they derived unit costs from the estimates of Robert Morris (1755), George Richardson (1792) and Robert Kerr (1865), to which we have already referred. From them, as a rough guide, the Stones concluded that the cost of living space in a medium-sized country house was, in the 1750s £40 per square, in the early 1790s £55, and in 1865 £58 or £83 for a £5000 or £20,000 house respectively, 'roughly the range' which concerned them.[81]

Two main observations may be made about these figures. First, they are minimal estimates. Architects had an interest in publishing rock-bottom prices, largely unrealisable in practice. Morris was providing estimates at £40 per superficial square (about £16 per square for the actual area of *living* space) for a two-and-a-half storey house which would have broken any contractor who attempted to match them. They can have been for little more than the case of his designs. Well might he warn builders: 'often through ignorance, or design, of the estimates, it [final cost] exceeds double, sometimes treble, the sum estimated'.[82] Secondly, in practice few houses were completed on estimate. As we have seen, clients changed their minds, finishes were finalised across the duration of a project and varied considerably in cost. In general, the larger the house, the more elaborate was its finish. Both Halfpenny and Kerr, writing more than a century apart, showed a range of cost three times from the cheapest to the most expensive finish.[83] First-rate ones, with wall and ceiling paintings, carvings, stucco, the extensive use of marble and statuary chimney-pieces, all requiring top-notch craftsmen, artists and sculptors to create them, were indeed expensive. Of course it is possible that simpler finishes, more tightly drawn contracts for all aspects of a house's construction and better managed workforces were all elements driving down real costs per unit. Against them must be set the marked advance of wages in the quarter century after 1850. It is, however, the difference in finishes between country houses which makes attempts to estimate cost from their square area difficult (Plate 74).

Do insurance policies provide alternative estimates of the cost of country houses? At first sight, they offer as rich a source for the valuation of country houses and their contents as those of early factories which have been used in studies of fixed capital formation in the rapidly growing textile industries after the 1780s.[84] Owners of houses insured against the hazard of fire from the early eighteenth century onwards. The registers of the Sun Fire Office (founded in 1710), the Royal Exchange (1721) and, at a regional level, the Norwich Union Fire Insurance Office (1797) and the Suffolk Fire Office (1802) include many policies relating to country houses – for fire in them was a well-recognised risk.

   In comparing the use of insurance policies in the valuation of factories and country houses, however, differences between industrial and domestic realities should be noted. The mill and factory data are from a critical, but nevertheless relatively short, period of industrial development. Against this, insurance valuations of country houses are being considered over a 150-year period. The vast majority of landowners were not thrusting industrialists, nor were owner-occupied mansions income-earning assets. Country houses, although the consequences of an uninsured loss could be damaging to an estate, were also not in the same high-risk league as factories. Furthermore, a search of the Sun and Royal Exchange indexes for policies relating to country houses also presents a problem of interpretation. It would be easy to provide a misleading picture because many policy-register entries, and hence indexes, record policies taken out by individuals at their country houses which do not provide cover for the insurance of that property alone. Where the house is covered it may be one of a number of separate classes of property including, perhaps, the contents of the house, out-buildings and estate farms. For example, the total policy cover in 1778 of John Berney Petre of Westwick in Norfolk was £4590.[85] Closer inspection of the policy itself, however, reveals that the house was insured for only £1200, contents, domestic offices and outhouses a further £650, whilst a long list of estate property, including tenanted farms, inflated the total to £4590. It is therefore essential to identify precisely the property covered in the indexed totals. We have searched only the indexed portion of the Sun and Royal Exchange registers and obtained valuations of over fifty houses in East Anglia and Yorkshire. For some a direct comparison between insurance values and the cost of building can be made. What generalisations can be drawn from them?

The earliest group of fire-insurance policies studied, based on the Sun index for 1714–31, includes cover for seven houses in Suffolk and four in Norfolk. These were early days for fire insurance. Of the ten which disclosed the sums insured, four were for £1000, five below £1000, and only one, Long Melford Hall, a substantial Elizabethan mansion owned by the appropriately named Sir Charles Firebrace, was for £3000.[86] These houses were clearly not insured for full rebuilding costs. This may be partly due to the imposition by the two companies of limits on the total risk insured. It may also reflect the perception of owners that total losses were unlikely and that the function of insurance was to provide cover against probable partial losses which, in the absence of an 'average clause', would be paid out to the insurance limit. To protect themselves, insurers were already separating different risks, limiting their exposure by writing specific policies for the main house, its contents and its outbuildings.

For the period 1766–93, insurance information has been obtained for twenty-six houses, ten in Suffolk, eight in Norfolk and eight in Yorkshire. For three houses, Denton, Tendring and Henham, the surviving building accounts are contempor-aneous with the insurance policies. For several others, incomplete but nevertheless useful cost estimates are available to compare with insurance values. Denton Hall was insured during construction in 1775 for £3000 plus £300 for its outbuildings. By 1782, well after completion, it was still insured for £3000, its stables, coach house and granary for £300, and its contents £1000.[87] The house and stable block had cost at least £9459 to build, with a further £1082 spent on new furniture. Tendring, built for £12,428 (see Table 12), was insured for £8000; Shotesham, a similarly-sized Soane house, was insured for only £2000 on its completion in

1792.[88] Henham was insured during building in 1796 for £10,000. At this stage, the insurance value was comparable with the sum then expended on building, but the policy register indicates that cover remained unchanged at least to its renewal in 1812, although the house cost over £21,000 to build.[89] These houses were insured for a varying proportion of their building costs; Tendring for around two-thirds; Henham for under a half; Denton for a third; Shotesham for as little as a fifth.

When we turn to even larger houses for which some estimates of cost exist, insured values seem equally adrift. Castle Howard cost around £40,000 to build between 1699 and 1713, with a further £38,000 spent across forty years on its unusually lavish landscape features. A big west wing (internally unfinished until 1811) was added in the 1740s and 1750s, a stable block in the early 1780s. Yet in 1785 the house was insured for £17,000.[90] Temple Newsam, the Irwin's vast old house near Leeds, again very substantially remodelled in the second quarter of the eighteenth century, was insured for only £3000 in 1781.[91] At Ickworth in Suffolk the degree of underinsurance is precise. The fourth Earl of Bristol spent at least £14,593 on his eccentric house between 1796 and 1810. Its central rotunda and east wing were only completed by the fifth Earl in the 1820s spending a further £39,155. At the time of its occupation in 1829 the insurance valuation was £12,000.[92] As at Denton, Henham and Tendring, we have at Ickworth the underinsurance of a house by an owner well aware of the sums he had recently spent. All these valuations are clearly much lower than the historical cost of building.

The relevant cost for comparison with insurance values is of course rebuilding cost, not the original cost. Insurance companies would normally only allow cover up to the amount it cost to rebuild or reinstate a property to its condition before it was damaged.[93] The long-established practice of companies like the Sun, Royal Exchange or Phoenix assumed that insurance cover reflected replacement costs.[94] These differed from original building costs for a variety of reasons, apart from price changes. Account was taken of the likely salvage of brick and stone, the survival of at least the foundations of a house, its cellars, drains and outbuildings, and the possibility that the structural shell might also survive. Even if it was the objective of the insurance companies to value property on the basis of rebuilding cost, the above comparison of cost and insurance valuations suggest that, in the case of country houses, their goal was rarely achieved. All suggest a significant degree of underinsurance. Our reading of the minute books (the policies have not survived) of the Norwich Union and Suffolk fire offices suggests that by the mid nineteenth century values were more realistic. Owners, installing improved but not necessarily safer heating systems, and perceiving workmen as perennially negligent, afforded better cover of both their houses and contents. The companies, much more rigorous in the inspection of houses and the negotiation of policies, and sharing their risks with other companies more freely than they had in the eighteenth century, also allowed larger cover. Detailed research on surviving Victorian policies would be fruitful for architectural and economic historians alike. As with all policies, they certainly reveal a good deal of detail and precise dating about rebuilding and the progress of alterations, as well as some comparative indication of values.[95]

If insurance policies with their built in element of underinsurance, and contemporary estimates by the square, variable when examined in relation to individual houses, are imperfect guides in reckoning the cost of country house building, does interpretation of the building accounts of completed projects provide an alternative way forward?

Even if a country house is accurately measured and described, its cost can vary for the reasons already discussed. Consequently, the production of an index which might be used to state precisely the cost of a particular house is not possible. The estimation of the total investment in a given population of houses is a more credible objective. This involves the placing of individual houses, ordered by size and date, in cost bands derived from detailed studies. The conclusions are tentative, given the small number of accounts reconstructed, but they are supported by other evidence, and with the addition of more examples and further research, the calculations could be refined further.

We have calculated the volumetric costs of ten well-documented houses, and used the results empirically to construct a graph from which building costs can be predicted for a range of house sizes over time. Unit costs in our sample rise in date order with some exceptions (Table 15). In comparison, volumetric costs derived from Halfpenny's data (1742) show a range of 3.3d. to 10.6d., for houses between 13,000 (a small 'summer-house') and 372,000 cubic feet, while Kerr's estimates (1871) range from 8d. to 13.5d. for houses between 41,000 and 802,000 cubic feet in size.

The apparent lower cost of Brodsworth may be attributable to the undervaluation of reused materials, the employment of a single contractor working to an agreed price, and proximity to the source of stone. However, Eshton and Heacham appear particularly expensive. This is because their accounts cover only 'family accommodation', Kerr estimating that for a house the size of Eshton the unit cost of family accommodation was about half as much again as for servants. Moreover, at Heacham some internal reorganisation of the old house, converted to a service wing, is included in the accounts. The Sheringham unit cost reflects the interruption of the building project for over twenty years and may still be low because the accounts are incomplete. But the results of Table 15 suggest that a general relationship between date, size and cost can be derived. They also indicate that the unit cost of 'family' extensions to houses was generally higher than those for building complete houses.

Table 15. *Country house unit building costs, 1670–1870*

House	Main building date	Plan area in hundreds of square feet	Volume in thousands of cubic feet	Building cost £	Unit cost (d. per cubic foot)
Ryston	1670s	51	200	2800	3.4
Cusworth	1740s	112	317	5320	4.0
Heacham	1770s	27	81	4128	12.2
Denton	1770s	136	279	9460	6.0
Sledmere	1780s	119	618	20,548	8.0
Henham	1790s	125	500	21,370	10.3
Sheringham [a]	1810s–1830s	88	213	12,618	14.2
Eshton	1820s	57	200	13,906	16.7
Haveringland	1840s	144	431	21,380	11.9
Brodsworth	1860s	155	521	24,327	11.2

Note: a) See Table 12, note d.

Sources: See Table 12; for Sledmere, Hull University Library, DD SY 98/142; for Brodsworth, Yorkshire Archaeological Society, Leeds, DD 168.

Figures 4 and 5 have been derived to provide a basis for cost estimation from volumetric data. Figure 4 is based on the assumption that building costs increased in proportion to the rises in wage rates, and that unit costs increased with size at a rate following Kerr.[96] A best fit of the costs of eight of our houses (excluding the remodelling of Heacham and Eshton) has been used to locate the date lines. Figure 5 employs the same data to plot total building costs against house size over time. It must be stressed that the aim of the procedure is to estimate the cost of a given population of houses. The individual predictions from the graphs are intended to represent mean costs for which the majority of houses of a given

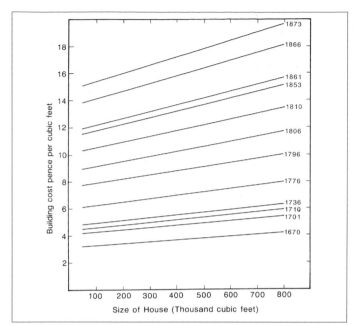

FIGURE 4.
Estimating the cost of building country houses: the variation of cost per cubic foot with house size and date.

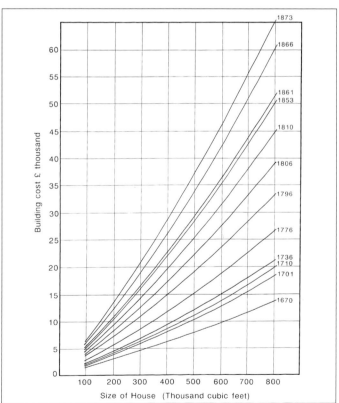

FIGURE 5.
Estimating the cost of building country houses: the variation of total cost with house size and date.

size and date could have been built, but not necessarily the actual costs for particular houses. These may have been higher or lower than the prediction, but the objective is to derive a credible overall figure for the sum of the costs of the houses.

A test of the fit of the data to the graphs in Figures 4 and 5 is to compare the actual costs of the houses for which expenditure is known with the predicted costs obtained from Figure 5. The results are shown in Table 16.

Table 16. *Comparison of actual and predicted building costs*

House	Building cost (£)	
	Actual	*Predicted*
Ryston	2800	2800
Cusworth	5320	7000
Denton	9460	8500
Sledmere	20,548	19,500
Henham	21,370	19,000
Sheringham	12,618	11,000
Haveringland	21,380	21,500
Brodsworth	24,327	30,500
Totals	117,823	119,900

Figure 5 overestimates the cost of two Yorkshire houses, Cusworth and Brodsworth. The absolute differences are a function of the way the graph has been fitted to the data, but the form of presentation will expose potentially significant relative differences. Given more costed houses, regional variations in building cost, for example, might be detectable. The wider application of the graph in its present form will depend on the studied houses being representative of a wider population, but the fit of the data is good. The *total* predicted cost of the houses included in Table 16 is within 2 per cent of the actual cost.

The evidence about the costs of country house building is unlikely ever to produce precise totals and indices. But approximation is a feature not unknown to economic historians in pursuit of statistical quantification in the two centuries after the Restoration. Measurement of houses from plans and large-scale maps is possible; estimates by the square and cubic foot for living and office accommodation across the 1740–1880 period can be broadly calculated, although different finishes make fine calculations impossible; insurance valuations provide a further comparative data set. For a given population of houses at county level it is possible to provide broad estimates about periods of construction and costs. It is clear that houses fall into three categories: a handful of great houses belonging to the top-flight peerage and the wealthiest newcomers to landed society such as Edwin Lascelles at Harewood in the 1740s to 1780s period or John Walter at Bearwood in the 1860s. Below came a second division of houses, usually designed by architects of national fame, belonging to the wealthier greater gentry. The great majority of country houses, however, were smaller affairs, costing probably little more than £3000 to £6000 when new-built in the eighteenth century or £7000 to £10,000 in the mid Victorian period. Of course, many houses were even more reasonably remodelled across the centuries.

The sums spent in total on major country house building projects, as well as on furnishings and landscaping, are nevertheless impressive when compared with fixed capital investment in the two principal textile industries and in canal construction during the first phase of industrialisation. The last thirty years of the eighteenth century saw a dramatic increase in the fixed capital investment in the cotton-spinning industry with the building of hundreds of Arkwright-type mills valued at between £3000 and £5000 each for insurance purposes. Contemporary estimates of the total fixed capital invested in spinning mills range from Colquhoun's £1,300,000 in 1787 to Watts's £2,500,000 in 1797.[97] Similarly, it is reckoned that £2,149,000 was subscribed to complete the 'first generation' of canal construction between 1755 and 1780, and a much greater £15,052,000 between 1780 and 1815.[98]

For comparative purposes we have estimated the investment in country house building from 1770 to 1800 in Cheshire, Gloucestershire, Norfolk, Northamptonshire and Suffolk. There were thirty new houses built during these years in the five counties and significant alterations made to another thirty. No extravagant palaces were erected, nor had the infiltration of industrial money into the countryside yet upset established conventions relating building expenditure to rank and estate size. A significant alteration has been judged to be the rebuilding of a front, the addition of a wing, or the provision of a new range of domestic offices, but not routine maintenance, redecoration, or the rearrangement of an interior without major structural changes.

The estimate of cost of the building events has been arranged by estate size, and the figures for new houses and alterations derived from Figure 5 are shown in Table 17.

Table 17. *Estimated average cost of country houses by estate size, 1770–1800*

Estate size (acres)	Size of house (cubic feet)	Cost of new house	Cost of alteration
Greater than 10,000	600,000	£22,000	£5,500
5,000 to 10,000	375,000	£12,500	£3,125
3,000 to 5,000	200,000	£7,000	£1,750

Note: The estates are ranked according to their size in the 1870s. The cost of a new house has been derived from Figure 2, at the mid band for 1776–96; alterations are assumed to cost 25 per cent of these figures.

The estimated expenditure on building and altering country houses in the thirty-year period in the five counties is then £571,000. Given that the estate owners in the sample counties represented about 15 per cent of the national total, an extrapolated figure for expenditure on country house building in England between 1770 and 1800 is in the region of £3,800,000. This figure, already large in relation to cotton-mill and early canal investment, does not represent the full impact of country-house spending. Houses were also being built on smaller estates – those of Bateman's squires holding between 1000 and 3000 acres – who outnumbered the peers and great landowners together.[99] And the estimate makes no allowance for the cost of work on parks and gardens (according to Kerr one-third of the bill of a landowner building a new house, though established owners would not start from scratch), or the cost of furniture. It is nevertheless an indication of the order of magnitude of the flow of money into building country houses. However, it must not be assumed that every thirty-year period saw spending on this scale, nor that it was evenly spread across all counties. It was not. Indeed, building was not even uniform in our five counties. Our figures suggest that around 9 per cent of the total rental income of the five counties was spent on country house building in the 1770–1800 period. Yet it is important to stress that to express expenditure as a relatively small percentage of total rentals is not confirmation that building was funded from rents alone nor that those who did not build had equivalent sums available to invest elsewhere. Availability of funds was not the only factor behind decisions to build, although it is more likely that the builders than the non-builders had money to spare. At least for the builders of new houses generally, it was not landed money with which they built. Building out of current rents was unusual and, if attempted, meant many years before the work could be completed. Hence much of the building money came from non-landed sources. If arguing that country house building was a wasteful diversion of potential industrial investment, it does not matter whether the money came from landed sources or not, although it is pertinent to note the scale of the fortunes made in trade, banking and the textile and other industries, hence the scope for generating capital for reinvestment without recourse to landed surpluses.[100]

This attempt to estimate country house building costs, founded on the study of building accounts themselves and local building chronologies, makes possible a firmer statistical basis for the key question of the personal consumption and industrial investment of the English landowning class. Moreover, country house building projects were themselves important economic processes. Opportunities for the highly flexible workforces employed in their construction were significant. The largest projects occupied hundreds, certainly scores, of men, over several years. Even in minor schemes, several day labourers plus, in turn, all the specialised craftsmen were employed. Old materials were laboriously cleaned for reuse, bricks made by the hundred thousand, timber sawed, stone dressed and carved, and goods constantly carted. Before the nineteenth century, virtually everything was made up on site, including wheelbarrows, ladders and scaffolding. Only the finest chimney-pieces, fittings and furniture were bought in London, second-quality ones being obtained locally. Prime craftsmen were hired in the metropolis and the major regional centres. Stimulation to local economies, especially when building activity in a neighbourhood was extended by emulation and general prosperity, was considerable.

A wider point may be made. It is clear that capital invested in country house construction, even when the vast and atypical which has always hogged the literature is put in context, was still significant. Before economic historians become too carried away by the aristocracy's contribution to the development of industry, agriculture and transport, proper stress should be placed on their investment in housing, furnishings and landscaping, and the way this sustained a superb craft culture that was such a feature of English employment until the late nineteenth century. While not every generation in a family of landowners produced a notable builder, collector or gardener, almost every one does seem to have bought land or at the very least managed their estates to provide increasingly ample settlements for their descendants. At the core of these strategies was the perpetuation of the country house, the great symbol of a landed dynasty's standing and power.

8

Building and Finance

'A vast house with four wings, of which two not yet built, and magnificently finished and furnished; all designed by Adam in the best taste but too expensive for his estate [Lord Scarsdale's].'

Horace Walpole on Kedleston in 1768.[1]

'There seemed on the whole more cost than judgement.'

Samuel Johnson on Kedleston in 1774.[2]

The Honourable John Byng's view of the world of the English country house in the 1780s and 1790s was from the inside. As a man of deeply conservative opinions, his judgements on it were invariably severe. Partly his way of thinking reflected his own family's experiences. The Byngs in the course of the eighteenth century had built large houses and consequently left themselves with impoverished estates. Such was their indebtedness that his elder brother, Viscount Torrington, had been forced to sell Southill to the Whitbreads in 1795. He himself was a disgruntled Commissioner of Stamps. Everywhere on his tours he tended to note houses shut up, timber felled, owners prodigally spending their landed incomes in London. 'What a folly it is', he scribbled on one tour, 'for people to overbuild themselves.' The ease with which property could be mortgaged had allowed owners to erect, he noted in a memorable phrase, 'mausoleums of vanity'.[3] Often houses were too big for their estates. Debt was the inevitable consequence. Did Byng exaggerate?

The findings of economic historians, trawling estate papers in the twentieth century, suggest that he did. Debt they argue was a near-universal feature in the finances of landowners. Stoked by personal extravagance, sometimes by immoderate building ventures and big land purchases, but above all by the increasingly generous provision for their families within the framework of settled land arrangements, aristocratic and gentry debt mounted across the period as incomes to service it grew. It was fuelled by low interest rates and by the supply of funds landowners could tap with increasing ease: mortgages; personal loans; and eventually the provision of banks, usually London ones specialising in the needs of landed clients; and increasingly in the nineteenth century, cash-rich insurance companies. Yet debt seldom reached breaking point, even for the most profligate landowners; major sales of land, at least before agricultural depression began to bite in the 1880s, were uncommon; bankruptcy was a very rare event indeed.[4]

Since the finances of many thousands of landowners, from duke to parish squire, were each different and all highly complex in their particulars, it is difficult to present a balanced appraisal. Some landowners were excellent managers, watchful of their obligations, eager to improve their family's long-term financial position; others were fearfully extravagant, spending way beyond their incomes, submerging their estates in debt. The literature has focused upon atypical aristocrats in the nineteenth century: the finances of the Dukes of Devonshire, Sutherland and Bedford, the Marquess of Ailesbury and Earl Fitzwilliam; and notably the spectacular bankruptcy of the second Duke of Buckingham in the 1840s.[5] In this discussion of debt, the unravelling of the effects of the strict settlement of land and the investment strategies of the aristocracy, the precise contribution of building costs has become somewhat underplayed. At first sight this is surprising. The physical impact of a great house is enduring testimony of ostentatious consumption, the provision of annuities and portions made each generation for the children of its owners is not. Yet building costs in comparison with these arrangements for generous family security seem to have placed less strain upon the finances of landowners. This is for two reasons. First, by no means all owners built extravagantly. Against this, conspicuous consumption was endemic, the provision of charges for the support of widows and children universal features of landed budgets. Secondly, it is argued that usually building was achieved out of annual revenue: 'It is a common impression that while great estates were purchased out of capital, great houses were paid for out of current income.'[6] This apparently was a well-established principle. In the sixteenth and seventeenth centuries, 'many builders seem to have been largely successful in financing the bulk of their works out of current income'. This meant that the progress of building country houses in this period was inevitably slow. Moreover, special conditions applied to the prodigy houses of prominent courtiers bent on making the biggest splash. As a consequence, 'the estates of a few noble families were plunged into debt as a result of building, but for the builders of the smaller country houses the consequences were rarely disastrous'.[7]

Are these conclusions more tenable than Byng's first-hand impression of the deleterious effect of building costs upon landed incomes? The basis for building larger and larger houses across the centuries was never as precise as a straight relationship with rental incomes. The means to build were always more diverse, major building activity being usually spurred by big non-recurrent items of funding. To unravel further the sources of finance expended upon the English country house in our period, and to examine spending both upon the houses themselves and upon the indebtedness of their owners, it is imperative to match sets of building accounts with parallel ones disclosing total income and expenditure. Good fits of both are rare. Here we categorise within our sample of accounts four basically different patterns of income generation and look at them in tandem with major building projects. First, we comment on those of five builders, who either built on the grandest scale (Burley-on-the-Hill, Dyrham, Castle Howard and Holkham) or remodelled a great old house (Audley End) in the late seventeenth and eighteenth centuries. All relied in varying degrees upon the fruits of office and patronage unavailable to the large majority of builders. Secondly, Sledmere, Henham and Haveringland provide examples of three middling-sized country houses, two of the 1780s and 1790s and one of the 1840s, built by second-rank landowners reliant upon neither office nor place. Thirdly, the increasing number of houses built by newcomers to landed society are represented by Harewood, Dodington, Brodsworth, Orchardleigh and Denton. Lastly, we look at the builders of three houses built upon smaller estates, Hovingham, Heacham, and Strelley, to examine the impact of their construction upon their builders' finances. Together, they are representative of the income patterns and building projects of the large majority of country houses built in England between the Restoration and the late nineteenth-century depression in agriculture.

Great houses had always been built from the fruits of political office, but the triumph of the Whig aristocracy at the Glorious Revolution, and the opportunities created by the wars against France, brought fortunes to politicians, military leaders and financiers alike. Consolidated through marriage and the purchase of many aristocratic estates, this instigated a surge in country house building between the 1690s and the 1730s. Burley-on-the-Hill, Dyrham and Castle Howard are amongst the boldest statements of political and social ambitions by their thrusting owners. How were such grand edifices paid for? What burden did they place upon the finances of their builders?

Daniel Finch (1647–1729), second Earl of Nottingham, was not in terms of wealth a front rank member of the peerage.[8] Descended from a cadet branch of long-established Kentish landowners, his family's prospects had been transformed in the seventeenth century. His grandfather had been Speaker of the House of Commons; his father, the first Earl, Lord Chancellor. Their landed estates, however, were modest, perhaps realising no more than £3000 a year in the 1670s. The first Earl had concentrated more upon establishing his sons in the world than either building or buying much land. To this end he had contracted an excellent marriage for his eldest son with a co-heiress of the Earl of Warwick. Succeeding in 1682, the second Earl married for a second time three years later. Again it was an advantageous arrangement, his wife bringing him a £10,000 dowry. But his Buckinghamshire estate possessed no country house, his family spending much of their time at their home in Kensington (later vastly extended as Kensington Palace). Eager to enjoy the lifestyle of a great landed magnate, and becoming Secretary of State in 1689, he began to look round for a major estate in the Midlands. Eventually in 1694, after five years of protracted negotiation, he bought Burley-on-the-Hill for around £50,000 from the trustees of the late Duke of Buckingham. Oddly, given Lord Nottingham's requirements, it possessed no sizeable house, an earlier one having been burned down during the Civil War. Immediately he set about building, by measured work and probably largely to his own designs. He anticipated that the house would cost him about £15,000. In the event, in 1710, its final cost, a decade after he had moved in, was just over twice that amount (Plate 113).

It is clear that neither the estate was paid for out of capital nor was the house built out of regular income – together a massive £80,000. Inheriting nothing from his father beyond land and chattels, Burley appears to have been bought with his second wife's dowry (£10,000), the net £25,000 to £27,000 he earned as Secretary of State between 1689 and 1693 (exactly the years he was negotiating to buy the estate) and £19,000 from the sale of the Kensington house to William III. On the other hand, his accounts show that even with the benefit of the Burley rentals his landed income in the late 1690s did not exceed a net £7000 a year. His family's living expenses were in the region of £5500. A surplus of £1500 per annum was insufficient to build even a £15,000 house, for its final cost (including stables and landscaping) averaged some £1803 over the seventeen years the building accounts run (1694–1710), no less than £14,074 (46 per cent of the total) being expended in the four years before the family moved in. Since wages, the principal element in

PLATE 113. Burley-on-the-Hill, Rutland (Lord Nottingham and John Lumley, 1694–1710).

a house's cost, had to be settled regularly, there was no escape by deferring payment. In these years Lord Nottingham was therefore forced to borrow, sums repaid by the £18,000 sale of outlying Essex property from his first wife's dowry. Further relief came with a second period as Secretary of State (1702–4), providing him with around £12,000. Once finishing the house and landscaping could be undertaken at a more leisurely pace than during the key period of construction between 1696 and 1700, his rental surplus covered the average payments of £1257 made each year between 1702 and 1710 except when, after a fire, the great stables of the Duke of Buckingham were rebuilt and extended in 1705.

Lord Nottingham was capable and prudent in money matters. He was also ambitious for his thirteen surviving children who, untypically, escaped the demographic crisis which even-handedly pruned even peerage family trees in the century after 1660. The Grand Tour of his son cost over £3000; portions totalling £52,000, a larger sum than spent either upon buying Burley or building the house, were provided for his eight daughters. Lord Nottingham was also fortunate both that his marriage settlements gave him a very large degree of control over his estates, and that in the year of his death he inherited the titles and property of the senior branch of his family, the Earls of Winchilsea. He did need to borrow for family settlements, but the debts of about £22,000 on his death in 1729 were modest by peerage standards. Yet, however great his competence in financial matters, or his cleverness at juggling resources to launch his children, the estate and house were bought and built out of the proceeds of sales (at least £49,000) and public office (a net £40,000-45,000). Surplus recurrent income played a minor role except in the final years of finishing the house. There is also evidence that his original visions for both the house and gardens were curtailed by the serious inroads his large family made into his income after the late 1700s.

William Blathwayt (1649[?]–1717) was an exact contemporary of the second Earl of Nottingham (Plate 114).[9] He was, however, an administrator not an aristocrat,

PLATE 114.
William
Blathwayt, by
Michael Dahl.

firmly belonging to Pepys's London world of government business, money making and good living. John Evelyn wrote of him, he 'raised himself by his industry from very moderate circumstances'. In fact he was brought up by his uncle, Thomas Povey, who held several government posts in the 1660s and whose luxurious house in Lincoln Inn Fields the aspiring Pepys drooled over. Unlike his uncle, Blathwayt was competent, industrious and dull (his enemies would have added avaricious). He shared, however, the same desire for possessions. Already making a good career for himself, he married a thirty-six-year-old Gloucestershire heiress in 1686. It was a marriage of convenience brokered by Sir Robert Southwell of neighbouring King's Weston, Blathwayt's one-time superior and mentor at the Plantations Office. Although the estate produced little more than £1000 net, it was sufficient to launch Blathwayt into the world of the Gloucestershire gentry at little cost.[10] The Tudor house was in poor condition and, even before the marriage settlement was signed, Blathwayt had plans to completely rebuild it and lay out £2000 on linen and plate. Since his career went from strength to strength, he could well afford to do so.

At first his offices were modest, Secretary to the Lords of Trade (1679–96) and Auditor General of Plantations (1680–1717), but in 1683 he became Secretary at War (1683–1704), then Clerk of the Privy Council (1686–1714). Surviving the Revolution of 1688 to catch William III's steely eye, he acted as Secretary of State (1692–1701), accompanying the King on his annual expeditions to the Low Countries. As early as the year of his marriage, Evelyn reckoned he was earning £2000 a year from office; at the height of his career (1692–1701), his income was well in excess of twice this sum.[11]

Few other houses reflect more faithfully the economic circumstances and character of their builders than Dyrham. Building started in the spring of 1692. In the five years after his marriage both his parents-in-law and his wife, who bore him four children, had died. Blathwayt was now in complete control. At first his schemes were relatively simple. His architect, Samuel Hauderoy, unknown and cheap, was mercilessly exploited. Blathwayt, used to ruling his government clerks with a rod of iron and himself immersed in business and figures, fondly imagined he could deal with those working at Dyrham in the same manner, demanding constant reports and total attention to work at the lowest rates. Impressive results were achieved in just over two years. A low, fifteen-bay building added to the partly remodelled old house with two long wings forming a *cour d'honneur* and linking it to the parish church were built. Then, after a four-year gap, a more extravagant campaign was commenced. Clearly, Blathwayt felt secure in the favour of the King. As a senior royal servant, he could secure the services of an architect in the Office of Works. Appropriately, his choice, William Talman, Comptroller of the Board of Works, was the leading country house architect of the Court of William III.[12] A big new stable-cum-service block in which Talman had at least a consulting role was erected first. Then the remnants of the old house were cleared away and a great east garden front, containing a set of state rooms, was built back to back, as was Hauderoy's west front, with that part of the old house retained to form a great hall and dining-room in the 1692–94 scheme. At the same time, in the hills facing Talman's east front, Blathwayt was creating one of the finest water gardens in England.

Blathwayt's career went into sharp decline following William III's death; by 1704 he had lost his two principal posts. Therefore Talman's state rooms on the east front were completed in the simplest fashion. The great cedar staircase, unlike that at Burley with wall paintings by Gerard Lancroon, was finished economically, its walls roughly marbled in sienna paint. The house, large but sparing in its finish, nevertheless cost as much as £10,000, a sum similar to that the Wentworths feared the great east front of Wentworth Castle would cost in 1709.[13] Many a builder would have completed their original scheme by borrowing. But Blathwayt was a cautious man, with seemingly no desire for his two sons to endure the same treadmill he had worked for almost forty years. The last decade of his life his biographer represents as one entirely free from financial worry.[14] He enjoyed a personal estate of some £20,000 invested in the public funds. Few great builders died less in debt. Yet the scale of his building and landscaping schemes in the late 1690s reflects the profits of office and the fees he could extract from running them, not the rent-roll of a moderately-sized Gloucestershire estate.[15] He burdened this with a very big house, so that for well over two centuries it remained largely preserved as William Blathwayt had left it in 1717.

As peers went, the third Earl of Carlisle (1669–1738) was not inordinately rich. The rent rolls of his large estates in Cumberland, Northumberland and north Yorkshire were, in comparison with those of similar acreages in more forward agricultural areas, confined. But in the 1690s, as a rising Whig grandee, he entertained the highest political ambitions and there seemed a good chance of their realisation in the late 1690s, the years when Castle Howard was planned on the grandest scale.[16] Reaching the top rung of the political ladder, Lord Carlisle briefly served as First Lord of the Treasury between December 1701 and March 1702. Then, like William Blathwayt, his career was blighted by the death of William III. Except for a second brief period as First Lord in the summer of 1715, it never recovered. Disillusioned by political in-fighting, he sought the increasingly welcome distraction of building to realise breathtaking schemes for his house and its innovative garden, and for the grandest mausoleum in England. How, if the rewards of office envisaged when it was planned in 1698–1700 never materialised, was this vast forty-year long programme paid for?

Again, like Lord Nottingham and Blathwayt, Lord Carlisle was an immensely capable man of business. Sir John Vanbrugh believed 'during the whole course of building, [he] managed all that part himself with the greatest care'. With his architects, Vanbrugh and Nicholas Hawksmoor, usually a couple of hundred miles away in London, such involvement was essential. As members of the peerage went he was competent in keeping his accounts, every six months totting up his income and expenditure so that building could more or less proceed to plan.

The profits of office appear to have been unimportant, providing an implausibly small 4 per cent of an income averaging some £7677 in the 1700s. This must have come as a blow, since the house had been planned on the trajectory of a promising political career. But Lord Carlisle was ferociously proud. The previous house had suffered a serious fire in 1693. There was no going back, for building had begun a few months before his political career reached its brief apogee (frontispiece).

The surprising feature of Castle Howard is how its superb theatricality and scale were achieved from Lord Carlisle's relatively limited finances. The house was built to a sectionalised plan, one ideal for building in stages. Expenditure upon its construction between 1700 and 1714 was remarkably level, running at some £3000 a year. Since this consumed around a third of the earl's income, it nevertheless caused major strains upon his finances. By the first half of 1705 these were becoming seriously adrift, disclosing an income of £1866 3s. 11d. against an expenditure of £3206 5s. 6d. When building was at its peak (1704–9) he had therefore to resort to a variety of stratagems. Economy was not amongst them, though at one point he seriously considered letting his fine town house in Soho Square. His accounts disclose that rentals provided no more than 60 per cent of his income in the 1700s. It was made up from a range of other sources. Since the returns of office (he remained a Gentleman of the Bedchamber) were so disappointing, he had resort to sales (6 per cent) of horses and jewellery as well as very modest amounts of land, to realising savings (16 per cent) and, when in

London, to the gaming table (7 per cent). In 1707 Vanbrugh reported that he had 'won Two thousand pounds of the Sharpers, and is gone downe again to lay it Out in his Building'.[17] His luck seems generally to have held, for he won more by gambling than he derived from office. More positively, he appears to have exacted an increased estate income through more efficient administration by the late 1700s. The house reflects these somewhat hand to mouth features of Lord Carlisle's affairs:

> In the light of knowledge of Lord Carlisle's financial circumstances, the extent to which the main pile of Castle Howard is a surface skin, in which all the sculptured effect is concentrated only on these parts which are immediately visible, and the way that the ground plan is arranged to create an immediate dramatic impression upon the arriving spectator, begin to be seen in terms of a taste for extravagance and display financed by an income which could not easily afford it.[18]

It seems that his third daughter remained unmarried because he could not provide a dowry commensurate to her rank. Moreover, the house was never completed to Vanbrugh's designs (Plate 115). Two-thirds finished in 1714, the west wing had to wait almost a century before Charles Tatham made Sir Thomas Robinson's big Palladian shell of the 1750s finally habitable.

Presumably, completing the house in the late 1710s would have seriously constrained Lord Carlisle's plans to create perhaps the most remarkable landscape in England, 'a garden of fantasy and wealth and ostentation': the setting out of Ray Wood, the great obelisk from which miles of avenues radiated, seven miles of stout park wall, the castellated Carrmire gate, a pyramid, a parterre and terrace alive with obelisks, urns and statues, two temples and, the crowning glory, Hawksmoor's mausoleum, itself costing more than the vast majority of country houses. In all some £38,000 was spent on these works (Plate 20). There seems to have been no overall plan, paradise emerged as Lord Carlisle's and Vanbrugh's ideas developed and 'as and when workmen or funds permitted'.[19] In other words, Lord Carlisle found he could spend an average of around £1000 a year on his garden and park across the forty years of its creation, less before 1714, more afterwards. In the end, he ran out of time rather than money. The mausoleum was completed by his son; his remains had to wait seven years before they could be reinterred there. It was a fitting resting place for the master of the art of pushing ostentation to the limits of a finite purse.

We have seen how heavily the imprint of the Grand Tour was stamped upon

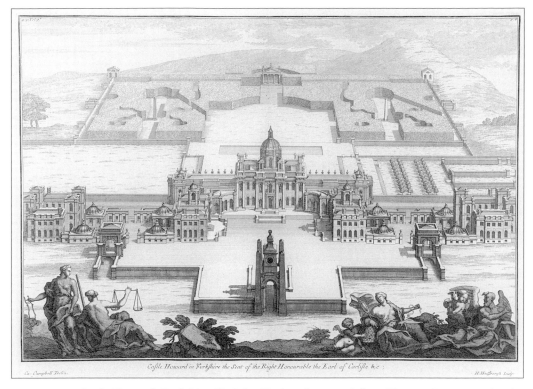

PLATE 115. Castle Howard, Yorkshire (Sir John Vanbrugh, 1701–12) from *Vitruvius Britannicus* (1725).

Holkham.[20] Contemporaries were invariably impressed with the grandeur of its scholarly Palladianism; they also frequently wondered when the house would ever be completed. Was Lord Leicester's leisurely progress (he died in 1759 after forty years of planning and building, with the house unfinished) due to his perfectionism, or did progress reflect his economic and family circumstances?

Holkham is habitually quoted as *the* great house built slowly out of estate income. The truth is more complex. Certainly, Lord Leicester became the possessor of fine estates, worth almost £10,000 a year, on his coming of age in 1718. The Norfolk ones especially were capable of early improvement. Investment in them was never stinted; portions of land adjacent to them were regularly purchased. During Lord Leicester's possession of them between 1713 and 1759 they showed an increase in rent of 44 per cent. He was also fortunate in that he had to make, unlike most landowners, so little provision for his family with but two sisters and an only son. His estates were never all settled. On the death of his son, a complete waster, in 1753, he had total control of their disposition.

From these facts it might be assumed that Lord Leicester's financial position was buoyant. Far from it. Within two years of his coming of age he was £15,000 overspent. The following year he lost at least £37,928 in the South Sea speculation. In 1722–23 he was making interest payments of £2565 out of an income of £10,501. Fortunately, recovery was faster than those who prophesied doom anticipated. The death of his grandmother in 1722 added further landed income of £1200 a year; in the late 1720s he acquired through his marriage settlement a right granted by Charles II to collect the dues on shipping passing Dungeness lighthouse. The privilege netted him around £1500 a year. In addition, he secured for his lifetime the office of Postmaster-General, worth some £1000 annually. Even though he faced the 1730s with a lighter heart than the 1720s, 'the building of the great house at Holkham was certainly not undertaken as a consequence of overwhelming prosperity'.[21] Indeed, its commencement in 1734 had been seriously delayed by the perilous losses from South Sea speculation. But once building began large sums were poured into the venture: an average of £2700 a year between 1732 and 1765; £20,000 in the years 1732–41; £23,000 in 1742–51; and £42,000 in 1752–61. This accelerating rate of expenditure was an unusual feature in country house building. It was probably explained by Lord Leicester's realisation that time was running out (he left provisions in his will for £2000 a year to be spent by his widow on the house's completion) and heavy expenditure upon the sumptuous Marble Hall. Like Castle Howard, the house was built, if even more slowly, in stages. The construction of family and 'stranger' wings allowed him to move out of the old manor house onto what was in effect a permanent building site for the rest of his life (Plates 31–33).

With big debt charges never cleared, sales of land were inevitable. Between 1749 and 1756 those from outlying estates realised £60,000, although land costing at least £22,830 was bought to add to the core of Norfolk property. Lord Leicester died as he had lived, in debt. His executors uncovered borrowings of £90,974: £60,357 on mortgage; £30,617 on bond. With no direct heirs, he was untroubled. His dream of creating paradise on a vast Palladian scale after four decades of effort was near realisation. It is possible to argue that it was achieved from the dues of a Kent lighthouse and the profits of the Postmaster Generalship.

The restoration of Audley End by Sir John Griffin Griffin (1719–1797) between 1762 and 1797 was outstanding (Plate 116).[22] The house, once perhaps the grandest in England, was in a sorry state when he succeeded to it in 1762. Briefly an unloved royal residence between 1666 and 1701, it had been burdensome to its

PLATE 116. Sir
John Griffin
Griffin Bt by
Benjamin West.

owners, the Earls of Suffolk, since the day it was completed in 1614 at a reputed mammoth cost of £200,000. Substantial demolition had taken place in the early eighteenth century; restoration of the rest had been piecemeal. Not only was the house in poor condition on the death of the tenth Earl of Suffolk in 1745, but the surrounding estate of around 6500 acres was split, after considerable legal wrangle, between three descendants of the third Earl, Sir John's mother, his aunt and the Earl of Bristol. The aunt, the Countess of Portsmouth, 'as proud as Lucifer; no German princess could exceed her', was determined to save the home of her ancestors. She bought the house in 1751 to prevent it from being razed to the ground, and left it to her nephew on her death in 1762. His inheritance was a daunting one. The house, in spite of further demolition and rationalisation by the countess, was still very large and in need of further repair. Equally disconcerting was the fact that the estate was now a mere 3257 acres, realising little more than £2000 a year. Sir John's vision and determination in the next thirty-five years equalled those of the Earls of Carlisle and Leicester, his management skills superior.

It is possible to reconstruct the restoration of both the house and estate in these years because of the unusual amount of accounting material which has survived. Again the crucial point to emerge is that appreciable spending upon house, household and land was supported by a multi-sourced income.[23] Sir John's expenditure after 1762 is set out in Table 18 below.

Table 18. *The expenditure of Sir John Griffin Griffin Bt, 1762–97 (to nearest £)*

		Total
Audley End	72,780 + 13,424 (furniture)	
London House [a]	8157 + 2255 (furniture)	96,616
Household expenditure	105,677	105,677
Estate	96,100 (land purchases 54,384)	
Home Farm	21,627	117,727
Miscellaneous [b]		38,966
		£358,986

Notes:

[a] Inherited from Lady Portsmouth in New Burlington Street.

[b] Largely 'personal expences, some election expences and the payment of annuities'. Ibid., p. 117. Williams's figures for Sir John's spending are difficult to reconcile precisely because a large sum 'remains unaccounted for in terms of provision spending'.

Source: Williams, 'Finances of an Eighteenth-Century Nobleman', pp. 116–18.

It is clear that expenditure on this scale could not be achieved from such a modest landed base. Inheritance by Sir John during his long life was unexceptional (no more than £20,000); his two marriages netted £18,000. Expenditure upon the estate and home farm was covered by the income from them and this seems to have included the £54,384 he spent upon additional land purchases. To create a bigger park, land had to be bought from Lord Bristol, and there were scores of

PLATE 117.   Audley End, Essex, by William Tomkins (1788–89).

transactions to round out his estate in this part of north Essex, at this date largely unenclosed. In addition, ancestral properties were purchased in Northamptonshire as well as sizeable tracts in Norfolk and Suffolk. Alterations to the house and park were extensive. Robert Adam created a suite of eight rooms. Although squeezed into the low ground floor, they were nevertheless in the van of neo-classical taste (Plate 118). The saloon was refitted with a series of ancestral portraits and a picture gallery created. A thirty-year programme, originally planned with the aid of Capability Brown, was undertaken to create a more extensive state-of-the-art park, with shelter belts, ha-has, a diverted river, temples, menagerie, Elysian and kitchen gardens (Plate 117). The close-on £10,000 a year average income to sustain Sir John's expenditure between 1762 and 1797 was made up essentially from two non-landed sources: his sixty-year military career (he ended

PLATE 118.   Audley End, Essex. The decoration of Robert Adam's little drawing room.

up as a field-marshal); and, above all, the income from five east coast lighthouses inherited from his aunt and continued by royal grant, provided him with over £3000 a year.[24] Like the building of Holkham, a considerable part of Audley End's restoration was the consequence of a rapidly growing coastal trade. Industrial expansion and the realisation of landowners' dreams were sometimes linked in unexpected fashion.

There were, as always, more personal features in explaining Sir John's successful management (he died solvent) of the resuscitation of Audley End and its estate. As an attorney's son, he balanced business acumen with the fierce pride of his maternal ancestors. The abeyance of the Howard de Walden barony was terminated in his favour in 1784.[25] Four years later he was created first Lord Braybrooke. House and park reflected his advance. But there was nothing rash in Sir John's make-up. Throughout he remained a careful accountant. True, he had no children to provide for, nor annuities to pay after 1772. In a sense this makes his vision and persistence the more extraordinary.

The creations of the four great late seventeenth- and early eighteenth-century houses and the extensive restoration of Audley End were not achieved from landed income. Inherited land alone was insufficient to realise their builders' ambitions. Even the less extravagant remodelling of Raynham Hall in Norfolk between 1724 and 1731 by William Kent and Thomas Ripley, costing around £15,000, was only undertaken so long as its owner, Viscount Townshend, held public office.[26] The profits of office, patronage and inheritance, or at least good prospects of them, were essential foundations upon which to realise integrated strategies for building, landscaping, purchasing more land and providing family settlements. How did the greater gentry, usually without the likelihood of great office, match their building schemes with more modest incomes?

We can be precise about the building histories and costs of Sledmere, Henham and Haveringland. All three houses were the confident schemes of prosperous members of the greater gentry. Did their construction pose problems for the finances of their builders?

Sledmere was a wholesale remodelling of a seven-bay, solid and rather old-fashioned house built by the Sykeses in the early 1750s.[27] Merchants in Leeds and later Hull, they had acquired the Sledmere estate through marriage in 1748. The builder's nephew Sir Christopher Sykes (1740–1801) became life tenant of the estate in 1770. On the death of his father, the first Baronet and vicar of Roos, in 1783 he began to extend the 1750s house. John Carr and Lewis Wyatt produced schemes to transform it, but it was Sir Christopher's own plans to convert it into an H-shaped affair by the addition of substantial cross wings which were finally drawn out by Wyatt. Although therefore Sledmere bears a loose Wyatt imprint, Sir Christopher acted as his own architect and clerk of the works (Plate 119). Joseph Rose, the celebrated plasterer, was later closely involved not only on site but also acting as Sykes's agent in London for many of the house's fittings. Built between 1787 and 1792, the additions, including the great library (Plate 120) which Rose thought 'will be one of the finest rooms in the Kingdom', cost £20,547 12s. 3½d.[28] Precision indeed.

Sir Christopher Sykes was an unusual landowner. The blood of business ran deep in his veins. Although a notable builder and book collector, his foremost interests were those of a passionate agricultural improver. His brief obituary in the *Gentleman's Magazine* captures something of his acumen. 'His early rising and great activity, both of body and mind, prompted the conduct of every plan of amending the state of the country, whether by drainage or inclosure, building or navigation.'[29] He planted a thousand acres of trees; he enclosed 18,000 acres of Yorkshire wold setting out numerous new farmsteads; he sought at one stage advice from Richard Arkwright about the construction of a cotton and carpet

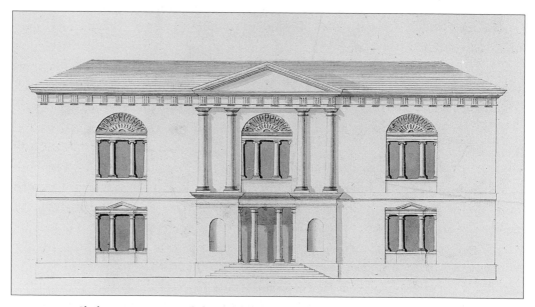

PLATE 119. Sledmere House, Yorkshire (1787–92). Sir Christopher Sykes's drawing of the south front.

PLATE 120.   Sledmere House, Yorkshire. The library by Thomas Malton, *c*. 1795.

manufactory. On the rising tide of agricultural prosperity, he founded the East Riding Bank in 1790 with branches in Beverley, Malton and Hull. His partner, Richard Broadley, was a Hull merchant, shipowner and dealer in land. And Joseph Denison, a famed London financier with whom the bank kept its London account, was also a major purchaser of East Riding land after 1790. The trio were a close and formidable force in East Riding land transactions, each benefiting enormously from the process of enclosure and improvement of the wolds.[30]

Although Sir Christopher's meticulous account book (which runs from 1770 to 1800) contains few references to his banking activities, it provides a detail of building expenditure in relation to estate income and spending unmatched by other landowners' accounts. Entries for the years 1787–1800, covering major extensions to the house, are summarised in Table 19 below.

Building expenditure was grouped with household expenditure. Sir Christopher then struck a balance against rental and investment income before other forms of income and expenditure were considered. He then calculated his net financial

PLATE 121. Sir
Christopher and
Lady Sykes, by
George Romney.

per cent in the peak year, 1789. Considerable additional sums, more than twice
that spent on the house, were expended on estate improvement. Consequently,
there were deficits in seven of the eight years from 1787–95, although over the
whole period even estate improvements were covered by rental income. He was
also active in buying and selling estates, making a net new investment of £46,000
between 1787 and 1800. Borrowings increased substantially, although his loans

were easily serviced from income, including indebtedness to Lady Sykes and their younger children (which did not carry interest). His capital position deteriorated by over £44,000 in the period, close to the net new investment in land.[32]

Sir Christopher was exceptional both in his income and in his single-minded vision. Yet when he represented Beverley in Parliament for half a dozen years he communicated none of his genius for agricultural improvement to his fellow Members, for he appears never to have spoken in the House.[33] Seeing the great financial benefits of enclosing hitherto marginal land, he created one of the greatest estates in the east of England. At its heart was his rebuilt house with its superb library. It was the fitting centrepiece of his creation, comfortably achieved within income.

The unusual feature of the building at Henham is how long Sir John Rous was before he began rebuilding the family seat. Here, as elsewhere, building, however pressing the need, had to wait until the owner's economic circumstances were right. The Rouses, unlike the Sykeses, were of old gentry stock, possessing their Suffolk estate since the 1550s and becoming baronets a century later. Sir John Rous (1750–1827), sixth Baronet, succeeded in 1771, the year he came of age. Two years later, through the carelessness of an inebriated butler, the big brick quadrangular house built by Charles Brandon, Duke of Suffolk, was burned down. Sir John retreated to a secondary house half a dozen miles away and acquired a set of grand, but 'very old-fashioned designs' to rebuild Henham from the architect, *cicerone* and dealer, James Byres.[34] He did not proceed with them, finance seeming to have been the principal bar. The uninsured loss on the old house was a reputed £30,000, and correspondence between Sir John and Eleazar Davy in the 1780s constantly bemoans his lack of income (disclosed as £3600 per annum in 1787). In the following year, when he wanted to buy a neighbouring farm, he wrote to Davy: 'by so doing I must lessen an income already too small to live upon, [by] full fourscore pounds a year. As to the day of my growing rich, I do not expect it this century.' He could only think of it 'as an exchange, by selling some other farm in Suffolk to pay for it'. He made calculations about the superior return – almost a third – on government stock in comparison with land, leading him to the conclusion that it was always sensible to sell 'whatever outlying farms you had, whenever you can get over twenty-five years purchase'.[35] Representing Suffolk in the Tory interest between 1780 and 1796 he complained of the cost, envying the wealth of his opponent in the election of 1790, Sir Gerard Vanneck of Heveningham ('it was impossible to keep pace with him in expense'). He would have liked a peerage (applying in 1790 and 1794, and successfully at the 1796 dissolution) but believed in 1785, that he had 'certainly not an income to support it'.[36] His gloominess was well founded: by that year he had debts of £16,542. Building seemed a distant prospect (Plate 56).

In the next four years Sir John's finances were transformed by three events. The precise chronology is important in relation to the building of Henham. First, in 1788 he married the co-heiress of a County Limerick landowner. She lived for only a couple of years after the marriage, but by it Sir John obtained an Irish estate of 17,000 acres, although he reckoned he would have appreciably to increase its rentals (£1939 gross) since they barely covered outgoings.[37] Secondly, around the time of his wife's death (June 1790), he appears to have persuaded his mother to sell her Norfolk estate in return for a £900 annuity. The transaction realised him a capital sum of £40,000 net.[38] At last, he could contemplate building. In December 1790 Humphry Repton was surveying the park for a good site; in the spring of 1791 James Wyatt was producing plans for a house costing £12,000. Work did not commence until March 1792, significantly a month after a third event, when Sir John netted a further £21,000 on his brokered second marriage. By its completion in 1797 the house had cost £21,340 – seven times Sir John's income from his Suffolk estates in the mid 1790s (£3030 net).[39] Clearly, without the proceeds of two marriages and the sale of a distant estate, Sir John could not have considered a Wyatt house suitable to his dignity built from the rentals of his Suffolk estates. At least not in 1792. Later, with high wartime price levels and some additional purchases, these increased appreciably: in 1799 the gross Suffolk rent roll amounted to over £5500; by 1809 it was over £8000; and by 1819 was nearly £11,500.[40] At last, this was an income to sustain the Rous family's passion, horse racing (he won the St Leger in 1801), and his advancement, after persistent jogging of the Prime Minister's memory, to the earldom of Stradbroke in the coronation honours of 1821.

If Sledmere was built by Sir Christopher Sykes from a large marriage portion, speculation by his father in government stocks and the enclosure and improvement of the Wolds, and Henham was financed by the sale of outlying land and the proceeds of a couple of advantageous marriages, Haveringland was built by Edward Fellowes (1809–1887) from the coffers of a century's landed wealth. By the second quarter of the nineteenth century there were many large landowners whose families had never had a whiff of the profits of government office, but whose surplus incomes from land, now often bolstered by the rewards of industrial and urban expansion, were well able to sustain major building programmes. Edward Fellowes inherited two substantial estates on his father's death in 1837, Ramsey Abbey (Huntingdonshire) and Haveringland (Norfolk). The former had been bought out of legal and East India Company fortunes around 1730; the latter was acquired half a century later. In 1883 they totalled a formidable 20,021 acres.

Although the Felloweses had, like so many landowners, continuously bought additional land to round out their initial purchase, they had, more unusually, also accumulated considerable investments in securities. When he died in 1837, Edward's father left a massive £130,854 in government stock and Pennsylvanian bonds to be shared by his widow and three other children.[41] The unspecified residue as well as personal effects and all the real estate were left to Edward. Through this inheritance and the good marriages they made the three brothers were known in London society, with rather obvious humour, as the 'Lucky Fellowes'.[42] Certainly, Edward's endowment was so comfortable that he could immediately summon Edward Blore to Ramsey and then, between 1839 and 1842, completely rebuild his secondary house in Norfolk. In all, within nine years, some £15,000 had been spent at Ramsey: on alterations to the house and stables (£10,039) and on furniture (£4815). At Haveringland £31,973 was expended on building the house and fitting it out.[43]

Unfortunately, Edward Fellowes's cash flow cannot be reconstructed, as his household and personal accounts have not survived. But the receipts from land in the fifteen parishes which comprised his Huntingdonshire estate do exist for the years of major building activity, 1836–45. They produced, as agricultural incomes at last began to improve from the post-Napoleonic wars depression, £142,004, or on average £15,778 a year. From them £77,596 was transferred to other accounts, and if calculations (based on Bateman's 1883 return) are made for the smaller inferior Norfolk estate, his average net income from land was around £10,286.[44] As much as five years of Fellowes's net landed income was spent on his ambitious building schemes. It was a high proportion of his income, but Fellowes was a bachelor, only marrying in 1845, and possibly careful in his other expenditure. He could just about have afforded to build from his way above average landed income, but he also had a considerable capital in government stocks to raid if necessary.

In each of these three examples taken from the greater gentry, building a large house meant that even for them the 'lumpy' pattern of payments over as long as a decade required careful planning. Sir John Rous could not contemplate starting until he had two marriage settlements and an appreciable sale of land under his belt. Sir Christopher Sykes's building of Sledmere, if made possible by a superb marriage and his clerical father's speculation in government bonds, was rolled up in a massive venture of land speculation and improvement undertaken in tandem with two other bankers and land dealers. He was a quite outstanding businessman in juggling these multifarious transactions. Edward Fellowes was fortunate enough to inherit both large estates and investments. He was able to remodel his main seat, build a big new secondary one and yet, it seems, barely dent his finances. Only when these ambitious schemes were completed did he think it time to marry.

Although these three houses are good examples of the building range of the greater gentry, they date from relatively late in our period. Even though their foundations were laid from additional sources of income, they were built on the trajectory of rising rents after the 1780s. Each of their builders was a Member of Parliament, two of them were raised to the peerage, but none of them tasted the profits of office. All three were confident about the future, well aware of the benefits of agricultural improvement and industrial advance. Into this scenario for the greater gentry extensive building and landscaping fitted easily.

When the building schemes of newcomers to landed society are matched with their incomes it is evident that they fall into two categories. The majority acquired run of the mill estates and rebuilt or remodelled their houses as their means allowed. Buying land was their prime agenda; building was often left to later generations. On the other hand, in most counties by the 1870s, there were a handful of great estates which had been acquired by the super-rich who built on a scale many peers could not compete with. Since the sources of wealth of both groups were diverse – city finance and banking, the law, colonial plantations, the East India Company, a wide variety of mercantile and industrial activities – the process of newcomers acquiring land was evident across the 1660–1870 period. It went on until the great depression of 1873–96, political reform and the establishment of a sound stock market altered perceptions about land forever. The building of Harewood, Dodington, Orchardleigh and Brodsworth illustrate the compass of the super-rich.

The Lascelleses were an old Yorkshire family, although when they bought the Harewood estate in 1739 their wealth was of recent origin. Its purchaser, Henry Lascelles (1690–1753), had made a large fortune as a plantation owner, victualling contractor and Collector of Customs in Barbados between 1715 and 1730.[45] Supposedly, he and his brother pocketed half the island's sugar duties. Henry returned to England in 1733, set up as a sugar factor, and bought the Harewood estate in 1739 for £63,827 (suggesting a holding of around 6000–8000 acres). Five years later he was still sufficiently in funds to put up £90,000 for the government loan of 1744. With expenditure on this scale, no wonder Lascelles's conduct of the Barbados customs was questioned after the fall of Walpole. Shrewdly, he defended himself from a House of Commons base, having acquired the pocket borough of Northallerton for £23,000. When he died in 1753, his elder son, Edwin (Plate 122), inherited the major portion of his vast £284,000 fortune (including the Harewood estate).[46]

PLATE 122. Edwin Lascelles, Lord Harewood, by Sir Joshua Reynolds (1768).

He set about building the new house at Harewood.[47] Gossip in London in the mid 1750s was that Edwin Lascelles was seeking to build a £30,000 house – the best country house commission of the decade. Capability Brown and Sir William Chambers were involved in drawing up preliminary schemes, but in the end the man-on-the-spot, John Carr, who had already built the stables in 1755–56, was responsible for the exterior, Robert Adam for its interiors. Given Lascelles's great wealth, work proceeded quite slowly: the house took twelve years to complete (1759–71). In the peak year of activity, 1767, costs exceeded £4000. Altogether the house (not including Adam's fees or the work of Angelika Kauffmann and Biagio Rebecca) cost £37,000, plus £6839 paid very leisurely to Thomas Chippendale, some of whose men worked throughout most of the 1770s fitting the house out to perfection, and an almost identical sum to Capability Brown.

Visitors to Harewood, as at Fonthill, were not invariably impressed with the outcome. Sir Richard Colt Hoare in 1817 was dismissive; a few years earlier the Revd Richard Warner found 'nothing within interests the mind; no production of the arts, unless the labour of the gilder and upholsterer may be considered as describing that character'. However expensively the house had been finished, it certainly had made no inroads on Edwin Lascelles's finances. When he died in 1795 (he had been raised to the peerage five years earlier), 'he left a fortune of at least £50,000 per annum – £16,000 per annum in Yorkshire, and at least £25,000 a year in the West Indies, £20,000 in the 3 per cents, besides a variety of other property'.[48] His successor, a nephew, Edward Lascelles (1740–1820), provided similar information to Pitt when he applied for his childless uncle's recent title to be remaindered in his favour, 'being of a very ancient family in this county ... an old Member of Parliament [Northallerton had been a good investment], and heir in entail to Lord Harewood's landed estate etc, which is one of the largest in England, as likewise heir presumptive to almost the largest monied property'.[49] In the space of sixty years Henry and Edwin Lascelles had put together a large estate, built the most influential Yorkshire house of the second half of the eighteenth century, and – there could be no greater testimony of their standing – represented the county in Parliament. By the 1790s they had come to rival the interests of the Rockingham-Fitzwilliams, *the* Yorkshire political dynasty for most of the eighteenth century. These were feats which could not possibly have been achieved from the Harewood rent-roll alone.

Other great houses, which like Harewood were pre-eminent in their regions, were built from non-landed sources of wealth. Samuel Whitbread, London's leading brewer, transformed Southill (Bedfordshire) into the epitome of Regency light and good living. Christopher Codrington built the showiest house of its period in the west country at Dodington (Gloucestershire) in the 1800s.[50] His endeavours are instructive for two reasons. First, it underlines the fact that the distinction between old and new wealth is not always easy to make in this period. The Lascelleses considered themselves 'of very ancient family'; the Whitbreads had deep Bedfordshire roots. Certainly, Edwin Lascelles and Samuel Whitbread, father and son, were recognised everywhere as men of capability, standing and worth. Similarly, the Codringtons had held Dodington since the sixteenth century, but the estate had changed hands by purchase within the family around 1700. The new branch derived their wealth from the owner-ship of sugar plantations in Antigua and Barbuda. Secondly, however rich men like Edwin Lascelles and Christopher Codrington were, they seem to have linked building expenditure in some loose way to the rentals of their landed estates. The building accounts at Dodington allow us to explore these two points further.

The inheritance at Dodington in the 1790s was a troubled one.[51] Sir William Codrington (1719–1792), owner of the estate since 1738 and an MP for almost as long, disinherited his son and heir in favour of his great-nephew, Christopher (1764–1843). Both men enjoyed an interest in landscape gardening which the dramatic position of the house, at the intersection of two combes on the Cotswolds escarpment, encouraged. In 1792 Christopher Codrington inherited a middling-sized estate of 4240 acres, a fortune of £108,500 and the valuable West Indian plantations.[52] Immediately, he summoned William Eames and John Webb to rework Capability Brown's landscaping of thirty years previously. Then in 1796 he engaged James Wyatt to replace the 1550s house. It was to be Wyatt's most

PLATE 123.   Dodington Park, Gloucestershire (James Wyatt, 1796–1812).

notable neoclassical country house, although the plans were conceived at the same time as he was working out Gothic schemes considered by the 1790s to harmonise more naturally in such landscapes as Dodington (Plate 123).[53] It was an expensive house, its halls and main staircase being incredibly extravagant in the use of space. The parish church was also completely rebuilt and linked to the house by a quadrant greenhouse.

Like those of so many landowners, the extant building and estate accounts at Dodington are difficult to interpret with precision. Although the former cover costs to 1814, they rarely specify the objects of expenditure. Also, since it was built by measured work, details about the size and origins of most of its workforce remain unknown. There is also an account of estate income running from 1799 to 1812, years which encompass the period of peak building activity; no information about earnings from the West Indian plantations appears to survive. The four main building accounts are summarised in Table 20.[54]

Table 20. *Expenditure on the building of Dodington (Gloucestershire), 1796–1814 (to nearest £)*

1796–September 1804	40,484
Michaelmas 1804–Lady Day 1807	8055
Lady Day 1807–Michaelmas 1811	13,502
Michaelmas 1811–January 1814	6437
TOTAL	68,478

Source: Gloucestershire RO, D1610/A96–7.

Supposedly, a further £60,000 was spent on the interior which was not completed until the 1820s (gas lighting, amongst the first in a country house, was installed in 1828).[55] This sum seems unlikely: although finishing did not begin before 1805, some of its costs must have been included in the above figures. There is no doubt, however, that Dodington with its giant portico, church and its interior of 'sombre splendour' was an extravagant house.[56] As was common practice, brick and lime were made on site and much estate timber was used, but the house was built in Painswick and Portland stone which cost £2616 plus carriage of a further £2418. The use of marble in both house and church was lavish; a top London plasterer was employed; the finest inlaid mahogany doors were hung. Codrington scribbled across the entry of Westmacott's bill for the drawing-room chimney-piece, 'including the ornaments, exclusive of carriage, erecting it etc., cost the enormous and shameful sum of £228 18s. 10½d.' In 1800 no less than £7689 in total was spent.[57]

The estate accounts are difficult to reconcile with these sums.[58] Rentals, farm income and casual profits produced £8203 a year on average between 1799 and 1812 (inclusive) with 'spending' running a not disastrous £300 ahead. The account appears to have produced £34,801 towards 'new building', or just one-half of the total expenditure on the house to New Year 1814. The house was not, as has been suggested, 'built by estate labour out of income' if income equates with the net rent roll of Codrington's Gloucestershire and Wiltshire estates.[59]

Yet Dodington was certainly built slowly. Wyatt, who got on well with Christopher Codrington (the architect was killed in a coach accident when they were returning to London together in 1813), was notoriously lackadaisical. But Codrington's cash flow does seem to have been carefully measured. In only two years (1800 and 1802) was more than £4400 spent, and after 1805 (when the shell was complete) costs fell to no more than £3200 on average between 1805 and 1813.

After 1813 the final fitting out of the house progressed even more unhurriedly. Presumably, he worked on the premise that building bills in most years could be met from the cash flow generated by estate rentals. Returns from the West Indies were less predictable. Edwin Lascelles, much richer than Codrington, had proceeded in the same fashion at Harewood half a century earlier. Even before he began the house Lascelles wrote in 1756: 'I am playing Ducks and Drakes with the income of my estate and spending half the rents before they become due.'[60] His expenditure on the house was spread over many years, his bills were paid so leisurely it protected his cash flow while it must have nearly wrecked those of his creditors. But at Dodington, in the long term, neither building and additional land purchase nor Codrington's lifestyle could be met from the landed estate he inherited. Between 1793 and 1809 he spent £78,340 on land and legal fees and a further £50,500 between 1814 and 1819.[61] Sums of this extent were met by the sale of investments and from plantation profits. The aim seems to have been to put together a 5000-acre estate centred upon Dodington itself, an objective undertaken when land prices were rising sharply. By 1873 (there were intervening land sales in the 1840s) the estate was 5023 acres producing a rental of £7210 (by contrast the Harewood estate had been built up to over 29,000 acres in the West Riding).[62] With colonial sugar prices at rock bottom greatly diminishing the Codrington's income from the West Indies in the late nineteenth century, it was fast becoming inadequate to sustain such a large house. Great houses were built

PLATE 124. Orchardleigh Park, Somerset. William Duckworth had the building of his new
house in the 1850s recorded in photographs and watercolours. This view (1856) shows both the
old house and the new one under construction.

from non-landed wealth: their subsequent upkeep was difficult if those sources
dried up and the surrounding estate did not match the scale of a house conceived
in different economic circumstances.

Orchardleigh Park (Somerset) built by William Duckworth in the late 1850s
was not on the scale of Harewood or Dodington (Plate 124). But his purchase of
the estate in 1855 and the construction of the house underlines a feature which
altered the boundaries for newcomers to the world of large-scale landownership.
Land was becoming increasingly expensive. By the mid nineteenth century very
sizeable fortunes were necessary both to purchase land and to rebuild country
houses. Whereas in the eighteenth century the likes of country merchants had
shrewdly put together small estates, and they or their descendants had built
modest houses within the Halfpenny-Morris price range, Orchardleigh illustrates
how expensive similar operations had become a century later. It suggests that,
unless newcomers were totally emulative of the landowner's way of life (and
many were), such large and relatively unproductive expenditures were better

invested in the stock market and in houses which went with much less land than the traditional country estate.

The source of Duckworth's wealth is difficult to locate. Although they claimed ancient Lancashire descent, their entry in Burke's *Landed Gentry* went no farther back than George Duckworth's purchase of the manor of Over Darwin, Blackburn, in 1811.[63] He died four years later leaving two sons, Samuel (1786–1847), later a Master in Chancery and briefly MP for Leicester in 1837, and William (1795–1876), the purchaser of Orchardleigh. The Lancashire property was ripe for development, and when William drew up an account of his wealth and income in 1824, the year before his marriage, his fortune of £52,192 included £8000 worth of building land, some cotton trading interests (in 1856 he still owned a mill in Manchester valued at £14,500) and debts. He also owed £10,350 to his brother. For the rest of his long life he made an annual calculation of his property and income.[64] Those for selected years are given below.

Year	Property £	Net income £
1824	51,642	1600
1834	94,013	4091
1847	145,745	6819
1856	412,784	12,757
1864	425,269	12,552
1876	529,779	18,370

The turning point in his fortunes was the inheritance of his brother's wealth in 1847. By the mid 1850s he reckoned the value of his shares, bonds and annuities, principally held in the stock of the Great Northern railway company, was almost £225,000. On the verge of sixty, he decided to buy the Orchardleigh estate. Obviously, finance was no problem – he simply sold shares – but the 2174 acre estate bought for over £46 an acre or almost thirty-nine years' purchase was very expensive.[65] Immediately Thomas Wyatt was summoned to design a house with ample, segregated space for visitors. Eventually, an estimate of £17,824 was agreed upon. Costs soon outran estimates. By February 1860 Duckworth entered in his note book, 'New house and stables cost to this date £34,435'. He had spent no less than £133,325 on the estate and the house, later described as 'large ... tedious inside and out'. In 1883 the estate produced a gross annual rental of just over £4000.[66] Of course Duckworth was untroubled; shortly before he died, in 1876,

he reckoned he was worth over half a million pounds. Moreover, he had achieved
his ambitions: he was a justice of the peace and Deputy Lieutenant; his four sons
were educated at Eton; his heir had married into the peerage. Another landed
dynasty had been launched. But it had not come cheap. Rich men rightly paused
before they undertook similar ventures.

   Both Brodsworth (west Yorkshire) and the source of its builder's wealth are
remarkable. Charles Thellusson (1822–1885) shared the proceeds of the famous
will of his great-grandfather Peter Thellusson, who had died in 1797 (Plate
125).[67] His portion was worth about £600,000 of which three-quarters was in land
(Lord Rendlesham, his cousin, fared a little better). In 1859–60 Thellusson thought
of remodelling Brodsworth, a big plain mid eighteenth-century house north of
Doncaster which Peter Thellusson, a highly successful Swiss-born banker and

PLATE 125.
Charles Sabine
Augustus
Thellusson in
1878.

PLATE 126. Brodsworth Hall, Yorkshire, from a watercolour possibly by Philip Wilkinson, *c.* 1861.

plantation owner, had bought in the 1790s. In the early spring of 1861 he turned to two young men, an Italian sculptor, the Chevalier Casentini from Lucca, and an unknown architect practising in London, Philip Wilkinson. They designed and built for Thellusson an expensive Italianate house two hundred yards from the old one, as symmetrical and classical as anything else built in the 1860s (Plate 126). Like Dodington, with three large halls and a broad corridor, it was incredibly wasteful of space. A London contractor, Longmire and Burge, working to a tightly-drawn contract with penalty clauses, was employed; a Bond Street firm, Lapworths, supplied furniture, carpets and curtains (Plate 127). Casentini negotiated the purchase of marble for two dozen statues for the house and a similar number for the garden. The house cost £20,500; or, if fees, stable block, laundry, gardener's cottage, lodge and road (all built by Longmire) are added, £31,000. Lapworth's bill came to £7300. The house had been completed within two years; within four everything was shipshape. The total bill, with work on the gardens, was in the region of £50,000. Such speed would have been inconceivable a century earlier. Those neighbours who were building and improving would have been endlessly consulted; numerous designs would have been procured and discussed. Even the immensely rich Edwin Lascelles had built and finished Harewood slowly and with infinite care, discussing every stage with John Carr, Robert Adam, the two Joseph Roses, Thomas Chippendale and his top men, Samuel Jones and William Reed. By contrast Charles Thellusson seems to have bought his statuary in a job lot from the Dublin Exhibition of 1865.

PLATE 127.   Brodsworth Hall, Yorkshire. The drawing-room *c.* 1890 showing many of the furnishings supplied by Lapworths.

Between 1859 and 1870 Thellusson spent £105,000 on Brodsworth and on improvements to the estate. This sum was around 70 per cent of his net rent roll in these years.[68] He also cleared the considerable debts (£59,000) of his father who, realising he was not going to benefit from Peter Thellusson's will, simply spent as if he had – chiefly on racehorses. Although Thellusson had inherited some 10,707 acres (plus a thousand acres of unvalued woodland) in five counties, producing a net rental of £13,219 in 1857, it was obviously inadequate to meet expenditure on the scale of the 1860s. In 1863, the peak year of activity, Thellusson spent about £25,000, far outdistancing estate receipts of £14,300. To bridge the gap between income and expenditure, sales of outlying land (sold well at more than forty years purchase between 1859 and 1864) realised £82,000 and of investments some £100,000. By 1865 the value of the latter had been diminished to around £70,000. It is clear that building the house, improving the estate and liquidating inherited debt was not achieved from regular income but from the sale of land and investments. In 1870 Charles Thellusson was still a great landowner with around 9000 acres. Nevertheless, his agent in the early 1870s worried that income and expenditure were already adrift by between £1000 and £3000 a year. This was before agricultural depression set in. Little wonder that the house was preserved in aspic for the next 120 years. In a region of open-cast coal mining, its survival in the family to 1990 was a miracle.

The moral for all these super-rich landowners was that, although they could build on a scale to match the best, the subsequent upkeep of the house and maintenance of lifestyles required the backing of a very large landed estate, unless they carefully nurtured their holdings of consols, bank and 'blue-chip' stocks. For non-landed sources of wealth, like plantation incomes, might dwindle, the profits of office did not flow regularly between the generations in families, and inherited investments, like those of the Thellussons, were all too easily dispersed.

Men such as Samuel Whitbread and Edwin Lascelles, who bought major estates and built on the grandest scale, were amongst the minority of newcomers who came to large-scale landownership between 1660 and 1880. Big estates such as they bought came less frequently onto the market. The majority, whatever the sources of their wealth, had to be content with smaller purchases of land, but if their more modest fortunes were not unduly overstretched, if family demographic circumstances were right, and if the capacity of their heirs was sound, they built up estates which gave them access to all the benefits of county society. Often their wealth was insufficient for them simultaneously to buy land and to build. Often, like the Bagges at Stradsett, they possessed a keener eye for acquiring land than for building. A good estate at Stradsett was put together over a century after 1760, the house built at the turn of the sixteenth century was gradually remodelled and a park created.[69] At Weston Longville in central Norfolk, John Custance, a merchant and twice mayor of Norwich, bought an estate for £5000. Eight years later it was described as 'six messuages, one dovehouse, eighty acres of meadow, 100 acres of pasture, 400 acres of [arable] land, twenty acres of wood, 400 acres of heath ... ten acres of marsh, twenty acres of alder carr'.[70] Custance continued to live in Norwich. His son served as High Sheriff of Norfolk in 1753, but it was not until the next generation that John Custance, the squire of Parson Woodforde's diaries, built a new house (1779–81) out of the proceeds of his marriage settlement with the daughter of Sir William Beauchamp-Proctor of

Langley Park, and emparked 300 acres of heath with plantations.[71] In Victorian England newcomers had less need to build from scratch, buying estates, such as Weston Longville, that had been put together over the previous 150 years. The Gurneys, whose wealth was derived from a highly successful Norfolk Quaker banking operation, came to own numerous Norfolk estates in the nineteenth century; but, with the exception of Keswick, a William Wilkins house of the 1810s, they were not notable builders of new houses.[72] When Felbrigg, the ancient seat of Windhams changed hands in 1863, the purchaser, John Ketton, a successful manufacturer of cattle food from Norwich, bought the house, its contents and half the Windham's estate, and changed nothing.[73] Lesser newcomers did build, but behind their schemes often lies a complex financial history which the historians of landownership have not really unravelled. Denton provides a well-documented example which allows a discussion of building costs related to income and dynastic ambitions (Table 9).

Denton Hall, built in ashlar limestone for Sir James Ibbetson (1746–1795) by John Carr in the early 1770s, cost £9460 (Plate 128).[74] Its foundations were raised upon two West Riding mercantile fortunes, those of the Ibbetsons of Leeds and

PLATE 128.   Denton Hall, Yorkshire (John Carr, c. 1770–75).

the Caygills of Halifax. Trading in cloth since around 1600, the Ibbetsons' fortunes had, like those of many merchants and financiers, taken off during the wars of William III and Queen Anne with Louis XIV. In 1717 Sir James's grandfather, James Ibbetson (1674–1739), had purchased the 2000-acre Denton and Askwith Wharfedale estate from the Fairfaxes and conveyed it to his eldest son, a barrister-at-law. James Ibbetson himself inherited valuable urban property in Leeds and continued to buy numerous investments in land scattered across the cloth-producing area of the West Riding. He, however, remained in Leeds, building a fine town house in 1715 and, a few years later, a good villa five miles away. He continued to trade in cloth, as did his younger son (created a baronet in 1748 for services in the '45 and as High Sheriff of Yorkshire), although Sir Henry married twice into prominent north country gentry families. The doors of the counting house only closed on his death in 1761 when the lucrative farming of the Aire and Calder Navigation tolls and coal-mining ventures, jointly undertaken with Peter Birt, also came to an end.

When Sir James Ibbetson (1746–95) came of age in 1767 the West Riding was at his feet. In the following year he inherited Denton from his uncle and married the sole heiress of Halifax's leading merchant. Twelve months later he served as High Sheriff of Yorkshire and, as soon as he had finished his undemanding duties, John Carr was summoned to build a smaller-scale version of nearby Harewood.[75] Although Sir James was a rich young man, financing the house was a complex operation. In terms of the Denton and Askwith estate income (a mere £1100), the house cost the equivalent of over nine years' rentals. This troubled the trustees of Lady Ibbetson's marriage settlement, who thought the building of the house, and even more of the church Sir James erected a little way along the valley, inadequate security for her jointure. The estate had also to support Sir James's three younger brothers who, now that the Ibbetsons were no longer merchants, were without vocations but possessed of expensive tastes. Sir James in addition had to pay his cousin, Lady Orwell, £4853 to rid himself of encumbrances on the estate. Steps were therefore taken to realise settled property in Leeds and elsewhere, a process already begun by Sir Henry by a private Act of Parliament obtained in 1755. A second one was procured in 1776. Together they enabled Sir James to raise around £15,500. This allowed him to build a house way beyond the proceeds of his rent roll and also to enclose and improve the estate, as well as developing a secondary one at Gomersal for industrial purposes and coal-mining ventures. Yet at times Sir James, like so many country house builders, was also driven to borrowing: £3600 on mortgage in the early 1770s; £2500 from the Wakefield merchant, Richard Slater Milnes in 1781. Part of the problem was that property prices slumped after the onset of the American War of Independence. The Ibbetsons' Leeds house, on the market for £2200 in 1770, realised only £1200 when finally sold eleven years later. The building of Denton was not met from the rentals of a modest estate but from the proceeds of an advantageous marriage and the sale of largely urban property released by private Act of Parliament from settlement. Putting together a landed estate and building a house to match the Ibbetsons' ambitions had taken three generations.

When we turn to examine the finances of those smaller landowners who were motivated to build, we move away from the territory of the rewards of royal service and government office, big non-landed sources of wealth, and the depth of landed incomes which allowed the likes of Lord Leicester and Sir Christopher Sykes to borrow and to build extensively. The lesser gentry were faced with tough agendas. They required considerable management skills to juggle the proceeds of limited rent-rolls to provide a country lifestyle, to buy and to improve land, and to make appropriate family settlements. When it came to their building enterprises, they were often content unpretentiously to remodel their houses to conform with shifting architectural styles, changing family requirements and the impact of social changes. Some, however, were bitten with a more serious strain of the building virus, the result perhaps of a good marriage, abiding memories of the Grand Tour, the emulation of neighbours, or rising rentals after the 1790s and the returns of enclosure. What effect had the financial circumstances of the lesser gentry on the scale of their building schemes? The accounts of Thomas Worsley of Hovingham (north Yorkshire), Edmund Rolfe of Heacham (Norfolk) and Thomas Webb Edge of Strelley (Nottinghamshire) provide a framework for an answer to the question.

When he succeeded his father at Hovingham in 1751, Thomas Worsley (1710–1778) already had grand building schemes in mind.[76] This was not surprising since he had spent the years between 1735 and 1737 on the Continent deeply immersing himself in architecture. He had also acquired a fine collection of architectural books and, unusually for an amateur architect, was a competent draughtsman. By the time he settled back in England in the 1740s he was steeped in the Palladian concepts which, under Lord Burlington's leadership, were beginning to excite those members of the Yorkshire gentry interested in architecture. He produced plans for stables for a couple of friends; he designed a Tuscan temple for his father in 1750. They were ventures which paled besides those undertaken to replace the small manor house his grandfather had built in the 1680s.

The Worsleys, of old Lancashire gentry stock, had moved to Hovingham around 1610. Their fortunes, like those of so many landowners, took a turn for the better after the Restoration. By 1750, after two generations of well-connected marriages, the Worsleys were thoroughly established at the heart of the north Yorkshire gentry. Their estate, however, largely confined within the parish of Hovingham, was a small one. From the outset Thomas's vision was bounded by his economic circumstances. His father had died 'many Thousands in debt'; his step-mother lived several years to enjoy her jointure. His own marriage to his half-sister's maid, the orphaned daughter of an impoverished clergyman, reads more like an extract from a Samuel Richardson novel than the usual hard-nosed marriage settlement of members of Worsley's class.

None of this, however, seems to have deterred Thomas Worsley's building ambitions. These were additionally fuelled by his other great passion besides architecture, the schooling of horses in a ménage. North Yorkshire had long been celebrated for its horses and in Geneva Worsley had acquired a profound knowledge in *haute école*, the practice of schooling them. In the early 1750s he therefore planned to erect stables, a riding school and a pavilion with a couple of entertaining rooms before building a new house on the site of its 1680s predecessor. But in

PLATE 129.   Hovingham Hall, Yorkshire (Thomas Worsley, *c.* 1755–78). The house as originally intended; the south wing to the right was never built.

1755 this scheme was abandoned in favour of one which uniquely combined
stables, riding school, family apartments and state rooms (Plate 129):

> Hovingham, as Worsley intended it, should be read as a standard Palladian stable
> quadrangle – with Diocletian windows in blank arches and small windows above –
> into which were grafted the three domestic pavilions, one at each end of the wings
> and one in the centre.[77]

When Arthur Young visited Hovingham on his northern tour in 1769 he was
bemused by the result. At first sight he thought the house, standing in the middle
of the village, was a hospital. But it was the proximity of the best rooms in the
house to the riding school and stables beneath them, and the prospect of a rising
odour in summer, which he found entirely novel, although he typically conceded,
'nothing should be condemned because uncommon'.[78]

Thomas Worsley's building schemes involved him for the entire twenty-seven
years of his tenure of the estate. They progressed slowly because plans constantly
evolved: the riding school was completed only shortly before Young's visit; the
stables were removed from the main part of the house; and the disposition of
some rooms changed in the last few years of his life. Building also went on slowly
because he had limited sums at his disposal for this purpose.

The building accounts for the house are not quite complete. For three years
they are missing altogether, in others only either the steward's or Worsley's own
accounts have survived. They tail off suspiciously sharply after the mid 1770s.
Those which remain add up to £6430. Probably the house cost around £8000 in
total. In the third quarter of the eighteenth century it was an expensive affair for
a small estate. There were other features which reduced the final cost. Although
Worsley's love of contrasting stone work is everywhere evident, the stone was
conveniently quarried on the estate. Finally, not only did he act as his own
architect but also as his own clerk of the works.

Three features stand out in an analysis of Thomas Worsley's accounts. First,
throughout the construction of the house his finances were under considerable
pressure. Until at least the early 1770s Worsley's borrowing was on a substantial
scale. Interest and debt repayments (averaging just over £500 a year) exceed those
spent on building (£330). One of his difficulties was that annuity payments remained burdensome at least to the mid 1760s. Between 1753 and 1772 they averaged
£390. Secondly, they reveal that Thomas Worsley was a competent man of affairs
and not unduly extravagant except in building a house rather beyond his means.

His household-book reveals an expenditure of around £555 for these years when both his own and the steward's reckonings are extant. Even his stable accounts ran to no more than £167 each year on average, presumably because his horse dealings were remunerative. Later he bragged that the riding school and the new stables of the 1770s had been built by profits from them. Thirdly, although Worsley struggled to build his dream house, carefully apportioning a few hundreds each year across two decades, constantly juggling his debts and living relatively modestly, he was saved by becoming Surveyor General of the Works in 1761 shortly after George III's accession.

He owed the office to his life-long friendship with the Earl of Bute as also his placeman's membership of Parliament for Orford (1761–68) and Callington (1768–74).[79] Horace Walpole described him on his promotion with his usual asperity: 'a creature of Lord Bute, and a kind of riding-master to the King'.[80] In fact Worsley, with his first-rate knowledge of architecture and building, was far better suited to the office than his predecessors, who had simply used it as a stepping stone to more lucrative political sinecures. Until personal tragedy and chronic illness struck after 1769, he was a competent and assiduous surveyor.[81] The returns from the office were estimated to be around £900 a year, plus rent-free accommodation in Scotland Yard and Hampton Court.[82] For those years in the run of accounts for which income entries exist, there was indeed an increase of this order from around £3375 in the last years of the 1750s to £4200 in the mid 1760s. His household accounts show that the profits of place were partly offset by the increased costs of living in London for long periods during the 1760s and early 1770s. Political office might have saved Worsley financially. It did not alter his plans for Hovingham beyond that metropolitan craftsman employed by the Office of Works increasingly replaced York men in the finishing of the house.

Although work proceeded almost to the end of Worsley's life, on his death in 1778 the house was still not completed: several rooms were not fitted up and the matching south wing was never built. Even the old 1680s house was not demolished until the 1830s. Indeed Thomas's successor appears to have lived in it, and for half a century the new house remained in wraps before final completion in the 1830s. Many times Thomas Worsley had lamented that his income did not match his architectural dreams. After visiting Studley Royal he came away cursing his birth: 'why was I not descended of a long race of droning Lords? Rich esquires at least, for even then I might have hopes.' On the keystone of his house he had inscribed, *Pro viribus non pro votis erexit* (he built according to his means not his wishes).[83] Although the house cost no more than a tenth of the sums expended at Holkham, his dogged realisation of a profound classical vision was just as remarkable as that of Lord Leicester.

The extensive additions to Heacham Hall in the 1770s typify the building endeavours of those thousands of smaller landowners in England whose fortunes improved in the eighteenth and nineteenth centuries.[84] Their origins were often modest, their social ambitions frequently limitless. To underpin the latter a policy of economic advancement sometimes over several generations was essential. In the Rolfes' case they were leading members of the elite which ran King's Lynn from the Restoration to the Municipal Reform Act (1835). Three generations were town clerks between 1654 and 1726, latterly managing Sir Robert Walpole's electoral interests in the borough. In the 1690s they acquired a 230 acre estate and manor house seven miles away on the eastern margins of the Wash. They remained, however, like so many members of flourishing urban elites, hybrid creatures – half landowners, half urban men of business. Certainly Edmund Rolfe I (1700–1774) was a true-to-type member, keeping wonderfully detailed accounts. He mostly lived at Heacham, but was also involved in Lynn affairs as an attorney negotiating the loans of its merchant oligarchy. Yet as 'Squire' Rolfe at Heacham he entertained grander notions. When a distant cousin, a prominent Norwich attorney, left him 1100 acres of scattered property, and £16,000 out on loan, he could begin to realise them. We have seen how his only son Edmund II (1738–1817) was dispatched on the Grand Tour. Within two years of his return he married a neighbouring baronet's daughter, the co-heiress of a Lynn mercantile fortune. Their fourteen folio marriage settlement, creating a trust fund of £23,719, was an extended declaration to found a landed dynasty. But the Heacham estate, now running to 420 acres, and the old manor house, little more than a single-pile Norfolk farm house probably rebuilt in the mid 1730s (when it was insured for £300) with the village common close behind it, was hardly sufficient to realise the Rolfes' ambitions. The house was the summer retreat of a merchant, not the country seat of a county family. Their agenda was now specific: to acquire more land in Heacham; completely to rebuild the manor house; and to set out a park, kitchen garden and plantations to improve its environs. Edmund I, generous as he was to his son, stood in the way. Having led a hell of a life, widowed once, separated from his termagant of a second wife, now with an income of £1400, he decided to enjoy himself in his last years. With four servants, he sampled high life in Epsom for a year, then rented a country house in south Norfolk before returning to Lynn. Meanwhile his son at Heacham, with an average income of £1797 in the same decade as his father restlessly did the rounds of London, Bath, Bristol Hot Wells and Great Yarmouth, planned his strategy.

Until his father died, enabling the release of capital, there seems to have been no question of major building at Heacham. Yet Edmund was not inactive. He served the office of High Sheriff of Norfolk in 1769 (his father gladly paid the £420 costs). He looked after the home farm, and rerouted the Hunstanton road to create a small park and kitchen garden. He also bought – an unusual departure for such a marginal gentry member – a London house in Wimpole Street. He visited Bath; he spent a lot of time at the gaming tables there and in London. He acquired more land near Heacham: two big farms of 1735 acres taken on a renewable twenty-one year lease at a low rent from the Dean and Chapter of Norwich Cathedral in 1769. Six years later he bought a similarly sized 670 acre farm from Lord Orford. They were light-land farms capable of great improvement by the new methods of agriculture advocated by Arthur Young and, later, Coke of Holkham. On Edmund I's death in 1774 the Rolfes, therefore, owned 1100 acres in and around Heacham, 1086 acres scattered across Norfolk inherited in 1754, and 1735 acres leased from the Dean and Chapter. In total this made up a sizeable estate of almost 4000 acres. Edmund II could think big in 1774.

Like many other country house building projects, Heacham involved the extensive rebuilding of an existing house. The new part was a brick-built, seven-by-four bay rectangular block of two and a half storeys. Behind it the old house was converted into an extensive set of domestic offices and a refurbished 'new room'. The big addition provided an entrance hall and staircase, dining- and drawing-rooms, a library and ante-room with best bed and dressing-rooms on the first floor. There is no mention in the accounts of an architect beyond an earlier payment of ten guineas made in Bath to 'Mr Wood'. Presumably, this was for an unexecuted plan by John Wood the younger made for Edmund while he kicked his heels there in 1767 (Plates 4–5).

The house was built between 1774 and 1778 at a cost of £4128, plus a further £1025 for new furniture and upholstery.[85] His accounts show that he could not have financed this out of estate income alone. Not unusually, the expenditure represented some four to five years of net rentals, these averaging £1173 per annum from 1775–80. Including income from investments, he had in these years an average of £2616 at his disposal. His accounts reveal, however, that routine expenditure ran to £2738, including £1954 per annum on his domestic account.

Indeed his current account was in deficit even before building began. Essentially, the house was paid for out of the capital that became available on his father's death.

Edmund Rolfe's capital position can be estimated in two ways: interest receipts suggest that between 1774 and 1780 his net capital fell from around £17,600 to £7500. Analysis of his cash flow indicates a net withdrawal of about £12,800. The main charges were £5153 spent on the house and furniture and £5014 used to pay legacies. The estate was also being extended and improved. Enclosure in 1781 vitally allowed the common which ran behind the kitchen garden to be eliminated. It cost £1049 and added ninety-two acres to Rolfe's holding in the parish. A further 132 acres were purchased in the next decade and, in 1782, when land prices were low, a 230-acre farm, the property of a bankrupt farmer, was acquired.

Both building and land purchase appear to have caused serious financial problems for Edmund Rolfe in the short run. The American war (1775–83) led to a collapse of the land market and the price of agricultural products. Landowners were deeply concerned, none more than Rolfe. By 1781–82 he was borrowing short numerous small amounts on bond in Lynn. In two years, 1781–83, he raised £5335 by these means; in 1784, although he paid off £1300, he borrowed a further £4500. In the following year, he approached his brother-in-law, Sir Martin Folkes, for £1000. Several small sums in the Funds were realised, and even the £100 lent to the Lynn Turnpike trustees was called in. By 1785 he was living more economically (albeit with five servants) in Bath. The London house was let; Heacham Hall, so recently completed, was closed, only opened up for Edmund to enjoy three weeks of partridge shooting each September. Stable expenses were cut to a minimum. In the five years, 1777–81, personal and household expenditure had averaged £2043; during his period of residence in Bath (1783–91) it was reduced by over a third to £1355. His son, Eton-educated, required an annual allowance of £250 and, in 1788, the purchase of a lieutenancy in the Blues. Four years later, his daughter went off to marry a member of the Yorkshire gentry with a £10,000 dowry in her baggage.

Again, building, land purchase, the whole process of gentry conversion, did not come cheap. Edmund Rolfe survived his financial difficulties in the 1780s because, when land prices had somewhat recovered, an outlying 637 acre farm near Norwich inherited in 1754 was sold in 1790 for £12,000 to Robert Fellowes of Shotesham, after it had been touted round the Norfolk gentry for eighteen months. This allowed him to repay his loans and to return permanently to

Heacham. Above all, he was saved by the prosperity of agriculture during the French wars (1793–1815); by 1805 he was able to afford £19,250 to buy the 894-acre adjoining Sedgeford Hall estate.

Even a small house like Heacham was not built out of rental income. It was only afforded through a fortuitous inheritance two decades earlier and a £8500 marriage settlement (although specifically this was not to be laid out on non-income earning building). Its construction and maintenance caused real problems for Edmund Rolfe's finances during the 1780s. Yet he had a great affection for his creation. When his son went to live at Sedgeford Hall, the family's attractive secondary house after 1805, Edmund constantly reminded him about his role at Heacham. On one occasion he wrote:

> I hope no consideration will induce you to give up Heacham as your residence. It is your birth-right; settled upon you by the Consent of both your Grandfathers; and the place you are bound to live at, in justice both to yourself, your tenants, and your poor parishioners. Your ancestors are buried there, and every reason urges you to live there as they have done before.[86]

For a landowner without a drop of aristocratic blood in him, it is a fine expression of common gentry sentiments about status, responsibility and place.

The Edges of Strelley, which they owned for over three centuries from the 1660s to the 1970s, were a typical English gentry family.[87] Their roots were urban and legal. The real founder of the family fortunes, Ralph Edge, was town clerk and mayor of Nottingham on three occasions in the 1660s and 1670s. He purchased the manors of Strelley and Bilborough, no more than four miles from the town, from the Strelley family. Thereafter the progress of the Edges was classic. The estate survived two descents through the female line; their record of public service became exemplary. Six generations in turn served the office of High Sheriff between 1709 and 1904, each of them also acting as county justices.[88] But their building activities were as unremarkable as those of the majority of the lesser gentry.

For well over a century they were content to live in the old manor house, in their worship each week seemingly unmoved to emulate the Strelleys who in the fourteenth century had erected a splendid chancel in the parish church to contain their monuments.[89] Only in the late 1780s did Thomas Webb Edge (1756–1819), who had succeeded to the estates as a minor in 1766, decide to rebuild substantially. He executed plans which must have been long in gestation. First, he moved the centre of the village, building new cottages to replace those he

PLATE 130.   Strelley Hall, Nottinghamshire (Thomas Gardner, 1789–90) in 1791.

had demolished close to the house. By this time, his family had accumulated a good estate of 3133 acres in four Midlands counties from which he enjoyed an income of around £2500 a year.[90]

Sir Nikolaus Pevsner describes Strelley as 'a large, absolutely plain brick house seven by five bays two-and-a-half stories now all rendered (Plate 130).'[91] Webb Edge had gone to a Midlands architect and builder, Thomas Gardner of Uttoxeter, for his plans.[92] Economy seems to have been Edge's constant watchword. The old house was to be partially demolished and many materials reused.[93] The parts which remained were to be stuccoed to conform with the new south and east fronts. The new building included a hall, dining-, drawing- and breakfast-rooms, with chambers and attics above and a service range, but the former dining-room was to be divided to create a butler's pantry and passages, the old staircase retained, and the truncated medieval tower converted into a study (Plate 131). The whole was to be finished 'ready for painting' in sixteen months. Gardner agreed to carry out all these alterations for £1656. In the event his bill came to £2763, the extras including a stables and best staircase of Stanton stone.[94] Since

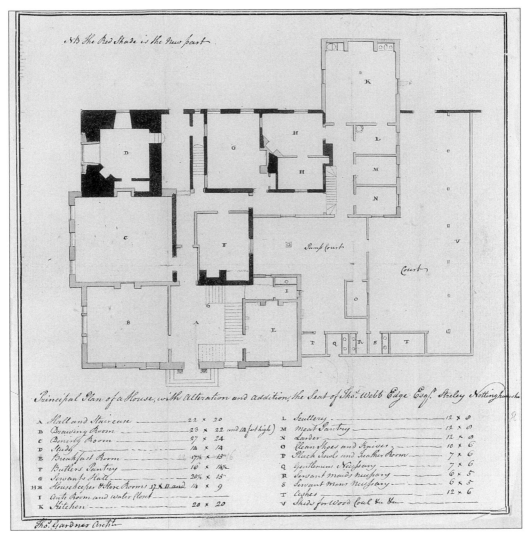

PLATE 131. Strelley Hall, Nottinghamshire. Thomas Gardner's plan of the principal floor. The darker shading indicates the incorporation of parts of the old house.

Edge supplied most of the materials the total cost of the house must have been close to £5000, or around two years of Edge's rentals.

Strelley was far from an extravagant house: it appears not to have caused the slightest problem for Edge's finances; it was little altered in its subsequent history.[95] This building chronicle is standard for the schemes of the lesser provincial gentry in the 1660 to 1830 period, or at least those who relied upon landed rental for their income. Only in the post-1830 period, as John Dobson commented about country house building in Northumberland, did they invariably turn to the architectural profession to carry out major rebuilding projects.

This survey of the finances of sixteen builders, drawn from across the spectrum of landowners, suggests that the English country house was seldom built from landed rentals alone. The big extensions to Sledmere or Edward Fellowes's house at Haveringland might conceivably have been, and Strelley certainly was, but elsewhere other sources of income were essential for owners to realise their building ambitions. For the peerage and some larger landowners it was the rewards of office and the procurement of sinecures obtained in the rough and tumble of the politics of patronage which were of key significance, at least before the reforms of the nineteenth century. Then many of them were to enjoy, as few of their members previously had, the benefits of industrial and urban development in the form of ground rents, mineral rights, and canal and railway company shares. Good marriage settlements, the savings of earlier generations and the sale of outlying lands were also important. Newcomers – not all of them men of 'new' families – to large-scale landownership and country house building were leaders in trade, finance, industry and the professions. Some like the Lascelleses brought great fortunes with them; more usually, like the Ibbetsons and Rolfes, they augmented them over the years. Even the lesser gentry, relying almost entirely upon landed rentals, usually needed some additional financial fillip for them to embark upon major remodelling or building a new house.

None of this is surprising because the calls upon estate income were becoming increasingly multifarious and sometimes burdensome. All the evidence shows that rentals were required to maintain lifestyles – increasingly often in London (this was Byng's gripe) as well as at county level: to buy more and more land, to enclose and improve estates, and to make larger and larger family settlements. With borrowing almost always necessary at one stage or another to undertake these activities, it is easy to see how rentals became entirely consumed by them. Mortgaging and borrowing were undoubtedly easy to arrange on the security of rising rentals. Yet the mounting interest payments could seriously erode incomes unless debt was carefully managed. To embark on major building schemes therefore required additional sources of finance to initiate them. Then constant juggling was required to meet the regular pattern of payments: heavy initial costs across the first two to five years for the case of the house to be completed, usually easing across the period of finishing. Table 21 reveals how difficult it was to fit this sequence into an income based upon landed rentals alone.

Table 21. *Comparison of building expenditure with rental income* [a]

House income	Building period	Years	Building cost £	Total rental income [b] £	Percentage of rental income spent on building	
					Overall	Peak year
Brodsworth	1861–63	3	31,200	44,400	70.3	92.9
Sledmere	1787–94	8	17,600	84,500	20.8	39.7
Eshton	1825–29	5	13,900	20,900	66.5	94.2
Haveringland	1839–43	5	21,400	85,800	24.9	29.1
Heacham	1775–80	6	4100	7000	58.6	160.8
Henham	1792–99	8	21,400	37,400	57.2	93.7
Sheringham	1815–17	3	8000	3000	222.2	— [c]

Notes:

[a] Only rental income is considered. The building period is that over which the main payments were made and is generally longer than the actual construction period. The costs exclude major work on parks and other estate property. If for Haveringland only Norfolk rents are considered, building consumed an estimated 178.3 per cent of rental income, and 208.3 per cent in the peak year.

[b] During the building period.

[c] The Sheringham rental of £1200 per annum is a best estimate for a time when rents fell in the post-war depression after 1815. An optimistic rate of £2000 per annum would still leave 133 per cent of rental income spent on building.

Sources: Brodsworth, Yorkshire Archaeological Society, Leeds, DD 168; Eshton, Yorkshire Archaeological Society, Leeds, MD 335, box 18; Leeds University Library, MS 417/34; Haveringland, Norfolk RO, MS 8595 20B; Cambridgeshire RO, Huntingdon, Acc. 2470; Cambridge University Library, Add. 3955; Heacham, Norfolk RO, HEA 480 256 x 3, 489 256 x 4, 488 256 x 4, 591 257 x; Henham, Suffolk RO, Ipswich, HA 11; Sheringham, Norfolk RO, UPC 37 640 x 4, 55 641 x 8; Sledmere, Hull University Library, DDSY 98/142.

Some houses were constructed slowly not because they were built solely out of landed incomes, or there were shortages of labour and materials, but because the finances of builders such as Thomas Worsley or Lord Leicester were tight even before they began; or such as the first Lord Braybrooke whose task of refurbishment at Audley End was so daunting; or such as Lord Carlisle whose schemes at Castle Howard were so grandiose. What is remarkable, in these times of high mortality, is the sheer extent of their ambition and vision. By the early nineteenth century however, with the emergence of the professional architect and the contract builder, the task for the landowners enjoying increasing incomes seems to have become easier.

Ruin as a consequence of building, like the fate of the absurdly extravagant second Earl Verney of Claydon, was comparatively rare. Occasionally, the destiny of those who employed the Wyatts was unenviable. Colonel T. R. Gale Braddyll, a member of a wealthy Lancashire landed family, commissioned Philip Wyatt in 1821 to build him a great Gothic house, Conishead Priory. Working drawings were not produced on time, and supervision was so lax that Wyatt was dismissed in 1829. By the time the house was completed in 1836 it had cost £140,000, a sum Braddyll could not possibly afford. In the following year the entire Conishead estate was on the market.[96] Another colonel, Lloyd Vaughan-Watkins, commandant of the Breconshire Militia, MP and Lord Lieutenant for the county, engaged Salvin to remodel Pennoyre entirely in an Italianate style between 1846 and 1848. Unlike Conishead, work was well supervised, but the £33,000 bill was too much for Vaughan-Watkins; he closed the house and went to live cheaply in a nearby hotel.[97] A less stringent form of economy than that of the two colonels was more usual. In 1784 the Gages of Hengrave Hall (Suffolk) 'do not', a visitor noted, 'entertain many people: they have been restoring an old-fashioned house, which is costing them a great deal and obliges them to economise'.[98] If building debts were more serious, houses were closed or let and families practised varying degrees of frugality in a secondary house, or more anonymously in London or at a watering place. Cecil Molyneux-Montgomerie (1846–1901) of Garboldisham in Norfolk, spurred on by an aristocratic marriage, engaged George Gilbert Scott junior to build a house in the Queen Anne style in the late 1860s. Almost immediately after its completion in 1873 the rentals of his Norfolk and St Kitts estates in the West Indies collapsed. Within less than a decade, the family were either renting a nearby manor house from an even more impoverished baronet, or retreating to the house the family had occupied and gently remodelled for over a century before engaging Scott.[99] Building helped to pile up debts for later generations, and large houses like Dyrham and Dodington, built from the profits of office and sugar respectively, were burdensome when supported, especially after 1880, by the rentals of moderately-sized estates alone.

In financial terms, building a country house was a poor investment, a poor monetary return for years of financial scheming. Some great houses, like Cannons, Horseheath and Eastbury, enjoyed only brief spells of glory before demolition.[100] Indeed 'the demolition of unwanted houses has been going on relentlessly throughout our history'.[101] Others were accidently burned down, and even when insurance of them became near universal after the mid eighteenth century, houses were generally underinsured. Thoresby (Nottinghamshire), a major house, was rebuilt no fewer than three times in the period. The William Talman house of 1689–91 was burned down in 1745; John Carr built a big villa after 1767 which was replaced by Anthony Salvin's grandest and most expensive country house between 1864 and 1875.[102] Audley End had reputedly cost £200,000 on its completion. Half a century later, in 1669, it was sold to King Charles II for £50,000, a sum never paid in full. In 1701 it was reconveyed to the Earls of Suffolk for a mere £20,000.[103] Little wonder Sir Christopher Sykes, a businessman to his finger tips, wrote off his rebuilding of Sledmere as consumption; or William Duckworth, who calculated the value of his investments with enormous care each year, immediately wrote down the cost of his new house and stables from £34,435 to £15,000.[104]

Country houses by themselves and without land were never sold before the early twentieth century. Indeed, an existing house might add little to the value of an estate. A mansion and all its appendages could attract a newcomer to landownership, but for the purchaser or heir already possessing a seat, a second house, perhaps obsolete and dilapidated, might be worth no more than the price fetched by its materials after demolition. When a house's redundancy was likely to be temporary, however, because of a family's economic situation, one of their periodic sojourns abroad, or during the minority of an heir, keeping house and estate together was important. In these circumstances letting was a better solution than leaving the houses gently to deteriorate: or, in the case of smaller manor houses (a common fate) to subside into ramshackle farmhouses. Demand depended very much upon the sociability and the hunting and shooting attractions of neighbourhoods, but 'To be let, for a longer or shorter period, furnished or unfurnished, was ... a part of the history of many British country houses'.[105]

The returns from letting houses were poor and the arrangements often troublesome, but the consequences for a house left unoccupied for long periods could be serious. Merton Hall (Norfolk) seems to have been neither occupied nor let between 1781 and 1831. By the latter date the 1610s house was incredibly old-fashioned. When Edward Blore surveyed it in 1831 he wrote to Lord Walsingham, 'to make it a suitable habitation ... it will be necessary to renew the interior ... the whole of the interior and the roof is in a state of absolute decay'.[106] Work costing £5926 was carried out between 1832 and 1837, and a further £2964 was spent between 1846 and 1848.[107] On the other hand, the risk of deterioration was much reduced if a house was heated and lived in. The cost of maintaining the house in tenantable condition fell upon the owner, but the tenant might be responsible for minor repairs, maintaining the gardens and keeping the game. Even so, an owner might still conclude that a house should not be let. Sir John Ingleby wrote from Munich in 1797 to his steward, John Hewitt, noting that his son would come of age in a few years and want his house (Ripley Castle in Yorkshire), or that he himself might return to England sooner than expected. With tax avoidance in mind, Sir John indicated that he was prepared to leave the house empty and locked, for if the windows were opened tax upon them would be due.[108]

For some owners letting was unavoidable. Broadlands (Hampshire) was let from 1758 to 1760 during the minority of the second Lord Palmerston for £100 per annum.[109] Sir Robert Davers, who found himself unable to pay the dowry of his sister when she married the fourth Earl of Bristol, let Rushrooke Hall (Suffolk) to the Duke of Cleveland in the 1760s.[110] Sir John Blois Bt (1740–1810), overfond of cards (a predilection his wife shared), lost large sums to 'a Mr Fitzgerald, a well-known Irishman ... "Fighting Fitzgerald" ... hanged in 1786', and found his estate assigned to trustees until he could settle with his creditors. His seat, Cockfield Hall (Suffolk), was let to Chaloner Arcedeckne (who was later to build a country house of his own, Glevering Hall) in the 1770s.[111] Sir William Middleton of Shrubland Park (Suffolk) was happily not under the same pressure, but found himself in the mid nineteenth century with a plethora of houses acquired by inheritance, marriage and purchase.[112] He let one of these Suffolk houses, Livermere Park, originally built about 1700, extended in the 1720s, and remodelled in 1795–96. Surviving papers quantify the financial considerations, revealing also that letting was a competitive business, with prospective tenants in a strong bargaining position.

The net annual loss to the estate when Livermere Park was unlet was estimated in 1856–57 to be £607.[113] Twenty years earlier, the house had been let for £500 per annum, but a decade later it was in poor condition. As much as one year's rent had to be spent on repairs to secure a three year let.[114] In 1848 new prospective tenants, Colonel and Lady Alice Peel, offered £500 for a year's tenancy, or £450 per annum for three, knowing that a previous tenant had paid £450, and that they had already been offered Redgrave Hall, also in Suffolk, for £400.[115] 'Certainly rather sharp as a lady of business', Lady Alice also disputed Middleton's contention that five men were needed to maintain his beloved gardens. 'Lady Peel', wrote her solicitor, 'has no objection to keep the head gardener in her service but she wished him to be distinctly informed that she does not intend keeping four gardeners under him, but considers two will be sufficient and if he thinks he cannot do with that number she will find someone who can.'

The Livermere figures show that if the income from letting houses is considered in the light of the cost of building and maintaining them, and the possible returns from the alternative cultivation of parks, the decision to let rather than demolish a house was rational only if future use by the family was envisaged. Net rental income was sharply reduced by the cost of repairs and the replacement of furniture. Rental income was a contribution to unavoidable costs, not a return on investment. For a £10,000 house, the net return would have needed to be some £400–500 per annum. If income maximisation had been Sir William Middleton's aim, pulling the house down and ploughing up the park would appear to have been his best course of action. That he chose to let the house, as did most owners of houses who were not living in them, indicates a strong reluctance to sweep away a potent symbol of landed status and, where owners had gone elsewhere to restore their fortunes, faith that the move was just a temporary one. Of course country houses were built with a variety of reasons in mind – dynastic or political ambition, status and emulation, a passion for architecture and a love of collecting, a sense of duty – but financial return was not amongst them.

PLATE 132.   Hill Court, Gloucestershire. Sir Francis Fust's scheme, perhaps in his own hand, for a new house to be called 'Paradise' (*c.* 1730).

9

Afterword

In 1728 Sir Francis Fust, the fifth Baronet, succeeded to the family's Gloucestershire estate, centred on the eponymous village of Hill. He dreamt of building a vast baroque palace to command a spectacular prospect to the west, embracing the Vale of Berkeley and the River Severn, and stretching to the hills of the Forest of Dean and distant Wales. His creation was to be called 'Paradise' (Plate 132).[1] It remained a fantasy, for even his family line was insecure. In the trough of the late Stuart demographic crisis, Sir Francis's father had married four times. The resulting two sons inherited in turn, but Sir Francis's only surviving son died in 1779 without producing an heir. With him the Fust line died out. The house to have been replaced by 'Paradise' was in ruins by 1807 and demolished in 1853. Many other landowners nurtured similar visions, often realising them in the two centuries covered here. Sir Francis's thwarted ambition, and the ultimate fate of his family and its seat, is a reminder that the building of the English country house was not, as modern myth would have it, an uninterrupted and painless progression in the creation of that rural arcadia, now forming the principal prop of our national heritage. Its evolution has been a very personal and calculated response to a constantly changing set of political, social and economic factors.

The character of both builders and their houses was always diverse. They ranged from the great territorial magnates to the parish squire, some of the former tracing their descent back to the Conquest and beyond, others having bought their way into large-scale landownership through the proceeds of office, a flourishing professional career or, increasingly, success in business and industry. All were united by the distinction of holding sizeable tracts of land and the advantages to be derived from it. Of course there were differences between them of rank and wealth, whether they had pretensions to figure on the national scene or operated merely within county or even parish confines. These social and economic boundaries were never precise, and were frequently crossed in practice. They were, nevertheless, evident enough to account for the great variety in the stock of English country houses, a feature historians have often neglected in their propensity to discuss the grandest examples of architectural distinction.

The ownership of land underpinned the aristocracy's national and local political power. This was at its height in the eighteenth century. Surprisingly, in an increasingly industrial economy, it was sustained until the reforms of the 1880s and beyond. Political authority was displayed in the houses they built, landowners using the discourse of architecture and planned landscape to demonstrate their ascendancy over tenant and employee alike. They built houses as the administrative centres of estates, as family homes, and as the focus of entertainment and display for relations, visitors and those friends and neighbours who formed county communities. Few estates remained unchanged over generations; debt or the failure to produce an heir brought varying amounts of land onto the market. The larger estates were the most durable and grew in size after 1660, as far-sighted landowners bought more and more land in parcels large and small. It was unusual for newcomers to break straight into the ranks of the largest landowners. Massive, growing wealth, a predilection to borrow, and extravagant emulative lifestyles, led to excess among a minority, but men built according to their rank and their means. They shared a common understanding in architecture, and immersed themselves in a rapidly expanding specialist literature, but it was the buoyancy of their economic circumstances which determined the scale of their building activities. A factor of ten would embrace the range of costs of all but the grandest houses, although thirty times as much might be spent on the palace of a great peer in comparison with the cut-price villa of a parish squire. Landowners shared the increasing prosperity of agriculture dating from as early as the 1690s. Yet, paradoxically, building a country house, the very symbol of landed authority, was not easily afforded from rental income alone. Contemporary advice that not more than one-and-a-half times or possibly twice the annual rental should be spent on building was usually ignored. The deployment of five times an estate's annual income was indeed not uncommon. In fact, there is no correlation between building activity, the general level of rents and the yields available from alternative investments. The value of a house was not viewed primarily in economic terms. It might, in adverse circumstances, be rented out, but generally owners wrote it off as an item of exceptional consumption, possessing, however, considerable social and political benefits.

The decision to build was a personal one, influenced by several factors. Estate owners, as tenants-for-life bound by strict settlements, were often land-rich but cash-poor. Living to the limit of, or beyond, their incomes, making provision for their families, investing in estate improvement, and servicing loans, their ability to indulge in house-building depended upon an additional boost – marriage, inheritance, the proceeds of office, or access to non-landed sources of income in the form of mineral rights or urban rents. Only a minority of heads of landed families, perhaps one in ten, ever built a completely new house in the two centuries after 1660. The rate of expenditure might be controlled by building slowly out of rents – indeed some houses were never completed to their original plan – but the usual strategy was to remodel and extend existing houses to meet a family's needs and reflect contemporary notions about consumption, social change and architectural style. This was a continuous process. Radical alterations were made without qualms. Additional floors were added as family size grew; houses sprouted wings of increasingly specialised domestic offices; a Victorian ballroom or *porte-cochère* might be bolted on to a regular, classical facade. Lesser landowners built more modestly and often later. About one-third of the seats of even the great landowners in the 1870s had not been completely rebuilt since the Restoration.[2] The survival rate of early houses on smaller estates, although more difficult to quantify, is likely to have been higher.

Epitomised by the experience of the Grand Tour, architecture inspired by the classical world was at the heart of the gentleman's education throughout the eighteenth century. In the surge of country house building, peaking in the 1720s and again in the 1750s, Italian idioms were translated for use in the English landscape, itself transformed into three-dimensional versions of the *Campagna* idealised in the eagerly collected paintings of Nicholas Poussin, Claude Lorrain and a host of lesser artists. The excitement of the new, and the participation of gentlemen-architects in the design process, before the emergence of the profes-sional architect, stimulated the desire to build. New building was, however, spread unevenly in time and across the regions. Different conjunctions of circumstances, not only variations in the existing stock of houses and the prosperity of potential builders but also in the examples set by the leaders of society, meant that the chronology of building could be quite different even in neighbouring counties. The rate of agricultural improvement was also not uniform across the country, and new industrial development tended to be concentrated in the Midlands and the north. A second significant peak in building activity from the 1770s to 1790s, curtailed by the French wars, presaged the end of the dominance of building by established landowners. As the nineteenth century progressed, the activity of 'new' men increased, with eventually the emphasis shifting from the country house as the centre of an agricultural estate, to a 'house in the country', which was primarily a recreational retreat, sometimes surrounded by no more than a few score acres.

The emerging professional architect dominated architectural design from the second half of the eighteenth century but it was the mid nineteenth century before significant changes in building technology and organisation had much impact on country house building. The cost of houses had always been difficult to control. The management of large gangs of local building workers, supplemented by specialist craftsmen often recruited from the metropolis at advanced rates of pay, and the organisation of the supply of materials, estate-derived and otherwise, taxed all but the most able clerks of the works. Owners often changed their minds and modified their original plans. Estimates, of doubtful validity anyway, were therefore frequently exceeded. The cost of decoration, furnishing and alteration, together with the landscaping of the house's setting, added to expenditure. Building employment was casual and unpredictable, but country house projects nevertheless made a substantial contribution to rural economies, typically returning as much as three-quarters of spending on them into the surrounding district. Only in the Victorian period did the general contractor, working to a fixed price calculated with the aid of precise specifications and costed bills of quantities, assume an important role in country house building.

The nature of the evidence about the costs of country house building is unlikely ever to produce precise totals or indices. An indication of total spending can nevertheless be derived from an empirical relationship between house size and cost, based on the most reliable of sources, surviving building accounts. An estimated £3,800,000 was spent in England on new houses and major alterations between 1770 and 1800, not only active years for house building but also ones which, for example, witnessed a dramatic increase in the construction of canals, and of mill buildings to accommodate the new cotton-spinning machinery. The sum expended on country house building is impressive compared with the £2,500,000 fixed capital invested in spinning mills in these years. The figure does not disclose the whole amount, because houses were also built on estates smaller than those we have considered. Nor is the sum inclusive. The cost of furnishings has not been taken into account, nor spending on gardens and parks. The order of magnitude of the flow of money into house building, and hence the importance of the boost to the rural economy, is nonetheless very apparent in these years, as indeed it was throughout the two centuries after 1660.

This boost to employment in the countryside had two further effects. First, upon consumption more generally. Post-Restoration society has been represented as one hooked on conspicuous spending, an addiction fuelled by the growing wealth of the upper and middling ranks of society, by the concept of 'politeness' with its constant emphasis upon public social display, and by a fast-growing literature of printed books and newspapers. Nowhere was conspicuous consumption taken further to extremes than in the building and furnishing of the country house. It became a prime cultural focus for the lesser gentry and the expanding, aspiring, commercial and professional classes. As the means of transport improved, they visited country houses in droves to look, to envy – and to copy. When they were in London, in Bath, and in every major provincial centre, they eagerly acquired cut-price versions of what they had seen. This provided a wonderful fillip for shopkeepers, struggling artists, furniture makers and skilled workers of every description. Secondly, country house building sustained the superb craft culture that remained as much a feature of the English economy as the progress of agricultural improvement, or as the slow advance to machine production brought about by industrialisation.

Increasingly as the nineteenth century went on, new men built country houses as retreats from business, often building in the fashionable nationalistic styles of architecture, Gothic or Jacobethan. They were centres for entertaining, recreation and sport, with the attached land as an agricultural enterprise of lesser importance. Established conventions about the relationship between the size and cost of a house, the status of its owner and the value of his estate, were discarded. Large houses were built on small estates. The edge-of-town villa was of course nothing new. Daniel Defoe enthused about its profusion on every side of London in the 1720s; Sir John Clerk of Penicuick, down from Midlothian in the same decade, was keen to see all the key Palladian examples.[3] Territorial magnates, active in national politics and court circles, had always maintained bolt-holes a few miles out of London, where they could relax from the cares of public business. One such house, Cliveden, bought for £30,000 in 1849 by the second Duke of Sutherland as a Thames-side retreat from London for his incredibly extravagant wife, symbolises, on a grand scale, the nineteenth-century 'house in the country' (Plate 133).[4] The Sutherlands, with well over one million acres in England and Scotland, and an industrial fortune to boot, were fabulously wealthy. They came to a house

PLATE 133.   Cliveden House, Buckinghamshire (Sir Charles Barry, 1851). The house and parterre *c.* 1860.

which had been rebuilt to William Burn's designs in the 1820s, only to lose the main part of the house to fire. A showy Italianate villa designed by Sir Charles Barry was then raised on the old foundations. Around the house were created 250 acres of formal and wild gardens: 'The very name of Cliveden', wrote the Sutherland's youngest son in 1884, 'recalls the hawthorn and the may, the fields in June, the carpets of primroses and violets, the scent of the cowslips and the thyme, the hum of bees, and the music of the feathered choristers in the woods.'[5] In the building of Cliveden, and the landscaping of its grounds, the Sutherlands created a haven of beauty and quiet which entranced visitors. As Lady Frederick Cavendish, a guest in the summer of 1863, wrote: 'When one lives in Paradise, how hard it must be to ascend in heart and mind to Heaven.'[6]

The 'New Domesday Book' of the 1870s, on which we have drawn to identify our house builders, was a by-product of agitation, the so-called Land Question, about the political and social influence of large-scale landownership.[7] Its findings were meant to test the assertions of the Radicals that the great owners enjoyed a 'practical monopoly of land'. Supposedly this concentration impoverished rural industry, made tenant farmers servilely dependant, held back improvement in the condition of agricultural labourer, and led to the extinction of the small landowner. The survey revealed the great landowners at their apogee, a mere 710 individuals owning a quarter of the area of England and Wales, and enjoying one-seventh of the nation's landed rentals. We have described house building in their golden age, from the Restoration to the 1870s, the eve of the decline in their political power, social status and economic viability. The agricultural prosperity of the mid Victorian period ended with acute depression in the late 1870s. This lasted, with only modest recovery after 1900, until the Great War, and then recurred, with an intensified severity, in the interwar years. It was this prolonged recession which fractured the economic foundations of the landed estate, especially those with arable farms dependent upon the price of cereals, and hit particularly hard those smaller landowners with few alternative sources of income besides their rentals. Debt which had been carried for decades was no longer easily serviced. Land lost its attraction as a secure form of holding wealth. The gentle ebbing of political power from the aristocracy earlier in the century became an irrevocable flood with the Third Reform Act of 1884–85, the reform of local government a few years later, and the emasculation of the House of Lords in 1911.

An enforced flight from the landed estate began. It continued for seventy years. Estates, or large parts of them, came onto the market at low prices. An unprecedented turnover in the ownership of land was set in motion. Country houses, once the greatest joy of their owners, became burdensome. They were let, shut up and increasingly, especially during the late 1940s and 1950s, demolished (Plate 134). It is a process, not novel as John Byng attested in the 1790s, which has now continued for over a century.[8]

Yet, 'country houses' were still being built in the twentieth century. Indeed, E. Guy Dawber, a future President of the Royal Institute of British Architects, observed in 1908 that 'probably more country houses are being built and more money and thought expended on them, than perhaps at any time since the days of the Stuarts'.[9] When Clive Aslet wrote about 'the last country houses constructed in Britain' in the period 1890 to 1939, he argued that they were not simply houses in the country, adding the crucial qualification that 'they to some degree functioned – or gave the illusion that they functioned' as the centres of landed estates.

PLATE 134.   Belhus, Essex. A Tudor house remodelled (1745–60) by Thomas Barrett-Leonard later Lord Dacre, seen here shortly before its demolition in 1956.

In fact, most were built, as have been those since the 1950s, to replace existing houses unsuited to the needs of their owners in the twentieth century.[10] The *raison d'être* of the country house had changed. Those newly created after the 1890s may well have created an illusion but it was just that, a dream of a bygone age. The country house that had been defined by the social and political position of the greater landowners from the Restoration to the end of the nineteenth century, with its armies of servants and scores of tenants, only survived fitfully through the twentieth century. In different degrees, depending upon the wealth of owners, a way of life gradually collapsed. Paradise, as Lady Frederick Cavendish encountered it at Cliveden in the 1860s, created across two centuries by the aspirations and prosperity of the English landed classes, was lost.

APPENDIX

The Chronology of Country House Building

Several authors have used Pevsner's monumental *Buildings of England* series as a basis for establishing the chronology of country house building.[1] Michael Flinn, in his discussion of the origins of the industrial revolution, observed that the chronology of trends in investment in country house building may have some relevance for the freeing of capital for more productive uses. Although conceding that the evidence was 'far too shaky to serve as a basis for working generalisations', he employed Pevsner as a starting point for a rough approximation.[2] Using the surveys for Durham, Hertfordshire, Middlesex, Northumberland, Nottingham-shire and Suffolk, he concluded that there were significant regional variations in building chronologies, and that there were two major periods of building activity: the 1690s to 1730s and the 1790s to 1830s. There was some revival in the third quarter of the eighteenth century but relatively little building after the 1830s. Jules Lubbock looked at a different group of counties: Dorset, Kent, Wiltshire and Northamptonshire.[3] He counted newly or substantially rebuilt manor and country houses from 1500 to 1930, datable to a decade or quarter century. He found a building peak between 1580 and 1620, but this level of activity was not reached again until a century later, between 1690 and 1710, and never matched in later years.

A more systematic quantitative national evaluation of English country houses and large landownership by Heather Clemenson was founded on Bateman's analysis of the 'New Domesday'.[4] She took a sample of 500 estates, representing the principal examples from each county in England, so that the balance of great landowner and greater gentry estates per county and for England as a whole, was a microcosm of the 1880 picture. A revival in the building of new houses in the 1680s and 1690s was apparent, with the rate continuing to increase in the early decades of the eighteenth century. After a fall in mid century, renewed activity came with rising economic prosperity. There was a concentration of eighteenth-century building in north-western and south-eastern counties. The relative isolation and insecurity of the most northerly English counties until the

Act of Union (1707) led to the survival of substantial, part-defensive pre-1500 structures, with relatively less Tudor and Elizabethan new building than further south. Many new houses were built in the nineteenth century (under-represented in studies based upon Pevsner), but in the sample group it was the number of alterations rather than new builds that stood out, for the completely new houses of the nineteenth century were largely for a different group of clients.

The differences between counties have been highlighted by Lawrence and Jeanne Fawtier Stone's detailed study of landed elites in Hertfordshire, North-amptonshire and Northumberland, representing three different situations: proximity to London; the rural heart of England, and the remote northern border.[5] The criterion for membership of their elite was the ownership of a house with at least 5000 square feet of *living* space.[6] Selecting subjects according to the size of their houses and not the size of their estates may not provide a representative picture of building by landowners as a whole. Nevertheless, the work is a valuable examination of the issues underlying the construction of houses on landed estates, and reveals the differences between counties in building patterns.[7]

The stock of early houses varied in the three counties. Northamptonshire had a reasonable complement of solidly built stone houses in the mid sixteenth century, whereas there were few equivalent country houses in Hertfordshire. Much of the county was under monastic control, released only at the Dissolution of the Monasteries. The picture was again very different on the northern border in Northumberland, still turbulent in the sixteenth century. There the main growth in country house building began in the second half of the seventeenth century. The authors were aware of the problem of distingushing between the building of a new house and the radical remodelling of an old one, and deciding what is a significant alteration introduces further subjectivity. They chose not to count service wings in their study, thus excluding some building activity, especially the often gross extension of domestic offices in the nineteenth century. Notwith-standing these reservations, some interesting differences between counties emerged. Building in Hertfordshire picked up during the Interregnum, perhaps through the activities of London merchants, and was then sluggish in the late seventeenth and early eighteenth centuries. There was renewed bustle through to the 1730s, in the period of major activity noted by Summerson. The 1740s and 1750s saw another low, but building boomed from 1760 to 1820, much of it undertaken by 'new' men. A slump from the 1820s to 1840s was followed by a sharp recovery.

Northamptonshire was quite different. A building boom of 1570 to 1610 had left the squirearchy overextended and overhoused. Activity increased after 1660, lasting until 1730 when it petered out. To explain the architectural lethargy of the Northamptonshire gentry from 1740 to 1860, the Stones castigated them in such general terms their censure might have applied universally to all county landed communities: it was 'for the most part a hidebound, dull, inward-turned, and stuffy society, obsessed with horses, dogs, and hunting'. Building was resumed only in the two decades after 1860.[8] In Northumberland building took off after agricultural improvement gathered pace from the 1730s. The county, like Hertfordshire, enjoyed a building boom during the Napoleonic wars. But except near London, the Victorian building boom was perceived to be something of a myth. However, the elite criteria, and choice of counties, omitted many eighteenth- and nineteenth-century *arrivistes* who bought estates and built new houses. Nevertheless, in seeking an explanation for the pattern of building the authors reasonably concluded: 'Major trends in the profits to be derived from land are all obviously important, but money flowed into the countryside from so many other sources, such as office, the professions, banking, war, marriage, and overseas trade, that there is no clear correlation between building and rents. Indeed this is hardly to be expected, since the decision to build is so highly personal a matter, dependent upon so many considerations.'[9]

The apparent absence of country house building in much of the nineteenth century has been thoroughly undermined by Mark Girouard's analysis of the building dates of no fewer than 500 country houses built between 1835 and 1889.[10] The number in five-year batches climbed steadily to a peak in 1870–74, with only a slight dip in 1840–44, reflecting the acute recession of 1837–42. After 1875, with mounting agricultural depression, numbers fell precipitously to their lowest point in 1885–89. Within the total of builders, those belonging to the 'new' families – that is who had not owned a country house for at least two generations – revealed a steady growth, starting well below those drawn from the 'old' families, overtaking them in 1860–64, and climbing away from them to their peak in 1870–74. Members of the 'old' families building also peaked in 1870–74, but the pattern of their participation was more variable. 'Old' builders outnumbered the 'new' three-to-one in 1835–40, whereas by 1885–89 the positions had been reversed and there were twice as many new builders as old. Jill Franklin's study of the gentleman's house of this period reveals the same pattern.[11] From 1835 to 1854 just over half of the new houses were built by 'old' families (in the study, those who had owned an estate for at least three generations). In a great surge of building activity between 1855 and 1874, the share of the 'old' families was down to one-third. The agricultural depression then took its toll, and from 1875 to 1894, 'old' families accounted for less than one-quarter of building activity. When they did build it was generally with non-landed income. The shift to 'new' men, as well as a decline in the reliance upon agricultural rents, is evidenced by the fall in the proportion of builders who owned at least 2000 acres. It collapsed from three-quarters in 1835–54, to just over one-half in 1855–74, and then less than one-third in 1875–94. By the turn of the century the 'house in the country' had triumphed over the country seat. From 1895 to 1914, the builders of two-thirds of the new houses in the survey possessed fewer than 150 acres of land.

Notes

Notes to Chapter 1: The English Country House

1. V. Sackville-West, *English Country Houses* (London, 1944), pp. 7–8, 47.

2. In the century after 1880, 50 per cent of the houses in Heather Clemenson's sample of landed estates were demolished. Heather A. Clemenson, *English Country Houses and Landed Estates* (London, 1982), pp. 136, 138, 144, 148.

3. For example, the late Sir John Summerson, Mark Girouard, Jill Franklin and Giles Worsley.

4. See especially, G. E. Mingay, *English Landed Society in the Eighteenth Century* (London, 1963); F. M. L. Thompson, *English Landed Society in the Nineteenth Century* (London, 1973); J. V. Beckett, *The Aristocracy in England, 1660–1914* (Oxford, 1986); L. and J. C. F. Stone, *An Open Elite? England, 1540–1880* (Oxford, 1984); and John Habakkuk, *Marriage, Debt and the Estates System: English Landownership, 1650–1950* (Oxford, 1994).

5. J. Summerson, 'The Classical Country House in Eighteenth-Century England', *Journal of the Royal Society of Arts*, 107 (1959), pp. 539–40. He might have looked more closely at those financiers linked to the South Sea Company. For their frenzied acquisition of landed estates and building activities around 1720 see John Habakkuk, *Marriage, Debt and the Estates System*, especially pp. 429–30.

6. M. W. Flinn, *The Origins of the Industrial Revolution* (London, 1966), pp. 47–48.

7. Clemenson in *English Country Houses* suggests four broad periods of activity for the construction of the houses of the greater gentry she considers in her sample, although she makes no attempt to calculate the extent of investment. Beckett, *The Aristocracy*, pp. 325–36, provides a list of the costs of around a score of the biggest houses, such as Blenheim and Wentworth Woodhouse, warning about the typicality. Jill Franklin, *The Gentleman's County House and its Plan, 1835–1914* (London, 1981), provides estimates of the cost of about sixty of the most stylish and expensive country houses built in the Victorian period.

8. Geoffrey Beard, *Decorative Plaster-Work in Great Britain* (London, 1975), p. 5.

9. The research project was supported by a grant from the Economic and Social Research Council, reference R000221311, 'The Economic History of Country House Building in England, 1660–1870'. The original proposal also included Hertfordshire and Lancashire but these counties had to be dropped because of funding constraints.

10. *The Shorter Oxford English Dictionary*, i (Oxford, 1959), p. 232.

11. John Bateman, *The Great Landowners of Great Britain and Ireland* (London, 1883; reprinted Leicester, 1971), p. 507; John Kenworthy-Browne, Peter Reid, Michael Sayer and David Watkin, *Burke's and Savills Guide to Country Houses*, iii, *East Anglia* (London, 1981); Roy Strong, Marcus Binney and John Harris, *The Destruction of the Country House, 1875–1975* (London, 1974), p. 189.

12. For example W. White, *History, Gazetteer, and Directory of Norfolk* (Sheffield, 1845), listing 'Seats

of the Nobility, Gentry and Clergy of Norfolk' (pp. 40–48), is a poor guide to the number of country houses, since it includes so many rectories and houses of the urban magistracy. E. Walford, *The County Families of the United Kingdom* (London, 1887), includes 327 'county families' for Norfolk. Besides a few errors, the list includes clerical patrons of livings who were clearly not always landed gentry, and all titled owners irrespective of whether or not they owned an appreciable amount of land.

13. County elites have been defined by the size of their houses by the Stones in *An Open Elite?* (see below, Appendix, pp. 362). But to select a population of country houses according to size would be inappropriate for our study. The qualifying size would have to reflect the development of country house design and the tendency for the typical example to become larger over time. However, specifying a limit to reject, say, the larger suburban villas, would lead to the exclusion of landowners who lived in small houses, because they had not built anew or added significantly to old houses. Such individuals are as relevant to our study as those who did build. Conversely, setting the qualification size too low would embrace house-owners who did not have a significant rural presence, compromising our aim to study the house-building activity of the landowning class.

14. Thompson, *English Landed Society*, especially pp. 109–18.

15. BPP 1874, lxxii, Return of Owners of Land, 1872–73 (England and Scotland); and Bateman, *Great Landowners*.

16. Habakkuk, *Marriage, Debt and the Estates System*, p. 572.

17. Ibid, p. 560. See also the entry by Richard Wilson in the forthcoming *New Dictionary of National Biography*.

18. J. A. Houseman, *A Topographical Description of . . . Part of the West Riding of Yorkshire* (Carlisle, 1800), p. 186. For descriptions of villas around Bristol, see A. Gomme, M. Jenner and B. Little, *Bristol: An Architectural History* (London, 1979), pp. 150–71; and for Wakefield, Tate Wilkinson, *The Wandering Patentee* (York, 1795), i, p. 200.

19. T. M. Williamson, 'The Archaeology of the Landscape Park: Garden Design in Norfolk, England, *c.* 1680–1840', *British Archaeological Reports*, 268 (Oxford, 1998), pp. 98, 157–58.

20. C. Morris (ed.), *The Journeys of Celia Fiennes* (London, 1947); G. D. H. Cole (ed.), *Daniel Defoe, A Tour Thro' the Whole Island of Great Britain* (London, 1927), i, p. 168, also pp. 164–70; and M. Beeton and E. B. Chancellor (eds), *A Tour Thro' London about the Year 1725* (London, 1969), pp. 81–88.

21. See the major contributions of Mingay, *English Landed Society*; Beckett, *The Aristocracy*; Stone and Stone, *An Open Elite?*; Habakkuk, *Marriage, Debt and the Estates System*; and Thompson, *English Landed Society*.

Notes to Chapter 2: The Builders of the Country House

1. W. S. Lewis (ed.), *The Yale Edition of Horace Walpole's Correspondence*, ix: W. S. Lewis and R. S. Brown junior (eds), *Horace Walpole's Correspondence with George Montagu*, i (New Haven, 1941), pp. 184–85.

2. Gervas Huxley, *Victorian Duke* (London, 1967); Mark Girouard, *The Victorian Country House* (New Haven and London, 1979), pp. 2–4; John Bateman, *The Great Landowners of Great Britain and Ireland* (London, 1883; reprinted Leicester, 1971), p. 472.

3. Richard Wilson and Alan Mackley, 'Founding a Landed Dynasty, Building a Country House:

The Rolfes of Heacham in the Eighteenth Century', in *Counties and Communities: Essays on East Anglian History Presented to Hassell Smith* (Norwich, 1996), pp. 307–25. See below pp. 77–79, 107–8, 340–43.

4. G. S. Holmes, 'Gregory King and the Social Structure of Pre-Industrial England', *Transactions of the Royal Historical Society*, fifth series, 27 (1977), pp. 41–68. See also P. Lindert and J. G. Williamson, 'Revising England's Social Tables, 1688–1812', *Explorations in Economic History*, 18 (1982), pp. 385–408.

5. F. M. L. Thompson, 'The Social Distribution of Landed Property in England since the Sixteenth Century', *Economic History Review*, second series, 19 (1966), pp. 505–17.

6. J. V. Beckett, *The Aristocracy in England, 1660–1914* (Oxford, 1986), pp. 33–38.

7. G. E. Mingay, *English Landed Society in the Eighteenth Century* (London, 1963), pp. 20–23.

8. Beckett, *The Aristocracy*, pp. 26–31. Technically, it was the English peerage to 1707, of Great Britain from 1707 to 1801, and of the United Kingdom after 1801. Scottish and Irish peers respectively elected sixteen and twenty-eight of their number to the Lords for each parliamentary session.

9. H. A. Doubleday, the Hon. Vicary Gibbs, Lord Howard de Walden, R. S. Lea and G. H. White (eds), *The Complete Peerage*, 13 vols (London, 1910–40).

10. This paragraph is based upon John Cannon, *Aristocratic Century: The Peerage of Eighteenth-Century England* (Cambridge, 1984).

11. Beckett, *The Aristocracy*, map 1.

12. Those peers owning large estates in Norfolk were Yarmouth (earls of first creation, extinct 1732); Townshend (barony 1661; viscountcy 1682; marquessate 1783); Albemarle (earldom 1696; only acquired their Norfolk seat, Quidenham, in 1762); Walpole (two baronies, Walpole of Walpole 1723; Walpole of Wolterton 1742; Earl of Orford, first creation, 1742); Buckinghamshire (barony 1728; earldom 1746); Walsingham (barony 1780); Suffield (barony 1786); Wodehouse (barony 1797; earldom of Kimberley 1866); Leicester (earldom, first creation 1744; second creation, 1837); the ancient barony of Hastings only passed to the Astleys of Melton Constable in 1841.

13. Mark Girouard, *Life in the English Country House* (New Haven and London, 1978), p. 182.

14. Cannon, *Aristocratic Century*, p. 177.

15. Maud, Lady Leconfield and John Gore (eds), *Three Howard Sisters: Selections from the Writings of Lady Caroline Lascelles, Lady Dover and Countess Gower, 1825 to 1833* (London, 1955), p. 242.

16. R. G. Wilson, *Gentlemen Merchants: The Merchant Community in Leeds, 1700–1830* (Manchester, 1971), pp. 154, 222–23; A. C. Edwards, *The Account Books of Benjamin Mildmay, Earl Fitzwalter* (London, 1977), p. 29.

17. J. H. Plumb, *The Pursuit of Happiness: A View of Life in Georgian England* (New Haven, 1977), p. 3.

18. Mingay, *English Landed Society*, pp. 21, 26.

19. Cannon, *Aristocratic Century*, p. 126.

20. Mingay, *English Landed Society*, p. 20.

21. This section is based upon Bateman, *Great Landowners*. Some peers (Howard de Walden and Cadogan) whose landed estates were below the Bateman's 2000 acres, £2000 margin, nevertheless had large incomes from their London estates. In the example of Hawke, the estates had passed to the earldom of Rosse through the female line.

22. Linda Colley, *Britons: Forging the Nation, 1707–1837* (London, 1994), pp. 147–93.

23. John Habakkuk, *Marriage, Debt and the Estates System: English Landownership, 1650–1950* (Oxford, 1994).

24. For a succinct discussion of the debate about strict marriage settlements and mortgages, see Cannon, *Aristocratic Century*, pp. 131–35. Controversy surrounding the debate was at its height in the reception of Stone and Stone, *An Open Elite?*. See especially Eileen Spring and David Spring, 'The English Landed Elite, 1540–1879: A Review', *Albion*, 17 (1985), pp. 149–66 (and Lawrence Stone's 'Spring Back', pp. 167–80); and Eileen Spring, *Law, Land and Family: Aristocratic Inheritance in England, 1300–1800* (Chapel Hill, North Carolina, 1993).

25. F. M. L. Thompson, *English Landed Society in the Nineteenth Century* (London, 1973), pp. 72–73; Colley, *Britons*, pp. 153–54; Bateman, *Great Landowners*, p. 375; *Complete Peerage*, vi (1926), p. 49. Beckett, *The Aristocracy*, pp. 206–86, provides the most detailed discussion of the aristocracy's financial rewards from industry, transport and urban development.

26. Habakkuk, *Marriage, Debt and the Estates System*, p. 225.

27. *Claydon House* (The National Trust, 1986); *Complete Peerage* (1959) v; Sir Lewis Namier and John Brooke, *The History of Parliament: The House of Commons, 1754–90*, iii (London, 1964), pp. 580–82, and information from Dr John Broad of the University of North London.

28. Habakkuk, *Marriage, Debts and the Estates System*, pp. 338–39.

29. Ibid., pp. 334–39.

30. Andrew Moore, *Houghton Hall: The Prime Minister, the Empress and the Heritage*, Norfolk Museums Service (Norwich, 1996), pp. 63–64.

31. R. A. Kelch, *A Duke Without Money* (London, 1974).

32. Habakkuk, *Marriage, Debt and the Estates System*, p. 292.

33. David Cannadine, 'The Landowner as Millionaire: The Finances of the Dukes of Devonshire', *Agricultural History Review*, 25 (1977), pp. 77–97. In the 1840s Earl Fitzwilliam had a gross income of £150,000 per annum, but his debts of £800,000 swallowed up interest payments of £45,000. J. T. Ward, 'The Earls Fitzwilliam and the Wentworth Woodhouse Estate in the Nineteenth Century', *Yorkshire Bulletin of Economic and Social Research*, 12 (1960), p. 22.

34. Thompson, *Landed Society*, p. 286; idem, 'The End of a Great Estate', *Economic History Review*, second series, 8 (1955), pp. 36–52.

35. Habakkuk, *Marriage, Debt and the Estates System*, p. 355.

36. Bateman *Great Landowners*, p. 515; Thompson, *English Landed Society*, pp. 109–50, discusses the figures in detail.

37. Bateman, *Great Landowners*, p. 43 (Colonel Tomline thought the figures 'very wrong'); Burke's *Landed Gentry* (London, 1937), Pretyman of Orwell Park and Riby Grove; John Kenworthy-Browne, Peter Reid, Michael Sayer and David Watkin, *Burke's and Savills Guide to Country Houses*, iii, *East Anglia* (London, 1981), p. 255.

38. Privately owned, day book of Davy Durrant, 1738–55; N. Pevsner and B. Wilson, *The Buildings of England: Norfolk*, i (London, 1997), p. 659.

39. Jane Austen, *Persuasion* (Nelson Classics, n.d.), pp. 1–2; E. J. Climenson (ed.), *Passages from the Diaries of Mrs Philip Lybbe Powys of Hardwick House, Oxon., AD 1756 to 1808* (London, 1899), p. 134.

40. Figures and the best general discussion appear in Beckett, *The Aristocracy*, pp. 31–47, 484–85, 489–91.

41. Austen, *Persuasion*, p. 1; Peter Roebuck, *Yorkshire Baronets, 1640–1760: Families, Estates and Fortunes* (Oxford 1980), p. 31.

42. Howard Colvin, *A Biographical Dictionary of British Architects, 1660–1840* (New Haven and London, 1995), pp. 829–31; Giles Worsley, *Classical Architecture in Britain: The Heroic Age* (New Haven and London, 1995), pp. 138–39; Roebuck, *Yorkshire Baronets*, pp. 269–70, 274–75; N. Pevsner, *The Buildings of England: Yorkshire, The North Riding* (Harmondsworth, 1966), pp. 309–10.

43. Pam Barnes, *Norfolk Landowners since 1880* (Norwich, 1993), pp. 85–87.

44. Figures compiled from Bateman, *Great Landowners*.

45. Beckett, *The Aristocracy*, p. 47.

46. *Gentleman's Magazine*, 57 (1787), pt 2, pp. 677–78 quoted in Beckett, *The Aristocracy*, p. 115.

47. Quoted in David Cannadine, *The Decline and Fall of the British Aristocracy* (New Haven and London, 1990), p. 300.

48. Beckett, *The Aristocracy*, p. 116.

49. R. A. C. Parker, *Coke of Norfolk: A Financial and Agricultural Study, 1707–1842* (Oxford, 1975), p. 24; J. Simmons, 'Georgian Somerset', in *Parish and Empire* (London, 1952), p. 63.

50. Stone and Stone, *Open Elite*.

51. R. W. Ketton-Cremer, *Norfolk Assembly* (London, 1957), p. 190.

52. Climenson, *Diaries of Mrs Philip Lybbe Powys*, p. 6.

53. J. Godber (ed.), 'The Marchioness Grey of Wrest Park', *Publications of the Bedfordshire Historical Record Society*, 47 (1958), p. 144.

54. B. Cozens-Hardy (ed.), *The Diary of Sylas Neville, 1767–1788* (London, 1950), p. 298.

55. Pevsner and Wilson, *Norfolk*, pp. 534–35.

56. N. Pevsner, *The Buildings of England: North-West and South Norfolk* (Harmondsworth, 1962), pp. 240–42.

57. Girouard, *Victorian Country House*, pp. 194–204, 402, 412; Barnes, *Norfolk Landowners*, pp. 32, 44–45; *Burke's and Savills Country Houses, East Anglia*, pp. 97, 100–1.

58. Quoted in Colvin, *Biographical Dictionary*, p. 155.

59. D. Stroud, *The Architecture of Sir John Soane* (London, 1961), pp. 29–64.

60. Colvin, *Biographical Dictionary*, pp. 317–19; Roderick O'Donnell, 'W. J. Donthorn (1799–1859): Architecture with "Great Hardness and Decision in the Edges"', *Architectural History*, 21 (1978), pp. 83–92.

61. We are grateful to Dr John Barney for information about Philip Case.

62. Account book at Honing Hall (the house was built in 1748 by Andrew Chamber, a Norwich worsted weaver). The cost of Salle Park is given in Norfolk RO, MC 65/1, 509 x 2, 'Memorandum Book 1808' (probably of Richard Paul Jodrell, 1745–1831). Building started on 11 February 1763 and the family moved in on 15 October 1765.

63. M. V. B. Riviere, 'The Revd William Gunn, BD: A Norfolk Parson on the Grand Tour', *Norfolk Archaeology*, 33 (1965), pp. 351–406.

64. H. M. Colvin and J. Newman, *Of Building: Roger North's Writings on Architecture* (Oxford, 1981), pp. 7–8. According to Huon Mallalieu, *Country Life*, 191, 11 December 1997, p. 54, Vincent inherited Fetcham Park (Surrey) in 1697, commissioned plans for a house there in 1699, but moved to Norfolk before it was completed and sold the estate in 1705. See also John Harris, *William Talman: Maverick Architect* (London, 1982), pp. 41–43.

65. HMC, Portland MSS, vi (1901), p. 65.

66. Climenson, *Diaries of Mrs Philip Lybbe Powis*, p. 20; D. Stroud, *Henry Holland: His Life and Architecture* (London. 1966), p. 57; C. Bruyn Andrews (ed.), *The Torrington Diaries: Containing the Tours through England and Wales of the Hon. John Byng (Later Fifth Viscount Torrington) between*

the Years 1781 and 1794, i (London, 1934), p. 288. Time lent enchantment. Sir Richard Colt Hoare, no mean critic, noted Wenvoe in 1803 as 'a modern castle ... a handsome and large stone building, grounds well dispersed and covered with wood'. M. W. Thompson (ed.), *The Journeys of Sir Richard Colt Hoare through Wales and England, 1793–1810* (Gloucester, 1983), p. 234.

67. Habakkuk, *Marriage, Debt and the Estates System*, pp. 383–84; Stroud, *Henry Holland*, pp. 127–31; Roger Fulford, *Samuel Whitbread, 1764–1815* (London, 1967), pp. 97–106. Christopher Hussey, *English Country Houses: Late Georgian, 1800–1840* (London, 1958), pp. 27–40.

68. Bateman, *Great Landowners* p. 329; F. M. L. Thompson, 'Stitching it Together Again', *Economic History Review*, second series, 45 (1992), p. 373; Girouard, *Victorian Country House*, p. 407.

69. From the dust-jacket of Stone and Stone, *An Open Elite?*.

70. W. D. Rubinstein, 'New Men of Wealth and the Purchase of Land in Nineteenth-Century Britain', *Past and Present*, 92 (1981), pp. 125–47; ibid., *Men of Property* (London, 1981), passim. For a counter argument see F. M. L. Thompson, 'Life after Death: How Successful Nineteenth-Century Businessmen Disposed of their Fortunes', *Economic History Review*, second series, 43 (1990), pp. 40–61.

71. Habakkuk, *Marriage, Debt and the Estates System*, p. 534.

72. David Watkin, 'Cambridgeshire' in *Burke's and Savills Country Houses, East Anglia*, p. 1.

73. Thompson, *English Landed Society*, p. 124.

74. Habakkuk, *Marriage, Debt and the Estates System*, p. 572.

75. Humphry Repton quoted in Dorothy Stroud, *Humphry Repton* (London, 1962), p. 69.

76. Wilson, *Gentlemen Merchants*, pp. 221–23.

Notes to Chapter 3: The Inspiration of Travel

1. E. Moir, *The Discovery of Britain: The English Tourists, 1540 to 1840* (London, 1964), p. 65.

2. C. P. Moritz, *Journeys of a German in England in 1782*, ed. R. Nettel (London, 1965), p. 104.

3. Paget Toynbee (ed.), 'Horace Walpole's Journals of Visits to Country Seats, etc.', *Walpole Society*, 16 (1927–28), p. 72.

4. This paragraph is chiefly based on Charles Saumarez Smith, *The Building of Castle Howard* (London, 1990).

5. Ibid., pp. 9, 12.

6. Quoted at the beginning of George Howard's *Castle Howard Guide Book* (4th edn, Castle Howard, 1965), p. 1.

7. Saumarez Smith, *Castle Howard*, p. 155.

8. Geoffrey Webb, *The Complete Works of Sir John Vanbrugh*, iv, *The Letters* (London, 1928), p. 25.

9. Lamport (Northamptonshire) provides a good example of a house continuously remodelled, in this case by one family, the Ishams, its owners since the late sixteenth century. Lamport was built post-1568, altered post-1610–11, again in 1650 (by John Webb) and wings were added *c.* 1732 and 1741. Henry Hakewill substantially rebuilt what remained of the Tudor house in the 1820s. In the 1840s and 1850s a conservatory was built and the domestic offices altered. The house was refronted, the north wing remodelled, the roof new slated and the windows re-sashed in the early 1860s by William Burn. Northamptonshire RO, IL 3086/3279.

10. The first chapter of Mark Girouard's immensely influential survey of the social history of the country house from the middle ages to the Second World War, *Life in the English Country House* (New Haven and London, 1978), is entitled, 'The Power Houses'.

11. Lord Leicester to Matthew Brettingham the younger quoted in James Lees-Milne, *Earls of Creation* (London, 1986), p. 262.

12. See Girouard, *Life in the English Country House*, for the classic, pioneering account.

13. R. Latham and W. Matthews, *The Diary of Samuel Pepys*, 11 vols (London, 1995).

14. C. H. Collins Baker and M. I. Baker, *The Life and Circumstances of James Brydges, First Duke of Chandos* (London, 1949), pp. 175–76; R. A. Kelch, *A Duke Without Money* (London, 1974), pp. 71–72.

15. H. M. Colvin and J. Newman (eds), *Of Building: Roger North's Writings on Architecture* (Oxford, 1981), pp. 26, 62.

16. Joyce Godber (ed.), 'The Marchioness Grey of Wrest Park', *Publications of the Bedfordshire Historical Record Society*, 47 (1968), p. 162.

17. Scottish RO, GO/18/2107, Clerk of Penicuik, 'Journey to London in 1727'.

18. John Summerson, 'The Classical Country House in Eighteenth-Century England', *Journal of the Royal Society of Arts*, 107 (1958–59), pp. 539–87. On p. 577 he writes: 'In the hands of these three [Ware, Taylor and Chambers] over a period of some twenty years, the English country house underwent a fundamental change of character, based on a reconsideration of the villa and financed not by country magnates but, very largely, by moneyed men from the towns.'

19. It is not possible to estimate total numbers of servants before the 1851 Census provides full data. However, a yearly tax introduced in 1777 of one guinea (£1.05) was payable on each male servant. It included gardeners and gamekeepers (but not day labourers), as well as indoor servants. 'The List of Persons in Yorkshire who Paid the Tax on Male Servants in 1780' was published in *Yorkshire Archaeological Journal*, 14 (1896), pp. 65–80. The majority of the wealthier gentry kept between five and fifteen male servants; only four great landowners kept more than twenty. The Marquess of Rockingham at Wentworth Woodhouse, employing sixty-five, was in a class of his own. Well-to-do merchants in Leeds, Wakefield or Hull employed between two and six, although William Garforth, a York banker, kept sixteen at nearby Askham Richard. Of the Yorkshire houses for which we have accounts (see index), sixteen were employed at Harewood, ten at Cusworth and Warmsworth (the two Wrightson houses), seven at Denton, five at Hovingham, four at Sledmere and two at Eshton.

     Sir John Rous kept twenty-four servants at newly-built Henham in 1797: twelve male (paid £280 1s. a year) and twelve female (£122 18s.) on a gross income of £5638. In J. T. Cliffe, *The World of the Country House in Seventeenth-Century England* (New Haven and London, 1999), appendix 1, there are 141 examples of numbers of servants in gentry households linked to the incomes of their employers: gentry of £3000 a year and upwards; £1000-£3000; £500-£1000; and under £500 a year.

20. This paragraph is based upon E. J. Climenson (ed.), *Passages from the Diaries of Mrs Philip Lybbe Powys of Hardwick House, Oxon., AD 1756 to 1808* (London, 1899). See especially pp. 128–44, 165, 178–90, 336. Langley Park in fact had been built by the Duke of Marlborough to the designs of Stiff Leadbetter in 1755. It was also admired on its completion by Lady Pomfret and Dr Pococke. See G. Worsley, *Classical Architecture in Britain* (New Haven and London, 1995), pp. 228, 232 and 236.

21. J. Beresford (ed.), *The Diary of a Country Parson*, 5 vols (Oxford, 1924–31). The Parson Woodforde Society published *The Diary of James Woodforde (The First Six Norfolk Years, 1776–1781)*, 3 vols (1981–84) in full. See also L. H. M. Hill 'The Custances and their Family Circle', *Journal of the Parson Woodforde Society*, 3, no. 4 (1970), pp. 1–56.

22. Godber, 'Marchioness Grey', pp. 22–46; Paget Toynbee, 'Horace Walpole's Journals', p. 70.

23. For the Houghton Congress see J. H. Plumb, *Sir Robert Walpole*, ii, *The King's Minister* (London, 1960), pp. 88–89; Godber, 'Marchioness Grey', p. 25.

24. John Gore (ed.), *Creevey* (London, 1948), p. 250.

25. Roger Fulford (ed.), *The Greville Memoirs* (London, 1963), pp. 5, 13; Cambridge University Library, Buxton Papers, letter from John Buxton to Robert Buxton, 29 September 1729.

26. Lytton Strachey and Roger Fulford (eds), *The Journal of Mrs Arbuthnot*, 2 vols (London, 1950); J. W. Croker, *Correspondence and Diaries* (London, 1885). See also Gervas Huxley, *Lady Elizabeth and the Grosvenors: Life in a Whig Family, 1822–1839* (London, 1965).

27. Gore, *Creevey*, p. 229. When the Marquess of Westminster entertained the King and Queen for the day at Moor Park (Hertfordshire) in 1833, 130 people dined in the house.

28. Strachey and Fulford, *Journal of Mrs Arbuthnot*, ii, p. 42.

29. Gore, *Creevey*, p. 236; Huxley, *Lady Elizabeth and the Grosvenors*, pp. 24, 43.

30. Jill Franklin, *The Gentleman's Country House and its Plan, 1835–1914* (London, 1981), and Mark Girouard, *The Victorian Country House* (New Haven and London, 1979), provide excellent guides to the subject.

31. G. Martelli, *Man of His Time: A Life of the First Earl of Iveagh, KP, GCVO* (privately published, 1957), pp. 210–21; see also the forthcoming *New Dictionary of National Biography*, entry for Lord Iveagh by R. G. Wilson.

32. For general introduction see Brinsley Ford, 'The Grand Tour', *Apollo*, 114 (December 1981), pp. 390–400; Christopher Hibbert, *The Grand Tour* (London, 1987); and Jeremy Black, *The British and the Grand Tour* (London, 1985). See also John Stoye, *English Travellers Abroad, 1604–1667* (rev. edn, New Haven and London, 1989); and P. F. Kirby, *The Grand Tour in Italy, 1700–1800* (New York, 1952). Andrew Moore, *Norfolk and the Grand Tour* (Norwich, 1985), provides an excellent local study.

33. A typical view is that expressed by Humphrey Prideaux, Dean of Norwich, about the twenty-five-year-old Ashe Windham of Felbrigg in 1699, 'a young gentleman of a very considerable estate in this countrey, but, haveing had an Italian education, is all over Italiz'd, that is, an Italian as to religion, I mean a down right atheist; an Italian in politics, that is a Commonwealths man; and an Italian I doubt in his moralls, for he cannot be persuaded to marry'. Quoted in R. W. Ketton-Cremer, *Felbrigg: The Story of a House* (London, 1962), pp. 81–82. See also Hibbert, *Grand Tour*, pp. 235–38.

34. This paragraph is based upon Lionel Cust, *History of the Society of Dilettanti* (2nd edn, London, 1914).

35. Quoted ibid., p. 36.

36. James Stuart and Nicholas Revett, *The Antiquities of Athens* (London, 1762). Further volumes by various editors were published in 1789, 1795, 1816, 1830; Nicholas Revett, *The Antiquities of Ionia* (2 vols, London, 1769–97). A third volume appeared in 1840.

37. For the building of Holkham and the first Earl of Leicester, see Lees-Milne *Earls of Creation*, pp. 219–63; Moore, *Norfolk and the Grand Tour*, pp. 32–39, 115–22; R. A. L. Parker, *Coke of Norfolk: A Financial and Agricultural Study, 1707–1842* (Oxford, 1975), pp. 1–65; C. W. Jones, *Chief Justice Coke: His Family and Descendants of Holkham* (London, 1929); Leo Schmidt, 'Holkham Hall, Norfolk', *Country Life*, 167, 24 January, 31 January, 7 February, 14 February, 1980, pp. 214–17, 298–301, 359–62, 427–31; idem, *Thomas Coke, 1st Earl of Leicester: An Eighteenth-Century Amateur Architect* (Holkham, 1980). See below pp. 306–8. A very similar

study of the impact of the Grand Tour on a country house and its collection could have been written about Leicester's neighbour and friend, the celebrated virtuoso Sir Andrew Fountaine of Narford (1676–1753). See Moore, *Norfolk and the Grand Tour*, pp. 26–31, 93–113.

38. For Felbrigg and William Windham, see Ketton-Cremer, *Felbrigg*, pp. 112–58; idem, *County Neighbourhood* (London, 1951); John Maddison, *Felbrigg Hall* (National Trust, 1995); Moore, *Norfolk and the Grand Tour*, pp. 40–47, 122–32; Peter Leach, *James Paine* (London, 1988), passim; Merlin Waterson, 'The Shipwright Squire?', *Country Life*, 180, 7 August, 18 September 1986, pp. 438–40, 904–6; John Cornforth, 'Felbrigg Hall, Norfolk', *Country Life*, 184, 5 April, 12 April 1990, pp. 138–41, 102–5.

39. Quoted in Ketton-Cremer, *Felbrigg*, p. 128. Roger North in *Of Building*, ed. Colvin and Newman, pp. 56, 132, was critical of the addition of William Samwell's west wing completed in 1686: 'the whole so different from the rest of the house that I am not, tho the generality are, pleased with it'.

40. Quoted in Maddison, *Felbrigg Hall*, p. 26.

41. This section is based upon R. G. Wilson and A. L. Mackley, 'Founding a Landed Dynasty, Building the Country House: The Rolfes of Heacham in the Eighteenth Century', in C. Rawcliffe, R. Virgoe and R. G. Wilson (eds), *Counties and Communities: Essays on East Anglian History* (Norwich, 1996), pp. 307–28. See also R. T. and A. Gunther, *Rolfe Family Records*, ii (London, 1914); and V. Berry, *The Rolfe Papers: The Chronicle of a Norfolk Family, 1559–1908* (Norwich, 1979).

42. Peter Mandler, *The Fall and Rise of the Stately Home* (New Haven and London, 1997), pp. 21–70.

43. See the preface to William Mavor, *The British Tourists; or Traveller's Pocket Companion through England, Wales, Scotland and Ireland*, 6 vols (London, 1798). Authors summarised ranged from Samuel Johnson and Arthur Young to 'a Gentleman of the University of Oxford'.

44. Climenson, *Diaries of Mrs Philip Lybbe Powys*, p. 165. For the best discussion of country house visiting since the eighteenth century see Mandler, *Fall and Rise*.

45. Mavor, *British Tourists*, ii, p. 355.

46. Norman Scarfe (ed.), 'A Frenchman's Year in Suffolk, 1784', *Suffolk Records Society*, 30 (1988), pp. 138–42.

47. Mavor, *British Tourists*, ii, p. 334; the Hon. Mrs Murray quoted in Ian Ousby, *The Englishman's England* (Cambridge, 1990), p. 81.

48. Paget Toynbee, 'Horace Walpole's Journals', p. 26; C. Bruyn Andrews (ed.), *The Torrington Diaries: Containing the Tours through England and Wales of the Hon. John Byng (Later Fifth Viscount Torrington) between the Years 1781 and 1794*, iv (London, 1938), p. 134.

49. Climenson, *Diaries of Mrs Philip Lybbe Powys*, pp. 200–1. Paris-made sofas at Heythrop cost 90 guineas each, chairs £30. Lady Shrewsbury told Sir John Dashwood furnishing the drawing-room had 'only cost £6,000'.

50. Few authors linked sentiment and the experience of the British tour more closely than 'a Gentleman of the University of Oxford' in his *Journal of a Three Weeks Tour through Derbyshire to the Lakes* (1797). He found Sir Brooke Boothby's monument (by Thomas Banks, RA) to his six-year-old daughter at Ashbourne, 'perhaps the most interesting and pathetic object in England ... The man, whom this does not affect, need not proceed any further on his tour. His heart is not formed to relish the beauties of nature or of art.' Certainly Queen Charlotte passed the test, suitably moved to tears when it was exhibited at Somerset House in 1793.

Mavor, *British Tourists*, v, pp. 214–15; Rupert Gunnis, *Dictionary of British Sculptors, 1660–1851* (London, new rev. edn, n.d.), p. 38.

51. Ilana Bignamini, 'Grand Tour: Open Issues', in *Grand Tour: The Lure of Italy in the Eighteenth Century*, Tate Gallery (London, 1996), p. 32.

52. Scottish RO, Clerk of Penicuik, GO/18/2107. See John Fleming, *Robert Adam and His Circle in Edinburgh and Rome* (London, 1962), pp. 15–44. The 1727 journey cost him, with two servants, the large sum of almost £300. Sir John made a similar tour in the late spring of 1733, visiting Norfolk and London, ibid., pp. 328–29.

53. This account of Lord Oxford's tours is based upon the 'travels' section of the Royal Commission on Historical Manuscripts, *Portland MSS*, vi (London, 1901), pp. 74–192. See also Lees-Milne, *Earls of Creation*, chapter 4, and *DNB*, viii, pp. 1278–80. The quotation comes from *Complete Peerage*, x, p. 267.

54. The following three paragraphs are based upon Godber, 'The Marchioness Grey of Wrest Park'. The travel journals of Philip Yorke are printed, ibid., pp. 125–63.

55. Paget Toynbee, 'Horace Walpole's Journals', pp. 9–80.

56. Ibid., p. 64; W. S. Lewis (ed.), *The Yale Edition of Horace Walpole's Correspondence*, ix: W. S. Lewis and R. S. Brown (eds), *Horace Walpole's Correspondence with George Montagu*, i (New Haven, 1941), p. 289, letter dated 19 July 1760.

57. Timothy Mowl, *Horace Walpole: The Great Outsider* (London, 1996), pp. 38–80. For Walpole's career see also R. W. Ketton-Cremer, *Horace Walpole: A Biography* (London, 1940); and Martin Kalbich, *Horace Walpole* (New York, 1971).

58. Lewis and Brown, *Horace Walpole's Correspondence*, ii, p. 278, letter dated 11 May 1769.

59. Ibid., p. 286, letter dated 27 August 1769.

60. Paget Toynbee, 'Horace Walpole's Journals', p. 64.

61. Climenson, *Diary of Mrs Philip Lybbe Powys*, pp. 154–55.

62. Sarah Markham, *John Loveday of Caversham, 1711–1789: The Life and Tours of an Eighteenth-Century Onlooker* (Wilton, 1984); J. E. T. Loveday (ed.), *Diary of a Tour in 1732*, Roxburghe Club (London, 1890).

63. See the four volumes of Andrews, *The Torrington Diaries*.

64. A good example of the type is the Suffolk antiquary, Davy. See J. Blatchly ed., 'A Journal of Excursions through the County of Suffolk, 1822–1844, of David Elisha Davy', *Suffolk Records Society*, 24 (1982). An impecunious member of a minor gentry family, Davy rarely commented on a great house (never numerous in Suffolk). What enthused him in his excursions across the whole county collecting material were, besides churches, the great stock of Tudor and Stuart houses, often partly demolished or in decay housing farmers, and the genealogies of their former owners.

65. M. W. Thompson (ed.), *The Journeys of Sir Richard Colt Hoare through Wales and England, 1793–1810* (Gloucester, 1983).

66. A note to this section on London is restricted to three excellent general volumes on its history and buildings. They also provide ample guides to further reading. Roy Porter, *London: A Social History* (London, 1994); John Summerson, *Georgian London* (London, new edn 1988); and Christopher Simon Sykes, *Private Palaces: Life in the Great London Houses* (London, 1989). For the London houses of the richest members of the late Victorian plutocracy, see J. Mordaunt Crook, *The Rise of the Nouveaux Riches* (London, 1999), pp. 153–212.

67. Sykes, *Private Palaces*, pp. 102–3, 152–53, 223, 257–66.

68. Summerson, *Georgian London*, p. 123.

69. Scottish RO, Clerk of Penicuik, GO/18/2107.

70. See the exhibition catalogue, *Rococo Art and Design in Hogarth's England*, Victoria and Albert Museum (London, 1984), which provides a superb guide to the mid eighteenth-century period.

71. Norfolk RO, HEA 480–81 and 458–59, especially HEA 489: 'Exp[ense] of Altering and Rebuilding the House at Heacham'.

72. Richardson specialised in interior decoration of an Adam character. One of his many books of design was *A New Collection of Chimney Pieces* (London, 1781). See Howard Colvin, *A Biographical Dictionary of British Architects, 1660–1840* (New Haven and London, 1995), pp. 810–11.

73. Louis Simond, *An American in Regency England* (London, 1968), pp. 81–82.

Notes to Chapter 4: Architect and Patron

1. Yorkshire, East Riding RO, Beverley, DDGR 41/3.

2. Cambridge University Library, Buxton Papers.

3. John Soane, *Plans Elevations and Sections of Buildings* (London, 1788), p. 6.

4. Yorkshire, East Riding RO, Beverley, DDGR 41/3, letter from Stephen Thompson in London 9 August 1746 to Thomas Grimston at Grimston (Yorkshire). Thompson's father, born in 1677, was still alive and lived to the ripe old age of eighty-three.

5. Howard Colvin, *A Biographical Dictionary of British Architects, 1600–1840* (New Haven and London, 1995), p. 672.

6. Colvin, *Biographical Dictionary*, p. 672; Lynn F. Pearson, 'Ormesby Hall, Cleveland', *Yorkshire Archaeological Journal*, 61 (1989), pp. 149–54.

7. Yorkshire, East Riding RO, Beverley, DDGR 41/3, letter from Stephen Thompson to Thomas Grimston, 22 November 1746.

8. Yorkshire, East Riding RO, Beverley, DDGR 41/4, letters from Stephen Thompson to Thomas Grimston, 11 December 1746 and 3 January 1746–47. No doubt Thompson was referring to Roger Morris (1695–1749), who rose from the rank of bricklayer to become Colen Campbell's assistant and then the collaborator of the architect Henry, Lord Herbert, afterwards ninth Earl of Pembroke, before appointment to posts in the Office of Works and Office of Ordnance. At the time Kirby Hall was being planned, Morris was engaged upon the building of Inveraray Castle for the third Duke of Argyll and could have easily stayed over in Yorkshire for consultations with Thompson. Colvin, *Biographical Dictionary*, pp. 665–69.

9. The house was built *c.* 1715 and demolished in the 1760s. K. A. MacMahon, 'The Beverley House of the Hotham Family: An Early Eighteenth-Century Building Project', *Transactions of the Georgian Society of East Yorkshire*, 4 (1956–58), pp. 37–49.

10. Yorkshire, East Riding RO, Beverley, DDGR 41/4, letter from Stephen Thompson to Thomas Grimston, 19 February 1746–47.

11. Colvin, *Biographical Dictionary*, p. 151.

12. Brett Harrison, 'Thorp Arch Hall, 1749–1756: "Dabling a Little in Mortar"', *Publications of the Thoresby Society*, second series, 4 (1994), pp. 1–39. See also Amanda Vickery, *The Gentleman's Daughter: Women's Lives in Georgian England* (New Haven and London, 1998), passim.

13. Harrison, 'Thorp Arch', p. 28.

14. Ibid., pp. 28–29.

15. It is tempting to ascribe Gossip's architectural diffidence to his mercantile background and

lack of appropriate education, but the listing of thirteen men who described themselves as merchants among the subscribers to Leoni's translation of Palladio's *Four Books* published in 1721 cautions against this conclusion.

16. The conventional Renaissance belief that architecture was the queen of the mechanical arts, quoted by Denis Cosgrove, *The Palladian Landscape* (Leicester, 1993), p. 214.

17. This section draws upon Eileen Harris, *British Architectural Books and Writers, 1556–1785* (Cambridge, 1990), pp. 23–44.

18. John Bold, *Wilton House and English Palladianism* (London, 1988), pp. 33–44.

19. Timothy Mowl and Brian Earnshaw disentangle the complex attribution of this house in *Architecture Without Kings* (London, 1995), pp. 48–59, but the conventional view remains that the house was essentially designed by Pratt with advice from the aged Inigo Jones.

20. Sir Gyles Isham, 'The Architectural History of Lamport', *Northamptonshire Architectural and Archaeological Society*, 57 (1951), pp. 13–28.

21. This section draws on Colvin, *Biographical Dictionary*, pp. 26–33.

22. R. T. Gunther, (ed.), *The Architecture of Sir Roger Pratt, Charles II's Commissioner for the Rebuilding of London after the Great Fire: Now Printed for the First Time from his Note-Books* (Oxford, 1928), p. 60.

23. Ibid.; Nigel Silcox-Crowe, 'Sir Roger Pratt, 1620–1685: The Ingenious Gentleman Architect', in Roderick Brown (ed.), *The Architectural Outsiders* (London, 1985), pp. 1–20.

24. Colvin, *Biographical Dictionary*, p. 27.

25. Roger North, 'Of Building', BL, Add. MS 32540, fol. 23, quoted by Colvin, *Biographical Dictionary*, p. 32.

26. Quoted by F. Jenkins, *Architect and Patron* (London, 1961), p. 45.

27. H. J. Habakkuk, 'Daniel Finch, Second Earl of Nottingham: His House and Estate', in J. H. Plumb (ed.), *Studies in Social History* (London, 1955), pp. 139–78.

28. Colvin, *Biographical Dictionary*, refers to Robert Hooke and William Hurlbutt working at Ragley, p. 509; and William Talman at Lowther Castle, ibid., p. 953. Cambridge University Library, Buxton Papers, letter from John Buxton to Robert Buxton, 5 September 1729. James Gibbs's *Book of Architecture* had been published the previous year.

29. Colvin, *Biographical Dictionary*, pp. 287–88, 419.

30. Mark Crinson and Jules Lubbock, *Architecture: Art or Profession?* (Manchester, 1994), pp. 22–26.

31. Brian Fothergill, *The Mitred Earl* (London, 1974).

32. Barrington Kaye, *The Development of the Architectural Profession in Britain* (London, 1960), p. 58.

33. Kathryn Cave (ed.), *The Diary of Joseph Farington*, viii (New Haven, 1982), p. 2887, entry for 16 October 1806.

34. Howard Colvin, 'Architect and Client', in Giles Worsley (ed.), *Georgian Architectural Practice*, The Georgian Group (London, 1991), pp. 6–11.

35. Alan Mackley, 'The Construction of Henham Hall', *Georgian Group Journal*, 6 (1996), pp. 85–96.

36. Entry for 2 February 1782 in S. H. A. Hervey (ed.), *Journals of the Hon. William Hervey, 1755–1814* (Bury St Edmunds, 1906), p. 324.

37. BL, Add. MS 19223, fos 166–67, letter from John Rous to Eleazar Davy, 1 December 1791.

38. K. Garlick and A. Macintyre (eds), *The Diary of Joseph Farington*, iii (New Haven, 1979), p. 914, entry for 2 November 1797. Wyatt did sometimes base his commission on building costs, as shown by the accounts for Dodington Park, the house he designed for Christopher

Codrington. Gloucestershire RO, D1610/A96–97. Soane Museum, ledger E, account with Purney Sillitoe, and ledger B, account with E. R. Pratt.

39. Margaret Richardson, 'John Soane: The Business of Architecture', in Giles Worsley (ed.), *Georgian Architectural Practice*, The Georgian Group (London, 1991) pp. 65–72.

40. Quoted in Colvin, *Biographical Dictionary*, p. 45.

41. Derek Linstrum, *West Yorkshire Architects and Architecture* (London, 1978), pp. 31–32; Jenkins, *Architect and Patron*, p. 113. For the similar career of John Johnson, see Nancy Briggs, *John Johnson, 1732–1814: Georgian Architect and County Surveyor of Essex* (Chelmsford, 1991).

42. Soane, *Plans*, p. 7.

43. Colvin, *Biographical Dictionary*, p. 905; D. Watkin, *Sir John Soane: Enlightenment Thought and the Royal Academy Lectures* (Cambridge, 1996).

44. Sir Balthazar Gerbier, *A Brief Discourse Concerning the Three Chief Principles of Magnificent Building* (London, 1662), p. 14; *Counsel and Advise to All Builders* (London, 1663), pp. 59, 61.

45. Colvin, *Biographical Dictionary*, pp. 24–25.

46. Alan Mackley, 'Building Management at Dyrham', *Georgian Group Journal*, 7 (1997), pp. 107–16.

47. Gunther, *Architecture of Sir Roger Pratt*, p. 47.

48. Howard Colvin and John Newman, *Of Building: Roger North's Writings on Architecture* (Oxford, 1981), p. 23.

49. Christopher Chalklin, *English Counties and Public Building, 1650–1830* (London, 1998), pp. 67–91.

50. Ibid., p. 78.

51. John Shaw, 'The Finance and Construction of the East Anglian Houses of Industry', *Proceedings of the Suffolk Institute of Archaeology and History*, 37 (1992), pp. 351–65.

52. Chalklin, *English Building*, p. 84; J. Mordaunt Crook, 'The Custom House Scandal', *Architectural History*, 6 (1963), pp. 91–102.

53. Mackley 'Dyrham'; Geoffrey Beard, *Craftsmen and Interior Decoration in England in England, 1660–1820* (London, 1986), p. 144. See also pp. 302–4 below.

54. Mark Girouard, 'Dyrham Park, Gloucestershire', *Country Life*, 131, 22 February 1962, p. 398.

55. J. A. Kenworthy-Browne (revised by J. Harris and N. Stacey), *Dyrham Park*, The National Trust (London, 1995), pp. 34–35.

56. Northamptonshire RO, OBB 12.

57. Colvin, *Biographical Dictionary*, p. 860.

58. Northamptonshire RO, Milton Plans 91, letter John Sharman to Earl Fitzwilliam, 10 January 1747/?48.

59. Northamptonshire RO, 2328.

60. Berkshire RO, Preston MSS D/EP1.

61. Colvin, *Biographical Dictionary*, p. 151.

62. John Summerson, *Architecture in Britain, 1530 to 1830* (Harmondsworth, 1953), p. 222.

63. Julia Ionides, 'Mr Pritchard of Shrewsbury', in Malcolm Airs (ed.), *The Later Eighteenth-Century Great House* (Oxford, 1997), pp. 156–71. See also Julia Ionides, *Thomas Farnolls Pritchard of Shrewsbury: Architect and 'Inventor of Cast Iron Bridges'* (Ludlow, 1999).

64. Colvin, *Biographical Dictionary*, pp. 882–90.

65. John Heward and Robert Taylor, *The Country Houses of Northamptonshire*, Royal Commission on the Historical Monuments of England (Swindon, 1996), pp. 256–62.

66. Northamptonshire RO, IL 4168.

67. Northamptonshire RO, IL 3965.

68. Andor Gomme, 'William and David Hiorn, 1712–1776, ?–1758: The Elegance of Provincial Craftsmanship', in Roderick Brown (ed.), *The Architectural Outsiders* (London, 1985), pp. 45–62.

69. Colvin, *Biographical Dictionary*, p. 752.

70. Ibid., pp. 391–92.

71. Lyall Wilkes, *John Dobson* (Stocksfield, 1980), pp. 99–110.

72. Colvin, *Biographical Dictionary*, p. 270; E. W. Cooney, 'The Origins of the Victorian Master Builders', *Economic History Review*, second series, 8 (1955–56), pp. 167–76.

73. Hermione Hobhouse, *Thomas Cubitt: Master Builder* (London, 1971); Cooney, 'Master Builders'.

74. A stream of price books flowed from the early eighteenth century. William Salmon's *Country Builder's Estimator*, published in 1733 and the first to be wholly devoted to builders' prices, was reprinted many times in the next forty years. Thomas Skaife Taylor's *Builders' Price Book* of 1776 was, in its many editions, a standard work for over a century. Harris, *Architectural Books*, pp. 43–45, 133.

75. Cooney, 'Master Builders', p. 175.

76. M. H. Port, 'The Office of Works and Building Contracts in Early Nineteenth-Century England', *Economic History Review*, second series, 20 (1967), pp. 94–110.

    Nash was chosen by King George IV for the reconstruction of Buckingham Palace (1825–30) but the expenditure became a public scandal and the architect was criticised by a Select Committee of the House of Commons in 1828 for his mismanagement. J. Mordaunt Crook and M. H. Port, *The History of the King's Works*, vi (London, 1973), pp. 263–302.

    The building contractor for Pell Wall House (Staffordshire), designed by John Soane for Purney Sillitoe, 1822–28, wisely had second thoughts about his agreement to complete the interior of the house for a fixed price. When it became clear that it could not be done for the contracted £4009, John Carline junior wrote to Soane that his father had made the estimate on work he knew too little about and 'thinks it right to communicate this much previous to the commencement as the execution of the work would be but deceiving Mr Sillitoe and yourself and ruin to my father'. Soane Museum, Pell Wall correspondence, J/8/1.

77. Soane, *Plans*, p. 7.

78. Writing years later the combative Robert Kerr was scathing of this amateur effort. For want of the mere elementary counsel of an expert, he asserted, it overflowed with errors – 'a warning indeed'! There was 'more imbecile conventional symmetry than even Palladianism itself would have produced'. Although allowing that the design was remarkably bold for its day, Kerr saw the result as a matter of regret to all who respected the memory of the designer. Robert Kerr, *The Gentleman's House* (London, 1871), pp. 427–30.

79. Nicholas Kingsley, *The Country Houses of Gloucestershire*, ii, *1660–1830* (Chichester, 1992), pp. 249–53.

80. Jill Allibone, *Anthony Salvin: Pioneer of Gothic Revival Architecture* (Cambridge, 1988), pp. 40–52.

81. Ibid., p. 84.

82. Lord de Grey's architectural activity did not end there. He was President of the Institute of British Architects and, as a leading Conservative peer, was a member of the commission charged with controlling expenditure on extensions to Buckingham Palace in the 1840s. He modified Blore's elevations for the new east wing, his interference leading to the architect's threat to resign in 1849. The connections within the building business are well displayed in Lord de Grey's unpublished memoirs: 'Blore was the architect, and I thought him a very inefficient man [not a commonly held view]. Thomas Cubitt of Belgravia was the builder,

and I thought him a very superior intelligent person; and Oliver who had [been] my clerk of the works at Wrest was the clerk of the works under Blore.' Mordaunt Crook and Port, *King's Works*, vi, p. 290, quoting Bedfordshire RO, CRT 190/45/2. See also ibid., pp. 229, 289, and James Collett-White, 'Inventories of Bedfordshire Country Houses, 1714–1830', *Publications of the Bedfordshire Historical Record Society*, 74 (1995), pp. 250–51.

83. Berkshire RO, D/EWal E12 (building accounts) and E13 (letters).

84. Hobhouse, *Thomas Cubitt*, p. 376.

85. Ibid., pp. 396–97.

86. Ibid., p. 463.

87. Patricia Spencer-Silver, *Pugin's Builder: The Life and Work of George Myers* (Hull, 1993), pp. 78, 86, 173.

88. Alan Mackley, 'The Building of Haveringland Hall', *Norfolk Archaeology*, 43 (1999), pp. 111–32.

89. Somerset RO, DD/DU127. See below, pp. 328–30.

90. Northamptonshre RO, IL 2765, N. i. 12; Mark Girouard, *The Victorian Country House* (New Haven and London, 1979), p. 420. Holland and Hannen took over the firm of William Cubitt and Co. in 1883.

91. Cheshire RO, DGN.

92. Somerset RO, DD/DU 127.

93. Somerset RO,. DD/DU 163.

94. Ranald C. Michie, 'Income, Expenditure and Investment of a Victorian Millionaire: Lord Overstone, 1823–83', *Bulletin of the Institute of Historical Research*, 58 (1985), pp. 59–77.

95. John Bateman, *The Great Landowners of Great Britain and Ireland* (London. 1883; reprinted Leicester, 1971), p. 348.

96. Quoted by Jill Franklin, *The Gentleman's Country House and its Plan, 1835–1914* (London, 1981), p. 245.

Notes to Chapter 5: A Pleasure Not to be Envied

1. Sir William Chambers, *A Treatise on the Decorative Part of Civil Architecture* (3rd edn, London, 1791), p. ii.

2. Rudyard Kipling, 'A Truthful Song', *Rudyard Kipling's Verse* (London, 1940), p. 654.

3. Sir Balthazar Gerbier, *A Brief Discourse Concerning the Three Chief Principles of Magnificent Building* (London, 1662), p. 3.

4. H. J. Habakkuk, 'Daniel Finch, Second Earl of Nottingham: His House and Estate', in J. H. Plumb (ed.), *Studies in Social History* (London, 1955), p. 152.

5. Suffolk RO, Bury St Edmunds, E2/23/5, letter from Henry Oakes to Sir Thomas Cullum, 15 January 1839.

6. Buckinghamshire RO, D/FR 22/1/1, letter from Henry Wilson to Sir Thomas Fremantle, Stowlangtoft, 16 September 1864. Quoted by Jill Franklin in *The Gentleman's Country House and its Plan, 1835–1914* (London, 1981), p. 121.

7. Detailed estimates were a late development. Nash told the 1831 Select Committee on Windsor Castle and Buckingham Palace that architects never made that sort of estimate in the first instance. J. Mordaunt Crook and M. H. Port, *The History of the King's Works*, vi, *1782–1851* (London, 1973), p. 145.

8. The evolution of the clerk of the works's role in royal service is discussed in R. Allen Brown,

H. M. Colvin and A. J. Taylor, *The History of the King's Works*, i, *The Middle Ages* (London, 1963), pp. 164–201, and H. M. Colvin, D. R. Ransome and John Summerson, *The History of the King's Works*, iii, *1485–1660*, part 1 (London, 1975), pp. 5–24. Their position in private practice has been neglected by architectural historians, except to note that in the evolution of the architectural profession, some clerks of the works emerged as architects in their own right. Alan Mackley, 'Clerks of the Works', *Georgian Group Journal*, 8 (1998), pp. 157–66.

9. William of Wykeham became a clerk of the works in 1356. By 1367 he was both Chancellor and Bishop of Winchester. Chaucer was clerk of the works from 1389 to 1391.

10. It is not certain that Nedeham was appointed for his technical knowledge but under Henry VIII there was a clear shift away from churchmen to the employment of paid laymen. Nedeham's successor, Richard Lee, may have come from a family of masons, advancing himself socially and financially in the post. Colvin et al., *King's Works*, iii, pp. 11–14.

11. R. T. Gunther (ed.), *The Architecture of Sir Roger Pratt, Charles II's Commissioner for the Rebuilding of London after the Great Fire: Now Printed for the First Time from his Note-Books* (Oxford, 1928), pp. 47–48.

12. H. M. Colvin and J. Newman (eds), *Of Building: Roger North's Writings on Architecture* (Oxford, 1981), p. 22.

13. Worsley's reward for his amateur enthusiasm for architecture came in 1760, when he was appointed by his old friend the Prime Minister, Lord Bute, to the Surveyor-Generalship of the Office of Works. Giles Worsley, 'Hovingham Hall, Yorkshire', *Country Life*, 188, 15 September 1994, pp. 90–93 and 22 September 1994, pp. 56–61. See pp. 336–40 below.

14. Cambridge University Library, Buxton Papers, letter from John Buxton to Robert Buxton, 1 May 1727.

15. Gordon Smith, *Cusworth Hall* (Doncaster, 1968), p. 6.

16. D. R. Hainsworth, *Stewards, Lords and People* (Cambridge, 1992), pp. 236–50.

17. D. R. Hainsworth and Cherry Walker (eds), 'The Correspondence of Lord Fitzwilliam of Milton and Francis Guybon, his Steward 1697–1709', *Northamptonshire Record Society*, 36 (1990); Hainsworth, *Stewards*, pp. 237–38.

18. Joan Wake and Deborah Champion Webster (eds), 'The Letters of Daniel Eaton to the Third Earl of Cardigan, 1725–1732', *Northamptonshire Record Society*, 24 (1971).

19. The Blathwayt papers, including letters and estate accounts for the period of the rebuilding of Dyrham, are in Gloucestershire RO, D1799. The project is discussed in Alan Mackley, 'Building Management at Dyrham', *Georgian Group Journal*, 7 (1997), pp. 107–16.

20. For example, William Atkinson at Lowther Hall in 1694 (Hainsworth, *Stewards*, p. 238). Samuel Popplewell, Edwin Lascelles's steward when Harewood House was built from 1755, found himself bewildered by the multiplicity of duties expected of him when adding the role of clerk of the works to his other tasks. Mary Mauchline, *Harewood House* (Newton Abbot, 1974), p. 30.

21. Howard Colvin, *A Biographical Dictionary of British Architects, 1600–1840* (New Haven and London, 1995), pp. 818–20.

22. Ibid., pp. 354, 721, 978, 1124; Derek Linstrum, *West Yorkshire Architects and Architecture* (London, 1978), p. 31. The process continued from father to son. When William Etty, clerk of the works at Castle Howard, died in 1734, his son John (who was to die in 1738) was recommended by Hawksmoor to Lord Carlisle as 'sober, carefull, ingenious, and industrious'. Geoffrey Webb, 'The Letters and Drawings of Nicholas Hawksmoor Relating to the Building of the

Mausoleum at Castle Howard, 1726–1742', *Walpole Society*, 19 (Oxford, 1931), p. 148. James Paine employed his own son as clerk of the works at Thorndon Hall (1764–70). Malcolm Airs, *The Tudor and Jacobean Country House: A Building History* (Stroud, 1995), p. 72, discusses the emergence of surveyors from craft backgrounds in the seventeenth century.

23. Richard Wilson and Alan Mackley, 'Founding a Landed Dynasty, Building a Country House: The Rolfes of Heacham in the Eighteenth Century', in Carole Rawcliffe, Roger Virgoe and Richard Wilson (eds), *Counties and Communities: Essays on East Anglian History Presented to Hassell Smith* (Norwich, 1996), pp. 307–25.

24. For Henham there is the rare survival of a near complete set of clerk of the works's reports: Suffolk RO, Ipswich, HA11, Rous family papers, C7/1–2. The Henham project is described in Alan Mackley, 'The Construction of Henham Hall', *Georgian Group Journal*, 6 (1996), pp. 85–96. The Marsdens appear to have been an estate family. An Elizabeth Marsden travelled the twenty-one miles to Great Yarmouth in January 1795 to buy a feather bed, blankets and a coverlet 'for the greenhouse', the cost being charged to the building account. A Rufus Alexander Marsden began work in April 1796 at the boy's wage of one shilling per day.

25. Leeds University Library, MS 417/7, Mathew Wilson's day book, 1823–25, entry for 24 December 1824.

26. Dorothy Stroud, *Henry Holland: His Life and Architecture* (London, 1966), p. 131.

27. The correspondence between George Freke Evans and Humphry Repton is in Northampton-shire RO, X. 2830A, Freke Evans (Laxton) collection.

28. The building of Sheringham Hall is described in a journal kept by Abbot Upcher, Norfolk RO, UPC55. The building accounts are in UPC27 and 38, 640 x 4. Extracts from the journal have been published as Susan Yaxley (ed.), *Sherringhamia: The Journal of Abbot Upcher, 1813–16* (Stibbard, 1986).

29. Cheshire RO, D2781.

30. Colvin, *Biographical Dictionary*, pp. 1121–23.

31. The dispute between Lord Sherborne and Lewis Wyatt is documented in Gloucestershire RO, D678/322, Sherborne Muniments, Sherborne Family Settlements.

32. Lord Sherborne compiled a long list of defects in the structure and its finishing and asserted that for at least two years he and his family had been harassed and 'kept in a state worse than houseless'. The arbitrators were London architects Thomas Allason (for Lord Sherborne) and Joseph Kay (secretary of the London Architects' Club), with recourse to Sir Robert Smirke if they failed to agree. The penalty is noted by Clive Aslet, in 'Sherborne House, Gloucestershire', *Country Life*, 179, 20 March 1986, pp. 720–23. Wyatt's habitual detachment from his projects is further indicated by his writing about Oulton Park (Cheshire), which he altered from 1817 for Sir John Egerton. In 1821 he stated that he had very little information about what had been done in the previous twelve months, and in 1822 he could not calculate his commission because he lacked information about expenditure (Cheshire RO, DEO 200/4).

33. Nicholas Kingsley, *The Country Houses of Gloucestershire*, i, *1500–1660* (Cheltenham, 1989), p. 154; David Verey, *The Buildings of England, Gloucestershire*, ii, *The Vale and The Forest of Dean* (Harmondsworth, 1970), pp. 385–86; Jill Allibone, *Anthony Salvin: Pioneer of Gothic Revival Architecture, 1799–1881* (Cambridge, 1988), p. 165.

34. The correspondence between Antrobus and Wyatt is in Cheshire RO, D2781.

35. Cheshire RO, D2781/152, letter 1 February 1828, from Lewis Wyatt to G. C. Antrobus.

36. Peter de Figueiredo and Julian Treuherz, *Cheshire Country Houses* (Chichester, 1988), p. 233.

37. Norfolk RO, MS 8595 20B, Haveringland Hall building accounts. A complete set of the clerk of the works's reports has survived, supported by numerous account books.

38. Richard Armstrong was also alert to the value of a discount. Samuel Thomas, a Birmingham locksmith, wrote to him on 9 January 1843: 'In answer to yours of the 6th inst. that an allowance of 5 per ct will reduce my slender profit very seriously but for prompt cash payment I will make the sacrifice feeling grateful for your kindness.' The net sum was £67 15s. 6d., for goods supplied between 25 April 1841 and 12 November 1842. Thus the 'prompt' payment was, in part, for goods supplied nearly two years before (Norfolk RO, MS 8595 20B, box 2).

39. Three stonemasons, paid 3s. 6d. per day, enjoyed another 6d. when they moved to Shadwell (Norfolk); and two others increased their pay from 2s. 6d. to 3s. 6d. One plasterer moved to Shadwell for the same wage and another increased his from 3s. 4d. to 4s. Moving to Haveringland entailed a drop in pay from 4s. 4d. to 3s. 6d. for John Hughes when his work ended at Ramsey (Huntingdonshire), another house of the Fellowes family altered by Edward Blore, although he received 1s. 6d. per week lodging allowance in 1839 and £5 per annum rent allowance thereafter. Edward Blore's accounts for Merton, Ramsey and Shadwell, Cambridge University Library, Add. MSS 3937–38, 3949–50.

40. Specific references to the remuneration of clerks of the works early in the period, when the job was often done by men holding a salaried position on an estate, are rare.

41. At Oulton Park (Cheshire) in 1819–20, when supervising alterations by Lewis Wyatt for Sir John Egerton, James Rigby was paid 6s. per day, while the highest-paid plasterers (from Manchester) and carpenters received 5s. and 4s. 2d. respectively (Cheshire RO, DEO 200/4).

42. On the emergence of the general contractor see Richard Price, *Master, Unions and Men* (Cambridge, 1980), p. 23; M. H. Port, 'The Office of Works and Building Contracts in Early Nineteenth-Century England', *Economic History Review*, second series, 20 (1967), pp. 94–110; Hermione Hobhouse, *Thomas Cubitt: Master Builder* (London, 1971). At the time that he wrote *The Gentleman's House* (London, 1871), Robert Kerr concluded that it was the norm for country houses to be built by general contract.

43. *The Builder*, 9 October 1852, p. 647, quoted by Hobhouse, *Thomas Cubitt*, p. 265.

44. The role of the clerk of the works in the late nineteenth century is described in G. G. Hoskins (revised by H. P. Hoskins), *The Clerk of Works* (8th edition, London, 1914).

45. Yorkshire, East Riding RO, DDGR 41/4, letter from Stephen Thompson to Thomas Grimston, 20 June 1748. The elevation, at least, has been attributed to Roger Morris, in association with the third Earl of Burlington (Colvin, *Biographical Dictionary*, p. 668), but Thompson's letters show that he developed his own design, with advice from Colonel Moyser (who recommended that he consult Morris). As late as February 1747, Thompson wrote: 'Morris nor no architect but Payne [James Paine] has seen it' (Yorkshire, East Riding RO, DDGR 41/4, 19 February, 1746/47). The first brick was laid on 6 September 1747.

46. The building process in the Georgian period seen from the viewpoint of the craftsmen is covered by James Ayres, *Building the Georgian City* (New Haven and London, 1999).

47. Charles Saumarez Smith, *The Building of Castle Howard* (London, 1990), p. 63.

48. Anthony Dale, *The Wyatts* (Oxford, 1956), p. 68.

49. F. M. L. Thompson, *English Landed Society in the Nineteenth Century* (London, 1963), p. 92.

50. Franklin, *Gentleman's Country House*, p. 125.

51. L. Jacks, *The Great Houses of Nottinghamshire and the County Families* (Nottingham, 1882), p. 161.

52. Clive Aslet, *The Last Country Houses* (New Haven, 1982), p. 188; Jane Brown, *Lutyens and the Edwardians* (London, 1997), p. 235. The foundation stone was laid in 1911 and the last stone placed at the end of 1925.

53. P. Nunn, 'Aristocratic Estates and Employment in South Yorkshire, 1700–1800', in S. Pollard and C. Holmes (eds), *Essays in the Economic and Social History of South Yorkshire* (Sheffield, 1976), pp. 36–39.

54. Wolterton Hall MSS, 3/1/1, day book of Richard Ness, 1738–44.

55. Wolterton Hall MSS, 3/1/1. No detailed labour accounts survive before 1738.

56. Cambridge University Library, Buxton Papers, letter from John Buxton to Robert Buxton, 7 July 1728.

57. A seven by five bay house faced with Bath stone on three fronts, with domestic offices grouped around a rear courtyard, and a separate stable block. Additions were made in the 1850s to the designs of the former clerk of the works, Richard Armstrong. The house is featured in R. H. Mason, *Norfolk Photographically Illustrated* (Norwich, 1865).

58. Norfolk RO, MS 8595 20B. The clerk of works's pay-bills are analysed in Alan Mackley, 'An Economic History of Country House Building, with Particular Reference to East Anglia and the East and West Ridings of Yorkshire, *c.* 1660–1870' (unpublished Ph.D. thesis, University of East Anglia, Norwich, 1993), ii, appendix 20, pp. 382–96.

59. For the period 1500–1640 the discussion is based upon Airs, *Country House*, especially pp. 147–70.

60. Leicestershire RO, DG 4/598, wages book for the building of East Carlton Hall, 30 April 1777 to 26 August 1780. See also Nancy Briggs, *John Johnson, 1732–1814: Georgian Architect and County Surveyor of Essex* (Chelmsford, 1991), pp. 29–32.

61. Airs, *Country House*, p. 75.

62. Habakkuk, 'Daniel Finch', p. 150.

63. Alan Mackley, 'Building Management at Dyrham', *Georgian Group Journal*, 7 (1997), pp. 107–16.

64. Dorset RO, D/BUL/M8, account book, Baruch and Thomas Fox in account with Sir William Oglander, Bt. Parnham, near Beaminster, was a sixteenth-century house, remodelled in 1807–11 to designs by Nash, at a cost of about £25,000.

65. Nottinghamshire RO, DD4P/70/55/9, letter December 1745 from James Osborne and Thomas Ince to Henrietta Cavendish, Countess of Oxford, at Welbeck Abbey. These masons, having just been discharged from working by the day, petitioned to be allowed to continue to work by the piece, 'both having families and destitute of work for the winter'.

66. The only freestone in East Anglia is carrstone, a soft red sandstone found near Snettisham in north-west Norfolk and employed for the stables at Houghton. The Suffolk firm of masons John and Benjamin De Carle of Bury St Edmunds did building work at country houses, including Culford Hall for Lord Cornwallis in 1794–95, and at Ickworth in the 1820s, but their contracts were generally for maintenance, and for monumental masonry. Suffolk RO, Bury St Edmunds, De Carle letter book, 468.

67. Sidney Pollard, 'Labour in Great Britain', in Peter Mathias and M. M. Postan (eds), *The Cambridge Economic History of Europe*, vii, part 1 (Cambridge, 1978), p. 103.

68. Ibid., pp. 108–10.

69. Gloucestershire RO, D1799/E236, Agreement between John Povey and Robert Barker, 2 June 1693. Payment was also made for one day preparing to leave London, travelling time and the carriage of tools.

70. Annette Bagot and Julian Munby (eds), ' "All Things is Well Here": Letters from Hugh James

of Levens to James Grahame, 1692–95', *Cumberland and Westmoreland Antiquarian and Archae-ological Society Record Series*, 10 (1988); Northamptonshire RO, Fitzwilliam (Milton), MSS plans 94; Leicestershire RO, Finch MSS, DG/7/1/128; Robert Machin (ed.), 'The Building Accounts of Mapperton Rectory, 1699–1703', *Dorset Record Society Publication*, 8 (Dorchester, 1983), p. 9.

71. Geoffrey Beard, *Craftsmen and Decorative Artists in England, 1660–1820* (London, 1986), p. 133–37.

72. Ibid., p. 138.

73. Charles Saumarez Smith, *The Building of Castle Howard* (London, 1990), pp. 63–66.

74. Ibid., p. 95; Beard, *Craftsmen*, p. 149.

75. Geoffrey Webb, 'The Letters and Drawings of Nicholas Hawksmoor Relating to the Building of the Mausoleum at Castle Howard, 1726–1742', *Walpole Society*, 19 (Oxford, 1931), pp. 128–29. See also Saumarez Smith, *Castle Howard*, pp. 95–104.

76. Mary Mauchline, *Harewood House* (Newton Abbot, 1974), pp. 73–93.

77. Peter Leach, *James Paine* (London, 1988), pp. 22, 147, 220–21.

78. At Haveringland the number was fifteen out of 243 (6.2 per cent).

79. Airs, *Country House*, pp. 142–43; Peter Nicholson, *An Architectural Dictionary* (London, 1819), ii, p. 518.

80. John Summerson, *The Unromantic Castle* (London, 1990), p. 161.

81. Cheshire RO, DCR/15/12, letter from John Crace, at 38 Wigmore Street, to Lord Crewe, 16 January 1869. Crewe Hall was rebuilt by the general contractor W. Cubitt and Company to E. M. Barry's designs, after a disastrous fire in 1865.

82. Pollard, 'Labour in Great Britain', p. 133.

83. Cambridge University Library, Buxton Papers, letter from John Buxton to Robert Buxton, 17 July 1727.

84. Blathwayt's experience at Dyrham is based on letters in Gloucestershire RO, D1799/E239–242. Nottingham University Library, Denison MSS, DE/H5, letter to John Pate, 31 January 1781.

85. The labourers Jonathen Snell and William Robbins, for example, were fined 6d. of their 1s. daily wage for loitering. Gloucestershire RO, D1799/A105, Samuel Trewman account, 2 June to 28 July 1694.

86. Dorset RO, D/BUL/M8, account book, entries dated 6 and 27 August 1808.

87. C. R. Dobson, *Masters and Journeymen* (London, 1980), appendix A, pp. 154–70.

88. Franklin, *Gentleman's Country House*, p. 126.

89. Hull University Library, DDEV 56/285, account book for alterations to Everingham, the seat of William Constable Maxwell.

90. Suffolk RO, Bury St Edmunds, FKB 941/30.

91. Franklin, *Gentleman's Country House*, pp. 127–28.

92. Leeds University Library, MS 417/8, Mathew Wilson's day book, 11 February 1826. The apparent absence of any such celebrations at Haveringland in the 1840s parallels Pollard's observation that in the early stages of industrialisation employers feasted their employees but within a generation it was the shareholders who were feted and the relationship with workers took on an entirely different character. Sidney Pollard, 'Factory Discipline in the Industrial Revolution', *Economic History Review*, second series, 16 (1963), p. 257.

93. Thompson, *English Landed Society*, p. 92.

94. Sir John Rous paid 2s. to Coleman, a mason, in 1796, and the same sum to joiners in 1797. Suffolk RO, Ipswich, HA11, C7/1/37–38; Dorset RO, D/BUL/M8, 24 December 1808.

95. Airs, *Country House*, p. 198.

96. E. H. Phelps Brown and S. V. Hopkins, 'Seven Centuries of Building Wages', in E. M. Carus-Wilson (ed.), *Essays in Economic History*, ii (London, 1962), pp. 168–78.

97. E. J. Hobsbawm, *Labouring Men: Studies in the History of Labour* (London, 1964), p. 346; Donald Woodward, *Men at Work: Labourers and Building Craftsmen in the Towns of Northern England, 1450–1750* (Cambridge, 1995), pp. 176–80.

98. Some men listed as craftsmen in building accounts may have been labourers or boys in craft groups, members of one family recruited as a team. At Haveringland in the 1840s, for example, there were three stonemasons named Baker who arrived together from Tewkesbury, three masons named Stanley, four bricklayers called Gass, and four Richards who were plasterers, their wage rates being 3s. 6d., 3s. 4d., 2s., and 6d. respectively. Norfolk RO, MS 8595 20B, Haveringland building accounts.

99. Gloucestershire RO, D1799/A104, Samuel Trewman's accounts, 18 June 1692.

100. Phelps Brown and Hopkins, 'Seven Centuries of Building Wages'.

101. One joiner was paid 2s. 2d., one carpenter 2s. and two 1s. 8d. Somerset RO, DD/TB, box 13, FL1, wages book for the building of Crowcombe, 1724–27. Thomas Carew's old house was rebuilt by Thomas Parker and later work by Nathaniel Ireson began in 1737.

102. Leicestershire RO, DG 4/598, wages book, 30 April 1777 to 26 August 1780.

103. Suffolk RO, Ipswich, HA11. Arthur Young in *General View of Agriculture in Suffolk* (London, 1813), pp. 223–24, 428, quotes (for 1803) 1s. 4d. in winter, 1s. 6d. in summer and 2s. 10d. at harvest for Suffolk farm labour, although noting that most work was done by the piece in which earnings were usually higher. He observed that average day rates for winter and summer rose by about 21 per cent between 1790 and 1803.

104. Dorset RO, D/BUL/M8, account book. There were eventually twelve London carpenters working there; and four London painters, who were also paid 4s. 6d. per day and a lodging allowance.

105. Price, *Masters*, p. 34.

106. Philip J. Roe, 'The Development of Norfolk Agriculture in the Nineteenth Century, 1815–1914' (unpublished M. Phil. thesis, University of East Anglia, Norwich, 1975), appendix 4, table 1. He quotes labourers' weekly wages for the period 1839–42, drawn from five different sources, ranging from 9s. to 12s., with a mean of 10s. 4d., or 1s. 9d. per day assuming a six-day week.

107. E. J. Hobsbawm, *Labouring Men*, p. 74, quotes unemployment levels in 1842 in the north-western town of Bolton as 87 per cent for bricklayers and 84 per cent for carpenters.

108. Price, *Masters*, p. 83.

109. Northamptonshire RO, IL 2765, 'Journal of the Works Executing at Lamport Hall, the Seat of Sir Charles E. Isham Bart, 24th June 1861'. Holland and Hannen secured the contract for rebuilding the north-west front and other alterations by competitive tender. The price was £3083 and with extras the contractor's bill came to £3737 4s. 7d. A supplementary account was submitted in 1862 for £419 14s. 0d. The architect's fees and expenses were some £220.

110. Northamptonshire RO, IL 2786.

111. Wolterton Hall MSS, 3/1/1.

112. Suffolk RO, Ipswich, HA11 C7/1/37–8, C7/2/4, Rufus Marsden's pay-bills, 1796–97.

113. Dorset RO, D/BUL/M8, Account Book, 19 December 1807 and 8 October 1808.

114. Norfolk RO, Kimberley 14/205.

115. Dorset RO, D/BUL/M8, account book.

116. Gloucestershire RO, D1799/F92, agreement between William Blathwayt and John Harvey of Bath, 1 November 1710.

117. Gloucestershire RO, D1799/E241, letter from William Tyler to William Blathwayt, 28 May 1701.

118. Norman Scarfe, *Innocent Espionage* (Woodbridge, 1995), p. 211.

119. Isaac Ware, *A Complete Body of Architecture* (London, 1756), p. 95; Colvin, *Biographical Dictionary*, pp. 1020–23.

120. Royal Commission on Historical Monuments in England, *An Inventory of the Historical Monuments in the County of Northampton*, vi, *Architectural Monuments in North Northamptonshire* (London, 1984), p. xlii. Blake Tyson, 'Transportation and the Supply of Construction Materials: An Aspect of Traditional Building Management', *Vernacular Architecture*, 29 (1998), pp. 63–81, shows that in hilly Cumbria quarries were rarely more than one and a half miles from the building site. Longer distances and greater costs were tolerable for higher value materials such as slate. Stone could be moved in winter if the ground was frozen. The article is a useful guide to the allocation of transportation costs to the different stages in a journey.

121. W. J. Reader, *Macadam: The McAdam Family and the Turnpike Roads, 1798–1861* (London, 1980).

122. Hainsworth and Walker, *Correspondence of Lord Fitzwilliam of Milton*, p. 124.

123. This section is based on Eric Pawson, *Transport and Economy: The Turnpike Roads of Eighteenth-Century Britain* (London, 1977), p. 22.

124. Norfolk RO, MC 84/72, 524 x 7, letters from James Wilson, Goods Manager's Office, Great Northern Railway, York, to William Amhurst, 23 September and 5 and 9 October 1863.

125. Norfolk RO, MC 84/77, 524 x 7.

126. Buckinghamshire RO, D/FR 22/1/1, letters to Sir Thomas Fremantle from Henry Wilson, Stowlangtoft, 19 September 1864, and G. R. Wright, Woolpit, 23 September 1864.

127. Gloucestershire RO, D1799/E234.

128. Mauchline, *Harewood House*, p. 20.

129. Leeds University Library, MS 417. Mathew Wilson's house was rebuilt from 1825–27, and the domestic offices in the 1830s, by George Webster of Kendal.

130. Leicestershire RO, Finch MSS, DG 7/1/129.

131. Suffolk RO, Bury St Edmunds, 468, De Carle ledger, 1794–96.

132. J. Chambers, *A General History of the County of Norfolk* (Norwich, 1829), p. 922; Wilson and Mackley, 'Founding a Landed Dynasty', pp. 307–28.

133. 1856 price list for Messrs Randall & Saunders, quarry owners, reproduced in K. Hudson, *Fashionable Stone* (Bath, 1971), pp. 83–101.

134. Somerset RO, DD/TB, box 13, FL1, wages books for the building of Crowcombe, 3 volumes, 1724–27.

135. Somerset RO, DD/TB, box 13, FL1. A labourer paid 1s. per day received an additional 8d. per day for the use of his horse.

136. Gloucestershire RO, D1799/E239, William Blathwayt's annotation of letter from Charles Watkins at Dyrham, 30 July 1698.

137. Suffolk RO, Bury St Edmunds, 941/30, letter from L. Jackaman to J. H. Turner, Lord Bristol's agent, 15 July 1873.

138. Gloucestershire RO, D1799/E239, letter from Charles Watkins at Dyrham to William Blathwayt, 30 July 1698.

139. Suffolk RO, Ipswich, HA11, C7/2/2.

140. Norfolk RO, WAL 1429, letter from Thomas Ripley, 17 December 1724.

141. Cheshire RO, D2781/158, letter from Lewis Wyatt to G. C. Antrobus, 21 November 1827.

142. F. O. Morris, *A Series of Picturesque Views of Seats of the Noblemen and Gentlemen of Great Britain and Ireland*, ii (London, 1880), p. 65.

143. Gloucestershire RO, D1799/E241, letter from Charles Watkins to William Blathwayt, 31 May 1701.

144. Hobhouse, *Thomas Cubitt*, p. 9. The term 'builder's merchant' had reached provincial market towns by the 1840s, W. Bartram & Sons, of Aylsham, Norfolk, describing themselves as such when supplying Edward Fellowes at Haveringland Hall, Norfolk RO, MS 8595 20B.

145. Brett Harrison, 'Thorp Arch Hall, 1749–1756: "Dabling a Little in Mortar"', *Publications of the Thoresby Society*, second series, 4 (1994), pp. 1–39.

146. Suffolk RO, Ipswich, HA11, C7/2/1.

147. Norfolk RO, HEA489, 256 x 4, Edmund Rolfe's accounts for the building of the house at Heacham, 1774–80. The reuse of ship's timbers is not to be expected in country houses but, for the arguments against their use in building generally, see P. S. Barnwell and A. T. Adams, *The House Within: Interpreting Medieval Houses in Kent* (London, 1994), p. 2.

148. Although Edward Miller in *The History and Antiquities of Doncaster* (Doncaster, *c*. 1805), p. 278, loyally described the three quarries in the village as being equal to any in the county of York for building or burning to lime. The Brodsworth limestone weathered very badly, as the restorers of the house in the 1990s were also to find. See also Mark Girouard, *The Victorian Country House* (New Haven, 1979), p. 237; G. Smith, *Cusworth Hall* (Doncaster, 1968), p. 22; and Kate Jeffrey (ed.), *Brodsworth Hall* (London, 1995).

149. Quoted by Linda Clarke, *Building Capitalism* (London, 1992), p. 137.

150. Gerard Lynch, *Brickwork History, Technology and Practice* (London, 1994), i, pp. 4–15. Nineteenth-century manufacturers of brick-making machinery promoted their goods to estate brickworks, with claims for performance and cost-savings, as their literature in the Gisburn (Yorkshire) papers shows. Yorkshire Archaeological Society, Leeds, MD335, box 10.

151. Somerset RO, DD/TB, box 13. F. L., Crowcombe wages books (3 volumes), 1723/24–27.

152. Robert Malster, 'Suffolk Brickmaking', in *Suffolk Review*, 5 (1983), pp. 173–86; Norman Smedley, *East Anglian Crafts* (London, 1977), pp. 106–13; R. Brunskill and A. Clifton-Taylor, *English Brickwork* (London, 1977), p. 15.

153. Sir Balthazar Gerbier, *A Brief Discourse Concerning the Three Chief Principles of Magnificent Building* (London, 1662), p. 52.

154. Colvin and Newman, *Of Building*, p. 36. Cambridge University Library, Buxton Papers, letter from John Buxton to Robert Buxton, 14 June 1726.

155. R. Campbell, *The London Tradesman* (London, 1747; reprinted 1969), p. 169.

156. Norfolk RO, BUL 11/89, 615 x 8, cash book 1793 – *c*. 1801.

157. Norfolk RO, MS 8595 20B, box 3, Richard Armstrong's pay-bill no. 7.

158. BL, Add. MS 19223, fos 112–13, letter 16 March 1791.

159. BL, Add. MS 19223 fos 118–19.

160. Thomas Wilsford in *Architectonice: The Art of Building* (London, 1659), pp. 1–5, estimated that 6000 bricks could be made per man in five hours. N. Lloyd in *English Brickwork* (London, 1934), pp. 19–21, quotes a letter of the 1680s which states that a man, with assistants tempering the clay and carrying away the bricks, could mould 2000 in a fourteen- or fifteen-hour day, and 'an extraordinary man', 3000. Nicholson in *Architectural Dictionary*, i, p. 77, reckoned that

an industrious man, working from five in the morning until eight at night, could mould 5000 in a day. He would be assisted by a team of six, preparing the brick earth and stacking the moulded bricks. Clarke in *Building*, p. 101, concluded that a gang of six to eight men could produce around 12,000 bricks per day, although 22,000 was possible. Such a team could produce one million bricks in a four-month season.

161. Lloyd, *English Brickwork*, p. 21.

162. West Yorkshire Archives Service, Leeds, Ingleby MS 2662, brickmaking agreement, 23 November 1733.

163. Ibid., BW A/159, box 3, cash book 1725–58.

164. Norfolk RO, BEA 337, 438 x 7.

165. Some of this coal may have been used as fuel elsewhere on the site. The excise duty on brick had been 5s. 10d. per 1000 since 1833.

166. Lynch, *Brickwork*, i, pp. 20–21, considered that an ox pulling a cart in the middle ages would do well to transport 200–300 bricks ten miles in one day. In the nineteenth century a horse-drawn cart could only carry about two tons, between 600–800 bricks, a similar distance.

167. M. W. Thompson (ed.), *The Journeys of Sir Richard Colt Hoare through Wales and England, 1793–1810* (Gloucester, 1983), p. 70.

168. Habakkuk, 'Daniel Finch', p. 149.

169. Gloucestershire RO, D1799/E239, 241.

170. Northamptonshire RO, IL 2785. If the pressures of fashion overrode considerations of quality, problems could arise. A reaction in London against Portland stone used in classical buildings, coupled with a renewed interest in medieval models, led to the shipment of stone from Caen for the remodelling of Buckingham Palace in 1845–53. The Caen stone was cheaper but its choice proved disastrous, decayed masonry falling from the building within a very short time. Hobhouse, *Cubitt*, pp. 400, 421.

171. Northamptonshire RO, Fitzwilliam MSS, Milton Plans, 98. This stone was expected to cost a further £300 to work and set.

172. Cheshire RO, DEO 213/1, Oulton building accounts, 1824–28.

173. Hudson, *Fashionable Stone*, p. 52.

174. Stone was relatively cheap at Eshton and brick, delivered at a cost of at least 34s. per 1000 with some bought at over 40s., seems to have been expensive. However, on a volumetric basis, brick even at this price was cheaper than local stone. Assuming eighteen bricks to the cubic foot, the cost per cubic foot was less than 10d.

175. This was about one-third of the amount spent on brick. A duty of 20 per cent *ad valorem* was imposed on coastal movements of building stone in May 1794. Rous's first five shipments seem to have escaped it.

176. Norfolk RO, Kimberley MSS 14/205. The slate was priced f. o. b. London plus £1 5s. 0d. per ton for sea freight to Norwich. It is an example of a material (like lead) where the value far exceeds the cost of its fixing. The delivered cost for slate and nails was £346 11s. 1½d., whereas the slaters' wages plus accommodation cost only £17 2s. 9d. This was not a unique example of London men arriving on site before their materials. Lord Peterborough visited Dyrham in 1701, coming from Dodington where bricklayers had arrived weeks before bricks were even made; Gloucestershire RO, D1799/E241, letter from Charles Watkins at Dyrham to William Blathwayt, 4 June 1701.

177. A quotation obtained from 'Mr Webster' (presumably of the Kendal family of masons and

architects) by the Revd Eaton for Sir Martin Folkes Bt of Hillington, Norfolk (Norfolk RO, MC50/21, 503 x 5, letter dated 17 October 1774). Nicholson, *Architectural Dictionary* ii, p. 701, quotes the Kendal price as £1 15s. per ton for the best quality, of which 1 ton 6 cwt would cover forty-two square yards.

178. West Yorkshire Archives Service, Bradford, 68D 82/5/204, 18 May 1838.
179. H. S. K. Kent, 'The Anglo-Norwegian Timber Trade in the Eighteenth Century', *Economic History Review*, second series, 8 (1955–56), pp. 62–74.
180. Leicestershire RO, Finch MSS, DG7/1/129, letters from John Landsdell to the Earl of Nottingham, 14 May and 11, 22 August, 1696.
181. Blathwayt's unusual imports from the American colonies in 1693 included various berries and nuts, and two rattlesnakes in a cage. Gloucestershire RO, D1799/E234.
182. Mauchline, *Harewood*, p. 57.
183. Emily J. Climenson, *Passages from the Diaries of Mrs Philip Lybbe Powys of Hardwick House, Oxon., AD 1756 to 1808* (London, 1899), p. 132.
184. Norfolk RO, HEA 489, 256 x 4. The chaldron was a customary volumetric measure which varied according to district. By the eighteenth century the imperial chaldron, used in London, had settled down to the equivalent of 1.32 tons. In 1776, with the kiln-building cost paid, lime was charged to the building account at 7s. and 6s. 3d. per chaldron. Nicholson, *Architectural Dictionary*, ii, p. 199, estimated that one bushel of coal was needed to produce three bushels of lime.
185. Suffolk RO, Ipswich, HA11, C7/1/37–38, C7/2/1,3. The materials included thirty-four barrels of 'composition', a form of cement for ornamental mouldings, made of powdered whiting, glue in solution and linseed oil.
186. Gloucestershire RO, D1799/E239.
187. A house at Meriden by the Warwick architect Francis Smith. Beard, *Craftsmen*, pp. 34–35.
188. 'An Account of the Several Sums Expended in the New House at Denton', in the possession of Mr J. F. Goodchild of Wakefield.
189. Suffolk RO, Ipswich, HA11, C7/2/5.
190. Suffolk RO, Ipswich, HA11, C7/2/3, clerk of the works's accounts, and C7/1/35, letter to John Rous, 28 April 1796. About 3960 square feet of glass was needed for the house, the largest single pane being about three square feet in area.
191. Leeds University Library, MS417/7, Mathew Wilson's day book, 1 October 1824.
192. The historical review of glassmaking is based on T. C. Barker, *The Glassmakers: Pilkington, 1826–1976* (London, 1977).
193. Roger Dixon and Stefan Muthesius, *Victorian Architecture* (Oxford, 1978), p. 139.
194. Girouard, *Victorian Country House*, p. 226.
195. Dixon and Muthesius, *Victorian Architecture*, p. 96.
196. Suffolk RO, Ipswich, HA11. The Henham blacksmiths were not local men, being paid a lodging allowance. Ironmongery was bought from several local sources, and an iron colonnade fixed between the hall and the kitchen came from Norwich. £1176 was spent on ironmongery (excluding wages and carriage), representing about 5 per cent of the cost of the house. Alan Mackley, 'An Economic History of Country-House Building', p. 339.
197. Pamela A. Sambrook and Peter Brears, *The Country House Kitchen, 1650–1900* (Stroud, 1996), pp. 92–115.
198. A range supplied by one of the best-known London smiths, W. H. Feetham, is still to be

seen in the old kitchen at Holkham Hall. Feetham was also favoured with an order for the supply of a grate for the luncheon room at Buckingham Palace (Hobhouse, *Cubitt*, p. 403).

199. Advice probably in 1695 from Sir Henry Sheeres, surveyor of the ordnance, quoted by Habakkuk in 'Daniel Finch', p. 149. The carcase of the house was brick, and stone was used for the foundations, outer coverings to the walls, and ornamentation.

200. Hobhouse, *Cubitt*, p. 385.

201. Suffolk RO, Ipswich, HA11, C7/1/40, account, 20 October 1798.

202. Lincolnshire RO, Thorold MSS, 6/3/1–5, invoice 'for work done at the New Building at Syston Park', 8 February 1766 to 26 February 1772. The bill for £351 was not settled until 10 February 1775. Langwith at times employed as many as four men besides himself; he provided no materials.

203. Joyce Godber (ed.), 'The Marchioness Grey of Wrest Park', *Publications of the Bedfordshire Historical Record Society*, 47 (1968), p. 153.

204. Gloucestershire RO, D1799/E243, letter from William Blathwayt to his agent Charles Watkins, 6 April 1703; Godber, 'Marchioness Grey', p. 140.

Notes to Chapter 6: The Pattern of Building

1. G. Webb (ed.), *The Complete Works of Sir John Vanbrugh*, iv (London, 1928), p. 25.

2. Lilian Dickins and Mary Stanton (eds), *An Eighteenth-Century Correspondence: Being the Letters to Sanderson Miller, Esq., of Radway* (London, 1910), p. 397.

3. Ibid., pp. 394–98.

4. Thomas Coke, first Earl of Leicester, died the year after Lyttelton's visit, and Holkham Hall was not completed until 1764.

5. Matthew Brettingham remodelled Euston Hall in Suffolk in 1750–56 for the second Duke of Grafton. The Elizabethan house had been rebuilt in the seventeenth century for Lord Arlington but, in continuing to use the original, low-lying site, the duke failed to set a fashionable, inspirational example for other builders in the county. In addition to Holkham, Norfolk offered Sir Robert Walpole's spectacular Houghton Hall, completed in 1735, his younger brother Horatio's Wolterton Hall, completed in 1741, and more than a dozen other houses built since 1700 by significant landowners.

6. Derek Linstrum, *West Yorkshire Architects and Architecture* (London, 1978), p. 65.

7. Paul Nunn, 'Aristocratic Estates and Employment in South Yorkshire, 1700–1800', in S. Pollard and C. Holmes (eds), *Essays in the Economic and Social History of South Yorkshire* (Sheffield, 1976), pp. 28–45. Edward Waterson and Peter Meadows, *Lost Houses of the West Riding* (Welburn, 1998), p. 21.

8. John Summerson, 'The Classical Country House in Eighteenth-Century England', *Journal of the Royal Society of Arts*, 107 (1959), pp. 539–87. One hundred and forty-seven of the houses were datable: twenty-one (1710–14); twenty-two (1715–19); fifty (1720–24); twenty-two (1725–29); twenty-one (1730–34); eleven (1735–39); a further eighty-three (1740–60).

9. John Beckett, *The Aristocracy*, pp. 326–29.

10. That is, the 'Great Landowners'. Bateman, in updating the survey of 1872–73 for his fourth edition of 1883, may nevertheless have missed some estates created with new wealth in the intervening years.

11. F. M. L. Thompson, *English Landed Society in the Nineteenth Century* (London, 1963), p. 112.

12. Peter de Figueiredo and Julian Treuherz, *Cheshire Country Houses* (Chichester, 1988); Nicholas Kingsley, *The Country Houses of Gloucestershire*, i, *1500–1660* (Cheltenham, 1989); idem, *The Country Houses of Gloucestershire*, ii, *1660–1830* (Chichester, 1992); J. Heward and R. Taylor, *The Country Houses of Northamptonshire*, Royal Commission on the Historical Monuments of England (Swindon, 1996).

13. G. Baker, *The History and Antiquities of the County of Northamptonshire*, 2 vols (London, 1822–41); J. Bridges (ed. P. Whalley), *The History and Antiquities of Northamptonshire*, 2 vols (Oxford, 1791).

14. K. J. Allison (ed.), *A History of the County of York: East Riding*, ii (Oxford, 1974).

15. See John Beckett's summary in *The Aristocracy*, pp. 326–29.

16. Houses were selected by the RCHME for publication in *The Country Houses of Northamptonshire* on the basis of size and the social status of their early owners. They observe that very few houses of any size and importance were built after 1800. In fact, only two of the fifty-nine houses discussed were built after 1660: Dallington Hall (1720) was erected soon after the estate was bought by Joseph Jekyll. It was let from 1766 to the mid nineteenth century, becoming a secondary house of the Spencers. Sulby Hall (1793 by Soane) was built by Rene Payne soon after he bought the estate, but the extravagance of a grandson forced its sale in 1847.

17. That the seats of the larger estates of the 1870s tend to be earlier than those on the smaller estates is consistent with the propositions that the more successful estate owners had built earlier; and that a house was less likely to be rebuilt if the estate remained in the same family.

18. Christopher Hussey, 'Dalham Hall, Suffolk', *Country Life*, 54, 1 September 1923, pp. 280–85.

19. Marcus Binney, 'Worlingham Hall, Suffolk', *Country Life*, 147, 12 March 1970, pp. 624–28.

20. Kingsley, *Gloucestershire*, ii, p. 127.

21. Ibid., p. 219.

22. Lindsay Boynton, 'Newby Park: The First Palladian Villa in England', in Howard Colvin and John Harris (eds), *The Country Seat* (London, 1970), pp. 97–105.

23. Estates of over 10,000 acres accounted for 40.4 per cent of the estates in the sample. In the whole period 1660–1879, 39.8 per cent of new houses were on these estates. In the 1690s to 1720s, however, the percentage was higher at 45.2.

24. Three new heirs built: Sir Thomas Broughton at Doddington; Henry Cornwallis Legh at High Legh; and William Egerton at Tatton Park. New houses for other long-established families included Hooton Hall for Sir William Stanley and Delamere House for George Wilbraham. Bostock Hall, totally rebuilt for Edward Tomkinson, was sold in 1792.

25. Bevan bought Riddlesworth around 1785, rebuilt the house and sold it in the early nineteenth century. West Wretham was another new house soon sold. Long-established builders included Hare and Gurdon, at Stow Bardolph and Letton respectively since the sixteenth century. The Prestons, at Beeston St Laurence since the early seventeenth century, also rebuilt their house.

26. Baker, *Northamptonshire*, p. 18.

27. Norfolk RO, Walsingham MSS 21554, LXI/31, 430 x 6, handwritten note to Lord Walsingham.

28. See Chapter 8, note 65.

29. W. D. Rubinstein, 'New Men of Wealth and the Purchase of Land in Nineteenth-Century Britain', *Past and Present*, 92 (1981), pp. 125–47.

30. F. M. L. Thompson, 'Life after Death: How Successful Businessmen Disposed of their Fortunes', *Economic History Review*, second series, 43 (1990), pp. 40–61.

31. Anthony Howe, *The Cotton Masters, 1830–1860* (Oxford, 1984), pp. 29–31.

32. J. Mordaunt Crook, in *The Rise of the Nouveaux Riches* (London, 1999), discusses the issues of style and status among the very rich in the Victorian and Edwardian periods. He observes (p. 75) that most of those who built country houses were 'extraordinarily obtuse in their choice of architect' and quotes Margot Asquith, writing in 1922, 'Rich men's houses are seldom beautiful, rarely comfortable, and never original', p. 78. From the late 1870s, 'Instant fortunes were more instantly translated into status symbols in the metropolis than in the countryside', ibid., p. 155.

33. C. Bruyn Andrews (ed.), *The Torrington Diaries: Containing the Tours through England and Wales of the Hon. John Byng (Later Fifth Viscount Torrington) between the Years 1781 and 1794*, iii (London, 1936), p. 318.

34. The landowner's decision whether to rebuild or remodel a house is discussed in Chapter 7, pp. 271–85.

35. For the discussion of rents this section draws on M. E. Turner, J. V. Beckett and B. Afton, *Agricultural Rent in England, 1690–1914* (Cambridge, 1997).

36. Norfolk RO, Walsingham MSS, WLS XLV/7/4, 425 x 2, letter dated 1 April 1804.

37. Turner, Beckett and Afton, *Agricultural Rent*, p. 179.

38. BL, Add. MS 19223, fos 33–34, letter to Eleazar Davy from Bath, 9 June 1788.

39. M. H. Port, 'Town and Country House: Their Interaction', in Dana Arnold (ed.), *The Georgian Country House* (Stroud, 1998), pp. 117–38.

40. Andrews, *Torrington*, iii, p. 134.

41. Ibid., p. 143.

42. Port, 'Town and Country House', p. 138.

43. Andrews, *Torrington*, iii, p. 209. Boughton was bought in 1528 by a successful lawyer, Edward Montagu (*c*. 1486–1557). Ralph Montagu began a major transformation of the old house in the late seventeenth century and his son John, second Duke of Montagu, continued the work; but by the second half of the eighteenth century the house was one of several seats owned by the family and never again occupied continuously. The estate passed by marriage later in the century to the Dukes of Buccleuch. Seward and Taylor, *Northamptonshire*, p. 94.

44. R. Strong, M. Binney and J. Harris, *The Destruction of the Country House* (London, 1974); M. Binney and K. Martin, *The Country House: To Be or Not To Be*, SAVE Britain's Heritage (London, 1982).

45. David Watkin, 'Cambridgeshire', *Burke's & Savills Guide to Country Houses*, iii, *East Anglia* (London, 1981), p. 1.

46. J. Collett-White, 'Inventories of Bedfordshire Country Houses, 1714–1830', *Bedfordshire Historical Record Society*, 74 (1995), p. 4.

47. Andrews, *Torrington*, iii, pp. 200–1.

48. George Gilbert Scott, *Remarks on Secular and Domestic Architecture, Present and Future* (London, 1857), p. 141.

49. Baker, *Northamptonshire*; Bridges, *Northamptonshire*.

50. Figueiredo and Treuherz, *Cheshire*, p. 1.

51. J. Blatchly (ed.), 'A Journal of Excursions through the County of Suffolk, 1823–1844, of David Elisha Davy', *Suffolk Records Society*, 24 (1982), p. 89.

52. Andrews, *Torrington*, iii, p. 220.
53. Thompson, 'Life after Death'.
54. The following discussion draws upon Kingsley, *Gloucestershire*, and Figueiredo and Treuherz, *Cheshire*.
55. The end date of 1830 for Kingsley, *Gloucestershire*, ii, excludes Victorian houses built on new sites, but the replacement of existing houses is generally covered.
56. Ibid., ii, pp. 7–8.
57. Geoffrey Scard, *Squire and Tenant: Life in Rural Cheshire, 1760–1900* (Chester, 1981), p. 15.

Notes to Chapter 7: The Cost of the Country House

1. William Halfpenny, in the preface of *A New and Complete System of Architecture* (London, 1749).
2. Robert Kerr, *The Gentleman's House* (London, 1871), p. 390.
3. 'Catalogue of Books Made Out Aug. 1791. Robert Fellowes.' See also Christie's South Kensington Sale Catalogue, 24 September 1979; Norfolk RO, Fellowes MSS, Fel. 716, 1079, 1115; Burke's *Landed Gentry* (1937); D. Stroud, *The Architecture of Sir John Soane* (London, 1961), p. 32, plates 23–27.
4. There are twenty-two letters from Fellowes to Soane, the earliest dating from September 1786, in the library of the Sir John Soane Museum, private correspondence, I, F, 2. Soane's drawings for Shotesham are in the Norfolk RO, Fel. 1115/P157C.
5. Norfolk RO, Fel. 716, Royal Exchange Insurance policy, dated 10 January 1793, for Robert Fellowes's 'Brick built and tiled mansion house'. Tendring Hall (Suffolk), a rather grander contemporary Soane house cost £12,050 (see Table 13); like Shotesham, it was new built and the cost included stables and kitchen garden walls.
6. L. Dickins and M. Stanton (eds), *An Eighteenth-Century Correspondence: Being the Letters ... to Sanderson Miller, Esq., of Radway* (London, 1910), p. 136.
7. *Leeds Intelligencer*, 9 February, 15 March 1768; R. G. Wilson, 'Merchants and Land: The Ibbetsons of Leeds and Denton, 1650–1850', *Northern History*, 24 (1988), p. 92; N. Pevsner, *The Buildings of England: Yorkshire, the West Riding* (Harmondsworth, 1959), pp. 50, 178; C. Hussey, 'Denton Hall, Yorkshire', *Country Life*, 86, 4 November 1939, pp. 470–74.
8. See pp. 40, 56 above; E. J. Climenson (ed.), *Passages from the Diaries of Mrs Philip Lybbe Powys of Hardwick House, Oxon., AD 1756 to 1808* (London, 1899), pp. 145–48.
9. R. Warner, *Excursions from Bath* (Bath, 1801), pp. 189–90.
10. R. L. Winstanley (ed.), *The Diary of James Woodforde: The First Six Norfolk Years, 1776–1781*, Parson Woodforde Society (1984), ii, p. 176; John Beresford (ed.), *The Diary of a Country Parson, 1758–1802* (London, 1959), pp. 210, 227.
11. Kenneth Garlick and Angus MacIntyre (eds), *The Diary of Joseph Farington, 1793–1821*, 15 vols (New Haven and London, 1978–84); C. Bruyn Andrews (ed.), *The Torrington Diaries: Containing the Tours through England and Wales of the Hon. John Byng (Later Fifth Viscount Torrington) between the Years 1781 and 1794*, iii (London, 1936), p. 228.
12. Climenson, *Diaries of Mrs Philip Lybbe Powys*, pp. 166–67, notes that Fonthill Splendens, 'where is display'd the utmost profusion of magnificence', cost Alderman Beckford, £240,000; Farington cites £100,000. Fonthill Abbey cost £270,000 according to J. M. Robinson, *The Wyatts: An Architectural Dynasty* (Oxford, 1979), p. 85; F. M. L. Thompson, *English Landed Society in the Nineteenth Century* (London, 1963), pp. 88–89, suggests 'perhaps £400,000'. The figures for

Thoresby and Westonbirt are taken from Jill Allibone, *Anthony Salvin: Pioneer of the Gothic Revival* (Cambridge, 1988), and Jill Franklin, *The Gentleman's Country House and its Plan, 1835–1914* (London, 1981); for Bearwood see Berkshire RO, D/EWal E13, letter of John Walter to Robert Kerr, 23 June 1875; Wynyard and Conishead come from Robinson, *The Wyatts*; Eastnor from the *Eastnor Castle Guide*, p. 13; and Moor Park from Paget Toynbee (ed.), 'Horace Walpole's Journals of Visits to Country Seats, etc', *Walpole Society*, 16 (1927–28), p. 24.

13. W. Halfpenny, J. Halfpenny, R. Morris and T. Lightoler, *The Modern Builder's Assistant* (London, 1742).

14. T. Rawlins, *Familiar Architecture: Consisting of Original Designs of Houses for Gentlemen and Tradesmen, Parsonages and Summer Retreats* (London, 1768), p. v.

15. See Chapter 2, n. 59. Lawrence Stone, 'Cole Green Park House', and Lindsay Boynton, 'Newby Park, Yorkshire: The First Palladian Villa in England', in Howard Colvin and John Harris (eds), *The Country Seat* (London, 1970), pp. 75–80, 97–105. The total for Newby from Boynton's figures 'Newby Park' (p. 105), looks improbable with very few materials, probably estate produced, specified.

16. B. Harrison, 'Thorp Arch Hall, 1749–1756: "Dabling a Little in Mortar"', *Publications of the Thoresby Society*, second series, 4 (1992), pp. 1–39; L. F. Pearson, 'Ormesby Hall, Cleveland', *Yorkshire Archaeological Journal*, 61 (1989), pp. 149–54; Pevsner, *The Buildings of England: Yorkshire, North Riding* (Harmondsworth, 1966), pp. 276–77; Somerset RO, DD/TB, box 13, FL1.

17. E. Harris, *British Architectural Books and Writers, 1556–1785* (Cambridge, 1989), p. 124.

18. A. Bell, *Sydney Smith* (Oxford, 1980), p. 88; G. Worsley, 'Brockfield Hall Yorkshire', *Country Life*, 183, 9 March 1989, pp. 136–39.

19. Franklin, *Gentleman's Country House*, p. 124. Of course, a good deal depended upon the internal finish. If it was basic, prices might be driven down below Franklin's lower threshold. David Bryce built (1856–60) a bargain-basement country house, Shambellie, for William Stewart, a member of an old Kirkcudbrightshire landed family who owned 2400 acres in the county. The house cost, after inordinate disputes between client, architect and builder, £2984 10s. 9d. A. Rowan, *The Creation of Shambellie: The Story of a Victorian Building Contract* (Edinburgh, 1982), pp. 12, 14, 57.

20. John Beckett in *The Aristocracy in England, 1660–1914* (Oxford, 1986), a 500 page, deeply researched survey, devotes only a dozen pages to the building and landscape gardening activities of the nobility and gentry, although it was perhaps their greatest interest and finest achievement. In table 10.1 he cites the cost of a curious *mélange* of only sixteen houses, not differentiating between new and remodelled. The selection is entirely of top-flight houses; even those built by the three commoners included, Southill, Harlaxton and Bearwood, are totally exceptional.

21. Dickins and Stanton, *An Eighteenth-Century Correspondence*, pp. 230, 284–85, 292.

22. We are grateful to Dr John Barney for looking at Soane's practice records in the Soane Museum.

23. This section on Haveringland is based upon Alan Mackley, 'The Building of Haveringland Hall', *Norfolk Archaeology*, 43 (1999), pp. 111–32, where a full set of references to the building accounts and Edward Blore's accounts and drawings are located.

24. The issues considered in this chapter are discussed in R. G. Wilson and A. L. Mackley, 'How Much Did the English Country House Cost to Build, 1660–1880?', *Economic History Review*, second series, 52 (1999), pp. 436–68.

25. Dorothy Stroud, *The Architecture of Sir John Soane* (London, 1961), p. 83.

26. J. Mordaunt Crook and M. H. Port, *The History of the King's Works*, vi, *1782–1851* (London, 1973), p. 177 n. 3.

27. Cheshire RO, D2781/152, letter from Lewis Wyatt to Gibbs Antrobus of Eaton-by-Congleton Hall, Cheshire, dated 1 February 1828.

28. Alan Mackley, 'The Construction of Henham Hall', *Georgian Group Journal*, 6 (1996), pp. 85–96.

29. Some payments did not stay in the local economy, for instance the architect's fee, the cost of stone, sea freight, and brick duty (in all 17.1 per cent of the project cost). The cost of other materials from external sources amounted to 19.5 per cent. If the local merchants' gross margin was 50 per cent (out of which they paid their own local costs), another 10 per cent or so of project cost left the area. If all the wage payments were spent locally, some 73 per cent of total expenditure benefited the local economy. Some of the migrant workers (and the clerk of the works) will, however, have remitted part of their wages to families at home. The evidence suggests a minimum of fifteen migrants in a total of over 250 different men employed, although they worked a much higher proportion of total man-hours, and were paid a higher proportion of the wage bill (which was 46.6 per cent of expenditure, if jobbing accounts are included) than the numbers of men suggest. It is therefore reasonable to conclude that at least two-thirds of total expenditure was of local benefit.

30. For example, Terling Place (Essex), 1771–74, undated estimate for £5722, house and stables built for £5500; Sadborrow (Dorset), 1773–75, £2589; Kingsthorpe Hall (Northamptonshire), 1773–75, £3490; East Carlton Hall (Northamptonshire), 1776–80, £7400. Nancy Briggs, *John Johnson, 1734–1814: Georgian Architect and County Surveyor of Essex* (Chelmsford, 1991), pp. 20–32.

31. Soane Museum, Gunthorpe bill book, and ledger B, fol. 16, account with Charles Collyer.

32. Jules Lubbock, *The Tyranny of Taste* (New Haven and London, 1995), p. 60.

33. Robert Kerr gave advice, *Gentleman's House*, p. 381, on this as all other matters. Since it was a complex topic, with individual circumstances varying so much, he could offer only 'a series of notes'. His calculations were that a landowner should spend, like the middle classes, one-tenth of their rentals on their house. This meant that if an estate produced £5000 a year, then a notional 'rental' of £500, reckoned as a 5 per cent return, warranted a house costing £10,000. He also commented on the cost of living well in a house, reckoning this to be ten times its rental.

34. John Soane, *Plans, Elevations and Sections of Buildings* (London 1788), p. 6.

35. Halfpenny, Morris and Lightoler, *Modern Builder's Assistant*. See also Halfpenny, *Chinese and Gothic Architecture*; and R. Morris, *Select Architecture: Being Regular Designs of Plans and Elevations Well Suited to Both Town and Country* (London, 1755).

36. Kerr, *Gentleman's House*, pp. 390–92.

37. Berkshire RO, D/EBY E87, Richard Armstrong to Richard Benyon, 3 October 1888.

38. Kerr, *Gentleman's House*, p. 384.

39. Andor Gomme, 'Nightmare and Apotheosis: The "Finishing of Stoneleigh"', in Malcolm Airs (ed.), *The Later Eighteenth-Century Great House* (Oxford, 1997), p. 172. See also his 'Stoneleigh after the Grand Tour', *Antiquaries Journal*, 68 (1988), pp. 265–86.

40. Soane Museum, journal 1, fol. 19ff, and private correspondence, i, F2, 1–22; Norfolk RO, Fel. 1115/P167C.

41. West Yorkshire Archives Service, Leeds, BW/A/25 (box 1), 26 (box 1), 30 (box 1), 31 (box 1), 32 (box 1), 159 (box 3). See also Peter Leach, *James Paine* (London, 1988), pp. 53, 181–82.

42. B. F. Duckham, 'Canals and River Navigations', in D. H. Aldcroft and M. J. Freeman (eds), *Transport in the Industrial Revolution* (Manchester, 1983), p. 114.

43. David Watkin, *The Life and Work of C. R. Cockerell* (London, 1974), pp. 169–70.

44. R. T. Gunther, *The Architecture of Sir Roger Pratt, Charles II's Commissioner for the Rebuilding of London after the Great Fire: Now Printed for the First Time from his Note-Books* (London, 1928), p. 54.

45. Kerr, *Gentleman's House*, p. xi.

46. Gunther, *Sir Roger Pratt*, pp. 53–54, 61.

47. Berkshire RO, D/EWal, E13, letter from John Walter to Robert Kerr, 23 June 1875.

48. Cheshire RO, DCR/15/7, letters from E. M. Barry to Lord Crewe, various dates from 6 July 1866 to 16 February 1871.

49. Julia Ionides, 'Mr Pritchard of Shrewsbury', in Airs, *Later Eighteenth-Century Great House*, pp. 156–71; idem, *Thomas Farnolls Pritchard of Shrewsbury: Architect and 'Inventor of Cast Iron Bridges'* (Ludlow, 1999), passim.

50. Quoted in Allibone, *Anthony Salvin*, p. 39.

51. Colvin, *Biographical Dictionary*, pp. 391–92. For Cole Orton, see Colvin and Harris, *The Country Seat*, pp. 215–19; for Strelley, Nottinghamshire RO, DDE 46/58, 46/61, 46/62, 60/1–11.

52. Joyce Godber (ed.), 'The Marchioness Grey of Wrest Park', *Bedfordshire Historical Record Society*, 47 (1968), p. 114.

53. Gunther, *Sir Roger Pratt*, p. 54.

54. James Collett-White has edited an excellent collection in 'Inventories of Bedfordshire Country Houses, 1714–1830', *Bedfordshire Historical Record Society*, 74 (1995).

55. Ibid., pp. 250–51. Marchioness Grey's title died with her in 1797. Her daughter Amabel became the newly created Countess de Grey of Wrest Park in 1816. She died in 1833 and the title passed to her nephew, Thomas Philip, who rebuilt the house.

56. He was involved in some seventy-five remodelling commissions for county houses and twenty-three new houses. Allibone, *Anthony Salvin*, pp. 155–97.

57. Collett-White, *Bedfordshire Country Houses*, p. 249; Leicestershire RO, Bray of Stanford collection, 23D57/1747/8. Staveley's estimate is undated but relates to his letter to Sir Thomas Cave, 26 February 1768. The third Earl died in 1770. The old stables were demolished in 1771, the interior partly remodelled in 1776, and George Richardson's fine Gothic-style church built in 1783. See also John Nichols, *The History and Antiquities of the County of Leicester*, ii, pt 1 (London, 1795); N. Pevsner, *The Buildings of England: Leicestershire and Rutland* (Harmondsworth, 1960), pp. 234–37.

58. Leicestershire RO, 23D57/1647–8. The 1738 bill does not seem to include all spending because John Taylor, bricklayer, presented a bill for £568 18s. 7d. in 1739.

59. Emma Hazell, 'Matthew Brettingham, 1699–1769: "Great Man" or "Pretious Ass"?' (unpublished M.A. thesis, University of East Anglia, 1997), p. 39.

60. Ionides, 'Mr Pritchard of Shrewsbury', p. 157.

61. Soane Museum, Journal 1, p. 152ff; ledger B, fos 32–38, account with E. R. Pratt; private correspondence, iv, 9, B (1–7).

62. Dickins and Stanton, *Eighteenth-Century Correspondence*, pp. 111, 135, 190, 310–13, 401, 406.

63. Geoffrey Tyack, *Warwickshire Country Houses* (Chichester, 1994), pp. 9–15; idem, 'The Gothic Revival Country House in Eighteenth-Century Warwickshire', in Airs, *Eighteenth-Century Great House*, pp. 114–22.

64. Todd Longstaffe-Gowan, 'Two Great Eighteenth-Century English Landscapes: Trewithen and Weston Park', in Airs, *Eighteenth-Century Great House*, pp. 62–75. See also the continual alterations made to Lamport Hall (Northamptonshire), John Heward and Robert Taylor, *The Country Houses of Northamptonshire* (Swindon, 1996), pp. 256–62. John Harris describes a similar cycle of updating at Bulstrode Park (Buckinghamshire) in 'Bulstrode' *Architectural Review*, 124 (1958), pp. 319–20, and in his *No Voice from the Hall* (London, 1998), pp. 153–58.

65. Cheshire RO, D2781/156, letter from Antrobus to Wyatt, 4 January 1828.

66. Kerr, *Gentleman's House*, p. 296.

67. Suffolk RO, Ipswich, HH/93/3/222, 224. Norris's excessive remodelling of Rendlesham Hall (Suffolk) was corrected by Henry Holland at the request of Soane. Dorothy Stroud, *Henry Holland: His Life and Architecture* (London, 1966), p. 58.

68. For example Horace Walpole, quoted in Paget Toynbee (ed.), 'Horace Walpole's Journals of Visits to Country Seats, etc.', *Walpole Society*, 16 (1927–28), p. 58; Kerr, *Gentleman's House*, pp. 52–53, 290, 426–27.

69. Kerr, *Gentleman's House*, pp. 279–99.

70. Gunther, *Sir Roger Pratt*, p. 61; Howard Colvin and John Newman (eds), *Of Building: Roger North's Writings on Architecture* (Oxford, 1981) p. 7; Richard Neve, *The City and Country Purchaser and Builders Dictionary* (2nd edn, London, 1726), p. 59.

71. Paget Toynbee, 'Horace Walpole's Journals', pp. 17–19, 52, 64. Walpole's opinion of Donnington Park was almost exactly echoed by Byng; the house was 'of a capacity for a gentleman of £2000 a year, squatted in a hole of most ugly building; and what was added by the present earl is of the worst taste, a low dining-room, with a tea room above it, like a mean addition to a villa near London'. Andrews, *Torrington*, ii, pp. 75–76.

72. B. Cozens-Hardy (ed.), *The Diary of Sylas Neville, 1767–1788* (London, 1950), entry for 31 December 1781.

73. Norman Scarfe (ed.), 'A Frenchman's Year in Suffolk, 1784', *Suffolk Records Society*, 30 (1988), pp. 139–41.

74. Colin Platt, *The Great Rebuildings of Tudor and Stuart England* (London, 1994), p. 32.

75. See the essays by John Harris and Tom Williamson in Andrew Moore (ed.), *Houghton Hall: The Prime Minister, the Empress and the Heritage*, Norfolk Museums Service (Norwich, 1996).

76. A. C. Edwards, *The Account Books of Benjamin Mildmay, Earl Fitzwalter* (London, 1977), pp. vii–viii, 28–64. Having suffered from use by the military during the French wars, and being surplus to the family's requirements, the house was demolished in 1809. We are grateful to David Cubitt for bringing this source to our attention.

77. Cambridge University Library, Buxton papers, letters from John Buxton to Robert Buxton, 30 November 1726 and 1 May 1727. Gentlemen's discussion of the choice of site for a house could also be informed by their awareness of early writers such as Andrea Palladio (1508–80) who stressed the importance of convenience, health and prospect. Andrea Palladio, *The Four Books of Architecture*, trans. Robert Tavernor and Richard Scholefield (Cambridge, Massachusetts, and London, 1997), pp. 121–22. The importance of such considerations was reiterated by Isaac Ware in, *A Complete Body of Architecture* (London, 1756), p. 95.

78. Mary Mauchline, *Harewood House* (Newton Abbot, 1974), pp. 15–19, 32–34, 108–9, 112.

79. Collett-White, *Bedfordshire Country Houses*, pp. 250–51.

80. Lawrence Stone and Jeanne C. Fawtier Stone, *An Open Elite? England, 1540–1880* (Oxford, 1984), see especially pp. 349–96 and appendix 2; idem, 'Country Houses and Their Owners in

Hertfordshire, 1540–1879', in W. O. Aydelotte, A. G. Bogue and R. W. Fogel (eds), *The Dimensions of Quantitative Research* (Princeton, 1972), pp. 56–113.

81. Stone and Stone, *An Open Elite?*, p. 440.

82. Morris, *Select Architecture*, preface.

83. Halfpenny, Morris and Lightoler, *Modern Builder's Assistant*; Kerr, *Gentleman's House*, pp. 390–407.

84. S. D. Chapman, 'Fixed Capital Formation in the British Cotton Industry', *Economic History Review*, second series, 23 (1970), pp. 235–66; J. P. Higgins and S. Pollard (eds), *Aspects of Capital Investment in Great Britain, 1750–1850* (London, 1971), p. 15; D. T. Jenkins, *The West Riding Wool Textile Industry, 1770–1835* (Edington, 1975). The use of insurance records in historical research is discussed in M. W. Beresford, 'Building History from Insurance Records', *Urban History Yearbook* (1976), pp. 7–14; D. T. Jenkins 'The Practice of Insurance against Fire, 1750–1840', in O. M. Westall (ed.), *The Historian and the Business of Insurance* (Manchester, 1984), pp. 9–38.

85. London, Guildhall Library, 11936/266.

86. Ibid., Sun policies 11936/12/524; 15/543; 18/228; 19/72; 21/26; 23/15; 24/208, 267; 25/508.

87. Ibid., 11936/266/321 and 291/633.

88. Ibid., 11936/342; Royal Exchange policy GL 7253/24/188.

89. Ibid., 7253/31/61.

90. Ibid., Sun policy 11936/329/318.

91. Ibid., 11936/290/359.

92. Suffolk RO, Bury St Edmunds, HH/500/2/2, 5; 941/30/114, 134.

93. Jenkins, *West Riding Wool Textile Industry*, p. 279.

94. Idem, 'Practice of Insurance', p. 28.

95. Another approach in ascertaining at least a ranking of country house values, by county and indeed nationally, is to consider the collection of the Inhabited House Duty introduced in 1778, much amended the following year, raised several times between 1789 and 1815, repealed in 1834, and reintroduced on the abolition of the Window Tax in 1851. Collections were sizeable: £900,000 gross per annum by 1815; £1,300,000 in the early 1830s. Parliamentary Papers reveal returns for 1822–23 and from 1861–62 onwards. Although the figures arranged in bands from £20 net annual value upwards should in theory reveal, since they ran to ones collected on more than £400 net annual value (1823) and £500 net annual value (1862ff), the stock of a county's country houses, they in fact disclose an extraordinary preponderance of valuable urban property. For example, the duty collected in 1822–23 on houses of above £50 net annual value was a mere dozen in Bedfordshire compared with 17,605 in London, Westminster and Middlesex and 2697 in Somerset (Bath and Bristol falling within its collection district). These returns after 1862 reveal the same picture. Clearly country house owners were able to demonstrate effectively to the local commissioners of the tax that the net annual value of a rented country house on the open market, once the costs of maintaining it were deducted, was low. See S. Dowell, *A History of Taxation and Taxes in England*, iii (London, 1884), pp. 178–98; *Parliamentary Papers*, 1824, viii, pp. 453–57; 1863, xxiv, p. 677; 1873, xxxvi, p. 247.

96. The rate of change of wage rates over time is based on E. H. Phelps Brown and S. Hopkins, 'Seven Centuries of Building Wages', in E. M. Carus-Wilson (ed.), *Essays in Economic History*, ii (London, 1962), pp. 168–79. The intervals in the scale are proportional to rises in craftsmen's rates, at dates which correspond to the start of relatively stable periods for wage rates. The

rate of increase in building cost with house size is derived from Kerr, *Gentleman's House*, pp. 381–408, with the same rate assumed for all dates.

97. S. D. Chapman, *The Cotton Industry in the Industrial Revolution* (London, 1987), p. 29. The figures were adjusted to include capital invested in mule spinning machinery.

98. J. R. Ward, *The Finance of Canal Building in Eighteenth Century England* (Oxford, 1974), pp. 74–75. According to Ward's calculations, peers and gentlemen (rural-based but not necessarily large landowners) invested some £340,000 per decade in canal construction in the 1755–80 period, and £950,000 in the 1780–1815 period, the heyday of canal building. In total, peers and gentlemen provided 23.7 per cent of the capital for inland waterway construction between 1755 and 1815 (figures based on the analysis of 54.8 per cent of investment in the first period and 25.2 per cent in the second).

99. Building activity is better documented for the larger estates but the evidence suggests that the construction of new houses there was generally earlier than on the small estates.

100. For example Sir Richard Arkwright (1732–92) died worth 'a little short of half a million', gathered in just over twenty years, and his son Richard (1755–1843) amplified this to over £3,000,000 by his death. See R. S. Fitton, *The Arkwrights: Spinners of Fortune* (Manchester, 1989), pp. 219 and 296. The estate of the flax-spinner John Marshall of Leeds increased from £2180 in 1793 to £716,965 by 1839, a rate of increase beyond the dreams of the most efficient landed-estate owner; W. G. Rimmer, *Marshalls of Leeds Flax Spinners* (Cambridge, 1960), p. 321.

Notes to Chapter 8: Building and Finance

1. Paget Toynbee (ed.), 'Horace Walpole's Journals of Visits to Country Seats, etc.', *Walpole Society*, 16 (1927–28), p. 64.

2. E. Moir, *The Discovery of Britain, The English Tourists 1540 to 1840* (London, 1964), p. 68.

3. C. Bruyn Andrews (ed.), *The Torrington Diaries: Containing the Tours through England and Wales of the Hon. John Byng (Later Fifth Viscount Torrington) between the Years 1781 and 1794*, ii (London, 1935), pp. 20, 121.

4. F. M. L. Thompson, 'The End of a Great Estate', *Economic History Review*, second series, 8 (1955), pp. 36–37, 50–52.

5. D. Cannadine, 'The Landowner as Millionaire: The Finances of the Dukes of Devonshire, *c.* 1800 – *c.* 1926', *Agricultural History Review*, 25 (1977), pp. 77–97; E. Richards, 'An Anatomy of the Sutherland Fortune: Income, Consumption, Investments and Returns, 1780–1880', *Business History*, 21 (1979), pp. 45–78; idem, *The Leviathan of Wealth: The Sutherland Fortune in the Industrial Revolution* (London, 1973); D. Spring, *The English Landed Estate in the Nineteenth Century* (Baltimore, 1963); F. M. L. Thompson, 'English Landownership: The Ailesbury Trust, 1832–56', *Economic History Review*, second series, 11 (1958), pp. 121–32; idem, 'End of a Great Estate'; J. T. Ward, 'The Earls Fitzwilliam and the Wentworth Woodhouse Estate in the Nineteenth Century', *Yorkshire Bulletin of Economic and Social Research*, 12 (1960), pp. 19–27.

6. H. J. Habakkuk, 'Daniel Finch, Second Earl of Nottingham: His House and Estate', in J. H. Plumb (ed.), *Studies in Social History* (London, 1955), p. 163. In this seminal study of building a great country house, Sir John went on to show that Burley was bought and built from the proceeds of high political office and the sale of property. See pp. 300–2 below.

7. Malcolm Airs, *The Tudor and Jacobean Country House: A Building History* (Stroud, 1995), pp. 82, 100–3.

8. This section on the financing of Burley-on-the-Hill comes from Sir John Habakkuk's study, 'Daniel Finch', pp. 141–78. See also James Lees-Milne, *English Country Houses: Baroque, 1685–1715* (London, 1970), pp. 112–18.

9. For Blathwayt's career and the building of Dyrham, see G. A. Jacobsen, *William Blathwayt: A Late Seventeenth-Century English Administrator* (New Haven, 1932); John Kenworthy-Browne, *Dyrham Park* (National Trust, 1995); James Lees-Milne, *English Country Houses: Baroque*, pp. 85–94; Mark Girouard, 'Dyrham Park, Gloucestershire', *Country Life*, 131 (1962), pp. 335–91, 396–99; and Alan Mackley, 'Building Management at Dyrham', *Georgian Group Journal*, 7 (1997), pp. 107–16.

10. Jacobsen, *William Blathwayt*, pp. 53–54; Gloucestershire RO, D1799/C8, letter from William Blathwayt to Sir Robert Southwell, 28 September 1686.

11. Jacobsen, *William Blathwayt*, pp. 435–68.

12. John Harris, *William Talman: Maverick Architect* (London, 1982), end page.

13. Lees-Milne, *English Country Houses: Baroque*, pp. 237–38; Mackley, 'Building Management', p. 112.

14. Jacobsen, *William Blathwayt*, p. 435.

15. Gloucestershire RO, D1799/100, inventories of William Blathwayt's estate in the public funds, 5 April 1705, 24 January 1714/15; 18 February 1714/15 and 26 June 1716. The estates (he obtained the reversion of the Wynter's Somerset estate in 1707) produced a gross £2263 in 1717, Gloucestershire RO, D1799/F92, schedule of estate, 20 June 1717.

16. This section on Castle Howard is based upon Charles Saumarez Smith, *The Building of Castle Howard* (London, 1990) and Laurence Whistler, *The Imagination of Vanbrugh and his Fellow Artists* (London, 1954).

17. Quoted in Saumarez Smith, *Castle Howard*, p. 75.

18. Ibid., p. 84.

19. Ibid., p. 149.

20. See pp. 70–72 above and Chapter 3, note 37. This section relies heavily upon R. A. C. Parker, *Coke of Norfolk: A Financial and Agricultural Study, 1707–1842* (Oxford, 1975), pp. 1–70.

21. Ibid., p. 23.

22. For Audley End see *Audley End* (English Heritage, 1997); J. D. Williams, *Audley End: The Restoration of 1762–97* (Colchester 1966); idem, 'The Finances of an Eighteenth-Century Nobleman', *Essex Archaeology and History*, 9 (1977), pp. 113–25; and idem, 'A Pattern of Land Accumulation: The Audley End Experience, 1762–97', *Essex Archaeology and History*, 11 (1979), pp. 90–100.

23. It was examples of incomes like Sir John's which led Sir G. N. Clark to conclude, 'it is hard to find a class of mere landlords', in *The Wealth of England from 1496 to 1760* (London, 1946), p. 159.

24. The identifiable total of his army pay and profits was £25,617 between 1763 and 1797. But over a period of fifty-eight years, which included thirty-six years after he had retired from active service, his income from this source was considerable.

25. Sir John had represented Andover in the House of Commons from 1749 until 1784.

26. J. M. Rosenheim, *The Townshends of Raynham* (Middletown, Connecticut, 1989), pp. 187–88.

27. The Sledmere estate is discussed in Barbara English, *The Great Landowners of East Yorkshire, 1530–1910* (Hemel Hempstead, 1990), passim; J. Fairfax-Blakeborough, *Sykes of Sledmere* (London, 1929); and J. Popham, 'Sir Christopher Sykes at Sledmere', *Country Life*, 179, 16 January, 23 January 1986, pp. 128–32, 188–91.

28. Popham, 'Christopher Sykes', p. 191.

29. *Gentleman's Magazine*, 71 (1801), p. 1049.

30. In the 1870s their descendants were amongst the top half-dozen east Yorkshire landowners; the Sykeses with 34,010 and Denisons (Lord Londesborough) with 33,006 acres were the county's leading owners. Harrison Broadley possessed 14,877 acres. English, *Great Landowners*, p. 31.

31. In addition, Sir Christopher's own rents from settled estates were £3275 and £401 from unsettled ones. Hull University, DD54 98/142, account book of Sir Christopher Sykes, 1770–1800.

32. See Table 19, note c.

33. L. B. Namier and J. Brooke, *History of Parliament: House of Commons, 1754–1790*, iii (London, 1964), p. 514.

34. A. Suckling, *The History and Antiquities of the Hundreds of Blything and Part of Lothingland in the County of Suffolk* (London, 1847), p. 350; R. Lawrence, *Southwold River: Georgian Life in the Blyth Valley* (Exeter, 1990), pp. 32–43; H. Honour, 'James Byres's Plans for Rebuilding Henham Hall', in H. M. Colvin and J. Harris (eds), *The Country Seat* (London, 1970), pp. 164–69.

35. BL, Add. MS 19233, fos 26, 28–29, 30–34, 37–38.

36. R. G. Thorne, *The History of Parliament: The House of Commons, 1790–1820*, v (London, 1986), pp. 56–57.

37. BL, Add. MS 19233, fos 46–47, 57–58, 96–97.

38. BL, Add. MS 19233, fos 90–91, 100–1, 126–27; Suffolk RO, Ipswich, HA11 C6/1/3, general account book, 1788–94.

39. Alan Mackley, 'The Construction of Henham Hall', *Georgian Group Journal*, 6 (1996), pp. 85–96.

40. Lawrence, *Southwold River*, p. 37.

41. Cambridgeshire RO, Huntingdon, Acc. 2470 R35/5/1.

42. Gervase Jackson-Stops, 'Englefield House, Berkshire – III', *Country Life*, 169, 12 March 1981, pp. 642–45.

43. Cambridgeshire RO, Huntingdon, Acc. 2470 R40/6/2; RB3/36–37 and 3/47–48; Norfolk RO, MS 8595 20B.

44. Cambridgeshire RO, Huntingdon, Acc 2470, RB 3/36–7; John Bateman, *The Great Landowners of Great Britain and Ireland* (London, 1883; reprinted Leicester, 1971), p. 160. In 1883 the Norfolk estate produced an average rental of 17s. 6d. per acre, the Huntingdonshire ones £1 8s. 5d.

45. R. Pares, 'A London West India Merchant House', in R. A. and E. Humphreys (eds), *The Historian's Business and Other Essays* (Oxford, 1961).

46. Romney Sedgwick, *The History of Parliament: The House of Commons, 1715–1754*, ii (London, 1970), pp. 199–200.

47. This account of the building of Harewood House is taken from M. Mauchline, *Harewood House* (Newton Abbot, 1974).

48. M. W. Thompson (ed.), *The Journeys of Sir Richard Colt Hoare through Wales and England, 1793–1810* (Gloucester, 1983), p. 124; R. Warner, *A Tour through the Northern Counties of England and the Borders of Scotland*, i (Bath, 1802), pp. 241–42.

49. Joseph Farington's Diary quoted in V. Gibbs (ed.), *Complete Peerage*, vi (London, 1926), p. 311.

50. For Southill, see p. 42 above; for Dodington see C. Hussey, *English Country Houses: Late Georgian, 1800–1840* (London, 1958), pp. 41–54; and N. Kingsley, *The Country Houses of Gloucestershire*, ii, *1660–1830* (Chichester, 1992), pp. 118–23.

51. Uniquely there are two Codrington of Dodington baronetcies, one dated 1721, the second created for Christopher Codrington's descendants in 1876, although the two previous generations had claimed and assumed the title of the older baronetcy.

52. Gloucestershire RO, D1610/E145.

53. Hussey, *Late Georgian*, p. 42.

54. Gloucestershire RO, D1610/A96–97.

55. Hussey, *Late Georgian*, p. 42, and Kingsley, *Gloucestershire*, ii, p. 119. Wyatt was paid over £4000, which suggests an £80,000 commission, if the sum does not include travel.

56. Hussey, *Late Georgian*, p. 53.

57. Gloucestershire RO, D1610/A96–97.

58. Gloucestershire RO, D1610/A76–77, E145.

59. Hussey, *Late Georgian*, p. 42, repeated by Kingsley. Nor is it likely that the estate workforce was responsible for anything more than the usual labouring and routine tasks.

60. Quoted in Mauchline, *Harewood House*, p. 22.

61. Gloucestershire RO, D1610/E145.

62. Bateman, *Great Landowners*, pp. 98, 207.

63. Burke's *Landed Gentry* (15th edn, London, 1937), pp. 651–52.

64. Somerset RO, DD/DU163 inscribed by the Revd W. H. Duckworth, 'my father's valuation of his Property and Income'.

65. He initially seems to have borrowed £64,000 at 4 per cent, but by September 1856 sales of stocks and shares had allowed him to pay the remaining purchase money. He reckoned the estate, two manors and the advowsons produced £2500 net.

66. M. Girouard, The *Victorian Country House* (New Haven and London, 1979), p. 415; Bateman, *Great Landowners*, p. 140.

67. The building of Brodsworth was funded by the payout to Charles Sabine Augustus Thellusson of a legacy from the notorious will of his great-grandfather Peter Thellusson (1737–1797), a London banker and West India merchant of Swiss origin, who purchased the Brodsworth estate. After providing £100,000 for his wife and children, he left between £600,000 and £800,000 in trust to accumulate during the lives of his sons and grandsons, and any great-grandchildren living at the time of his death. On the death of the last survivor, the estate was to be divided equally between 'the eldest male lineal descendants of his three sons then living'. There being no great-grandchildren living at the time of his death, the trust was limited to two generations. Alarm that so vast a landed estate should be held by one family (one computation being that the accumulated value could be as much as £140,000,000) led to the passing of the 'Thellusson Act' (39 & 40 George III cap. 98) which prevented any testator from accumulating property for more than twenty-one years after his death. In the event, the value of the estate hardly increased at all, due, it has been argued, to 'accidents of management'. *DNB*, xix, pp. 589–90; *Notes and Queries*, eighth series, 12, pp. 183–84, and ninth series, 8, p. 53.

68. For Brodsworth see Girouard, *Victorian Country House*, pp. 236–42; C. Whitworth, *Brodsworth Hall* (English Heritage, 1995). Details about the building of Brodsworth and Charles Thellusson's income and expenditure are to be found in Yorkshire Archaeological Society (Leeds), DD 168 (individual documents are not numbered).

69. See pp. 38–39 above.

70. L. H. M. Hill, 'The Custances and their Family Circle', *Parson Woodforde Society Quarterly Journal*, 3 (1970), pp. 4–55. The estate was enclosed in 1825; in 1883 it was 2913 acres.

71. See p. 58 above. The five-by-five bay brick house by Thomas Rawlins probably cost less than £5000 to build. The similarly sized Terling Place, Essex, built in 1771–74 by John Johnson for John Strutt, a well-to-do miller, who had bought the manor of Terling Place and about 850 acres in 1761, cost £5722: the house £4053, the service wing £870 and the stables £809. N. Briggs, *John Johnson, 1732–1814* (Chelmsford, 1991), pp. 20–24. By 1873 the Strutts had built up a very sizeable 8632 acre estate. Bateman, *Great Landowners*, p. 377, see under Rayleigh.

72. J. Allibone, *Anthony Salvin: Pioneer of Gothic Revival Architecture, 1799–1881* (Cambridge, 1988), p. 159. Salvin's additions to North Runcton for Daniel Gurney in 1833–36 costing £4900 were modest.

73. R. W. Ketton-Cremer, *Felbrigg: The Story of a House* (London, 1962), pp. 267–77.

74. R. G. Wilson, 'Merchants and Land: The Ibbetsons of Leeds and Denton, 1650–1850', *Northern History*, 24 (1988), pp. 75–100, provides a full set of references. See also C. Hussey, 'Denton Hall, Yorkshire', *Country Life*, 86, 4 November 1939, pp. 470–74.

75. The old Fairfax house was, according to Ralph Thoresby *The Diary of Ralph Thoresby*, i (London, 1830), pp. 381, 386, being rebuilt in 1702. It was subsequently much modified by Samuel Ibbetson in the 1730s after the Fairfax's house had burned down.

76. This section on the building activities of Thomas Worsley is based upon Giles Worsley, 'Hovingham Hall, Yorkshire', in *Country Life*, 188, 15 September 1994, pp. 90–94, and 23 September 1994, pp. 56–60; H. M. Colvin, J. Mordaunt Crook, Kerry Downes and John Newman, *The History of the King's Works*, v, *1660–1782* (London, 1976), pp. 76–78, 137, 213; L. B. Namier and J. Brooke, *The History of Parliament: The House of Commons, 1754–1790*, iii (London, 1964), pp. 1410–13. Giles Worsley kindly let us see his abstract of Thomas Worsley's accounts in the Worsley papers at Hovingham.

77. Worsley, 'Hovingham', p. 57.

78. Arthur Young, *A Six Months Tour through the North of England*, ii (London, 1771), p. 88.

79. Namier and Brooke, *House of Commons*, iii, pp. 1410–13.

80. Quoted in Colvin et al., *King's Works*, v, p. 76. Worsley had acted as an equerry to George III when he was Prince of Wales.

81. Worsley lost three of his six children in 1769, including his eldest son and heir, when scarlet fever struck the family in London while his wife was lying-in. By 1774 he was suffering from excruciatingly painful attacks of kidney stone.

82. Colvin et al., *King's Works*, v, p. 74.

83. Worsley, 'Hovingham', pp. 56, 93.

84. For a full set of references to the Rolfe papers in the Norfolk RO, upon which this section is based, see R. G. Wilson and A. L. Mackley, 'Founding a Landed Dynasty, Building a Country House: The Rolfes of Heacham in the Eighteenth Century', in Carole Rawcliffe, Roger Virgoe and Richard Wilson, eds, *Counties and Communities: Essays on East Anglian History* (Norwich, 1996), pp. 307–28.

85. See pp. 11, 77–79, 107–8 above.

86. Norfolk RO, HEA 492, Edmund Rolfe to Edmund Rolfe junior, letter dated 17 June 1811.

87. The Edge papers are deposited in the Nottinghamshire RO; see especially DDE 46/58–59, 46/61–63 and also plans and elevations in DDE 60/1–11.

88. Burke's *Landed Gentry*, p. 680.

89. N. Pevsner, *The Buildings of England: Nottinghamshire* (Harmondsworth, 1979), pp. 391–92.

90. Nottinghamshire RO, DDE 63/5. Edge's landholding in Warwickshire, Staffordshire, Derbyshire and Nottinghamshire is given as 3133 acres in 1801. 'Old rents' had produced £2573 a year, 'raised rents' now returned £3533. In 1805 figures disclose that his income was almost entirely landed, £3551 out of £3823. He was then living entirely within his means, with expenditure of £2902. In 1883 the family owned 2758 acres.

91. Pevsner, *Nottinghamshire*, p. 392. All but the north front of the house was rendered in the 1790s.

92. Howard Colvin, *A Biographical Dictionary of British Architects, 1600–1840* (New Haven and London, 1995) pp. 391–92.

93. Nottinghamshire RO, DDE 46/61.

94. Nottinghamshire RO, DDE 46/59.

95. See note 90 above and Nottinghamshire RO, DDE 14/76/1–2. In 1816 Strelley Hall was insured with the Royal Exchange (policy no. 297676) for £6000: the mansion, £3260; furniture, clothes, plate and books, £1030; glass and china, £100; pictures, prints and drawings, £100; the domestic offices and their contents, the balance.

96. J. M. Robinson, *The Wyatts: An Architectural Dynasty* (Oxford, 1979), pp. 122–23; Burke's *Landed Gentry*, pp. 226–27. The Braddylls then retreated to their second estate, Highhead Castle, which was sold in the 1870s.

97. Allibone, *Anthony Salvin*, pp. 92, 172; Girouard, *Victorian Country House*, pp. 415, 449.

98. Norman Scarfe (ed.), 'A Frenchman's Year in Suffolk, 1784', *Suffolk Records Society*, 30 (Woodbridge, 1988), p. 27.

99. Norfolk RO, MC 39/17 and 112/7; family papers kindly lent by the late Mrs Rosemary James; Burke's *Landed Gentry*, p. 1620; John Kenworthy-Browne, Peter Reid, Michael Sayer and David Watkin, *Burke's and Savills Guide to Country Houses*, iii, *East Anglia* (London, 1981), p. 115.

100. Baker and Baker, *James Brydges*; *The Victoria History of the Counties of England: A History of Cambridgeshire and the Isle of Ely*, vi, ed. A. P. M. Wright (London, 1978), pp. 71–72; J. V. Beckett, *The Rise and Fall of the Grenvilles: Dukes of Buckingham and Chandos* (Manchester, 1994), pp. 54–57.

101. Howard Colvin, 'Lease or Demolish? The Problem of the Redundant Country House in Georgian England', in Malcolm Airs, *The Later Eighteenth-Century Great House* (Oxford, 1997), p. 100. See above, pp. 226–28.

102. G. Worsley, *Classical Architecture in Britain: The Heroic Age* (New Haven and London, 1995), pp. 70, 229; Allibone, *Anthony Salvin*, pp. 87–90, 190; Girouard, *Victorian Country House*, pp. 421–22.

103. Colvin et al., *King's Works*, v, p. 131.

104. Somerset RO, DD/DU 163.

105. Colvin, 'Lease or Demolish?', p. 109. On p. 107, Colvin notes that between 1771 and 1824 at least twenty mansion houses in Norfolk were advertised in the county's newspapers for letting, with shooting being the prime attraction.

106. Norfolk RO, WLS XVIII/7/20, 410 x 8, letter dated 15 August 1831 from Edward Blore to the fourth Baron Walsingham.

107. Cambridge University Library, Add. MSS 3937–38, cash books, and 3955, Edward Blore's account book.

108. West Yorkshire Archives Service, Leeds, Ingleby MS Acc. 2662, letters dated 24 July and 1 October 1798.

109. Colvin, 'Lease or Demolish?', p. 104.

110. Suffolk RO, Bury St Edmunds, HD 1113.

111. Suffolk RO, Ipswich, S. Yoxford, unpublished manuscript; R. T. L. Parr, *Yoxford Yesterday*, iv, pp. 214–49.

112. In a little over two hundred years, the estates of the Lee, Acton, Fowle, Middleton, and Broke families were united by marriage and descent to the Barons de Saumarez, including the Suffolk seats Bramford Hall, Broke Hall, Livermere Park and Shrubland Park. Suffolk RO, Ipswich, HA93, 'Report on Further Family and Estate Papers of the Saumarez Family, Barons de Saumarez: Thirteenth to Twentieth Century', Royal Commission on Historical Manuscripts (London, 1987).

113. Suffolk RO, Ipswich, HA93/3/306 'An Estimate of Expenditure Incurred when Livermere Park is Unoccupied, 31 March 1857'.

114. Suffolk RO, Ipswich, HA93/3/314, letter dated 27 January 1837 from John Chevallier Cobbold (Middleton's solicitor) to Sir William Middleton.

115. Suffolk RO, Ipswich, HA93/3/315, letter dated 20 August 1848 from Lucy Cobbold to Sir William Middleton.

Notes to Chapter 9: Afterword

1. Nicholas Kingsley, *The Country Houses of Gloucestershire*, ii, *1660–1830* (Chichester, 1992), p. 290.

2. The 'great landowners' were those with more than 3000 acres of land.

3. G. D. H. Cole (ed.), *Daniel Defoe, A Tour Thro' the Whole Island of Great Britain*, i (London, 1927), pp. 164–70; Scottish RO, GO/18/2107, Clerk of Penicuik, 'Journey to London in 1727'.

4. James Crathorne, *Cliveden: The Place and the People* (London, 1995).

5. Ibid., p. 98.

6. Ibid., p. ii.

7. David Spring, 'Introduction', in John Bateman, *The Great Landowners of Great Britain and Ireland* (London, 1883; reprinted Leicester, 1971), pp. 7–22.

8. C. Bruyn Andrews (ed.), *The Torrington Diaries, Containing the Tours through England and Wales of the Hon. John Byng (Later Fifth Viscount Torrington) between the Years 1781 and 1794*, iii (London, 1936), p. 209. For a full recent discussion, see F. M. L. Thompson, 'English Landed Society in the Twentieth Century', *Transactions of the Royal Historical Society*, fifth series, 40 (1990), pp. 1–24; sixth series, 1 (1991), pp. 1–20, and 2 (1992), pp. 1–23.

9. Clive Aslet, *The Last Country Houses* (New Haven and London, 1982), p. 2.

10. Ibid., pp. 2–3. John Martin Robinson, *The Latest Country Houses* (London, 1983), has also looked at twentieth-century building since the Second World War, defining the country house as 'the capital of a functioning agricultural estate'.

Notes to Appendix: The Chronology of Country House Building

1. N. Pevsner, *The Buildings of England* (Harmondsworth and London, 1951–98).

2. M. W. Flinn, *Origins of the Industrial Revolution* (London, 1966), p. 48.

3. Jules Lubbock, *The Tyranny of Taste* (New Haven and London, 1995), pp. 55–56 and p. 377 n. 54.

4. Heather A. Clemenson, *English Country Houses and Landed Estates* (London, 1982). In John Bateman, *The Great Landowners of Great Britain and Ireland* (London, 1883; reprinted Leicester, 1971), the term 'Great Landowner' is used for owners of more than 3000 acres worth at least £3000 p.a. but Clemenson reserves it for owners of more than 10,000 acres.

5. Lawrence and Jeanne C. Fawtier Stone, *An Open Elite? England, 1540–1880* (Oxford, 1984).

6. Denton Hall (pl. 128) and Henham Hall (pl. 56), rated according to the Stones' criterion in units of 100 square feet, are both 150-unit houses and qualify comfortably as elite houses, but Heacham Hall (pl. 5) of about forty units is below the fifty-unit threshold and would therefore be rejected.

7. See especially reviews by Christopher Clay, 'An Open Elite?', *Economic History Review*, second series, 38 (1985), pp. 452–54, and R. G. Wilson, 'An Open Elite?', *Social History*, 11 (1986), pp. 105–8.

8. Stone and Stone, *An Open Elite?*, p. 385, state that the flurry of building activity lasted until 1770 but their fig. 11.8, p. 384, does not support this conclusion. Building peaked in the 1730s and then declined – with partial recovery in the 1790s – until the 1820s. Building activity rose steadily through the nineteenth century.

9. Ibid., p. 386.

10. Mark Girouard, *The Victorian Country House* (New Haven and London, 1979), pp. 8–9. Girouard does not say how he compiled his list of houses. It is not referred to as a 'sample'.

11. Jill Franklin, *The Gentleman's Country House and its Plan, 1835–1914* (London, 1981), pp. 24–38.

Index

Page numbers in italics refer to plates